Southern Voices from the Past:
Women's Letters, Diaries, and Writings

This series makes available to scholars, students, and general readers collections of letters, diaries, and other writings by women in the southern United States from the colonial era into the twentieth century. Documenting the experiences of women from across the region's economic, cultural, and ethnic spectrums, the writings enrich our understanding of such aspects of daily life as courtship and marriage, domestic life and motherhood, social events and travels, and religion and education.

Memories of a Georgia Teacher

Memories of a Georgia Teacher

Fifty Years in the Classroom

Martha Mizell Puckett

Edited by Hoyle B. Puckett Sr.

The University of Georgia Press

Athens & London

© 2002 by the University of Georgia Press
Athens, Georgia 30602
All rights reserved
Designed by Louise OFarrell
Set in 10.5/13 Bulmer by Bookcomp, Inc.
Printed and bound by Thomson-Shore
The paper in this book meets the guidelines for
permanence and durability of the Committee on
Production Guidelines for Book Longevity of the
Council on Library Resources.

Printed in the United States of America
02 03 04 05 06 C 5 4 3 2 1

Library of Congress Cataloging-in-Publication Data
Puckett, Martha Mizell.
Memories of a Georgia teacher : fifty years in the classroom /
Martha Mizell Puckett ; edited by Hoyle B. Puckett Sr.
p. cm. — (Southern voices from the past)
ISBN 0-8203-2259-8 (alk. paper)
1. Puckett, Martha Mizell. 2. Teachers—Georgia—Biography.
I. Puckett, H. B. (Hoyle B.), 1925– II. Title. III. Series.

LA2317.P83 A3 2002
371.1'0092—dc21   2001046465

British Library Cataloging-in-Publication Data available

CONTENTS

Contents

ACKNOWLEDGMENTS

Numerous people connect to create a publication. A memoir such as this one, which spans the late nineteenth century and all of the twentieth, has of necessity involved many individuals. My mother, Martha Puckett, wrote her manuscripts in longhand; she did not type. Her granddaughter, Martha P. Broderick, volunteered to transcribe the handwritten manuscript into typewritten format. Martha ceased writing in 1973 because of poor health. She died in July 1974. One of her manuscripts, "Snow White Sands," was published in 1975. It proved to be of immense local interest, and my sister, Mrs. Lawrenna P. Powell, has had several reprints made of the book.

Several years later Lawrenna and I were discussing the continued interest in the first book, and she mentioned that there was another manuscript dealing with Martha's teaching experiences in later years. She said that no publishers would look at it unless it was in a word processor format, and that she had been unable to get it retyped at what she thought was a reasonable cost for a book that would never turn a profit. She had given up the idea of getting it published. I, with inexperienced confidence, said, "That should be no problem. A text scanner would be able to convert typed text into a computer file." Lawrenna told me to take the manuscript and do what I could with it.

I spoke with some writers associated with the University of Illinois and soon found that their estimates of cost far exceeded what I was willing to invest. I then asked a friend who was doing desktop publishing to scan the typed text and produce a computer file. He did, and while he was scanning the text, he read the manuscript. He told me that I should get it published and that he admired the determination and ability of the writer, my mother. This friend, Dr. Rupert N. Evans, dean emeritus of the College of Education, University of Illinois, more than any other person, is responsible for my sticking to the task and finishing the editing of the original text. Every so often Rupert would ask me, "How is the editing coming along?" He would fire me up with a comment, "It's important. You should publish it."

My daughters, Ms Carol B. Puckett and Mrs. Kristina A. Puckett Berbaum, helped me convert the scanned pages to word processor files. The scanned pages had numerous errors. This amounted to a complete retype. Without their help I would probably not have completed the conversion.

When the text was half done, I took it to the University of Georgia Press. I asked Malcolm L. Call, senior editor, to look at the manuscript and tell me if the Press would be interested in publishing it. He took it and said he would read it. Several weeks later he let me know that he thought they could publish the manuscript, and he would like to see the remaining chapters as soon as possible. Now, after ten years and much prodding by friends and editors along the way, the manuscript is published almost forty years after my mother first put pen to paper and began to write.

Hoyle B. Puckett Sr.

Martha Isabella Mizell was the last of five children, two sons and three daughters, born to Jasper Pleasant Mizell and Susan Matilda Purdom Brown Mizell. Martha was born March 26, 1897, at home, a few miles east of Raybon, near the Big Satilla River in Wayne County, now Brantley County, Georgia. Jasper and Susan were each widowed; Jasper brought six children, three sons and three daughters, to the union, and Susan brought one, a son. Farm life at the turn of the century in any area was demanding, but the demands on people in the rural areas of Wayne County were perhaps greater because of poor transportation. It was a two-day trip from the Mizell home to Jesup, the county seat— if the rivers and creeks were not running too high to be forded or crossed on a ferry. Since Martha was the youngest, it fell to her to assist her father with the farmwork. Jasper spent much of this time discussing life's problems and possibilities with Martha. These father-daughter discussions enlightened her and shaped her thinking. It was an intellectual foundation that lasted a lifetime.

Jasper Pleasant Mizell was a Primitive Baptist minister and served several churches in the county (most ministers at that time had to support themselves and their family). He was well read in the arts and sciences. He believed that only well-educated men and women would be able to prosper in a free society and sustain their freedom. During Reconstruction, Jasper's father, Perry Stallings Mizell, had told Jasper, his youngest son, that when he voted to be very sure of his vote and to always vote, for he would be voting for his father and for his brothers. They had all served the Confederate army or supported the Confederate cause and were prohibited from voting. Jasper was born in 1857 and was not of voting age until 1878, but he accepted the advice of his father and always considered intelligent voting his prime civic duty. He also served in elected and appointed positions. Jasper spoke of his convictions of service to God, his family, and his country in the many conversations he and Martha had while performing tasks on the farm. These conversations with her father were Martha's first and most intensive courses in sociology and civics from which she learned the importance of education for our citizens and for our country. The relationship between Jasper and his daughter Martha was close and unique and is expressed in the name "Babe" by which he called her until his death in 1919. Throughout this book, the closeness of Martha to her father is expressed over and over.

Martha was fifteen years old when she began her teaching career. She had just finished the seventh grade at Strickland School and had taken the state test for schoolteachers, which was administered by the county school superintendent. She received a high score and asked for an assignment. She was assigned to a one-room one-teacher school in Burnt Bay, Georgia, on the periphery of the Okefenokee Swamp. The origin of the town's name is interesting, but I'll leave it for you to discover in her writings. Martha did not reach her sixteenth birthday until near the end of this first teaching assignment.

Martha continued to gain experience as she completed assignment after assignment. She gained confidence in her ability, recognized that teaching was what she wanted to do, and planned her life to make teaching her profession. She was recognized early on as an excellent teacher, able to handle difficult situations, and was given greater responsibility with each appointment. Her desire to teach surpassed all else in her life. Trustees of the schools often asked if she would finish the term and said that they did not want "courting" to interfere with schoolwork. She usually responded that she was there to teach and that she was not "husband hunting." Such was the case until the fall 1920 term. That is when my father-to-be began to pay her serious court. He asked her to be his wife, but she put him off because of her plan to be the best schoolteacher she could be. He persisted, and they were married. She now had a ready-made family, with six children, ages three to fourteen. She bore my father two additional children. My sister, Lawrenna, was born in 1921, and I was born in 1925. Her family was now her whole world. She had set aside her plan to teach and, instead, tended her brood of eight. Life was near perfect.

By 1929, the year of the stock market crash, the boll weevil had destroyed the Sea Island cotton industry. The crash hit the farmers hard and caused many to fail. Other businesses, dependent upon the farmers, soon followed. My father's railroad construction business had had no work since 1927. What had been a comfortable life for my family turned into a cash-strapped existence. I have no strong memories of the hard times of the 1930s. The simple wants of a small child were well accommodated. I had adequate clothing, food, shelter, and a loving family. I never really wondered or thought about what was being done to sustain the family. The life we had was all I ever knew.

By 1932 the depression was hitting hard on all fronts. There were many mouths to feed and essential expenses to be met. The house, in good repair, was always full of kinfolk. There was plenty of homegrown food, enough for all. Rarely did you go to the filling station and say, "fill-it-up"; instead, it was, "one gallon please." Only when I read my mother's memories did I realize what a traumatic time it was for her. She kept her troubles to herself and kept doing for others in spite of all the problems.

The most difficult time for her was when she had to accept a teaching position to bring in some money for the family. My father had no work and no prospect of any. Money was needed; so she accepted the teaching position. It had been twelve years since she had taught school. She had been a wife, a mother, and a homemaker. Now she had to leave this life she had created and return to the teaching profession. The trauma of this change so affected her that she knelt in prayer, seeking help from God to understand why all this pain and hardship should befall her and separate her from her family who so needed her. The answer came, "Because I have need of thee." From this point on, she never looked back but kept pressing on till the day she retired from teaching and set about recording her memories.

Education in Georgia at the turn of the century was provided primarily by the local citizens. State funds were meager to nonexistent. In 1913 the state of Georgia subsidized local schools at the rate of one dollar per student per month for three and a half months per year. Local schools were provided by local subscription on a per child basis. Room and board for teachers were furnished by the families from which the children came. This made classroom activities at the neighborhood school a highly personal matter. Local families paid close attention to what and how their children were taught. As time passed, the number of months for which the state subsidy was paid gradually increased, until, by the 1950s, it was nine months. State financial support of education in Georgia remained comparatively low until the late 1940s. In the thirties the state had no money, and teachers were not paid except where local systems were able raise enough money for salaries. A few of the larger schools paid at least partial, if not full, salaries to their teachers. The small low-enrollment rural schools could give only support in kind (room and board and very little more).

When WLOP, the Jesup radio station, first went on the air in the fifties, Martha obliged them with a story-telling program, which was aired each Saturday morning for about an hour. She also had a story-telling time at the local library, a small frame building on East Cherry Street. She would tell children's stories and stories that her mother had told to her as a child. This endeared her to a wide audience of children and adults. Libraries are a source of continuing education and enjoyment to all. She worked tirelessly to build a great library in each school and a public library in Jesup for all to use.

State support of public education changed more in concept and substance between 1932 and 1948 than in any earlier sixteen-year period. The full impact of the agricultural depression and the failure of the stock market culminated in a full-blown depression by 1932. A cash-starved economy failed to function. With no business activity and no wages being earned, there was little tax money coming to government to support essential services. Education received very little, and teachers in rural community schools got nothing. Governor Eugene Talmadge won his election in 1932 in part because he said he would pay the teachers. In 1933 he was not able to obtain funds to pay the teachers. In 1934 he tried to "borrow" funds from other accounts to pay the teachers, but the legislature would not go along, and the legislative session was allowed to end without a budget authorizing state funds.

For the next two years, Talmadge struggled with the legislature. Although he was successful in getting some money to the state school superintendents to pay bills in 1934 and 1935, it was not until 1936 that funds were released to pay teachers, who had not been paid full salaries since 1932. In addition, beginning with the fall 1936 term, and funded by this money, free textbooks were distributed to all schoolchildren in grades one through six.

E. D. Rivers, an influential state senator, was elected governor in 1936 and took office on January 12, 1937. During his administration, legislation was passed to provide free textbooks to all public schoolchildren. The economy was improving, and the state was now in better financial condition. Georgia's commitment to improving education in the state is evidenced by the strong statement supporting education that has been included in each Georgia state constitution approved since 1941.

Martha's approach to education was through the heart as much as through the mind. She used examples rather than pronouncements to guide students and their parents to the correct conclusions. She believed that you could achieve a lot more if you didn't make a big issue of who gets the credit for a particular accomplishment. This method encouraged all to seek true and correct conclusions. Her teaching methods did not fit a textbook on pedagogical procedures, but they were well suited to the social environment and business conditions. Her methods were anything but haughty and formal. To teach her students, she appealed to their senses. She used repetition and storytelling to excite their imaginations. She wanted them to enjoy learning for the sake of learning and to know the whole world not just a small facet of it. She encouraged students to interact with each other in play periods and at school functions. She stimulated their desire to learn history and sociology and helped her students learn who they were individually and collectively through field trips to historic sites that related to their time and families. She always tried to get parents involved in their child's learning process, believing that the interest of their parents stimulates students to try harder and gives them immediate rewards for their efforts.

It is important to realize in reading these memories that this text was written by Martha after she retired, and there is no claim of irrefutable evidence to the accuracy of names and dates. While her body had weakened with advancing age, her mind was clear and quick, and I assume that where accuracy was important her memory is the most reliable source, for even written records in the county files are not without error. Check your birth certificate. Is all the data correct? Most of her writing was done in her early seventies. She was seventy-seven years old March 26, 1974. She died July 9, 1974.

Martha Isabella Mizell Puckett accumulated several honors in the course of her life. She was named a Master 4-H Club member for her outstanding work for rural youth as a club leader. She was named teacher of the year in Pierce County, Georgia, in 1957. In 1995 the Wayne County Board of Education named a new middle school for her in appreciation of her many years of service to the schools of Wayne County. From 1913 until her retirement in 1962, her teaching license never lapsed. Although she earned a lifetime four-year teaching license, it was not from the University of Georgia: by the time she had accumulated enough credits, the university determined that her two quarters in residence were too old to count for a degree. The state of Georgia still gave her the lifetime four-year license. Martha considered herself an alumna, and she made sure that her daughter and son went to and graduated from the University of Georgia. The most outstanding award she received was the tribute paid her by her former students—from gray-haired great-grandparents to just graduated teens. Her service had spanned four generations.

Memories of a Georgia Teacher

CHAPTER 1

My School in the Okefenokee Swamp

Dawn had crept over the jungle on the south banks of the Big Satilla Swamp, and now, in the cold frosty morning air, the sun was shining through the tall yellow pine trees on the higher ground of the riverbanks. My mother was putting the last hairpin in place in the lovely knot of wavy black hair atop my head, placing the huge black comb at the right angle so my small plumed hat would set at the right slant. She and my cousin Alice Highsmith had spent nearly two full weeks trying to coax the long black curls that had hung down my back all the days of my life into a hairdo befitting a schoolmarm.

My father called in his clear, loving, yet commanding voice, "Babe, all is ready; time is wasting. We must be going if you expect to catch that early morning train to your school." He had the faithful old red mare with two white feet all shined, and harnessed to the family carriage. The little square tin trunk was tied securely behind the backseat with two good strong plow lines. He stood holding the lines of the shining harness as my mother and I came rapidly down the walk to the front gate, where Father had stopped after driving from the buggy and harness shelter. Father had placed a sack of shelled corn under the buggy seat. He planned to take it to the mill to grind for meal and grits after he put me on the train. He pushed the sack aside and placed my hand grip on the floor of the buggy also. I kissed my mother good-bye and hugged her dearly as I laid my head on her shoulder one more time. I was her baby, the youngest of twelve children, going away to the great Okefenokee Swamp to teach school. I felt the hot tears on my face. I kissed her once more, and my father helped me into the buggy. Oh, he was so genteel, with his well-kept Vandyke, deep-set black eyes, and the ways of a true French nobleman, the Honorable J. P. Mizell. I waved as long as I could see Mother standing by the gate. Every now and then I would see a corner of her apron go up to her face as she waved with the other hand.

[1]

When the road curved around the long dense cypress pond, past mighty alligator cave, I could see her no more. I then spoke to my father and told him that there were two things my mother had told me never to forget: first, that I am your daughter and bear your name to honor or dishonor, whichever I choose; second, that I am the child of God until I give myself to the Devil. She said that if I always remembered these two things I would be safe in the Okefenokee Swamp or any place else.

Although I was only fifteen years of age, I had taken full advantage of the educational opportunities offered by our local school, the Strickland District School of Wayne County, Georgia. I had read all the books on teaching methods that I could lay my hands on, books such as Page's *Theory and Practice*, Dutton's *School Management*, the works of Horace Mann, and many others. After leaving school, I traveled to Jesup, our county seat, and appeared before the county school superintendent, the Honorable B. D. Purcell, and the county board of education to take a written test given by the state of Georgia and known as the "teacher's examination." I passed it and was granted a teacher's license.

So now I was on my way to the little railway station in Raybon, four miles down a long white sandy road on the south ridge of the Big Satilla River basin. To get there we had to cross two deep tributaries flowing into the Satilla, Washe's Branch and Millard's Branch, each named for the gentleman who lived hard by and maintained a water mill upon it. I worried that water would dip into the buggy, wetting the corn and my hand grip, and asked my father had he not better reach for the bag of corn and put it on the seat beside us. His reply was, "No need to worry. There has been a long dry spell in these parts, and the dams were holding back all the water and needed more." We were expecting winter rains every day.

We talked of many things as Nellie, the old mare, trotted swiftly along. The farmyards and front porches were filled with happy robust cousins as we passed along in the early morning light, and they would shout hearty, joking greetings and farewells to me. They told me not to let the big black bears catch me and not to let any of those tough Okefenokee schoolboys throw me out the window. They warned me to be sure not to take on to their ways of courting and find out how Lydia Stone had made her millions off the old sow and pigs her father had given her. And be sure, they said, to mark the road to the "cow house" and to "Billy's islands" so I would know the way out of the swamp. They said to keep a list of the alligators I killed so I would know how much more I could make catching alligators than I could teaching school. These boys and girls were my first cousins, the Highsmiths, Willises, Smiths, Purdoms, and Lewises. They thought the joke was on me. Here they stayed on the Big Satilla Ridge, highly cultured since Revolutionary War, and I was off to the great Okefenokee Swamp to teach school.

During the lulls between the family farms, my father kept up a stream of talk. He told me many things. First he told me not to be sad over my mother's farewell. It was their desire to see me well established in life before their time of going, which was around sixty in those days. Although I was the youngest child, it did not mean I was not to have the opportunity to reach out and explore and find my place of usefulness to all mankind. Second, he told me I was going into a great profession to try to lead needy boys and girls out of darkness, ignorance, and superstition into the way of truth, light, love, and knowledge. He said I should never do or say anything that would not be helpful to their young lives and to the teaching profession. I have done my best to remember that well.

By this time we were to the little railway station. The usual crowd gathered around. Many fine trains from the north, east, and west, including the new Jesup to Folkston short line, passed this station by. Only one stopped, a little local passenger and freight train known as the "Bogey." It was operated by John Donaldson, engineer; Dewey Bryant, fireman; J. H. McPipkin, conductor; Sidney Bennett, flagman; and J. A. Grubbs, expressman, better known as the great "accommodator" up and down the line. He would bring you anything from a Kabo corset to a bottle of prescription medicine, lace for shroud, or a set of stovepipes and elbows if you gave him the measurements and the money to buy them.

My father waved the train, as there was no stationmaster and only a little platform by the track to load and unload freight and luggage. He helped get my little tin trunk onto the platform. I had tied the trunk key to a handkerchief in the bottom of my purse beside the eight dollars I had borrowed from my uncle Wash Willis to go to my first school. I was to repay him the total amount out of my first month's salary of twenty dollars.

The shouts and laughter died down. I boarded the train, the jibes still ringing in my ears. My father stood there waving his black felt hat toward my window for as long as I could see. I was on my way.

The train stopped at my cousin John Brown's siding to unload supplies of flour, beans, peas, bacon, sugar, brogans, calico, snuff, tobacco, 666's (a patent medicine), Fletcher's Castoria, and the like, and to take on lumber, turpentine, crossties, cattle, and other products.

We chugged on to Nahunta, the junction of the Brunswick and Western Railway and the short line. Here, we in the passenger compartment, sat on a spur while the engine shifted the freight cars to the B & W line destined for the Downing Company and the Lott Company at the bustling port of Brunswick. The empty freight cars were picked up and carried down the road to the numerous business sidings from Nahunta to Folkston and to the two giant companies at Hickox, the P. S. Knox Lumber Company and the Gautier Retort Company, now Hercules.

By and by all this shifting and placing was finished, and our passenger coaches were hitched on behind a long line of empty flatcars, boxcars, and stumpcars, and away we huffed and puffed the last three miles to Hickox, my destination. My train ride had been a total of eight miles and cost twenty-five cents. It was now near noontime. The trip would have been much quicker with a horse and buggy except for great Buffalo Creek, a mighty tributary of the lower portion of the Big Satilla River system. Since it was so deep and wide, there was no way to cross it with a horse and buggy, and there was no bridge. You either swam the stream or stayed on the other side—which is what we usually did.

As we came to a halt at Hickox, I saw a depot and an unloading platform. I got off the train and, with my little satchel in my hand, stood and watched until my trunk was placed on the platform. I went into the depot and had a seat (as my father had told me to do) and waited until the stationmaster finished his numerous duties. I watched the train engine pull off with its long string of freight cars, taking them to a place where they would be picked up in the afternoon and taken to Nahunta on their way back to Brunswick. The passenger cars were left sitting.

After a while I saw the stationmaster back in his office, and I walked over to the window, introduced myself, and told him I was Martha Mizell of Lulaton, Georgia, the daughter of J. P. Mizell, a very good friend of his father, Mr. Allen Mattox of Jesup, Georgia. I asked him was he not Mr. Harvey Mattox, Mr. Allen's son. He said he was. So I told him I was going to the Okefenokee Swamp to teach school and asked had he seen any of those people from there who were coming to meet me. His reply was, "No, but the P. S. Knox tramline goes right by there." I told him they were to meet me at the station. So he said, "If they said so, never fear, they will be here by and by, so just have a seat and wait." That I did.

Not many minutes had passed before a long tall gentleman appeared. He was wearing high-top boots with spiked soles and carrying a four-plait leather cow whip with a short handle on one end a fine horsehair cracker on the other. He went up to the stationmaster and asked, "Have you seen anything of my school-teacher?" Mr. Mattox replied, "There she sits." I stood up and Mr. Mattox introduced us. He was Mr. John Morgan, the son of Mr. Gordon Morgan, with whom I had been corresponding about the school. Mr. Morgan took my satchel and, with hat in hand, said, "I have come for you."

We stepped out the station door, and there I saw a large two-wheeled cart, floored with tie scores loosely laid on, and a yoke of beautiful red and white piebald oxen hitched to the tongue. (Tie scores are the sides of the tree that are cut off to square the log for use as railroad ties.) The oxen were gently standing, chewing their cuds so patiently. He took my baggage check, got my trunk, and strapped it to the axle. He placed a large bag of corn shucks in front of it and said, "This is your seat." He gallantly helped me over the high wheels after taking his red bandanna and wiping all the mud off the wheel. I sat down. He handed me my satchel and told me to hold on tight, for we had some mighty rough roads to travel. He climbed up on the tongue of the cart, sat at the front of the cart, cracked his whip, and away we went—in one mud hole and out into another, one high wheel up and the other down for some three miles.

This was a tie-and-timber road into the very heart of the great Okefenokee. Soon we came to a deep, deep swamp, where the road was cut far below the level of the earth and was filled with mud and slush. The oxen waded in; directly they stopped. Mr. Morgan called to them, coaxed them, petted them, but no go. There they stood in the muddy water. Time was passing; the sun was getting lower. Mr. Morgan said, "I hate to ask you, but you will have to get off the shucks." I thought surely he was going to feed them, for I was almost hungry enough to eat shucks myself; but nay, he lighted them and crawled out on the tongue of the cart, telling me to hold on to the cart axle standards with both hands for dear life. He stuck a lighted shuck to the belly of each ox. Zip! They jumped. And away they went through the long muddy ford and over the rise to higher ground, up to a large double gate that was swung wide by two beautiful dark-eyed girls, Rena and Viola Morgan. Then there came four more lovely girls, Kansas, Verdie, Jeremey, and Dora Morgan, to welcome their new teacher.

The oxen trotted on up to the back porch, where I was helped down just as gently as I was helped on, although I was now quite as mud spattered as the cart wheels and the driver. From the kitchen came that greatest of all aromas, that of frying catfish. Out stepped a lovely lady, Mrs. Laura Wainwright Morgan, her substantial husband, Gordon Morgan, and their nine-year-old son, Eddie Morgan. I was told that Kansas was to be my bedfellow, while Rena, Viola, Jeremey, and Dora occupied the other two snow-white beds in the large, airy freshly scrubbed bedroom. I was told to use the basin and pitcher to get the swamp mud off me and freshen up a bit before supper. The whole countryside would soon be there to see their new teacher.

So I put on my cream serge dress with the ecru lace collar and my white kid high-top button shoes, brushed my hair, and came out for supper. Of all the food I ever ate in my life, I believe that meal was the best. It was the first mouthful of food or drink I had eaten since before daybreak at my father's home. I was about twelve miles from home, but it had taken all day to get there. Supper was wonderful. Everyone was so kind and pleasing. Mr. and Mrs. Morgan knew my father and had heard him preach and thought him true to the faith.

Soon young folks were coming from every direction, and old folks and children also, to see the teacher who was to teach for them in the new little log cabin some three miles further in the swamp. Soon the young ladies of the community were playing the organ, and people were singing sacred songs, love ballads, and sad event songs such as "Baggage Coach Ahead," "Did He Ever Return," "Barbara Allen."

While all of this was going on, Mr. Morgan and other parents, often called "patrons," were giving me instructions about the school. Three good schoolhouses had burned down in recent years. This little log cabin—with two windows, one door, a step block at its entrance, peg-leg benches, and desks made of tie scores supported by wooden pegs that had been driven into the wall—was their last attempt to have a school. At that time the state and county did not pay for construction of school buildings or for equipment. They contributed only one dollar a day toward a teacher's pay. I was asked to try to be friends with everyone, to do anything they asked within reason, and to know that if things got too rough, it would be no disgrace to quit. They were used to that.

Sunday was spent quietly. We had a good dinner of chicken and dumplings, potato pie, fresh greens with ham bone, pickle preserves of all kinds, and a beautiful coconut cake to celebrate my coming. More patrons and pupils came in the afternoon. There was more organ playing and singing and still more directions on my duties. I was told that, above all, I must get along, or this schoolhouse would suffer the same fiery fate of the last three. In the past, if they didn't like the teacher, they would burn the schoolhouse; hence the name Burnt Bay.

Monday morning, January 6, 1913, came clear and cold. School opened for class at eight o'clock sun time. (Although "standard time," or "train time," could be determined from the courthouse clock, we often told time by the position of the shadow made by the flagpole, thus "sun time.") I was there early to greet the patrons and students. I was to teach grades one through seven, eight lessons per day. Many students were much older and larger than I. How did I do it? It can be done. I was brought up in a school just like that and knew all about it.

The trustees talked. Then the patrons talked. Then I asked to talk. I told them I had only one rule, and that was for all of us to do right, to try to find out the truth and knowledge that we needed to make us better friends and neighbors. I told them that I was ready to begin work. The parents signed their children into my care and gave them their last instructions, telling me how severe to be for their children if they did not comply. The parents all left, and we began work on the day's lessons. The blackboard, some planed lumber painted black, was quickly put to use to explain the lesson assignments. At ten o'clock we stopped for recess and went to get fresh water from a dug well, using a scrubbed cypress bucket with brass hoops, and long-handled gourd dippers for drinking cups. A ball game was soon begun, and the fifteen minutes passed pleasantly and quickly.

After recess, we returned to more lesson assignments. Spelling, reading, arithmetic, and English were completed in the first two hours. Afterward came the geography and history periods. Just as we were all settled down for work, in walked a gentleman with a handlebar mustache and a long-barrel rifle. He took a seat on the little peg-leg bench by the door, his gun across his lap.

I was up front at my table and walked back to introduce myself. He told me that he was Mr. Miller Crews, a trustee of the school, that he knew my father and thought a great deal of him. He had two students in my school, Nellie and Lucy, and he wanted them to learn well. He had been busy with his stock that morning and could not come earlier, but he said he would be by from time to time to see how they were doing in their work. He would always like to hear them read or spell, work arithmetic, or recite in some way when he came. I told him, "Yes sir, I would be glad to comply." I had Lucy spell several pages and then read quite a long story. She was an excellent reader and speller, grade five. Then I called Nellie up, and she spelled at length then read a nice story from her book, grade three. She also read well for her age. He seemed well pleased and said Lucy wanted to be a teacher just like me, and he hoped I would help her all I could. I promised him I surely would.

Then he told me he wanted me to come to his home every Tuesday and Thursday night throughout the whole school term. They would be expecting me. Again I said, "Yes, sir," remembering the instructions Mr. Morgan had given me. I told him I would surely be there at the appointed time unless prevented by illness, which I did not expect, since I was pretty strong and healthy. Although I had been told they lived in a one-room log cabin, I went as promised.

They had divided the back end of the cabin off from the front end with sheets, and divided it again with more sheets to make two sleeping rooms. I slept with Lucy and Nellie, and Mr. and Mrs. Crews slept in the other bed with the baby child. My bed was soft and downy, with clean white sheets and pillowcases and pretty, soft handmade quilts. The house was always cleaned until it glistened. The food was excellent: hand-ground hominy, sweet potatoes, winter vegetables, dried peas and beans; wild game, good plump chickens, ham, and sausage; fresh eggs, milk, butter, and cream; wild honey, Georgia cane syrup, and tea cakes. I tell you it was mighty good fare. I received only twenty dollars per month and had to board around for my lodging. I was always glad when my nights came to go to the Crews family, and I never failed to fill them. We became very good friends. Mr. Crews liked to hear me talk on different subjects, and he liked to come to school to hear his children recite as well as to hear the other children.

Noon came. We stopped working and went outside to have our midday meal, eaten from tin dinner pails that we had hung on pegs on either side of the front of the cabin. The students chose sides and captains, and a real ball game was begun. At one o'clock the bell was rung, and we returned to the classroom, where singing, Bible reading, and prayers were on the program. Then we entered into health, talking, studying, and planning and read from our physiology book. At 2:15 P.M. we all went out to play again and to get fresh water. At 2:45 P.M. the bell rang for lessons. We wrote in our copybooks and learned the different forms of writing. The blackboard was in continuous use during this hour from 2:45 P.M. to 3:45 P.M. Then all stopped. The officers of the day scrubbed all the slates, washed out the sponges, and hung them on pegs above the desk at each student's place. They also made sure that there were fat splinters available and lightwood knots to start a quick fire in the pot-bellied stove, as well as a big chunk or so of gum or oak for a long slow-burning fire. They swept the floor with the palmetto broom, poured the water out of the bucket, and turned it upside down. At four o'clock the day was done. All lessons learned and recited, slates cleaned, school dismissed, and away we hurried hither and yon, across swamps and islands to our various homes.

I went to the home of Miller Crews every Tuesday and Thursday night as I had promised. He lived in a little log cabin some three miles away. The food was cooked on a wide, open hearth and was so good. The feather beds were deep and soft, and the quilts were soft and warm—all handmade. The floors were scrubbed to snowy whiteness. Mr. Crews made his living tending hogs, cattle, timberland, and a small farm with corn, cotton, potatoes, peas, the usual garden, fruit, poultry, wild honey, berries, and grapes.

My board was to be had among my patrons. So I also spent many nights at the home of Mr. Cage Crews, a relative of Miller Crews. He had three daughters, Laura, Lovey, and Versey, and a son, Monroe, who married Gordon Morgan's daughter Beulah. Mr. Owen Strickland, another of my patrons, had a son so tall he could walk up to one of the swamp cow ponies and throw his leg over him without ever using the stirrup. He also had a daughter, Cora. Both were older and larger than I. We all had a good time together. There was a Mr. Rhoden with several small children, a Mr. Lee, with several children, and a few more families I don't remember so well.

We lived, learned, loved, and played together and saw the P. S. Knox tram trains go by loaded with giant virgin yellow pine and cypress trees that were so long it would take two flatcars to hold them. They were brought from the heart of the swamp by great teams of oxen. Twenty yoke to the team, all driven by highly trained teamsters. The logs were loaded on skids by a smaller team to be taken to Hickox and the P. S. Knox lumber mill. I taught at this school until the end of the term and closed it at Easter time. Our terms were short, our hours long. Both students and parents sought after our teaching. At school-breaking time, we had speaking, singing, dinner on the ground, and a wonderful egg hunt enjoyed by both young and old. They marveled at the beauty of the colored eggs. There were community sings, peanut hullings for seed to plant in the springtime, quiltings, fish fries, and church days for pastimes. I went home once. After I left the school, other teachers taught there for many more years, until, finally, when the roads to Hickox were good enough, the school was consolidated with the Hickox school. It was never burned again.

In the great Okefenokee Swamp, among the bears, hoot owls, spring frogs, deer, turkey, alligator, violets, butter cups, ty ty, gallberry, dog-tongue, and many other flora, fauna, and lovely, honest people, my teaching career began fifty years ago, January 1, 1913.

CHAPTER 2

To Jack Petty's to Teach

In the fall of 1913, our county and state supported public schools about three and a half months a year, paying twenty dollars a month in gold for each teacher. The balance of the teacher's salary was paid from tuition paid by the parents. The patrons of the school provided board, lodging, transportation, laundry, and other amenities for the teacher. Parents paid according to the number of children they had enrolled in the classroom. They could pay at once for one long board and lodging period or for shorter periods, round and round as their time came, whichever way they preferred. Parents also supplied all the books; ofttimes two children would share one book if they were at anywhere near the same scholastic standing. Slates, pencils, a small amount of writing paper, and pen and ink made up the rest of the school supplies, which were purchased with parents' tuition payments.

Because there was no state or county money for buildings, schools were constructed and maintained by the local community. All labor for the school building and furniture was gratis. The ladies of the community prepared a big dinner the day the schoolhouse was to be raised. Although the building was put up in one day, much work had to be done beforehand, such as cutting the rafters, ridge poles, and laths; preparing the shingles, doors, and window frames; and hauling and pounding clay for the chimney and fireplace. A well had to be dug, and furniture had to be made—benches, the teacher's desk, a long desk for the older students, and a blackboard. That night, after the building was finished, there was a big party.

A school was usually a log cabin with a stick-and-clay chimney across one end, where giant logs were burned to heat the entire building. The doors and window frames were made of hand-rived cypress. The seats were peg-leg benches, each made of a log split in half by gluts, wedges, and malls. The split side faced up, and the round side faced down. The peg legs were placed in holes sufficiently deep to hold the pegs good and tight, yet not so deep they marred the smooth side of the bench. If the men of the community were not public-spirited enough to build this type of schoolhouse, classes could be held only if a vacant cabin could be found. This did not happen often, as houses—empty or not—were scarce in those days.

It really took cooperation of everyone in the community to bring a school building into being. When the job was finished, it was revered and pointed to with pride. The person who gave the land, usually one acre, would get it back, or the donor's estate would get it back, when the property was no longer needed for school purposes.

Mr. Jack Petty belonged to the same faith and order of church as my father and mother. He lived in the Knee Knocker Swamp community in Pierce County, between the Satilla River and the Okefenokee Swamp. The settlers on this fertile hammock were few and far between. It was a wilderness of pine and cypress timber and countless small fur-bearing animals, such as raccoon, opossum, gray squirrel, bobcat, black bear, panther, and thousands of alligators. Timbermen and their outfits came and went, but these swamp settlers stayed on, making a good living from their fruitful land, from the sale of timber and the furs of animals they trapped during the winter season. Homegrown corn, sweet potatoes, sugarcane, pumpkins, small fruits, tame and wild honey, beef, pork, milk, and vegetables the year round provided a wonderful diet for these people.

Schooling for these settlers' children was a most difficult task. The community never had come together to build themselves a schoolhouse. They lived so far apart that it was difficult to achieve the necessary cooperation.

Mr. Jack Petty seemed to be the man most determined to do something about the situation. He had been to Blackshear, the county seat, to see the school superintendent, a Mr. Howard, who told him that if he could get as many as twenty pupils, the county would pay the state's allotment of one dollar per pupil per month for a three-month school term, that was if the community could furnish the house. So Mr. Petty told Mr. Howard he would see to it that there was a house, even if he had to give his own, and he would get the twenty pupils signed up.

Mr. Petty returned home, secured the twenty pupils, and donated one of his own cabins for the schoolhouse. In the meantime he had seen my father and asked him if one of his daughters would come to the swamp as a teacher. He promised our father he would make sure whoever came would be well taken care of and treated with respect and kindness by all concerned.

So Father came home and told us about Knee Knocker, the type of people who lived there, and how isolated it was. He said that if there was any place in the land where a real teacher was needed it was this community and that he would like to see one of us go. My sisters Lula and Ellen had been teaching for some time. They were good teachers, very much in demand, and had their choice of the best schools in Wayne County. I had taught only one term, but I told my father I would try it. So the contract was made with Mr. Howard. He hired me at twenty dollars a month for three months on the condition that Mr. Petty secure the house and twenty pupils. He set the date for me to go and said he would write to Mr. Petty. I was to write Mr. Petty also. School was to begin as soon as all could be brought together.

The day came for me to go. Father took me to Lulaton. The station there had been rebuilt after the War between the States. It had been destroyed in an attempt to prevent the Union soldiers on the gunboats at Brunswick from getting to the rich Satilla River plantations, but they came anyway. They walked on the torn-up road and swam the streams where the trestles had been burned. I was to go to a station called Coon Bottom, at the edge of Knee Knocker Swamp, where there was always some kind of timber business going on: crossties, pilings, sawmills, turpentine, and cordwood. The Brantley Company, founded in 1857, the same year Pierce County was founded, had its railroad tracks built into the lush hammock banks from which they took the sand that was added to commercial fertilizer in their great factory at Blackshear. The cars were filled with this rich earth each day by Negro laborers using hand shovels. Freight engines pulled the cars out each night through Waycross to Blackshear. Empty cars took their places to be filled the next day. This work was continuous year in and year out.

All the laborers supporting the many types of business at Coon Bottom were Negroes. The managers were white. There was always a good Negro school here each year. The Brantley Company and other businesses saw to that.

My train arrived at Coon Bottom at nightfall. There was no depot or agent or anything like that. The conductor helped me off the train, handed me my grip, and wished me luck with my Knee Knocker teaching adventure. The train was waved ahead and was gone. There I stood with what seemed to me hundreds of Negroes everywhere. I looked for someone to come forward to take me into the swamp, but no one came. The Negroes all melted away into the darkness; directly they were gathered around a great log fire some distance from the railway track. Here they were carrying on their laughing and storytelling. I stood there by the tracks. No one came. The air was chill, the night black, and the wind beginning to blow.

Although I was just sixteen, I came to my reasoning and told myself I could not stand there all night. So I picked up my grip and walked over to the campfire where the Negroes were gathered. I spoke to them with as brave a "Good evening" as I could muster. Most of them stood there spellbound. The oldest man in the crowd said, "Good evening Ma'am. Would you like to come up to the fire and warm?" I thanked him, and I stepped a few steps forward, set my grip down, and said, "I am Martha Mizell, youngest daughter of the Reverend J. P. Mizell of Lulaton, Wayne County, Georgia, and I have come to teach school in Mr. Jack Petty's community in the great Knee Knocker Swamp section out from Coon Bottom. He was to have met me, but he has not come."

The older Negro told me Mr. Petty had butchered hogs the day before, as the weather was near freezing, a good time to butcher. The man said he had helped Mr. Petty with the butchering and that Mr. Petty had told him they were trying to get them a school together. Mr. Petty had said he had not yet heard from the superintendent that he was going to send someone to him. He had gotten busy killing hogs that weekend and had not gone for his mail on Saturday as usual.

I asked the Negro man who was doing all the talking how far it was to Jack Petty's and if there was any way for me to get there. He told me it was some three miles into the heart of the swamp, the road was wet and bad, and there was no way of getting there except walking. Mr. Kirkland, the Brantley Company business manager, had the only driving horse and buggy, and he had gone down into Wayne County to see his girlfriend. It was usually close to daylight before he returned. I knew who his girlfriend was, a Miss Lilla Herrin, some twenty miles away, near my home.

I asked the man if he would show me the way. He told me Mr. Petty's was the closest white family to the railway stop. He told me how far it was. The way was bad, with a deep branch and poor foot logs to cross on. I told him I was used to walking, that I had walked three miles to school all my days. I did not mind, and I would surely appreciate it if he would go with me and show me the way. I knew my father would appreciate it also. They knew him, as my father always tried to see that the Negro had fair treatment and educational and religious opportunities as well as work opportunities. I well remember how bitterly my father was opposed to the Georgia white primary. I told them I knew Mr. Kirkland, and his lady friend was one of my near neighbors and dearest friends.

So off we started. The night was dark except for the brilliant stars. I remembered again, "He made the stars also" (Gen. 1:16). The road was all wet and full of puddles. The fall rains had come and gone, and now it was fair and cold. The man took my grip in one hand and held a long stick in the other. When we got to the edge of the Knee Knocker Swamp and had to attempt the first frosty foot logs, he stopped and cut me a stick from a stout sweet bay standing near by. It surely did help me get across those slippery logs without falling in the mud and water, and it helped me along the uneven road, over the roots, the mud holes, and lumps. So I continued to use it the rest of the way. We made good time. He soon realized that I was a brisk walker. I offered to take my grip part of the way to rest his arms and hands, but he said he did not mind, that he was used to carrying a load heavier than my grip every day all day long. He was a gum dipper in the turpentine plantation at Coon Bottom.

After a while we came to a somewhat higher rise of ground. This was the rich hammock on which Mr. Petty lived. We could see the small home and the barns as they shimmered in the starlight. We went up the lane to the house. I had never heard so many dogs in all my life. Blue speckled hounds. They stayed on their side of the fence, and we did the same. The old Negro man hollered and hollered. Finally Mr. Petty roused up and said, "Who is there?" "Isaac? What do you want this time of night?" and Isaac said, "Mr. Petty, I have your schoolteacher." Mr. Petty said, "What?" And Isaac answered, "Your schoolteacher."

By this time Mr. Petty was up and had tossed lightwood knots in the fire, and a brilliant light glowed as he threw open the door, calmed the dogs down, and told Isaac to bring me in. Isaac sat my bag down. I tried to give him a quarter, but he would not have it. He said he was sorry I had to walk through all those roots, mud, and slush. Mr. Petty thanked him graciously and told him he would see him later. So Isaac departed, to return to his friends. Mr. Petty turned to me and told me how sorry he was, that he had been so busy butchering hogs that he had not gone for his mail at Hoboken

Mrs. Petty was there in the bed in the front fireplace room. Mr. Petty stepped out on the porch to mind the hounds off of Isaac, and Mrs. Petty arose, dressed, and offered to fix me supper, I thanked her kindly and told her I had eaten an early supper before had I left my home to catch the train at Lulaton. Of course this was some six or seven hours later, but I surely was not going to expect anyone to fix me any supper that time of night.

Mr. Petty returned to the fireplace and remarked about how the chill was coming down and would be so good on his meat. Then he told Mrs. Petty to fix me a bed for the night. She went to one of the shed rooms of the cabin and adjusted the sleeping children around until she had a bed for me all by myself. She fixed it with nice clean sheets and pillowcases and the prettiest pattern quilts I had ever looked at. She fixed me a pan of water for washing and some drinking water in a pitcher and glass. Then she piloted me to the outdoor toilet. We had a nice friendly chat on the way out and back. She lamented that I was not met and had to walk. I told her not to mind, that I was used to walking and that I lived in the country also. I knew all about not getting the mail when things were too busy on the farm. She wished me a good night and told me when breakfast would be served the next morning. I told her if she did not hear me up and about on time to please call me.

My! How good that deep featherbed felt and how soft and warm those pretty pattern quilts were. I was so tired and quickly fell asleep.

Morning came all too soon. Breakfast was at the crack of dawn. My! How good! Plenty of home-ground hominy grits, plenty of fresh pork sausage well seasoned with homegrown sage and red pepper. Hot buttermilk biscuits, fresh butter, new Georgia cane syrup, and plenty of good cold sweet milk. I never drank coffee and do not to this day. I said to myself, "This may be in the middle of the great Knee Knocker Swamp, but the breakfast here is fit for a king. After breakfast, Mr. Petty and I talked about school. He told me it had been a long time since he had inquired of Mr. Howard about the possibility of having a school, and not having heard from him, he had let someone move into the cabin that he had intended to use for a school building. And now he just did not know what to do. He said he would try to get the man to move out if he could find the man another place to which he could move.

Well there I was, ready to teach but with no school. So I told him I had an uncle, Jim Craven, up on Big Creek, out from Schlattersville, and that I could go stay there while he made arrangements about the schoolhouse. He and his good wife decided that was the best plan, so he hitched up his mule to his buggy and took me to my Uncle Jim's, where I spent a week with my sixteen-year-old cousins. It was a good week of visiting.

Mr. Petty never got his house back for school purposes. I think the man and his family had moved in to help Mr. Petty harvest his enormous cane crop, and Mr. Petty wanted him to stay. So after waiting a week, I returned by way of train to my home.

I was sorry I did not get to teach in this Knee Knocker Swamp community. My experience there is still a joke among my family at home. When they want to get the best of me, they will say, "I suppose she wants to go to Mr. Jack Petty's to teach school."

My Short Stay in the Long Ford Community

In 1913, after my disappointing trip to the Knee Knocker community, the Wayne County school superintendent, B. D. Purcell, asked me to go to the Long Ford community, some thirteen miles south of Jesup. Miss Minnie Bennett, the teacher there, had been taken ill with a severe case of pneumonia and was not able to return in time to finish the school term that year. Mr. Purcell wanted me to take her place.

I was very happy to get this school. Mr. Harley Smith, one of the school trustees, met me at Broadhurst (a small railway station on the Jesup short line). He had his mule and wagon with him. Soon he had my trunk and grip in the back of the wagon and had helped me over the front wheels to a place beside him on the wagon seat. We were quickly on our way, through the cold dark night. Some four miles due north we soon crossed the Little Penholloway Creek bridge and turned to the right, where our road followed the bank of the creek to Long Ford. We did not have to cross the creek, as he lived on the side of the creek on which we were driving.

He had a nice little country home, a good farm, where he butchered native beef and home-raised hogs for the local markets at Jesup. He also raised quite a bit of cane and made good Georgia cane syrup for market. He seemed quite prosperous for that day and time. Any off time he had, he cut and sold firewood and cook-stove wood, also in Jesup.

He had a lovely wife; formerly she was a Miss Knight. They had several small children. The two oldest were to go to my school. The boy's name was Marvin, and I think the girl's name was Maize. They worshiped at New Salem Wesleyan Methodist Church, which was near by. I attended church with them and enjoyed the music, Sunday school classes, and devout sermons very much. When it was not church day in Long Ford, Mr. Smith would let me have the mule and buggy, and the two older children and I would go across the ford to Little Creek Baptist Church, where I met a lot of nice people, Harpers, Bennetts, Spells, and Knights among them. I made friends there that I still have, some sixty years since that far-distant day.

The school was a large frame building without a ceiling. It had one small heater, a few long benches, and a blackboard. That was all the equipment. Most of the children were beginners, in the three primary grades. We got on wonderfully, learning, playing, and enjoying ourselves. School continued in fine weather and good attendance through a beautiful Indian summer. My students were Smiths, Drawdys, Knights, Spells, Stricklands, and Wilsons. All were bright children. I visited with a good many of them for overnight stays. I always enjoyed visiting with their parents. Our school was on the bank of the creek, and some of the children had to walk across it on long foot-logs each night and morning.

When Christmastime came I went back to my home for the holiday season. I was to return on the first of January 1914 to start a new full-length term of five and a half months. When I got home, my father had already promised the trustees of Dowling School, some fifteen miles west of home, on the Big Satilla River, that I would teach for them. Father thought I would be well pleased to be so much nearer home. I regretted disappointing my newfound friends at Long Ford, and I very much disliked breaking my promise to them. But I did what my father asked me to do and accepted the Dowling School position. I wrote a letter of regret to the people at Long Ford, telling them that my parents wished me to work nearer home. My father saw how much I regretted not going back to those whom I had promised to teach, and he never asked me again to go back on my word to those whom I had given my promise. I taught for only six weeks at Long Ford, but they were six lovely weeks. Many of the young students I taught there have been my lifelong friends, and we still enjoy talking of those happy days long ago.

CHAPTER 4

Aunt Sara's Secret for a Happy Home

In January 1914 I went some fifteen miles from my home to teach at the Dowling School. This was a small one-room school where the snow-white sands of the south basin of the great Satilla River narrows to a very small ridge giving way to the rich hammocks of the dense Knee Knocker Swamp. There were some five or six families along the river ridge and about the same number in the swampland of the Knee Knocker. The river ridge folks were the Matthews, Robersons, Dennises, Dowlings, Jim Herrins, and others. The swamp folks were the Jim Lewis family and several Crews families. The school was located in a beautiful live oak grove near the long-established river road that ran some fifty-six miles between Brunswick and Waycross.

My boarding place was with the Dennis Dowling family, which consisted of the father, the Honorable Dennis Dowling, and his good wife, Sara Roberson Dowling; three sons, Charlie, Wiley, and Willie; and five beautiful daughters, Agnes (she was married to Albert Strickland), Eulalie (she was married to Newton Strickland, a first cousin of Albert), Mamie (she was married to Rembert Thornton), Hattie (she was married to Frank Raulerson), and Mizell. Mizell, the youngest daughter, attended the school I had come to teach.

Of the many homes I lived in during my fifty years of teaching in the rural schools of Wayne County, I must say this was the best ordered, run with the most timely schedule, and never any hurry, rush, or overly burdensome work on any member of the family. Their living was made from the production and sale of their many farm crops and animals, and sale of the fine timber products from their well-cared-for timberlands in the two nearby swamps, the Satilla and the Knee Knocker. Timber for such products as pilings, saw logs, crossties, heart cypress shingles, and barrel staves was always ready to be harvested and sold when the need arose. This work was usually done through the winter months.

The men of the farm would arise early, do the morning chores, and have a hearty breakfast. The timber choppers would leave for the day with a well-packed lunch. At the end of the day, they returned, full of the satisfaction of a good day's work and with some merry tale about their day to tell the homebound family.

Here they would find Aunt Sara with all the evening chores completed. The cattle, horses, and mules had been brought in from the pasture, watered, and well taken care of for the night. The chickens, turkeys, and geese were housed and latched up from the ever-preying foxes and owls. Eggs were gathered, cows milked, fattening hogs fed and watered, cotton weighed and stored in the cotton houses. All the animals were secure for the night, and all the gates were closed and tightly pegged. Wood was in neat stacks for the fireplaces and cookstove. Plenty of water had been drawn-up for the night supply and for the morning washups. Beds were all neatly made, their covers spread according to the feel of the weather, based just on long years of observation, as there were not any weather bureaus or radio reports in that day and time. The lamps were all filled, washed, polished, and burning brightly.

A steaming hot supper was ready and waiting to be placed on a well-set table as soon as the men arrived from the forest and were washed and ready to eat. Oh! Could they eat. Have you ever seen timber choppers eat? If not, you have missed one of the great joys of life.

All this was carried on under the direction of Aunt Sara. Every task was done well and on time. No one behind schedule, and there was time to spare to do the nice extras, such as baking delicious pies, cakes, cookies, and jelly-rolls for school and for the timber choppers' lunches. Or for putting in a new quilt to be quilted for warm cover or for a son or daughter who was to be married soon. There was time to cut and make a lovely dress, or to clean, brush, and press all the ladies' and men's winter suits and to hang them correctly. There were no laundry or pressing clubs anywhere then. The women washed and ironed all the family laundry. All those sons and Uncle Dennis wore snow-white shirts when they went out to church, out visiting, to funerals, or to attend to business.

There was never any clutter. Everything was in place. The family enjoyed each other and the company that was always coming, whether expected or unexpected. They were always received with a hearty welcome, well cared for during their stay, and invited to return again when they could. I lived in this home and watched the ease and efficiency of its care and production from day to day, and the joy that ran through everyone every day of their lives. No one was ever worried or harassed because some task was not done.

One day I asked Aunt Sara to tell me the secret of this happy home. Here is what she said: "Love, trust, obedience, thrift, saving, and always striving to do our best at what is needed to be done and to do this with all our might. When the day is done, we quit, rest, enjoy ourselves and are ready to do the same the next day. And if tomorrow does not come, there is no need to worry over what we did not get done. We keep everything in order." This is one of the best pieces of teaching philosophy that I have ever gathered, whether it be from a college professor, an educational text, or a teaching seminar. It never failed me, and I used it from that day forward.

I never knew an evening in that home that was not joyous, though there was also a serious side of life, planning of the work to be carried on and the affairs to be attended to the following day. From the oldest to the youngest, each contributed to the happy home. No matter what the weather, there was a task to fit the occasion. Like the day of the big ice storm, no one could go anyplace. All day long, we sat around the great roaring fire, shelled North Carolina peanuts for spring planting, had a feast at the noonday meal. Early in the evening, we had a big candy-pulling, roasted peanuts, and sang. We went to bed early, slept warm, rose the next day, and resumed our regular schedules. We were all in a fine mood for our day off on account of heavy weather.

Never a fret or a worry. A much-needed task would be accomplished, and there would be no worry about peanut seed when the dark nights in April came, and it was "pender" planting time in the snow-white sands of the great Satilla Ridge. All would be ready in this household.

Then there would be the cold, drizzly afternoons of shelling, by hand. And selecting the seed corn for spring planting, always saving the cobs for Aunt Sara to bake her pound cakes and then taking the ashes to make the lye for soaking the corn kernels to make big hominy, which was eaten with sausage, sweet potatoes, pickles, and greens. It would take one evening or day of heavy weather to cut Irish potatoes for seed. There was never any hurry or weather worrying. When the seasons came, everything was in readiness to go forward in a joyous working plan for pleasure and profit.

There grew up a great love between me and this entire family, but my teaching took me to many other communities far from this section of the county, and I would not get to see them very often. Yet the love and friendship between us lingered on, and I would always be invited to Aunt Sara's birthday. I well remember her ninety-sixth birthday celebration, which was at the home of her daughter Agnes, Mrs. Albert Strickland. Aunt Sara told me she milked the cows that morning and that she made egg custard pies for the dinner, just like I always liked them. We had such a blessed day talking, remembering the good times we had in her home. Uncle Dennis had passed away, and Aunt Sara now lived with Agnes.

I loved all of her children and counted them among my best-loved friends. I so well remember her oldest son, Charlie. He was many years my senior, and I always thought him so tall and handsome and so kind and gentle to everyone, always looking out for everyone's happiness wherever he might be. I remember a party that the community gave for my brother Bob after he came home from his tour of duty in the service. He had been in the Philippines and Hawaii. They wanted to hear him talk about the wonderful places he had been and what he had seen. I was not yet old enough to go to such affairs, as I was only thirteen (sixteen was the usual age at our home when girls were allowed to keep company with older boys and girls and go to their parties). My brother begged my mother and father to let me go. He said he wanted me to go and enjoy the party with him, that he would take good care of me. So I made my debut into our social set that evening. My brother was quite attentive for a while, and then he got so involved in the merriment that I was left quite alone.

Square dancing was the order of the evening. The neighborhood musicians did their best with their toe-tapping music, with the fiddle and bow and the ever-tinkling banjo. Charlie Dowling saw that I was just sitting out the party, and he came and asked me to dance. I told him I knew nothing of the figures, that this was my very first time to attend a square dance. He told me he would be glad to teach me. I was still very standoffish, telling him I did not believe I could do it. So he suggested that if I got three of my young girlfriends who, like me, did not know the figures, he would get three other young men who knew all the steps well. His brother-in-law, Newt Strickland, would call figures. Then, he said, we would go into another section of the house to practice. So we had our first lesson in square dancing. All this took a good portion of the evening, but Charlie seemed to enjoy it and was happy to help a group of giggling young girls have a pleasant evening. He was just as thoughtful of elderly people in seeing they were included in the gatherings. From that day forward I was able to square dance, but I never cared much for such a pastime. I had more serious plans for my life, but I was glad that I had the opportunity to learn.

Charlie married a lovely teacher many years before I was married. He raised a good family and was a good provider and a wonderful husband. He was seventy-six years old when he passed away. I went to his funeral early, hoping to get to see and talk with some of the family. There I saw Aunt Sara with her daughter Mrs. Eulalie Strickland. Aunt Sara said to me, "There lies seventy-six years of my joy, such a sweet pretty baby, such a loving lively lad, such a noble obedient son, faithful father and loving husband, and such a faithful man to his church, his God, and his community, my son Charlie, my eldest. He had been such a blessing wherever he went. I loved and honored him and I will miss him so." She lived many years after that, but I never did get to see her again. She passed at 102. Let us say with the Holy Writ:

Who can find a virtuous woman? For her price is far above rubies. The heart of her husband doth safely trust in her, so that he shall have no need of spoil. She will do him good and not evil, all the days of her life. She seeketh wool and flax; and work them willingly with her hands. She is like the merchant ships; she bringeth her goods from afar. She riseth also while it is yet night, and giveth meat to her household, and a portion to her maidens. She considereth a field, and buyeth it, with the fruit of her hands she planteth a vineyard. She girdeth her loins with strength, and strengtheneth her arms. She perceiveth that her merchandise is good, her candles goeth not out by night. She layeth her hands to the spindle, and her hands hold the distaff. She stretcheth out her hands to the poor, yea, she reacheth forth her hands to the needy. She is not afraid of the snow for her household; for all of her household are clothed with scarlet. She maketh herself coverings of tapestry; her clothing is silk and purple. Her husband is known in the gates, when he sitteth among the elders of the land. She maketh fine linen and selleth it, and delivereth girdles unto the merchant. Strength and honor are her clothing, and she shall rejoice in time to come. She openeth her mouth with wisdom and in her tongue is the law of kindness. She looketh well to the ways of her household; and eateth not the bread of idleness. Her children rise up and call her blessed; her husband also, and he praiseth her. Many daughters have done virtuously, but thou excelleth them all. Favor is deceitful and beauty is vain, but a woman that feareth the lord, she shall be praised. Give her the fruit of her hands and let her own works praise her in the gates. (Prov. 31:10–31.)

Sara Roberson Dowling was my dearly beloved friend whom I cherished and loved from my early youth until her passing in 1967, more than fifty years of earthly joy in having known her and being guided by her wisdom, love, and kindness.

CHAPTER 5

Penholloway School

This school is where I came into my own and found that teaching would be my lifework and my life happiness. In late October of 1914 our school superintendent, B. D. Purcell, wrote and asked me to go to Penholloway School in the Big Cypress Swamp, where a new school building had been erected in this community that had not had a day of school in more than twenty years. The families that lived there were surrounded on every side by the great cypress swamp, and it was difficult for them to get their children out to neighboring schools, so they just didn't go to school or to many other places for twenty years.

I visited Mr. Purcell and got his ideas on what teaching really meant. He felt I was the person for the job, and if I could not make a go of it, he would not hold it against my teaching career. I accepted the challenge. He gave me a box of crayon, some white chalk, a book list, and a box full of old school magazines. He took me to the railway station on a Monday morning and put me on the Bogey, the train that ran on the Jesup short line. It was made up of a long train of freight and one passenger car to serve all those from Jesup to Folkston. My destination was Broadhurst again, only this time I arrived in the early morning. Mr. Andrew Manning, one of my new school trustees, met me. He had his brother Mr. Monroe Manning's fine mule and buggy. We were soon loaded up. I had no trunk, just my suitcase. I had been advised by my superintendent not to take a trunk until I decided that I could stay and work at this school and community. We went some four miles due east after crossing the big Penholloway Creek. As I remember the timber road trail that we traveled, it was out of one mud hole into another.

It was almost noontime when arrived. We had a good country dinner of rutabaga, turnips, corn bread, hot biscuits, sweet potatoes, country sausage, new Georgia cane syrup, butter, and milk. After the meal, we went to Monroe Manning's home and his big cane-grinding. There, the whole community was gathered to see the new teacher who had come to teach their school. The trustees and I had a conference, and they wished to know about my plans. I told them the salary I was to receive and showed them my contract with the county board of education. The last school they had was on a tuition basis, where every parent paid so much for each child he signed up. I explained that this was a free school, and all who wished to come were welcome at no cost at all. I also gave them a letter from the superintendent naming some things they had promised him they would provide for the children: a good pump for water, four-foot-wide graded walkways, good smooth-hewn logs across the waterways, and good poles to use when crossing the streams. They were to make sure that plenty of wood was available for the heater, to see that the books were gotten at the very first opportunity, and to take good care of me. Mr. Purcell told them he would be down to see them in a few days. I also showed them my teaching license to let them know I was a bona fide teacher. They wished to know when I wanted to begin. I told them I had come to work and that I would like to begin at eight on the morrow if they could get the word around. They said they would.

I told them I had a book list and the price for each. I asked that they go for the books as soon as we could gather the order together. Monroe Manning said he would close his cane-grinding for the next day to help get the school going. He would take his mule and buggy and go to Jesup, thirteen miles away, to get books, slates, pencils, paper, pens, and ink.

Bright and early the next morning we were all there. I rang my brass bell at eight. Everyone came in and sat quietly. I told them my name, where I was from, who my father and mother were, and why I was there. Many of them knew my father, as he had been on the county board of education for many years and had also been county commissioner at another time, and some of them had heard him preach. Now I asked the trustees to tell the people about their plans for the school and the work needed to be done. These were some of the best school community talks I have ever heard. I asked the older people to express themselves if they wished to do so. Some made a few remarks; most of them said they agreed with everything their superintendent had asked them to do, and they were willing to help the trustees get it done. Some two hours had gone by when I told them it was time for recess, for we never held children more than two hours at the longest sessions. I asked the children to go out quietly, to get themselves a drink, and to play until I rang the bell. All the parents came up and shook hands with me, telling me who they were, how many children they had, where they lived, and how often I must come to see them.

In some thirty minutes I rang the bell, and the children came in and quietly took their seats. I began to make up the book order. I had some forty-six students, aged six to forty-two. Not one could read or write a word, so my first book order was for forty-six school primers. They cost fourteen cents each. On another list I put down a slate, a pencil, a paper tablet and a slate pencil for each student. The parents came forward and gave me the money for the primers and writing materials. I made a combined listing of the above and gave it to Monroe Manning along with the money I had collected. Mr. Manning was there with his wife, Victoria, to register their children for school, but soon he was on his way to get the needed supplies.

I asked each parent to come forward and sign up their children, giving their names and ages and the distance and direction of their homes from school. We already had the grade of each child. As soon as this work was over, it was time for the noontime break, at which we would eat our lunch and play awhile. I also told them that after lunch I wanted to give all my time to the children to learn their names and let them know what I expected of them and what they could expect from me. The adults who were not students could stay if they wished, but my time and attention would be given to the children. I only had one rule and that was "to do it right," and it would be my job from day to day to help them do it right.

After noontime, most parents left to go home to see after their work. They admonished their children to be good, to mind their teacher, and to be home on time. I told them school would close at 4:00 and begin again in the morning at 8:00. Morning recesses were from 10:00 to 10:30, noontime from 12:00 to 1:00. Afternoon recess was 2:30 to 2:45. School closed at 4:00.

In the classroom after lunch we had time to play a few games and to talk some. I began with the six year olds. I asked them their names and about their families. Some would tell me; others would not say a word. I went all the way through the list, grouping them according to age. I felt that was one way to begin. Of course I knew that their ability to learn would soon place them in different groups as we went forward. When I got to those above eighteen, I put them in one group and took some time to find out why they wanted to come to school this late in life. I saw that I had my hands full without them, and if they did not have a good reason for being there and a determination to learn, we would not get very far.

Pretty Gussie said she wanted to learn to read and write so she could write and read her own letters to her boyfriends. She never knew whether her friend who read her letters to her was reading them correctly, and she never knew whether they wrote what she told them to write. Verdie was many years older than the others. She was a skilled home nurse, but she was handicapped by not being able to read the directions for medicines she had to give when there was no doctor nearby. She had to memorize the directions and tie different colored threads to each bottle to tell from which bottle to give medicine at morning, noon, and night. Also, she longed to teach in Sunday school and to be able to read the Bible for herself and for her family. John said he wanted to learn to read and write and figure so he could keep accounts on their farm and read the Bible for himself and write letters to his mother should he ever have to leave home. (Several years later John had to go away to fight in World War I. I was so happy that I had been able to get John to where he could write a good letter—to his mother or anyone.) Lige's desires were about the same as John's; they were brothers, whose father had passed away.

The other older ones gave valid reasons why they wished to come to school and overcome the handicap of not knowing the written form of their mother tongue. I saw they were in earnest. Although I could not count them in the daily average of school attendance, I told them to come to school. I would expect them to follow the same rules and regulations as the children. I talked to them at length and told them they could be a great deal of help to me in having a good school. They were all as grown as I was and knew how to behave and set good examples for the children.

By now it was time for our afternoon recess. It was just long enough for the students to relieve themselves, get a drink, stretch their legs, get all their things together, and all come in when I rang the bell. After the last session of that first day at school, I showed them how I wanted them to depart from the building.

We had only the one door at the front end, a window on each side of the door, three windows on each side of the building. The whole back end was used for the good slate blackboard. Our study seats were five rows of wide well-made benches on each side of middle aisle in the back section of the room. The benches were short enough so that walkway space was left between the far end of the bench and the outside wall. I told them the first row to the front would be the first to leave all day Monday, the second row would be next, and so on. On Tuesday the second row would be first to go out all day (and first row would be last). By Friday the fifth row would be first.

Other benches were arranged at the front for recitation. We had visitors' benches and, around the heater, warming benches, where we sat to get ourselves warm without having to disturb the study benches. I placed my desk, a handmade table, at the front of the room. My chair, also handmade, was hickory and had a cowhide bottom. The stove was in the middle of the building. I called the roll and asked them to stand so I could look right at them as I called their names. I told them I wanted them to be in their places the next morning as I called the roll and that I would know all their names by then. They all snickered. They got their lunch buckets, shoes, coats, hats, and other belongings and got in their correct places. When I dismissed them, they passed out as I had outlined to them, in quietness and order, and it was that way every day for the two years I was there. Never was a coat, hat, shoes, dinner pail, or book forgotten.

The next morning all forty-six were there, as well as Monroe Manning with our primers (in later years there would be special books for adult beginners), our writing materials, and some other supplies and aids for me. He delivered the material to me and told the children to study hard and to keep their books clean. He also told them to be sure to come to his cane-grinding, and especially to the big candy-pulling he was planning for the last night of the "cane-grinding season." He wished me luck and told me to come by for some cold cane juice after school. I boarded at his brother's and had to pass right by Monroe Manning's house on my way home. I told him I would, as I was very fond of cane juice.

My next task was to write the students' name on their tablets, slates, and books. With the sharp knife for that purpose, I sharpened their pencils. I began the day with a devotional from Genesis, reading from King James Version of the Bible. I sang "America" for them and told them I wanted them to learn it so they could help me sing, for I got very lonesome singing by myself. I repeated the first verse for them several times, and soon they were singing all four verses, in good time, melody, and harmony, and with quite a bit of gusto.

I began with the subject of reading, using the age groups I had worked out the day before. I used every educational method I had ever read of and quite a few of my own invention to get them to master the art of reading. I taught them about punctuation marks. I told them funny stories about the different letters of the alphabet. I worked diligently on "the spoken word" from the very first day of school. I would tell them enjoyable stories on different topics, and I would have them do the same for me each day. Directly we were reading and spelling; writing came more slowly. Work with numbers seemed to come the easiest of all.

Our days were full of happy exciting times. My older students were apt learners. They were diligent, happy, and well behaved. We sent for more advanced books for them by the first person going to Jesup. I took them up grade by grade in all subjects. So that their vocabulary would be well grounded, we first wrote our letters, then words, and then full sentences. We were soon got into the letter-writing business. I would set up the situation for the letters, then give them the correct form for the letter and the envelopes. My blackboard came in handy to set forth examples for this lesson. The younger students soon became good letter writers also. That is one of the blessings of a one-teacher school. If you pay attention and listen to what is happening around you, you will learn from it, never a moment of wasted time. It became a habit that anyone going to Jesup would come by the schoolhouse to find out if any books or other school supplies were needed. The older boys and girls galloped through their primers. Then came the first readers, followed by the second readers, spellers, little number books, and language books.

We also studied history, geography, and literature. Because the older students' desire was to learn to read, write, spell, and figure, I did not call those subjects by their names. Instead I broadened the range of reading material and listed the books I knew they could handle, and we did a lot of good "reading" in the many other areas of learning. The little folks' lessons came as regularly as the clock. I went round and round from one class to the next, never missing a one, from eight in the morning until four in the afternoon. It was not long until some of them had to have books more advanced than the primer. We did not have "pre-primers" in those days. What a blessing these young ones were. Our numbers were the most fun. I taught them to count by noses, fingers, toes, dinner buckets, pigs, chickens, and geese. Teaching them to write, including how to hold a pencil and where to place their paper, was also exciting. We learned songs and games, for indoors and outside. We had to learn the songs by memory because we did not have any music books. We learned of our great national heroes and of the days set apart to honor them. Everything was new to them and exciting to me.

Hon. J. P. Shedd was our county agent, and Mrs. Annie B. Bennett was our home agent. I had been a very staunch 4-H member before I began teaching, and I believed wholeheartedly in its motto, Make the Best Better, and its goal of enriching the head, heart, hands, and health. That was what I was trying to do here in this long-neglected community. So I lost no time in inviting the 4-H people to come to my school to set forth their plan of work, study, and training. Everyone between the ages of ten and eighteen was enrolled. And in the fall, everyone went to the fair in Jesup, each carrying his or her own exhibit.

Mr. Sherrod Manning rounded up two mules and a large turpentine-barrel-hauling wagon and took all the 4-H club boys and girls and me; the younger children went with their fathers and mothers in their horse-drawn buggies and wagons. We all loaded up when the time came and were on our way in the pre-dawn. We moved across the Big Cypress in our long parade, our wagonload of 4-H'ers and their carefully packed exhibits leading the line.

When we got to Jesup, we set up our exhibits and then had some time to meet new people and to enjoy the exhibits of others at the fairground. You see, we were newcomers. People had never heard of Penholloway before. We won first prize as a club for having every member present with a good exhibit of their project, 100 percent on both counts. By mid-afternoon we gathered our ribbons and prizes and got ready to leave, telling good-bye to newfound friends. The congratulations we received were well worth the long ride to the fair, but the long ride back was too short for near all the excitement to be told.

I could well realize then that tomorrow at school would be a reliving of the day at the fair. So right then and there I planned to use the experience as a wonderful day of learning by writing of our ten most exciting happenings of the day. I wish you could have read them with me. Our school was now in its second year, and the majority of the forty-six students could by now read, write, spell, and compose beyond the average rate of second-year students. Making the Best Better. This became the class watchword, and mine throughout my teaching career.

Our school year had now become five months per year, and our year ran from July 1 through June 30. We celebrated all the special days that came during our school term. For Halloween we had songs, poems, and fortunes. We took a walk to an old hollow tree where we knew some owls had nested and made jack-o'-lanterns from local pumpkins. After we spooned the flesh of the pumpkin out for pies, we placed candles inside them (I bought the candles). After recess judges selected the best jack-o'-lanterns and awarded Halloween candy to the winners. We had already planned that whoever received candy would share it with everyone. After we used them at school, each child took his lantern home to put on the gatepost or on the garden wall or doorsteps. But the best part of the celebration was the old witch who rode her broom into school and told everyone's fortune. She stole the show.

My older student Verdie was my witch. I helped her fix her costume and prepare a nice juicy fortune about each student. Everyone was so excited about the jack-o'-lanterns when we got them all lighted that no one missed Verdie. She slipped out to put on Grandmother Manning's dress, a tall hat, a floppy cape, and a billowy apron and to get her fortunes in order. The witch came knocking on the door. I let her in and invited her to sit at my desk. Then I walked to the back of the room to be among the students. The witch read the fortunes aloud before giving the students their fortunes to read at their desks. Everyone was so happy. In the meantime, away went the witch—out to the ladies toilet to change. She eased back into the schoolroom unnoticed and read her fortune along with the others. We were through by 4 P.M.

I had returned to the front of the room and had everyone get their wraps, shoes, and dinner pails, plus the lighted jack-o'-lanterns. They left the schoolroom in order and were soon on their way. I will remember all my life what a happy group of children they were going home through the dense pine forest in the late October evening.

Then came Thanksgiving. The patrons were there with baskets of their best food to go on the Thanksgiving table under the tall pines. We had a good country dinner of backbone and rice, baked ham, baked sweet potatoes, great bowls of fresh sweet rutabaga turnips, late field peas, ham hocks, hog's-head cheese, liver pudding, cucumbers, and little green watermelons. There were also pumpkins, egg pies, jelly cakes, pound cakes, sugar cookies, cane juice fresh from the mill, and hot coffee made on the fire nearby. I tried to eat something from everyone's basket. The chairman of the board of trustees graced the table. All the children had instructions about how to behave and how to ask some grown person to serve them. I saw to it that every little child was well fed if his mama got too busy visiting with her neighbor to wait on her child.

We had our program after the bountiful dinner. I thought the children did wonderfully well. Of course they had practiced their pieces and knew how to leave their seats and return as I called them forth to give their thankful blessings. The grown people gave theirs spontaneously from their seats. To open the program, the children sang "Over the River and through the Wood to Grandfather's House We Go." I told the story of the first Thanksgiving, and we closed with everyone singing all four stanzas of "America." I had sent copies of "America" to every home and asked the parents to memorize every word and to help their children do the same so we could all sing it together. Four o'clock came all too soon. Everyone was so happy, with both old and young telling me it was the best time they had ever had in their lives. I told them we would expect them to come to our Christmas program.

We had no holiday from teaching for Thanksgiving or for any other holiday, so we had school the Friday following Thanksgiving. In every class we commented on the different happenings of the day before. We used our Thanksgiving experience in our spelling, number work, writing, storytelling, sentence formation, and question-and-answer period.

I had not been in the community but one month before I had been in every home. Many people asked me to come back and spend the night. Quite a few of them lived in one-room log cabins. Some had added shed side rooms to their cabins. I always accepted their invitations to come at the time they stated. I will say right now that I enjoyed every one of those overnight visits. In the one-room cabins they would hang up sheets or quilts to partition the cabin into rooms. I always had a clean bed and usually had one of the older girl children as a bedfellow. The food was always good, even if it was home-ground hominy, bread, potatoes, greens, fresh pork, or well-cooked chicken. Sometimes there was beef or wild game, such as quail, squirrel, turkey, rabbit, possum, or raccoon. I shall cherish and remember those overnight visits all the days of my life. They were so happy to have me come and break bread with them and always seemed to enjoy having me talk with them. In fact I think I taught the patrons as much as I did the children about things they wished to know. They seemed so eager to learn.

At that time the teachers of Wayne County reported to their superintendent once a month to give him an account of our work, to receive instructions, and to receive our small check for the month's work. We turned in a written report of our attendance and enrollment. While we were in Jesup we did our meager shopping. I was now getting forty dollars per month, twice the salary I received when I started in 1913.[1]

To get to the teachers meeting each month my patrons would have to take me to Broadhurst, across the Big Cypress and through the pine forest over the deeply rutted timber road so I could get on the evening train. I would spend the night at a hotel in Jesup, go to the meeting the next morning, and do my shopping in the afternoon. Then I would catch a Southern train to Gardi and spend the night there with friends. One of my patrons would come for me some eight miles across Little Creek after they had struggled through the Big Cypress to get on the Gardi Road. I would get back to my boarding place by late dinnertime on Sunday. In the two years I taught at Penholloway School I never missed a meeting. While I was in Jesup, I always did a lot of trading for the ladies of the community, purchasing items such as thread, braid, buttons, laces, ribbons, and sometimes shoes.

After Thanksgiving, all turned to planning for Christmas. I got the students some little poems and taught three Christmas songs—"Up on the Housetop," "Silent Night, Holy Night," and "Away in a Manger"—by rote. I read them the Christmas Story from the Bible. I also told them the story of St. Nicholas, and his spirit coming to see little children at Christmastime until this good day. Of course I stressed the wise men bringing gifts to the Christ child. One day I told them about Christmas trees, pine, holly, and cedar. The very next morning one of my patrons, Mr. Sherrod Manning, came to tell me that there was a beautiful holly tree on his Penholloway Creek property and that we were welcome to it. He would cut it and bring it to us, but he wanted me to go see it first. So we set the next Saturday morning to look it over. I told him to bring Mrs. Manning and his two daughters, Nola and Lee. In fact the whole family came, and I brought some of my older schoolgirls with me, Etta Manning, Verdie Brooker, Dolly Wilkerson. We all met early, as Saturdays were always such busy days for me.

I had to do my laundry work and get my wardrobe ready for the next week. I also had to plan and prepare for the Christmas program as well as my work and daily schedule for next week. I can tell you that teaching so many students keeps you on the move if you keep them all working for eight hours every day. There is no time for planning in the schoolroom. You had better have it all ready when you arrive on Monday morning, or you will soon be so bewildered that you can't get anything done.

The tree was the most beautiful holly I had ever seen, so green and luxuriant, with red berries from the lowest bough to the very tip of its crown. He said he would bring it on his timber skidder with care so as not to bruise, crush, or shake off the beautiful waxy red berries. So I told him to have it at the schoolhouse on Monday, the last day before we began our Christmas holidays. I told him how to bring ropes and wires so we could make it secure in its position. Our school was a brand-new clapboard building, not yet ceiled. The tree would reach from floor to the very rooftop. We would have to be so gentle to get it in the door. I took him and Mrs. Manning to one side and asked them if they thought they could get him all ready to play Santa Claus.

Now I had to begin planning a program and the decorations in earnest. I took five dollars of my money and bought each of my students a ten-cent gift: colored crayons for primary students, handkerchiefs and pretty combs for the older boys and girls. With the forty cents I had left I bought candles and candleholders for the Christmas tree. (I tremble now to think that I had lighted candles on that beautiful tree.)

The Christmas program was well prepared. Every child knew his part. Every patron we had was there. They gathered early, as they wanted to get home before dark and cold covered the watery walkways we had to travel to and from school. We had my small gifts for the children, a few gifts the children got together for each other, and a few their parents contributed. The trustees of the school had an apple, orange, and some Christmas candy put in tiny paper bags for each child. We had wreaths of snow-white popcorn and paper chains for our tree. After we had the tree in place and all presents on the tree, I asked the children to go relieve themselves, to get a drink of water, and to stretch their legs by walking around until I rang the bell. While they were gone, Mr. Manning got himself dressed and climbed up back of the tree and sat quietly on a joist. I rang the bell, and the children came in quietly and sat on the front benches. (All books and pencils and slates and tablets had been packed in boxes and stacked at the back of the room so all space on the benches could be used for seating. Standing room was also filled to overflowing with friends and neighbors. The tree was beautiful.

I had a Christmas tree every year I taught, but I never had a tree more beautiful than this one.

I opened the program by reading the Christmas story from the Bible. Then I began our program with "Away in a Manger," then poems for the older children, Christmas acrostics for the younger children, and songs for everyone, beginning with the happy song "Up on the Housetop." Santa Claus came down with a "Ho! Ho! Ho!" and a "Ha! Ha! Ha!" and gave out the gifts after a couple of our older boys and girls took them from the tree and handed them to me at my table, where I had a brilliant Coleman lamp. Darkness came early in that dense pine forest, and my lamp, the lanterns on the walls in back of the room, and the candles on the tree were the only lights we had. Although we had begun by four, nightfall caught us on that cold December day. We distributed the gifts, and everyone was asked to stand to join us in singing "Silent Night, Holy Night." I closed the program with the best Christmas prayer I could remember from my young happy years in my childhood community.

After dismissal everyone came forward, telling me how beautiful the tree was, how happy they were, how proud they were of their children, and how much they enjoyed the program. They wished me a merry Christmas, a most joyous one. I thanked them and told them to have a wonderful Christmas. I told the children to be good until I got back on the first Monday of January to start school again. (I did not dare tell them how badly I wanted to be home to be part of my own family's Christmas festivities and age-old traditions.)

Except for the family with whom I lived, all friends and patrons were gone. The fire in the heater had burned to the last ember. Every candle was off the tree and out. I fastened down the windows with the window sticks that had been used to prop them up. Carrying the Coleman lamp with me, I locked the door and placed the key deep in my purse. We walked around the building to see that all was well. We even checked the outdoor toilets to see that there was no mischief stored up there. All was secure. We walked away home in the beautiful December twilight, tired but happy.

Early the next morning I was up and on my way to Broadhurst to catch the Bogey about 7:30 on Saturday morning. My father met me at Raybon with the buggy and Dolly, our beautiful red. I waved at my first cousins all the way down the road to our home. I was so happy to see my mother that I cried when I fell into her arms, just as I had done at Raybon when my father met me. The memory of his arms around me that day is one of the most precious of my whole life.

The two weeks of holiday passed all too quickly, with the usual family and community festivities, cousins coming and going, parties, dinners, and Christmas rides. But I had a job to do. So as soon as Christmas was over, I had to begin to make ready for leaving, to get my trunk ready to go back with me with my few accumulated teaching supplies and clothes enough to last me through a long cold winter and into springtime. As my term was now five and a half months long, I would not be through teaching until about mid April, having taught about two months before Christmastime. Because the Bogey did not run on Sunday, I would have to return on Saturday night to be ready to open school the first Monday in January 1915 as I had promised.

School opened on time, lessons went well, and learning progressed. Special days were remembered with proper stories, songs, and poems. On Robert E. Lee's birthday, we sang "Dixie" and "Bonnie Blue Flag." On Georgia Day, we sang "Georgia Land" and "No State Like Georgia" and told stories of General Oglethorpe and Tomochichi, the Yamacraw chief who befriended him. On Abraham Lincoln's birthday, we sang "Battle Hymn of the Republic" and "We Are Tenting Tonight on the Old Camp Ground."

Then there was Easter to celebrate in a big way. A long cold rainy winter was over. How happy we were to see the warm sunshine and all the beautiful flowers of the fertile soil of the Big Cypress. In the woods and on the creek banks, there were ty ty, huckleberry, chokeberry, and sparkleberry blossoms, buttercups, violets, and lilies. In the old-time yards, there were spirea, sweet shrubs, roses, and more as spring advanced. We had the beautiful story of the Resurrection, all earth rejoicing, and of course we had the Easter egg hunt. Here the crayons they received for Christmas came in handy to make all kind of beautiful colors and designs on their Easter eggs. We also used natural dye from buttercups and other flowers.

After I returned from Christmas holidays, I lived in the home of Mr. and Mrs. W. E. Bennett, who lived across Big Cypress on the road to Broadhurst. They had one little girl, Annie, who was of school age. The way to the school was too far and too dangerous for her to walk alone, so I was glad to stay with her family and go and come with her. So that we could walk more safely, they cut big pine trees and laid them for foot logs after scoring them smooth for about one foot across. We also had a long pole to help us balance our way across the deep water. We could stand it up against a big tree until we came back in the afternoon. No one ever bothered our hand poles as I remember. I enjoyed my stay there very much. Mrs. Bennett was Miss Rogers before she was married, the oldest daughter of one of Wayne County's most highly respected families. I always enjoyed visiting at her mother's home, where Mrs. Peggy Rogers lived with her two unmarried daughters, Miss Hattie Rogers and Miss Mamie Rogers.

While I was at the Bennett home, I had to return to my home in March for my sister Mary Ellen Mizell's wedding. She had been teaching in Camden County and married Benjamin Clifton Lang at our home on March 1. My good friend Mrs. Bennett sent a washtub full of beautiful roses from her garden to help decorate for the wedding. She laughingly told me she would do the same for me if I would just let her know when I was getting married. I told her okay but that I was not husband hunting yet for awhile. I had other things I planned to do. Her roses were planted in rows in her garden and were plowed and hoed like the rest of the garden. They were always so beautiful. Many a bouquet of them I had in my schoolroom, as well as other beautiful flowers from the forest and swamps and from my other patrons' yards and gardens.

This beautiful new school was a far cry from the little log cabin I had started to teach in at Burnt Bay. And my salary had been doubled. The school had been built by Hon. W. C. Rogers, Mrs. Bennett's brother, and given to the people of the Big Cypress, quite a few of whom worked in his timber business in the timberlands nearby. Mr. Rogers did not want any one of these people to feel they had control of the building, so he gave the key to the county school superintendent and told him to give it to the teacher who came to teach. So the key was given to me, and Mr. Purcell charged me to hold on to it faithfully.

The Wesleyan Methodists and a group of Missionary Baptists requested the use of the school for church services. I asked my superintendent, and he said yes, as long as their Sundays did not conflict and if I would unlock the door, stay through the service, and lock the door when they were finished. The Methodists chose the first Sunday and the Saturday before, with Rev. J. B. Lastinger of the Empire community and Rev. Buddy Drury of Camden County filling the regular appointments. The Baptists chose the third Sunday, with Rev. Linwood Little of Browntown filling the appointments. I always enjoyed their meetings—the singing, the prayers, scripture-reading, and the sermons—as well as visiting with the people before and after the services. Neither of these appointments ever resulted in a permanent church, but I understand that in years afterward the Presbyterian church people sent a missionary to come and live among these good people, and he did succeed in establishing a mission to be served by the minister from the Jesup Presbyterian Church. I do not know how strong it ever became, but I hear that some of the girls went away to nursing schools sponsored by the Presbyterian church.

As my 1914–15 term was coming to a close, I told my superintendent, Mr. Purcell, that I wanted to go to school for further teacher training. He recommended that I go to the University of Georgia in the summer quarter and return to work in the fall to accumulate some more funds to return to the university again the next summer for another quarter. So that is the way I set my plans. I completed the school term with a big school-breaking program, including dinner, a spelling bee, an arithmetic match, farewell speeches, and an invitation to return in September for my second term. My first term had been very successful, satisfying to me and to all the patrons and pupils. It had now come to a close. I had left everything in good order in the building after the children had taken all their books and other personal possessions home.

My next duty was to report to my superintendent. I turned the key over to him and told him of my invitation to return, saying that I desired to do so if it was agreeable to him. He assured me he would be delighted to have me return in September at a salary of forty-five dollars. He also gave me some advice about summer school and the courses he wanted me to take in child care, growth and development, and reading methods. He advised me to buy myself a railroad mileage book, one hundred miles for two dollars, so I would not get stranded away from home for want of funds for a railway ticket. (There were no buses or cars then, only horses and buggies and trains and boats for transportation.) He also told me that it would take about one hundred dollars to pay for my quarter of study. That included tuition, books, lodging, food, entertainment, infirmary fees, and laundry. I had saved my money the best I could after I paid my ten dollars per month board. I had done my own laundry and bought as wisely as I could, but I saw I would not have much to spend on shoes and clothes. I went home on the train to make myself some dresses and get everything ready for summer school in June. My older sister Lula, who also taught in the Wayne County school system, planned to go to summer school also.

My time had been happily spent in the Big Cypress Swamp. I had met some of the young people from Little Creek community, where there was a Missionary Baptist church, being one of the oldest communities and church services in Wayne County. This was on the fourth Sunday, and the Saturday and Saturday night before. Some of my friends would come for me most every time the afternoon before, and I would spend the whole weekend with them.

My older girl student Verdie Brooker insisted I go with her to visit her sister who had married a Harrison down in Glynn County. One Friday afternoon as soon as school was out, her brother, Mr. Saint Clair Brooker, took us south through the Big Cypress and a stretch of Watery Reedy Swamp they called the Cane Break. Then we journeyed on a few more miles to the AB&C Railroad (dismantled now). There we boarded a nice train and rode a few miles east, across the Big Buffalo, where we got off the train at a little way station. Verdie's family met us with a horse and wagon, and we rode several miles in the bright moonlight to a small farm on a beautiful hickory knoll with a nice little home that had a garden and a beautiful yard.

The next day, being Saturday, everyone was ready to give us a good time. They had large herds of cattle and hogs that ran semiwild in the Green Swamp, a thick luxuriant swamp and hammock place. They usually went there on Saturdays to feed and salt the animals. And we did so that day. I had never seen any cabbage palmetto before then. They cooked the buds from three tall trees. It was delicious. The swamp was arrayed in all its springtime glory with blooming crabapples, wild plums, jasmines, azaleas, giant buttercups, and violets on the hammock knolls throughout. I will never forget that ride into the wilds of that swamp and its sylvan beauty.

On Sunday we went to their small church, which was on the same hickory knoll as their home. Here were beautiful dogwood and jasmine. We had a good Sunday dinner, then back to the little wayside station to catch the AB&C for a ride across the Big Buffalo and on to our little way station where Verdie's brother, Mr. Brooker, met us. It was far into the night when we finally got home, but it had been a most joyous weekend. I shall always remember how the hoot owls laughed and hooted at us as we drove in the dark across the Big Cypress. It seemed almost like they were talking to us as they signaled each other through the dense darkness of the jungle swampland.

I had a little over one month at home. My mother, my sister Lula, and I spent this time talking, sewing, and making ready to get away to Athens to attend summer school. We left home in time enough to stop along the way to see some of the interesting places. We spent a few days at Indian Springs, where we stayed at the Elder House, not at the Hiawassee, the plush hotel, although we went in there to see the museum of Indian relics. The lobby was a regular showplace. We also visited the Varner House, once a stagecoach inn, the Indian Springs Camp Grounds. There were many other boarding houses there, as it was quite a health resort then. In fact it had been famous since Indian days for its medical waters. We went on to Atlanta to see Nathaniel Harris inaugurated as the governor of Georgia. I believe he was the last Confederate veteran elected governor of Georgia.

We got to Athens on a Saturday afternoon, all ready to register on Monday morning. I had only one problem: I could not take all the courses I wished to take. I went to school all day long. I never missed a chapel program during the whole session. There we sang and had various speakers. Chancellor Barrow would talk to us every so often. He was quite elderly then. Mr. and Mrs. Cunningham were our song leaders. I took in all the college plays. I saw *Macbeth, Taming of the Shrew,* and *Madame Butterfly.* I can't name all the players who came to perform for us. I also participated in the Georgia Pageant, put on by Miss Carolyn Cobb.

On Sundays Professor Ernest, who rode a bicycle to and from class, would take us sightseeing. He would walk with us. I went to my first Catholic church, to a synagogue, and to a big Negro church to a two-hour "spiritual songfest." I saw the tree that owns itself and went to the home of John Howard Payne, who wrote "Home Sweet Home" when he was Indian agent stationed in Athens. His sweetheart was Miss Evelyn Hardin. We also visited the cemetery on the banks of the Oconee River and were told of all the notables buried there. One Saturday we had an excursion on a little railroad that went up into the mountains at Helen. The dormitory gave us our lunch in a sack. We paid one dollar for our round-trip ticket. I did not use my mileage book there, as the one dollar rate was so much cheaper.

I remember my professors so well. I chose Sanford, Brown, and Smith for English. We were using their textbooks, and I wanted to know more of their methods. I had Reed, Kellogg, and Higdons while in school. I had geography from Dr. Sell. It was in his class that I had my first meeting with the environment, learning about what made us what we were. For instance, we had wood houses because we had plenty of trees; Eskimos had ice houses because all they had to use was ice. I had United States history from Dr. McPherson. What a great history teacher he was. I took reading methods from Mrs. Alexander and Mrs. Wilburn. They were both good. I took blackboard sketching from Mrs. Townsend. She used white chalk, charcoal, and colored crayons—if you could afford them. That was one of my afternoon classes. I received so much good from it. I found my plan for education had been a good one, and that gave me greater confidence in myself.

I never lost a minute from the time I arrived in Athens until I left. I burned the midnight oil working on my assignments. Although I had been allowed to enter without a formal high school education, I walked away with A's in all my classes. Dr. Joseph Stewart was head of the summer quarter, and he knew how scarce high schools were in Georgia when I was going to school, and he let me try out. I never failed him a single time. At that time we had to take a teachers examination to get our teaching license. I took mine and came through with the highest-grade certificate issued, which then was called "first grade." Your grades had to rank between 90 percent and 100 percent to make it. A "second grade" was from 80 percent to 90 percent, and a "third grade" was from 70 percent to 80 percent. When summer school was over I returned home very happy with my first quarter in college. I knew I was on my way to what I longed to do.

Once I got back to Penholloway I was very busy getting myself ready to return to my work for my second term. I had a few new little ones. My children were named Manning, Brooker, Flowers, Chancy, Taylor, Wilkerson, Bennett, and Harper. No new families had come, and none had gone, so we were soon hard at work, with regular classes, special holiday celebrations, and preparation for our 4-H club to go back to the county fair to win more ribbons.

Our Halloween, Thanksgiving, and Christmas programs were better and more beautiful than the year before. Friends and neighbors came from far and near to enjoy the occasions with us. My! What a wonderful time we had. Everyone said we had improved so much over last year, with more songs, stories, poems, and Christmas plays. Of course, I returned to my own home for the Christmas holidays, where I helped with hog-killing, sausage-making, and other necessary chores, and worked on my wardrobe, for my clothes were getting plenty of hard wear each day. I was to return to open school on the first Monday in January 1916 for our last little bit of the school year.

With a five-and-a-half-month term, four full months came before Christmas, and only six weeks remained afterward, until about February 14, so we planned a St. Valentine party for our farewell. We made valentines for each other, and the children made real lacy ones for their mothers. I bought the paper doilies for the foundation, which we placed over deep-red art paper. Each child wrote a beautiful verse on a piece of nice white linen paper, all tied together with a red satin ribbon bow. I bought some heart-shaped valentine-verse candies, and the ladies of the community baked heart-shaped sugar cookies covered with red and white icing and served red lemonade. We had a few lovely songs and poems, but most of our time was spent reading our valentines. I read from the second chapter of the Song of Solomon and also told them of the beautiful story of St. Valentine.

I never will forget how the children enjoyed learning the age-old rhymes I put on the board for their valentines. Ones such as, "As surely as the vine grows around the stump, you are my darling sugar lump"; "The river is wide, and I can't step across it—I love you, and I can't help it"; "Roses are red, violets are blue, sugar is sweet, and so are you," and "If you love me, like I love you, a sharp knife can't cut our love in two." Of course, they contributed valentine verses handed down by their families, and we had quite a collection of love verses before we were through.

We had been very busy with our daily lessons. All my older boys and girls had by now completed fourth-grade work. My regular students were coming on nicely, and quite a few of them were ready for the fourth grade, and I had quite a few promoted to third grade. All had gone well. I cast my bread upon the waters, and through these many years it has come back to me multiplied many times over.[2]

I left in mid-February 1916 after having taught eleven months. I left a group of lovely people who had treated me so well. I loved them every one and count them among my best friends to this good day.

I went to Jesup to turn in all records and the school key. I told Mr. Purcell that I had been asked back and would be glad to return, but he told me that he had other plans for me. That next fall he wanted me to take the AB&C Railroad to Browntown, where he had built a new school called Bamboo, bringing together three little log cabin schools: the Drawdy School, the Tom Lane School, and the Jacobs School. He needed me there to tie those three far-flung communities together into one fine county school. He said he knew I could do it. I would get an increase in salary to fifty dollars per month, to begin in September 1916. But now he wanted me to go to Sandy Hill in the Uncle Enoch Bennett community to finish out the three-month term of a teacher who had gotten sick and was not able to return to finish her term.

So thus ended my sojourn in the Big Cypress teaching my beloved pupils of the Penholloway School. They, too, are among my dearest friends. Never a year goes by that I am not called on to establish some of their ages for their social security and Medicare benefits.

CHAPTER 6

My Teaching at Sandy Hill

I finished my two full terms of five months each at Penholloway School early in February 1916. My superintendent asked me to go to the Sandy Hill community, between Screven and Jesup on east side of the ACL (Atlantic Coastline) Railway in the Enoch Bennett Settlement to finish the term of the sick teacher.

I arrived early on a Sunday morning on Train No. 189 from Jesup. I was met by a fine young lad named Ernest B. Bennett, the son of Mr. Braxton Bragg Bennett, with whom I was to board. He had a nice horse and top buggy. He could take my suitcase and me but could not manage my trunk. He said his father would come for it early Monday morning. We were soon on our way over a country road to the community. Out of one gallberry flat into another one, through the mud and slush; some four or five miles of this, not a house or farm in sight until we reached Sandy Hill, with its magnificent live oaks and clear-running streams making their way toward Little Creek and on into the Penholloway Creek and on to the Altamaha River.

Here we came to the log house of Rev. Enoch Bennett, a Confederate veteran, one of the six famous Bennett brothers of Wayne County who served in General Robert E. Lee's Army of Virginia. Close by was his son Labron's nice home, built of fine-sawed yellow pine lumber; the lovely little cottage of his daughter Mrs. Mattie Hewett; and the little home of his son John and his good wife, Ella. A few miles farther down the big sandy road were his daughter Mrs. Mattie Tyre and her lovely family, and across the stream, a little farther on, was his widower son, Braxton Bragg Bennett. I was to live with Braxton Bennett, his son Ernest, and his two daughters, Witsel, who later became Mrs. Carlton Griffis, and Annie, who became Mrs. Luther Beaver. In the great house lived Braxton's two younger daughters, Miss Julia and Miss Beatrice Bennett. He also had a daughter named Lou, who lived in a distant city with her family, and a son, Albert, who was an ordained Baptist minister. Albert served many churches of the Missionary Baptist faith, an order that extended throughout the country.

These were hard-working, well-educated, self-sustaining people. They had nice farms, with broad acres of heavily timbered lands, large herds of range cattle, flocks of sheep and goats, and droves of piney-woods hogs. There were bees, horses, and fields of corn, cotton, potatoes, peas, beans, pumpkins, melons; orchards of peaches, plums, pears, a few apples; vines of both black and white grapes; and an abundance of huckleberries, blackberries, chinquapins, hickory nuts, walnuts, and pecans.

They had large flocks of chickens, geese, guineas, and the finest of gardens year-round. They made their living from what they produced at home and lived abundantly. Owing no man, they were able to lay by a little cash week by week from the products they sold in the small village of Screven and at Jesup. They had personal savings accounts at the post office. Their money was always deposited there before they returned home from their day of sales, whether it be little or much, whatever they had above their necessary spending. They did not need much money, as almost all the necessities of life were raised on their homeplaces.

The ladies had chickens, eggs, fruit, vegetables, butter, milk, sausage, puddings, honey, jams, jellies, and preserves. They had their handwork, tatting, crocheting, fancy quilts, aprons, and bonnets; brush brooms, shuck scrubs, palmetto-fan brooms, and broom-sedge brooms. There were feathers, turkeys in season (Thanksgiving and Christmas), garden seeds for planting (peas, beans, okra, mustard, collards, squash, and tomatoes), multiplying onion sets, and cabbage plants. The men handled the sale of corn, potatoes, cotton, beef, pork, bacon, hams, lard, timber, cattle, horses, sheep, goats, and wool. There was always something for them to market. They were some of the thriftiest and happiest people I was ever among. Everything was attended to on time, and there was time for all good things to be done, always time to see the sick, help a neighbor, or enjoy yourself. Most of my students were grandchildren of the patriarch, Enoch Bennett, and his wife, Alice Street Bennett. And I had a few other families too: Shipes, Powerses, and Harveys.

The school building was a small frame building with one door and three windows, and a heater in the center of the room. The beautiful snow-white school grounds under the graceful live oaks that surrounded the building were filled with many songbirds at this season of the year. The children were happy, well behaved, and well advanced in their learning. My group was rather small beside the large enrollment I had at Penholloway. Here I had eight grades, with not more than two or three pupils to each grade. It was almost individual teaching, quite a different situation from where I had been. I delighted in the work. I was really very anxious to get into higher mathematics, grammar, history, geography, literature, and to see my students appreciating my knowledge of these more advanced subjects.

Ernest Bennett was far beyond the ordinary student in his mathematical knowledge. He told me I was the first teacher in several years that could give him any aid in mathematics. It seemed to be an obsession with him, to see how far he could go and where he could confound his teacher. He soon found he could not trouble me, for I knew my subjects well. One afternoon I asked him to stay after school, for I wished to talk over a matter of importance with him. He quickly agreed to stay. I told him how proud I was of his mathematical knowledge. It was a pleasure to teach him, but I also wanted him to apply himself to other fields of study as well. He was going to have to live in a world of people, and he should be able to communicate with them in both spoken and written language and always have the knowledge to talk or write on interesting subjects. I suggested that he set himself the task of writing for every situation he could think of; he liked the idea. He asked me to set up situations, and he would do his best to write about them. So I did, and before the term was up he had written 160 communications for all forms of business, social, family, and friendly types of correspondence. He wrote in a beautiful hand, learned to handle words well, and used the form to fit the occasion. I wish you could have seen and read the collection. It was a joy to behold. There were others in this advanced work in English communication, but none did nearly so much artistic work as he, or were as correct to form. He was exact with all his work. That was one reason he was so good in his mathematical studies.

In this same afternoon of planning I asked him to broaden his knowledge of history and geography to learn more of the people of the world. We discussed the field of literature. I introduced him to the writers Henry Wadsworth Longfellow, Washington Irving, Nathaniel Hawthorne, Mark Twain, Alfred Lord Tennyson, and Cotton Mather, and Charles and John Wesley, the great hymn writers, and many others. His world began to broaden. He set himself the task of learning everywhere he turned. I introduced him to the almanac on his father's mantelpiece, and he became fascinated with the knowledge it held about his universe, about rising and setting of the sun, and the moon's control of the tides and the seasons, about the pressure of blood in human beings and animals. The morning and evening stars and latitude and longitude were no longer bugbears to him. He finished all the schooling that the local district had to offer, and his father sent him away to school. He became a prominent businessman, with figures and the like work being his profession, but what joy he reaped from his great knowledge of history, geography, and the English language in the written and spoken word. He was a leader among men wherever he worked.[1]

There were a few others in this advanced class, but none more brilliant than Ernest. It is amazing how much material we covered in those three and a half months. There was never a moment wasted. I was going the "rounds" (eight per day for each child) to see if they had finished their term assignment of written communication forms or their extra reading in literature, history, and geography, story, poem, or factual account of the world's great events. Discipline was no problem. There was so much they wished to learn, and so little time in which to learn it. Most of the students were first cousins and came from well-adjusted homes, where they were loved and well provided for in every way, food, clothing, housing, books, religious teaching, happy pleasures, and plenty of good wholesome work. Never a dull moment the whole year round.

The community life of this school district is an important part of my story. All the people were devout Missionary Baptists, with their membership at Screven. They attended church on the first Sunday in each month and the Saturday before, but their religious life did not end there. Each Sunday afternoon there was Sunday school of prayers, songs, and Bible teaching for all ages at the little schoolhouse. On Wednesday nights, more time was put in on Bible study and prayers. Everybody came. I never missed a session during my whole three and a half months. The time was exceedingly profitable to me, and I learned much from the brilliant and devout Enoch Bennett and his explanations of some of the most difficult passages. I well remember many very strongly argued passages, but grandfather Enoch always came up with the most convincing statements.

There was a good organ in every home, and most every Saturday or Sunday evening there would be an ingathering of all the folks of the community for a couple of hours of happy singing of the great old hymns. Many had beautifully trained voices for sacred music, as summertime singing schools were still the order of the day for every community. You went to school for at least two weeks or a month and sang all day long, learning the notes and measures from a traveling singing master.

There were also the peanut-poppings to get the peanut seeds out of shell ready for planting. They usually ended up with a candy-pulling or candy-drawing after we had shelled the allotted bushels of peanuts. Sometimes there would be games and refreshments if they did not work us too late. If they did hold us at the task too long, the young folks would remember it and would not care to come there next time.

Time rolled merrily on. I spent several nights in every home, with good food, comfortable beds, and nice private rooms, and wonderful hours of visiting in the afternoon and evening with my patrons. I could always make myself useful, churning butter, folding clothes, setting the table, rocking the baby, telling stories to the knee-babies, or talking to the elderly people of the home.

The time began to shorten, and everyone, both old and young, began talking of a "school-breaking." It had been some years since they had one. I had plenty of material, songs, drills, marches, pantomimes, dialogs, recitations, and poems. So we began to lay our plans for the closing day of school. The trustees agreed to let me use the afternoon hours for preparing the program. Regular lessons would be until noontime each day. The lessons that usually came in the afternoon of each day would now come every other morning, and practice was begun just three weeks before closing date. The pupils could study their lines if they had finished their regular assignments during the morning hours, but no practice went on until after noontime, when all the students worked on their portions of the program.

The building was tiny, but we overcame that by declaring the building our dressing room and property wings. On the beautiful grounds was our stage, built all the way across the front of building level with front door and some ten feet wide. To build it, Ernest and his father saved enough green pine "Home Comfort" stove wood blocks for the sleepers of the floor to rest on and also enough of the same blocks to make bearings for the outdoor seats to rest upon. We scouted around from home to home and found enough good wide plank to make flooring for stage and planks for our outdoor seats. They had no backs, just the seats. It took only a few nails and a short time to erect our staging and seating. We practiced right on our stage just like we were going to have it that night. Of course we had to bring lamps and lanterns to light the scenes.

We were soon on our way to perfection, with a program of some three hours' length from the opening "Welcoming Song" to "Good Night Ladies." We began around 7 P.M. and were through around 10 P.M. We had many types of entertainment, but the numerous dialogs and fancy drills and marches seemed to steal the show. Every child in the school appeared several times in songs, dialogs, recitations, pantomimes, drills and marches. The patrons seemed well pleased with the performances of their children. They enjoyed the show along with their friends and neighbors from the surrounding communities.

Now it was all over. The lessons had been well learned. Some six or seven had been promoted to Screven High School. The term had been most profitable for the students, the teacher, and the community. All had ended happily and well. Good-byes were said, and off to home we all did go. I arose at the crack of day to go back to the school building with Mr. Brack (Braxton) Bennett and his son Ernest to see that the lumber was returned to the persons from whom it had been borrowed. It took many short trips to the homes nearby to get it all delivered. Then the green pine blocks were free and ready to be returned to Mr. Brack. While they were loading and carrying the lumber some of the schoolchildren and I had been busy, arranging everything inside the building in perfect order for the weekly Sunday school and Wednesday night prayer meetings. After we had finished within the building, we put into crocus sacks all the trash that might have been dropped the night before. Candy wrappers, chewing gum papers, and other waste. We loaded the sacks onto the wagon and carried them to Mr. Brack's to be burned around his wash pot the next washday. I would not dare light a fire in the stove or on the grounds for fear a spark might not be thoroughly outed, and I was fast preparing to be gone from the community. I surely did not wish any calamity to strike as I was leaving.

This story would not be complete without telling you of the wonderful home where I lived while teaching at this fine little school. It was a lovely home and very artistic. Mr. Bennett had married Miss Carrie Carter, an honor student at the Milikin finishing school for fine young ladies. She died, leaving him with three young children. Her home and the lives of her children reflected the wonderful training she had received and put into use in her young household. My stay was very pleasant. I had a small shed room opening into the large fireplace room of the two daughters. I had privacy to dress and to plan my schoolwork and could warm by their fire if need be. It was a far cry from some of the accommodations I had had at other times. They attended church, and I could always go with them. We went to Little Creek Baptist Church one Sunday, some ten miles to the east, where I had often worshipped while I was at Penholloway. We also went to Screven Baptist Church. Many happy weekends I spent at grandfather Bennett's with his two daughters.[2]

My trunk was packed, and when we returned from leaving everything in order at the school, the two daughters had a lovely noonday meal ready for us early so I could catch Train No. 82 at Screven to take me to Jesup, where I would make my report to Mr. Purcell.

As we were saying our good-byes to all, the family gathered round. Some began to get very sad and weepy, but I soon had them all laughing. I would expect to see them all at the fair the next fall, carrying off the coveted blue ribbons and top prizes in their chosen 4-H projects. They were all well advanced in this work. The community was known far and wide for its high score in quality and quantity of exhibits among both old and young. Our faithful home agent, Mrs. Annie

Bennett (some of their close kin), and J. P. Shedd, the county agent, always regarded Sandy Hill as one of their prize 4-H communities. I left them all in rolls of laughter when I told them I intended to use all my spare time this summer practicing walking round slippery foot logs across deep streams. You see, I had slipped off the foot logs one cold frosty morning in March and fell into the stream on my way to school. No time to turn back and dress again, I hurried on to school, got a good fire started, and dried myself out while the schoolwork was continued. Never a minute to lose to get those eight rounds by 4 P.M.

All were laughing and waving good-bye as I rode off, with my trunk and suitcase in the family wagon, and me on the seat beside Ernest. He and I talked about his future all the way to the train station. He thanked me over and over for letting him know that there was other learning that was important beside his beloved mathematics, and he told me how much he would always appreciate me and my outlook on life.

From Jesup I took Train No. 85 to Nahunta. There I caught another train on the Brunswick and Western Railroad to Lulaton, where my father met me. He took me by horse and buggy some five miles farther to our home. There urgent work was waiting for me.

Bamboo School and a War Begins

After my arrival home from the Sandy Hill community, the summer was well on its way. The gardens, orchards, and vineyards were bursting with an abundance of the most delicious fruits and vegetables. Although I was so anxious to return to the University of Georgia for my second session of study, it seemed that there were other things concerning our family that had to be done.

My sister Lula, who was older than I and had been teaching for many years, thought we should buy some land at Nahunta, a village some seven miles from our beloved home. So our first duty after she arrived home that summer was to select the site. We bought a five-acre tract in a beautiful virgin yellow pine forest on the outskirts of Nahunta.

Our plans were to build a home there for ourselves and our parents as soon as we were financially able. This would enable us to get to our father and mother with greater ease and speed if the need arose, as the new house would be closer to the railroad station. They were getting on in years and were quite feeble. Mother, reading "the handwriting on the wall," said we had better can, conserve, dry, and save all the fruits and vegetables we could that summer, as it might be our last chance to ever have access to such an abundant supply of our usual produce. So the summer was spent making jelly, canning and drying fruits and vegetables, gathering berries and mayhaw, and squeezing and jarring honey. We worked until every jar, crock, and barrel was filled. What a joyous summer it was. Of course there was a new supply of clothes to be readied for another year's work. We selected teaching materials and made our plans to use them in our next school session. Of course our daily duties included our tasks that kept the home and farm going. My! How quickly the summer passed. Autumn was soon upon us.

When I made my report to Mr. Purcell after teaching at Sandy Hill, he told me he would expect me at the Bamboo School not later than mid-September to teach in the new school organized there. It was a new frame structure with glass windows, a front stoop, and good steps. There was a clock and a lunch rack room, a good heater, blackboards, a good desk for the students, a teacher's desk, but no ceiling. The county now gave two hundred dollars per school toward building better schoolhouses if the patrons contributed labor to the construction. This they did, but the two hundred dollars gave out before the ceiling could be bought.

An academic standard was set up by the state board of education. If this standard was met, the state paid for seven months of school for that district. The superintendent's plan was for us to meet the requirements and so to have the longer school term. I enrolled some fifty students, and my salary was to be fifty dollars per month for seven months if we could meet the standards. Our first job was to get the building ceiled and to expand the curriculum to take in arts, crafts, and community activities as well as to continue with a strong academic program for every child of the district. I had to do a lot of visiting and talking to get the people interested in a longer school term, a broader course of study, and a better building and grounds. I had three distinct groups of people to bring together to work as one perfect group. I asked every person who agreed with me to get one more person to agree. So by and by I felt that our plans were strong enough to launch our first project, an attempt to raise the money to buy the ceiling and to get people to do the work.

We set Thanksgiving weekend as the time for a community ingathering program, a speaking, money-raising, and entertainment night. First we had a program by our schoolchildren, then the community speaking by our home agent, Annie Bennett, and our county agent, J. P. Shedd. They told of their 4-H club work and of the wonderful exhibits at the county fair just held in Jesup the last week of October. They said they would be looking forward to exhibits from the boys and girls and fathers and mothers of Bamboo come next fall. Everyone became very enthused over this work and began to plan right then and there what they could do for the next fair. The speakers were invited back as often as they could come to help with the projects.

Next on the program was our moneymaking projects. First we had an old-fashioned box supper, where the young ladies made beautiful boxes artistically decorated according to the season. Ours was a Thanksgiving theme. They filled the boxes with the choicest of foods for a bountiful, delicious meal for themselves and for whoever bought them on the highest bids from the auctioneer's hand. We had quite a few boxes, and they all brought fancy prices. We had a big live turkey gobbler in a crate and sold chances on it all evening. Our last event was a lovely gift of jewelry for the most beautiful young lady of the community as determined by vote that sold for one cent each. The voting was fast and furious and brought in quite a tidy little sum.

When the evening's entertainment was over, we had adequate funds to pay for the ceiling (we already had the cost of the item figured up from the list price sent us by the Zirkle Saw Mill Company, at Zirkle, on the AB&C Railroad and Little Satilla River). We had money left over that the trustees agreed to put toward a good library for our school, which was one of the required items for us to have our seven-month term. The trustees held their business meeting, counted the money, and commissioned me to buy the ceiling the next Saturday. I was also to select and order the books for the beginning of our school library. The crowd had had a wonderful time visiting with each other and talking with Mrs. Bennett and Mr. Shedd about their community projects for the year. Everyone was called to order. Someone announced how much money was made from the evening's entertainment and how the funds would be used. A wild cheer went up. Bamboo was a solid cooperative community from that day forth. We thanked the congregation for their attendance and invited them back for our Christmas entertainment. The ingathering was dismissed with a prayer of thanksgiving for such wonderful people and their fine behavior throughout the evening, and with a closing prayer that they would all be with us at Christmas.

About this time, our neighboring school, Hopewell, across the Big Buffalo Swamp to the east and north, invited us to their Christmas entertainment and fund-raising project. This was a well-established school of the Nails, Arnetts, Chapmans, Dubberleys, and Drawdys, among other families. It was taught by Miss Mattie Gainey, a highly trained and devoted teacher. Their community spirit was high, and their academic work was above average, having more high school and college graduates than any other community in the whole county.

Bright and early on the Friday after Thanksgiving, Mrs. Bennett and Mr. Shedd were at school with us to tell about the different types of work offered in their many clubs. Every boy and girl within the age limit (ten to twenty years) was enrolled. The agents' visit with the patrons the night before surely had paid off. They were so pleased with their visit and the hearty response they had received from the whole community. They had enlisted the adults for a community exhibit at the next county fair. They both stated they never had been able to reach these children or their parents when the three small communities from which this fine school was built had separate schools. We were now bonded together as one school community. Mrs. Bennett and Mr. Shedd finished their work with us and drove south to Waynesville and Rozier to check on the well-established 4-H club work in those communities, which had had county and state winners for several years.

Saturday morning came bright and clear and cold after a rainy, windy, and soggy Thanksgiving Day. I arose early, went to Zirkle, and purchased the lumber for the ceiling, which was to be shipped to Browntown, our nearest railway stop. It arrived in due time, and the men of the community planned to put up the ceiling during the two weeks of Christmas holidays. In the meantime, I had the lumber stored to one side of the school building to keep it out of the weather. It was installed, and the balance of our funds was put into good books for our children and their parents. So you see, we were getting closer and closer to becoming a standard school, a far cry from my first school term of two months at Burnt Bay.

My home was made with Mr. and Mrs. Osgood Poppell. They had a lovely group of children in school: Oma, Myrtle, Flora, Agnes, Marion, and Slayton. They were fine children and excellent students. I enjoyed them very much. In addition to the families mentioned earlier, I had children from the homes of Lanes, Drurys, Jacobses, Litties, Days, and Crosbys. All very good children. Irene Little Bennett, the mother of our present county clerk, Hon. Stetson Bennett, was among the AB&C class of 1917 in that school.

The only church anywhere nearby was a little log cabin Primitive Baptist church at Mount Zion. My father preached there often. I always was happy when he and Mother came across the Big Satilla River at Ammons Ferry for my father to preach there on the first Sunday and the Saturday before. He had to come with horse and buggy, quite a drive for him in his later years. We would also sometimes cross the Big Buffalo Swamp, miles and miles of water, to Hopewell Missionary Baptist Church on the fourth Sunday. We would leave real early in the morning light and drive there with horse and wagon. After church services we would be invited to the Nails', Drawdys', Arnetts', or Chapmans' for a late Sunday dinner. Then begin our slow trek back home—an all-day trip for one hour of church.

Time rolled by so rapidly. Monday morning after our big Thanksgiving program we set ourselves to preparing for our Christmas program. All the children promised to learn their Christmas poems at home as well as the Christmas songs we were to prepare. We would read the Christmas story from the Bible and distribute gifts.

At our December teachers meeting in Jesup, Mr. Purcell told us of plans to hold a countywide school fair in early April 1917 to promote arts, crafts, club work, and general academic work. He hoped to promote friendly competition between the schools and to show, by the number of schoolchildren and their ages, the need of high schools in the county.

Teachers and students would come to the fair by an Atlantic Coastline train from schools in all parts of the county: from Bachlott, Hickox, Burnt Bay, and Nahunta, where it would pick up people from Waynesville, Rozier, Linda, Drury, Atkinson, Lulaton, Wainwright, Knox, and Buffalo who had arrived on the early Brunswick and Western or by horse and wagon from nearby Pine Bloom and Nahunta. The train would proceed on to Raybon to get Dowling and Strickland, and on to Hortense (with no stop at Trudy, as that is in Pierce County) to get Satilla, Saw Grass, Oak Grove, Bamboo, and Hortense people who had come in on the early AB&C train, then on to McKinnon, Broadhurst, Jesup, Mt. Pleasant, Union, Winslow, Gardi, Hopewell, and Pendarvis. Odessa people would come in on the Southern from Brunswick; Neva, Brentwood, Odum, and Red Hill would come in on an early Southern train to Jesup. While Screven, Kelly, O'Quinn, Ritch, Farm Life, Oak Ridge, Liberty, Omar, Sandy Hill, Slover, Shady Dale, and Reddishville would arrive on an early train on the ACL from toward Waycross. Those on the Lanes Bridge road would have to come in wagons and buggies, as would those from Friendship, Piney Grove, Madray Springs, Goose Creek, New Hope, Spring Grove, Oglethorpe, Kicklighter, Little Creek, Penholloway, Bethel, Empire, Flint Branch, and Doctortown.

We were to make banners for our children to march under and to use the same banners over our display booths, which were to be placed in the ground floor of the Masonic Temple just as soon as we arrived. All our exhibits were to be packed in strong boxes with good handles so our own schoolboys could carry them from the depot to the exhibit hall, then back to our train. There was no charge for exhibit crates. They came as baggage. We had to pay excursion rates for tickets, one dollar for adults, and fifty cents for children over five.

Each school had been allotted a space, so we could go to work arranging our exhibit as soon as we arrived. The parade was to begin at 10 A.M., speaking was at 11 A.M. at the courthouse, and lunch was to be on the courthouse square at 12:30 P.M. Each school was to bring its own picnic lunch; drinks would be provided by the town. The judging would be done while we were on parade, at speaking, and during lunch. The exhibit hall would be open from 2 P.M. until 4 P.M. Then we would be allowed one hour to pack up exhibits, gather our children and patrons, get to the train, count noses, and be ready to leave. It all sounded wonderful to me, with my brand-new school that I was trying so hard to standardize. I knew it would mean hard work for all of us, but I was determined right then and there to get 100 percent participation from every child and patron of the school and to do the very best we could in the arts and crafts we could manage.

I had Christmas on my mind when I left the teachers meeting and hurried downtown to purchase candles for the tree and a ten-cent present for each of my pupils. I said to myself, here is my plan: For each of my girl students, I will buy a thimble, a five-cent pack of needles, and a few skeins of embroidery thread so she can begin her needlework for the fair as soon as we get started with our arts and crafts after Christmas. For each of the boys, I will buy a one-bladed 1 x 1 knife for ten cents so he will have woodwork to enter in the competition. All will be wrapped, tagged, and hung on the tree when the time came.

To get back to my school from Jesup, I had to take a late afternoon train from Jesup to Offerman to get the train to Browntown. Many teachers were on that night run from Jesup to Offerman, and everyone was talking Christmas and how could they manage off such small salaries to give gifts to all children. I told them that I did, always had, and always would. They wanted to know how in the world I could manage. I told them I never went over ten cents per pupil, and I never left any of my pupils off the list. So they wanted to know right away what in the world did I find to buy. I told them what gifts I had bought. They all said, Why could we not think of something like that in place of walking our legs off and spending too much and being not yet satisfied with our gifts and still have some students for whom we have yet to buy a present?

The Christmas program was to begin in late afternoon, as soon as it was dark enough for the candles to shine. By starting then, the children could get home with their parents by horse and wagon before too late in the evening, before the chill of the night got too deep. We could not take too much time from our academic work. So we planned to have regular lessons every day until little recess time in the afternoon; then we would practice until going-home time. We would begin again the next afternoon where we had left off the day before. We were to teach that year until Friday, December 22. But my trustee persuaded me to stay over for Saturday, December 23, and to have the Christmas tree on Saturday evening, after which I would leave to go home for the holiday.

Our Christmas program worked out beautifully. The children knew their pieces well and recited them beautifully. Their sweet young voices sounded so heavenly that night. I read the Christmas story as best I could from St. Matthew and St. Luke. Santa Claus did a magnificent job delivering the gifts. The children had drawn names. Each child had a gift from playmates, a gift from me, a gift from his or her parents, and a gift of fruits and candies from the trustees. Of course some of them had extra gifts from grandfathers and grandmothers or other kin or friends. I believe that all the patrons had given gifts to their husbands and wives. I surely was laden with gifts from my humble people—cured sausage, blackberry and mayhaw jellies, a piece of their fruitcake, or canned peaches. Our tree was laden with gifts, and many were on the floor at the foot of the tree. Finally every gift was delivered to its right owner, and the whole congregation sang "Silent Night." Then there was a dismissal prayer. The candles were outed; the fire in the heater was checked and double-checked. We made sure everything was in order and secure. Holding lanterns to light their pathways home, people told me it was the happiest Christmas they and their children ever had, and they felt like now they knew the real meaning of Christmas.

Had we stayed until midnight I think we could have sung "Joy to the World" and "The Lord Is Come" with full meaning. But I barely had time to get my grip and hurry to the flag station, where I would have to wave the train to come to a stop. Mr. Poppell and his family accompanied me to the train. I told the clerk at the Royal Hotel, where I spent the night, to awaken me in time to catch the four o'clock Brunswick and Western train the next morning for Lulaton. When I stopped at the desk to thank him for calling me on time and started out with my grip in my hand, he insisted that I set it down. He would have their night porter take it over to the depot for me. It was only about two blocks. I had paid my lodging the night before as I came in, so I let the clerk take it in the office and I went on. The train was loading and was soon ready to go, but no porter came with my grip. I just could not go on and leave all my Christmas gifts and my new Christmas clothes behind. So the train rolled out of Brunswick depot without me. I could see in my mind's eye my dear old father at the Lulaton depot waiting in the dark for me, his baby child; and I was not there and he knew not why. Afterward, Mother said he never had been so broken over any incident before as this one.

I went back to the hotel. The clerk who was on duty then said the clerk who had been on at night told him that he never could find their porter, and he had no way to get word to me. So I picked up my grip—even though the clerk pleaded with me to let the porter take it—and went to the depot. My train left around three o'clock, and I got to Lulaton a little before five. Of course, no one was there to meet me. I persuaded a friend to take me home. When I arrived after sundown, all my brothers and sisters were gone. Father and Mother rejoiced upon seeing me, happy to find that I was whole and hearty. I told them the story of being over-persuaded by my trustees to stay over for Christmas Saturday night and then getting so snarled in the Christmas rush that I had no Christmas with my own family—which I and they felt was my just and right duty. I had learned my lesson well. I never did let myself be overpersuaded again and deny my family their just rights to my companionship at Christmas. I would always do my duty by my schoolchildren and patrons, but it could not prevent me from getting home to my own family by Christmas Eve or earlier.

Before returning to school I had so much to do. I could waste no time. I had to have a few more clothes to help finish out my term. I also had many things to gather together for the arts and crafts work of my boys and girls. The *Savannah Morning News* had carried a whole page of embroidery designs that you could transfer to cloth for centerpieces, pillowcases, dresser scarves, or table napkins. You could fasten your design to a large windowpane, then place your cloth over the design and transfer your design nicely. We had large windowpanes in our new glass windows. I had planned to buy some nice finely woven homespun Sea Island cotton and let the girls try their hands at making pillowcases. I also gathered a lot of coarse white wrapping twine for them to use as padding under their embroider floss to make their designs stand out and look so rich and pretty. A few spools of sewing thread to use for hemstitching the pillowcases and sewing the seams, and I was all set for the girls' work.

Now I turned my attention to my boys. I had collected cigar boxes for them to use to use for their craft projects. I packed all this material in a large box and took it back with me on the Bogey train as baggage to Hortense, where I had to transfer to the AB&C train to Browntown and my Bamboo School. I did not have a week at home, as I had to leave on Saturday night to be at school Monday morning. The Bogey did not run on Sunday.

We did not have a teachers meeting in January. Our first meeting for the new year would be the first Saturday in February. We were then to report to our superintendent how much progress we had made toward the school fair and how much booth space was desired. We would have to build our own staging and would be supplied with a few rough shelves and a few stepladders to reach the upper wall space. We were to be through by ten o'clock so we could lead our children in the parade while the judges took over the building for judging. Everything was to be prepared for display before we arrived, because all we would have time for was to arrange the exhibit in the most artistic style that was possible for us to do.

While in Jesup at the February meeting, I secured material for my Valentine party. I had promised the children that if they would do their Christmas pieces as perfectly as they could, I would get red construction paper, narrow red ribbons, and lacy paper doilies for them to make valentines for their mothers. We would also have a valentine exhibit in our school fair. The mothers had asked if they could display their valentines in their club booth at the fair. We all thought that would be just fine. They also planned a display of handmade quilts, bed-spreads, pillowcases, tablecloths, centerpieces, fancy aprons, and baby dresses.

After our Christmas holidays, our schedule had to be set up so we would have time to do our arts and crafts and our academic work. Now as our school-house had been nicely ceiled and our new reading library had arrived, we were assured of a seven-month term. Our library had four nice shelves with glass doors and enough good books to fill the shelves. More shelves and books could be added as funds would permit. Regular rules were set up, and a regular period was set apart for library hour. A count needed to be kept on the books and their return on time. The older children had to give book reports on all the books. No child could borrow a book until he could sign his own name and be totally responsible for the book he had borrowed. We never lost or destroyed a book during the whole term, and the books were read and reread. We would permit the parents to borrow from the library if they came themselves or sent a note by an older child stating the name of the book they wished to read. We would hold the note for safe return of the book. We never lost a book there either.

Early in January I had a meeting with the trustees. I told them that at our February teachers meeting I had to report on the progress of our arts and crafts, on our academic work, on the community work we wished to exhibit at the school fair, and the amount of space we would need at the fair. I told them I could not go at it in a haphazard way. I had to know what I would be permitted to do and then try to do that. They asked what I wished to do. I told them I needed the first period after lunch one day a week—from lunchtime until little recess—for a class in the special work we were to do. This would give the children time to get their instructions and to work all they could at school. They were to work at home too. The next week we would have another work period. I had already asked for such a period for library to check books in and out. I think the trustees' eyes were beginning to open as to why we needed the seven-month term if we were going to give our children a broader, richer, and more enjoyable school day.

While I had the trustees together I asked them to let me have a club meeting like the one Mr. Shedd and Mrs. Bennett had suggested when they met with us at Thanksgiving so we could check regularly with the boys and girls on their club projects. They wanted to know how often I wanted this time and what good it was going to do their sons and daughters to have this club meeting. I told them I wanted the meeting once a month unless something special came up, such as if the club agents came to visit us. Then we would meet more often. I also asked for it to be first period after lunch on a day we would select. I listed the good it would do the students. Here is the list I gave of what the students would learn:

1. Learn to assemble quickly and quietly.

2. Learn to listen to a speaker.

3. Learn to know when to speak.

4. Learn how to select and elect their officers.

5. Learn to fill the office with dignity and reliability.

6. Learn to ask for needed information from the person who had that knowledge to give them.

7. Learn how to take notes for future use.

8. Learn how to make reports on work that they had agreed to do.

9. Learn how to state the reason why, if they had been unable to do the work.

10. Learn how to demonstrate, exhibit, and report publicly on a project.

11. Learn how to keep minutes, make motions, nominate and elect officers, open and close meetings, speak publicly when necessary, keep records, make accounts to show gain or loss.

They wanted to know where were they going to learn that and from whom. I told them from me and in the club meetings by actually doing it. Then they wanted to know where and how and from whom had I learned it. I told them in a 4-H club meeting from Mrs. Annie Bennett and Mr. J. P. Shedd, where I had learned early "to make the best, better." They all spoke up with one accord and said that is exactly what we want our boys and girls to know. But they did not want the meetings to be all hullabaloo and bedlam. I told them it would not be so if I were their teacher; it would be a lesson the same as any other of their classes, only, I hoped, the most profitable and enjoyable of all their learning periods of the month. So now had my authority to move into my expanded school program and go forward. I felt I now had as much or more than I could accomplish in the remaining four months of the school term. If you care to check, you may come to Jesup and hunt down the minutes of the Wayne County Board of Education in the early 1930s to find where I pleaded for every schoolchild of the county to have permission for one 4-H club meeting per month during schooltime to meet with their leaders. The request was granted, and the boys and girls still have that privilege to this good day throughout the county.

We called our first meeting to order, elected our officers, and held our meeting according to *Robert's Rules of Order*. Our main business was to plan for our school fair to come first of April. I told them that our request had been granted by our local trustees. (Then schools were controlled almost entirely by the local trustees; later on, the county board of education took over almost completely, and the local trustees' authority became less and less as the years went by.) We decided to meet the period after lunch each Thursday. The boys were to work on their cabinets and woodwork with their pocketknives, tacks, hammers, glue, paint, and shellac on the long bench by the east window. The girls were to work on their sewing and embroidering at their own desks on the west side of the building. The little ones were to play in the middle of the room. All this to be done quietly and diligently this whole period. My desk was in the middle section, and anyone was free to come to me if need be. But I preferred to go to them to help them with their difficulties, as they would not have to lay down their work and walk to me. The little ones could choose to play outdoors part of the time, but you see this was in the dead of winter, so they chose mostly to play quietly around my desk.

We had been gathering cigar boxes for their soft wood, which would be easy for the boys to work with. I had asked the clerk of the American Tie and Timber Co. general store at Browntown to save his cigar boxes for us, and he promised to do so. They planned to make dollhouse furniture, jewelry boxes, trinket boxes, glove cases, and work boxes for their mothers, and other nice little containers. They knew what they wanted to do and were eager to begin.

The girls had not been able to decide what to make, so they were slower to begin. I finally helped them to decide to make pillowcases from the material I had bought. They could make two pair each. I furnished all the material. They were to make me a pair and to keep a pair for themselves for their hope chests (you know, we do not have anything to make ladies from but little girls). I told them I would teach them how to stencil their designs by the windowpane method. We had large panes in our new building. I would teach them how to measure for the size of their pillowcases, how to draw the threads for hemstitching, how to make selections for centerpieces, dresser scarves, chair tidies, and pillowcases, all with matching designs. We had enough designs for each girl to choose a different one if she wished. They learned how to make the various embroidery stitches—buttonhole, blanket, chain, outline, wheat, popcorn, brier, cross, and seed—to perfect the motifs. They also learned the hemming stitch to make their hems, the straight stitch to sew up their pillowcases, and the couching stitch to be able to put in their twine for padding for the heavy work.

We got the calendar and counted our Thursdays, three more in January, four in February, five in March—twelve in all—just a dozen lessons. The completed projects had to be ready to pack in the exhibit box early in April. No one was to be left out, and everyone was saving pennies to buy tickets on that special train to Jesup.

While the trustees and I were having our meeting, they had asked me to take over the job of cleaning and beautifying our grounds. We had one acre in a beautiful native forest of live oaks, some large virgin yellow pine, quite a few young yellow pine saplings, palmetto fans, wiregrass, and some patches of beautiful carpetgrass. It bordered on the old post road from Savannah to St. Augustine, Florida, one of the oldest roads in all Georgia. It was called the post road because every mile of it was posted with the number of miles you had to go. They also told me I could use the scrap lumber that had been left over from the ceiling job for fuel. I told them I would be glad for us to do as much as we could, but our load was getting heavy, and our time was getting shorter every day. I wanted those nice ceiling pieces for our arts and crafts. We would stack them in a nice box and slip them under the back of the building out of the weather, so we could get them as needed. I also asked them to buy us a good ax, handsaw, and hammer with some money left over from our moneymaking project. We would trim the oak trees of all scraggly limbs and cut up all the scattered lightwood knots and fallen dead timber and stack it for our heater. We would borrow good weeding hoes, scalp the wiregrass, and rake it up in piles if one of the trustees would come haul it away. Mr. Drury spoke up and said he would gladly haul it away for bedding for his animals.

By springtime we had it all pruned, cleaned, and ready for the carpetgrass to take hold, which it readily did when the wiregrass and trash were removed. We pruned out the dead fronds of the palmetto fans and let them remain, as they were quite luxuriant and beautiful. Our soil at Bamboo was getting down toward the sea enough to be a little brackish, which is the delight of the palmetto palm.

Our academic work was going well, and everyone was so happy, getting ready for the fair and planning what type of work they were going to exhibit—whether a map, a chart, a collection of letters, arithmetic tables, diagramming in their English, or the story of their arts and crafts project. I told each student to contribute at least one piece of written work.

Our arts and crafts were moving toward completion. Some of it was rather crude, but I felt all had learned well. The little girls had learned how to wear a thimble, thread a needle, hold a pair of scissors, cut a piece of material straight with the weave; how to work quietly, share their tools and time with each other, and how to plan for the article they were to make. They all learned how to launder it good and clean and press on the wrong side so their design would stand out beautifully. I thought the best lesson of all was to be faithful to the end. We had only twelve lessons, but girls finished on time, got everything laundered and labeled. The story about each article was to be displayed right with it. All were put in a nice flat box and well tied so nothing was lost or rumpled.

The boys had a harder time packing. We assembled each boy's project in a small box well stuffed with paper packing. We packed their stories in with their articles. A larger box held all the smaller packages. Our two larger boxes were put into a stout wooden shipping box and tagged with my name for delivery to the Wayne County School Fair, Jesup, Georgia. You see, we had to change trains at Hortense—from the AB&C train to our fair excursion train on the Atlantic Coastline, and our boxes had to be of shipping strength. I also had to arrange for our mules and horses to be taken care of while we were gone from before daylight until late in the evening. I went to Mr. Ward Harvey, manager of the American Tie and Timber Co., and asked him if he could arrange for our countymen to stable their mules and horses in his giant feed lot at Browntown. He said he would be glad to do that for them; just bring the amount of feed they wanted their animals to have, and he would have his barn boy feed and water them at the correct time. When we returned that night, he would have lanterns there and would help hitch up the teams. I asked him to come to the schoolhouse and make that statement to the children, which he did. They all took the message home to their parents, even to the far corners of the district. Mr. Ward did not have any children in school—his oldest son, J. R., was just a wee baby then—but he was a wonderful friend to the school. Many of the patrons were his workers, chopping and hauling ties for his company from the giant timbers of Buffalo Swamp. I well remember once, when I was really sick with a terrible chest congestion, something like pleurisy, he and his good wife, Mizell, had me come and spend the weekend with them where she could nurse and doctor me, and by Monday morning I was very much improved. God bless their dear souls. I will always have a sweet memory of their kindness to me in that far distant day in that isolated community, far from doctors, drugstores, or like facilities.

At our March teachers meeting, we were assigned our display space and given our final instructions on what was expected of us in bringing our schools, patrons, and displays to the fair. Strong emphasis was placed on our school banners and yells, on our exhibit, and on the behavior of our children, especially on the homeward-bound trains. We each had to give a report on how far along we were with our exhibits.

The day finally came. Long before daylight my patrons, my schoolchildren, my box of exhibits, and my marching banner were standing ready to board the train. The banner was made by the children and me of two peeled-oak standards and a double-thick fold of white homespun Sea Island cotton cloth. Large letters of lapped and overlapped sewn-on bamboo leaves spelled out Bamboo School. It was very attractive and eye-catching, lightweight yet sturdy and easy to carry. It gave honor to our parade and drew attention to our exhibit in the display hall. Many schools had elaborately embroidered banners in brilliant colors, while others had commercial ones they had ordered from school supply houses, with their school colors in two or three colors of felt. None drew more praise or comment throughout the day than ours.

It had been a wonderful day; pupils and patrons from the some sixty-odd schools of the county made quite a crowd for the small village of Jesup. Something like five thousand schoolchildren joined by their parents and teachers marched down the middle of the sandy streets. There were no paved streets or sidewalks, but there was plenty of cooling shade under the spreading oak trees that stood so stalwart and beautiful as they lined the streets. The porch of the old Ingleside Hotel was the reviewing stand. The heavy taxpayers had been especially invited to view the schoolchildren of Wayne County from that place. Some of us had never realized before from whom we were asking for more tax dollars—and we are still asking to this good day. This was a well-planned affair to promote better schools for Wayne County and to show the type of work the children were doing. Our line of march ended at the courthouse. All the notables and speakers moved on over to the courthouse auditorium, and the patrons were invited to go with them. The schoolchildren were to sit on the lawn and rest until lunchtime. Here was where we were to eat the lunch we had brought. For our school this lunch would also be our closing day celebrations, as the trustees had decided that it would suffice as our last-day dinner on the ground. The town of Jesup was to provide us with barrels of cold lemonade to go with our lunches. Each school had to have one or more teachers stay with their group of children. One or two of the larger boys helped make the lemonade. The others could tell stories, play stick frog or such quiet games, but there was to be no noise to disturb the wonderful speaking going on upstairs for the betterment of Wayne County schools.

We had put up our exhibits upon arrival and had to vacate the building so the judges could go to work. We assembled for the parade, and now we were wondering what score we were going to get on our school exhibits. We just could hardly wait for 2 P.M. to come when we would be permitted to reenter the hall and view all the exhibits of the some sixty schools and note the individual scores as well as the total score for the whole school and community. I well remember the unique and beautiful, useful and artistic exhibits in that school fair. Liberty, Piney

Grove, Nahunta, Hickox, Union, Madray Springs, Consolidated, Hopewell, and many other schools had wonderful exhibits of the handiwork of their boys and girls. I surely would have dreaded to be one of the judges having to make the selections and write the scores. They did a thorough and magnificent job. Hopewell, our neighboring school, came up with the most artistic and the greatest number of first-place articles. It was an old highly cultured community of long-standing high ideals for home, church, school, and community. We were happy over that and rejoiced with them. We were given a perfect score for having 100 percent of our boys and girls exhibiting their handiwork. We and our patrons were all so proud of that. We received many commendable scores for our girls' pillowcase sets, our boys' dollhouse construction, our little boys' tops made from spools, and balls made from the yarn of old socks, the little girls' doll clothes, and the ladies' exhibits of handmade articles. I don't remember having gotten any handiwork from the men. They were too busy trying to get everybody to stop work long enough to take their families on the excursion. It was the first time many of them had ever been to Jesup.

The speaking was finally over, and our lunches were brought from the exhibit hall where we had stored them while we marched. We were now ready to spread the food and eat. It took some time to get around to all the good food— jars of pickles, big bowls of chicken and dumplings, rice, hams, salads, cakes, cookies, pies, and on and on. Bucket after bucket of cold lemonade from the numerous barrels around the courthouse lawn. The cold lemonade hit the spot. Lunch was finally over. The visiting and news of the day was being carried on in a joyful way. The speaking was being commented upon. I was busy talking to friends across the way and greeting pupils from schools where I had taught before. We counted noses. Then we cleaned up, which was a minor job. No paper napkins, plates, or cups; no throwaway forks and spoons to dispose of; no drink bottles or cans to put in the garbage. Always people wanting all the bones to take home to the faithful old blue-speckled hound they had left home to guard the place while they were gone on this long day. We counted noses again. There was not a child or grown person missing. Our baskets were all packed, and we moved on over to the exhibit hall.

My! The hullabaloo and excitement in the exhibit hall, everyone so anxious to see their own and their neighbors' exhibits as well as the exhibits of their new-found friends from the other school districts. The tour of the hall was finally over, and it closed promptly at four. The teachers and their patrons were responsible for taking their exhibits down, crating them, and carting them back to the train. We had to tote our own, as not near enough drays were available to carry the exhibits. We had rope handholds on our box, so our large boys were able to carry the two large crates, and a giant box holding our lunch baskets, to the baggage car. I saw that all was secure and well labeled. It was marked "Bamboo School Exhibit," and our furled banner was fastened under its ropes. The children were not ready to give up their banner, but I told them there were too many people about to try to carry it into the coach and that the baggage master could care for it better than we could.

The excursion train stood waiting for us. I don't think a horse and wagon or a buggy left until all the trains had departed. There was a train to Odum, Redland, Neva, and other points, also a train to Odessa, Gardi, Pendarvis, Union, Hopewell, and Mt. Pleasant. The train to Screven and Slover and to many large schools such as O'Quinn, Liberty, Oak Ridge, Ritch, Omar, and Reddishville was a long one. Our train, the train that went down the Jesup short line, was the longest of all; more than forty schools were on this run. It was fed at Hortense by AB&C line and at Nahunta by the Brunswick and Western line, and it extended from Jesup to Bachlott, some forty miles due south. There were many coaches. We had all of our party instructed to line up in front of the coach on which we had arrived, and to stand there until we could count them. Think what a terrible thing it would be to lose a child. It was a yelling, shouting, and banner-waving good-bye. For a while it was all chatter after we boarded the train. Everybody so happy and joyous. Then their tiredness and long hours of wakefulness began to overcome them.

Soon the younger ones were asleep. If "Miss Mizell" had been said once that day, I suppose it was said numerous thousands. I had been on the tightest duty ever since we had begun to gather at Browntown before daylight. I had been on duty at the exhibit hall displaying exhibits, storing lunch on the parade route, and helping to hold order and quiet on the courthouse lawn during speaking. Eating and keeping an orderly lunch was quite a task, and then there was checking children, viewing exhibits, packing and loading exhibits, "counting noses," and loading schoolchildren and patrons on the train. I was responsible for awaking and getting all off at Hortense and loaded on AB&C train for Browntown; then, finally, for getting everyone off at Browntown. It was now far into the night. The biggest job was getting them to their own wagons and helping to keep order while the hitching-up was done. I had to see that our exhibits were placed in the wagon and delivered to where I boarded. Monday morning I would take them back to school and give each one to the person who had made it.

It was a wonderful trip, and people's eyes were opened. They had never dreamed there were so many schoolchildren in Wayne County. Many changed their minds that day about the school taxes, and Wayne County began to pull to the forefront in school promotions, and still is among the leaders of the state till this good day. Jesup High School was selected as the outstanding school in 1970, and Miss Mary Ann Stanley was an award-winning teenager in 1971.

We had only a few short weeks now to finish up our term. Our schoolyard was all nice and trim, clean and beautiful in its native forest. We had no fence, as we still had open range for all livestock. No work had been done with the delicate shrubbery or flowers, and we had had no time to devote to window boxes, being too busy since first day of school.

Our plans were now set to get the school closed out in good form. All the children would finish their academic work and plan for their club work during summer, as Mrs. Bennett and Mr. Shedd were twelve-month helpers with club work. A great deal of their 4-H work was done in the summertime, including the country fair in Jesup, the Coastal Empire Fair at Savannah, the state fair at Macon, and the southeastern fair in Atlanta. All books were to be completed as best we could, ready to be taken home at the closing date of school. There were no free books then, so books were well taken care of, used down the line year after year by the next child in line and then loaned or sold to kinfolks or neighbors. (It just makes me hurt to see how these free books are treated and abused and destroyed today.) The last day came. We had everything cleaned up, grounds, toilets, cloakroom, desks. We wrote our lovely good-byes on the blackboard, with a wish for a merry and profitable summer. We had our regular noonday lunch under the shade of the trees, just like other times, weather permitting. We played our last games on our beautiful playgrounds. Everybody's books were all stacked and ready to take home. After lunch, the trustees, their wives, and many other patrons came. Each was given a chance to speak if they wished to do so. Most of them did. The trustees came last, commending us for being a good school, a well-behaved school. They told us how proud they were of their big new Bamboo School, how proud they were of me, and how they wished for me to come back the next year. I thanked them for all their lovely compliments and told them how I wished I could have done a lot better and a lot more for them and the children. They tried to pin me down about returning. I told them I had always left that up to my superintendent, that he always placed me where he thought I could do the most good in the county system. I would be glad to return if he saw fit to have me do so.

He had already told me he wanted me to go to the O'Quinn School community out from Screven, where he was having quite a bit of trouble with behavior problems (I did not know what kind) and also with attendance. There were enough children there for three teachers, but he could scarcely keep one. He had tried college graduates, both men and women, old ones and young ones, but with no luck. He wanted me to go there in September 1917, and he would raise my salary to sixty dollars per month.

School closed out at four. We had said our good-byes and departed to go our separate ways. I checked the toilets, locked the doors and windows, and gave the schoolhouse key to the chairman of our board of trustees, Mr. Poppell. I had toted that key for seven months and had given it back to the board with a much-improved building and clean, beautiful grounds.

I had to hurry, as my trunk had to be packed, strapped, tagged, and ready to load on the wagon before daylight the next morning to take to Browntown, where I would wave down the early AB&C train. I said good-bye to my people where I had lived those seven months. They hated to see me go. I loved them very dearly. When we were loaded up, and in the wagon and going, I looked back, and all were yet standing there waving at me. I had my trunk put in the baggage car and kept my grip with me. I would change at Hortense for the Bogey train to Raybon, where my father would meet me.

When I got on the train, I saw people in such a stir. The talk of war was on every lip. I then began to realize what had happened a few days before, on April 6, 1917, when Congress and President Woodrow Wilson entered us into the First World War to help England and France in their great struggle against Germany. The further I rode, the greater the excitement became, and the more disturbed the people seemed to be. My world changed then. I was so glad to be at home once more.

CHAPTER 8

World War I and My Work

I was very anxious to return to the University of Georgia for my second quarter of college work. My family thought differently. Our father was getting quite old and feeble, and he was not able to meet Lula and me when we came home on trains that arrived at our local stations at night, which it seemed most of them did. Neither was he able to work our farm anymore to advantage, and our only single brother, Jerry, was away in the Navy for seven years. All thought it best for us to try to build our home on our nearby property at Nahunta. I did not want to leave the farm, but it seemed that circumstance overwhelmed me. There was no summer school that summer for me, but instead, I had the task of getting the home built.

My sister Lula and I selected our house plans. The contractor was hired, a Mr. Broyles, who was a carpenter in the newly arrived L. S. Robb colony from Ohio. He made out the bill of material for the eight-room, two-story frame structure, and he and I went to Waycross, to the P. M. Harley Lumber and Hardware Co., and bought all the materials—brick for the pillars and chimney, lumbers for doors, windows, framing, siding, flooring, and ceiling. We had the sills hand-hewn, of heart cypress from our native swamps and hauled to us by ox teams. The other material was shipped by freight in boxcars from Waycross to Nahunta, then hauled by mules and wagons from freight depot to the building site.

It seemed necessary that I be nearby and easily reached for consultation with the contractor. We lived some seven miles away. There was no road, just a timber trail through the giant forest, not a settlement for the whole seven miles. The horse was needed at home for the last plowing of the crop, which was the last my father ever tried to make. My sister Lula and I had walked it several times, but that was slow and hard on us. So one day we were dining with our good friends Mr. and Mrs. Bill Roberson, and I said that I wished I had someplace where I could stay until the home was built. Mr. Roberson spoke up and said that he had the perfect plan.

Their good helper, Ella Strickland, had been begging Mrs. Roberson to let her off for the summer to go to Odum and stay with her uncle and aunt, Dr. and Mrs. T. G. Ritch, and attend the little normal school being run there in the Odum High School by Mr. Charles H. Shriver. She hoped to be able to thereby pass the county teacher examination and start on her career as a county schoolteacher. Nevertheless, so far, they had not found anyone to come stay with his good wife, Mrs. Sallie, and help her with her housework. She was a polio victim, paralyzed from the hips down, and needed help and companionship. So he said that if I would come stay with them, I could be there close by where I would be able to survey the progress of the work every day and keep in close touch with the contractor about needed supplies. Ella could go to summer school to work toward her teaching license. It would give the Robersons three months to try to find someone to stay with Sallie. He said they would be so glad to have me. Never a word was said about my duties, or my pay for staying, or their pay to me for helping out. Father and Mother liked the idea very much. So I got my clothes all ready. Father took me back to Nahunta in the buggy. He brought Ella, who was our next door neighbor, back to her home to get ready to go to her aunt's home. Ella was soon off to school for the summer. She passed the teachers examination for county license and began teaching that fall.

I stayed all summer, helping Mrs. Sallie with her household tasks, whatever they might be. Although she had to use a wheelchair, she could do any type of housework, such as cooking, bed making, washing, and ironing. She could even hang out her baby clothes. She had two sons, Joseph and Nolan, and three older children, Juanita, Eppie, and Edwin, by Mr. Roberson's first wife, who had passed away. She raised them all except Nolan, who passed away in the terrible flu epidemic of 1918–19.

Our home was completed and well built, only the chimney did not do so well. The contractor wished to use flues and heaters, and we insisted on the great old fireplaces of our southern style (I don't think he knew much about building chimneys). They never did draw properly. In other words, they smoked out at the fireplaces. Otherwise the building showed good workmanship. And before the summer was gone, the home was ready for us to move into, but alas, my money had given out. You see, I had not been teaching near as long as my sister Lula had, and therefore I did not have as much saved. When it came time to settle up, I lacked one hundred dollars toward the building price. I asked Mr. Broyles to let me give him a note for the hundred dollars until I could teach that fall and pay him the amount plus eight percent interest. He said no, the cold cash, or no key to the house. He had every door and window locked, and the key was in his pocket. So, there the house stood. Mr. Roberson wanted to know when we were going to move in, so I had to tell him the truth about the matter. He said right back to me that he would lend me the money, and he did. I paid the contractor, and Mr. Roberson took me home and told Mother and Father how happy he was to have Lula and me come to his village as neighbors, and he hoped we would soon move. By this time Ella was back and had told Mr. Roberson that she now had her teaching licenses and would be expecting a school by the late fall, as soon as cotton-picking was over. It was the custom to teach school in the slack times between farm chores, and they were closed when the farmwork had to be done. I well remember that our little district school always closed for two weeks in August for fodder-pulling time, and again in November for potato-digging time. People had to pay tuition for their children to go to school, and they wanted them to be there every day the school was in session. The teacher would always visit her family or do short-term schoolteaching during these stop periods.

Mr. Roberson now knew he would have to locate someone else to be their household helper and the companion of Mrs. Sallie. He located Miss Elizabeth Johns of the Bethlehem community across the Big Buffalo Creek. She was a very kind and efficient person, charming and jovial in her ways, and highly skilled in good housekeeping. She remained with them for many years, until she married Hon. J. W. Brooker, the postmaster and general merchandise store keeper. She was his second wife; his first wife, Mrs. Phodonia Brown Brooker, had passed away several years before. She made him a faithful, loving wife and bore him two children, Marjorie and Wilder. She was one of Nahunta's most beloved ladies for more than fifty years. She passed away a short time ago.

Moving was our next job. We had only one horse wagon, so the moving went slowly. My sister Lula and my mother rode with Father and the first wagonload, consisting of the cookstove, table, pots and dishes, two beds, and five chairs. Father got help unloading the furniture when he got there. He spent that night and drove back home the next morning. I had been left at home to attend to the cattle, hogs, chickens, goats, and other animals and to see after the garden and the field crops. The stove was gone, so I did all my cooking in the hearth pots. When Father came back, we would begin to pack up the next load. He would load as much furniture, bedding, dishes, and other household goods as the wagon body would hold, and then he would fill all the extra spaces with sacks of corn, potatoes, peas, syrup, canned fruits, meat, lard, honey, or what you have until he felt he had as much weight as the gentle horse could pull. We would go to bed early after our good hearth meal, with plenty of good milk, cream, and butter. I would arise early and milk the cows, sending my mother and Lula plenty of good fresh milk, buttermilk, and butter churned the day before as well as plenty of fresh vegetables in season and fresh eggs gathered. After a hearty breakfast, Father would be on his way. He would get to the new home, unload, and work on the barn shed he was building for the horse, two milk cows, a few fattening pigs, the buggy wagon, and harness shelter. He would spend that night with Mother and Lula and return to me the next day, when we would repeat the process. I worked every minute he was gone, getting things packed and keeping the stock well tended. Our neighbors would drop by to see us sometimes, but I spent those nights there alone. The thoughts of my childhood, with all my brothers and sisters and cousins and friends, rolled through my mind on those nights.

It took us more than a month to move. Everything was carefully handled—not one broken dish, cracked jar of fruit, or scarred piece of furniture—nothing was left behind. The chickens and pigs were crated, and I held the two milk cows by a halter as I sat in the back of the wagon. Our cousin Alice Brown Highsmith and her good husband, Erastus, were to look after our drove of cattle, hogs, and goats until Father could dispose of them profitably. They lived just across the way from us. They were to water them and pen them each night. You don't know how I wept when I left the dear old homeplace. It was one of the saddest hours of my whole life. My father called out and said, "Babe, it is now time for us to go." So we drove away. By late summer we were all set up in our new home. Our friends and neighbors had come with a picnic lunch and helped us get our premises all cleaned. Our father had used all the waste lumber to build the barn shed and a toilet for our personal use. There was no plumbing or waterworks in the village of Nahunta until many years later.

After we entered World War I, our young men began to be called into military service. Labor became scarcer and scarcer. Food began to be rationed, especially sugar and flour. Troop trains began to move, taking thousands and tens of thousands of our young men to the training grounds.

I had a good friend and neighbor, Mr. Fred Knox, who had a large acreage in cotton that was white unto harvest, and he could get no help to harvest it. Only growing boys and girls were available. They made a good work force if he could stay among them, but he had wide and varied interest and had to be hither and yon throughout the day. As the old saying goes, "When the cat is away, the mice will play." His cotton fields were being destroyed by the children frolicking through them and fussing among themselves. One day Mr. Knox was lamenting to my good friend Mr. Roberson what a plight he was in. It looked like the autumn rains would come before he could ever get his cotton crop gathered. The prices of cotton and cottonseed were climbing day by day.

So Mr. Roberson referred him to me. He said you go ask her to help you control your children, and I am sure your troubles will be over, and you will soon be well on your way to getting a good clean harvest. So he came and told Father what he wanted, and Father told him to speak with me and that he knew I could do it, and he thought I would surely agree. Mr. Knox told me his great need and asked would I consider the job; he would pay me well. I thanked him. He said he would go among his friends and neighbors and tell them to have their children ready for the next week, that he had employed me to take care of the children and to see that all went well in the cotton field. Come Monday morning, he was there by the crack of dawn. I had my lunch ready and was in my cotton-picking clothes. This was a windfall for me, as I had spent my last dollar on my portion to the contractor and still owed money to Mr. Roberson. I was wondering where my funds would come from until my first payday of the fall school term.

We were all soon in the snow-white cotton field of more than one hundred acres. Everyone had a cotton-picking sack and an emptying sheet. We had left our lunches at an old dwelling on the farm and had taken our jugs of water with us to the field. We went clear to the backside, where the children had frolicked over the rows and wasted the cotton. I told them we had come to gather the cotton not to destroy it. I had counted the rows and the number of pickers, and I knew the number of days until school would begin for all of us. Their school was at Nahunta, and mine at O'Quinn. I told them how hard we would have to work to get through on time. We would have the good pay for our work, and Mr. Knox would have the cotton to sell to benefit his crop year. The nation would have the cotton and the cottonseed to help win the war; so to picking we all went. I took the middle row. Some ten or twelve children were on each side of me. We were going right on down the row, no nipping or boll throwing allowed. By and by emptying time came. We all went to empty after we had gotten everyone's rows up even with the others. We chose two children to go to the well at the old house for water. Everyone agreed to give the water carriers a big handful of cotton to keep their rows up even with ours. This plan proved satisfactory throughout the harvest. Each emptying time, a different pair would be chosen to go for water. Soon they had rather stay and pick than go for water, since they were getting paid by the pound to gather the cotton.

By and by noontime came. We all went and had our lunch. I told them a wonderful story, and we all lay down to rest, usually about 2:30 P.M., as the noonday sun was bearing down too heavily for man or beast to try to withstand it. We would then return to field and pick as late as we could and still have daylight enough to weigh in our cotton. When the wagons came to gather it up to take away to the gins, I had every child keep a record of their weights day by day to show their parents at night.

Early rising, getting to the fields in the cool of morning, steady working hours, a long noonday rest, and late picking in the cool of the evening gave us plenty of working time. We kept everybody's row up and all rows cleanly picked. The evidence could be clearly seen, a brown field behind us and a snow-white harvest in front. In a few days we could begin to count how long it would take us to gather the crop (with good weather) and how many days we had until school time. We set ourselves to finish the task on time and we did.

I made some of the staunchest friends of my life from among the parents and children in this wonderful work experience. I often think what a happy time we all had. They would not miss a day from picking for anything. They did not want to miss the noonday story hour. Have you ever thought of the power of a wonderfully told story? It can sway children and grown folks, too, when everything else fails. We all had our money to spend as we needed it. The children bought new fall school shoes, clothes, books, and supplies. I used my funds to get to my next teaching position and to make my way up the ladder in my chosen profession. I often think how easy it was to bring order out of chaos, and success out of defeat, all by knowing how and being willing to do the required work to accomplish the job. I have always remembered this summer of 1917 as one of my most worthwhile ever. First, staying with the Roberson's to help them out in their time of need, then helping my dear father and mother and sister move, and finally, helping my friend and neighbor get his cotton crop gathered. I flung my bread upon the waters, and it surely came back to me manyfold.

When I got to O'Quinn and began to teach, I had new shoes and new dresses and money enough to last me until my first payday. When I sent a check to Mr. Roberson to make my first payment on the note, he wrote a nice letter of appreciation for my prompt payment and included the note marked "paid in full." I had received no pay while staying with them and helping Mrs. Sallie while our house was being built. I was willing to stay without pay, although I had worked every day. I had a place to stay, food to eat, and a bed to sleep in so I could be near the building of our home. I have always felt I was doubly paid for service.

When my dear father passed away in late 1919, I escorted his body to Nahunta on a train from the St. Joseph's Hospital in Savannah, where he had died. We arrived before day on Train No. 89. Who should be there to meet us but my good friend Fred Knox with his fine team of mules and good wagon to take the body to our home and on to the church when the time came, as there were no trucks or hearses in our small village. Never a cent of pay would he have. He said that the debt had been paid by me in days gone by.

I have dear memories of my teaching career and early womanhood, always remembering that everything works together for the good of those that love the Lord.

CHAPTER 9

O'Quinn School

As the busy summer of 1917 came to a close, it seemed that the tempo of the world had changed from a slow-moving, delightful pace to a whirlwind of exhilarating movements for everyone everywhere. Trains were going by continually, loaded to overflowing with troops. More and more automobiles were appearing: Ford, Buick, Overland, Hudson, Studebaker, Franklin, Cole 8, White Steamer, La Salle, and on and on. Horses and buggies were not fast enough. If you did not have a car, you hired your neighbor to drive you for a fee that you thought exorbitant. Your neighbor knew it was not enough to pay the cost of the trip, yet he would take you because he never tired of driving his car hither and yon.

My superintendent wrote and asked me to go to the O'Quinn community the first of August to meet the trustees and have a talk with them to learn what kind of a situation I was going to have to deal with. I took ten dollars of my cotton-harvesting money with which to make the trip. He was sure that when I got to Screven, if I would inquire at the J. W. Walker gin company, I would surely find someone from the community who would be glad to take me out and around to see all the trustees. But alas, the day I got there seemed to be the day people from that community were not at J. W. Walker. They were all Sea Island cotton growers. The head clerk, Mr. Wright, said it was fine cotton-picking weather, and he expected I would have to go to the cotton fields to find them, as he had not seen a soul from that community all day. I asked him whom could I get to take me, and his reply was that Mr. Henry Mikel, the local jewelry man, had a nice little car and often made trips for hire. He was sure I could get him to take me for a small fee. I went over to his shop to see if he would take me. I told him the names of the three men I wanted to see and asked him what would be his fee. He said not much, but he did not know exactly where they all lived, and he could not set his price until he saw how many miles he had to go and the type of road he had to travel. Away we went, bumping along from one deep rut and sand bed to another.

[73]

We went to the various fields where the men were among their cotton pickers. They graciously stopped to talk with me and told me the kind of teacher they were looking for. They expected one that would teach the lessons and not sit up there and crochet or tat all day long in place of helping the boys and girls with their difficult problems. That was what Mr. Johnny Graham told me. I assured him that I never did that during class time at school, neither did I read a newspaper or try to grade papers during the eight hours of class time. Mr. Ashley Purvis said he did not want a courting school going on, and all the boys and girls running away and getting married. His daughter Nellie had run away and married the year before, and he was still upset over it. I told him I was not in the matrimony business for myself or for my pupils. I felt that was the parents' duty to help choose their children's mates, that I was not in the husband-hunting business and would have no part in such an affair. My next stop was with a Mr. Bell, who did not want any partiality shown among the students. He said that his son Paul had been accused of everything that had been done wrong at the school for the last five years. I promised him I always tried my best to treat everyone fairly, and I surely would try to find out who did these troublesome things of which Paul was being accused. They all seemed to be satisfied with my statements, and we set the day for me to come. I told them I would like to come on ahead early for us to get the schoolhouse ready for the children.

I had to pass by the school building on my way from Ashley Purvis's farm to Johnny Graham's farm, and I had asked Mr. Mikel to stop and let me look it over. The deep open well was supplied with all kinds of trash, the windowpanes were out, the steps were in sad repair, and the benches and desks were all awry. The stovepipe had melted and telescoped far down on each joint. The entire building looked as if billy goats had used it as a convention hall for the entire summer. Under the beautiful oak trees, the cows had rested from their grazing, and their noonday droppings had been left for many months. It was still open range for stock everywhere. The hogs had wallowed by the well anytime they could find enough water to make a mud puddle, which seemed to be often, as many people watered their stock from this well during dry seasons. I saw much to be done before anyone could begin to think of having an orderly school day. I cast my eyes down back of the campus and saw that both outdoor toilets were turned over and in dire need of major repair.

I could not retrace my steps to the trustees' homes, as the day was far spent. I told Mr. Mikel I would write the trustees letters telling them the date I wished to arrive and asking them to meet me at the schoolhouse with tools and material to get the needed work done. My mind flashed back to my brand-new Bamboo

School—with its beautiful grounds, well-locked doors and windows, nice deep pump, pure clear water, and good, well-kept toilets—and the fifty or so well-behaved boys and girls who took care of it. Here I would have to struggle with more than a hundred students, and try to build and keep an attendance of ninety so as to hold a teacher helper for me, all with an increase of just ten dollars per month. But I thought of the old adage, If you never do more than you are paid to do, you will never climb in your profession, and I said to myself, I will do my best. The sun was sinking low when we returned to Screven. We had not stopped any-place for lunch, although we had been asked by several to have the noonday meal with them. I knew that Mr. Mikel wished to catch a train back to Jesup, where I could catch my faithful Bogey early the next morning.

When we returned to Screven I thanked Mr. Mikel for being so patient with me and for helping me find all three trustees of the school in one day. I asked for his fee. He figured the mileage and his time and expense of the car, and it came out thus: three dollars for his time, five dollars for mileage and the expense of his car. Well that left me just enough to get back to Jesup. This was the first and last time I ever got so far away from home with so little money. Thereafter, I always put my return fare in another section of my purse; and to me, so far as spending it for anything other than my return fare, I just did not have it.

I arrived in Jesup late that afternoon and went to spend the night with my good friend and faithful advisor Annie Bennett, our home demonstration agent. I told her where I had been and what a plight I was in, and I borrowed enough money from her to buy my ticket from Jesup to Nahunta the next morning. We sat and talked for a long time that night, and she gave me some of the best teaching advice I ever received. She told me to find out the students' desires and goals if they had any, and if they did not, to help them find some for themselves; and to keep them busy from the first day of school until the very last minute of the last day. A lot of the disturbance occurred in rural schools on the last day, when some children wanted to settle all old grudges. She said that if I did not keep them busy, the disturbance was my fault. There were enough good things in the world for a person to learn to keep him satisfied and busy for a thousand years. If I did not know enough, I should get myself busy and learn enough and more. She was sure I would as time moved on. She said she was so glad Mr. Purcell was sending me there, for they surely had had some mighty hard luck with unsatisfactory teachers in past years.

Fine people lived in the O'Quinn community, and they had fine boys and girls, if only they had someone to lead them onward and upward. Mrs. Bennett and Mr. Shedd had some mighty fine club boys and girls in that community, and they always came through and had good exhibits at the fair every fall, but the records and reports of their work were poorly prepared. Slothfulness and a lack of academic training showed in their written work, and their spoken work seemed to be just as poor. I saw right then and there that some hard teaching lay ahead of me.

After my visit to the O'Quinn community, I spent a few hours with Mr. Purcell and told him of the survey I had made and gave him the information I had received first-hand and from the trustees. When I told him the number of students anticipated in the district, he told me he would have a good assistant teacher there to help handle the situation if I thought I could meet the attendance requirement for the additional person. I told him I would do my best. I wrote to all three of my trustees and told them of this promise I had from our superintendent. I had planned to arrive at school on Thursday before school was to start on Monday. I hoped the trustees and I could meet at the schoolhouse early Friday morning to get the needed repairs made. We needed to clean out the well, scrub the schoolhouse, replace windowpanes, fix the doorsteps, right the toilets and make them more stable, replace the stovepipe, and arrange the desk and tables—and more. I also told them that I and the other teacher, the school superintendent's sister-in-law, Miss Carrie Hires of Redland, Georgia, would need a place to board.

I was more than busy for the next few weeks getting teaching material ready. I had promised the trustees that I would do the beginner class and the upper classes of older students. They had heard of the wonderful success I had had at the Big Cypress community Penholloway School, with my forty-two who could not read or write a word, and also of my further success at Bamboo School. So my reputation had preceded my visit among them. I had to get a good supply of first-grade material stored up in my mind as well as dig deep for plenty of plans for alert boys and girls near-grown. Some of them were almost as old as me, ready for work or mischief, whichever way I could turn their energy. I was determined that it would be work if I had the power within me to so direct their minds and talents.

I also had to look well to my wardrobe, for I would be gone from home seven months with only a short Christmas vacation. I would need fall, winter, and spring clothes. In those days you made all your clothes, except the heaviest of coats. I was going to live among well-to-do people, and there would be plenty of places to go—other churches and villages nearby, and Jesup was not too far away. I did not plan any extravagances in clothing. But I did want a nice substantial, good-looking, well-fitted, and attractive teaching wardrobe, as well as an always presentable business or social dress or suit. I was as busy as I could be, until the time to go came.

My father and my mother wished me much luck. They were both happy to see me rising so rapidly in my chosen profession. I was now twenty years old. I had been teaching for five years, and my salary had been raised each year. I now had another teacher to control and direct, double or more the number of pupils, and many more patrons to satisfy than ever before. My father gave me great encouragement, telling me to control myself and to do justly by all those that came under my care and love; he was sure I would get on well and be a blessing to all those I went among. He gave me the same rules and guidelines he had given me the morning he took me to the train in 1913 to go to my first teaching assignment. He told me never to do, say, or act at any time in a way that would not be a help, always to be an ornament to those I was trying to lead and direct; never to forget that I bore his name, and never to bring anything but honor to it; never to forget I was a child of God unless I chose to give myself to the Devil; and, above all, to remember that God was everywhere and knew everything and was always watching over me and caring for me wherever I went if I would only trust him. I fell on his neck as I kissed him good-bye at the station, the same as I did Mother before I left home. I told him I would remember all he said and thanked him for his advice and blessings.

Miss Hires, my assistant teacher, and I arrived at school on a bright September morning. I had gone to Jesup the night before on my faithful Bogey train and stayed at the Ingleside Hotel. I arose early the next morning to meet with Mr. Purcell to get my final instructions and school supplies such as a register crayon (all teachers had to buy that) and a book list and prices. (Patrons had to buy their own books for children. It was some seventeen years until some free textbooks were available.) I also met with Miss Hires at the superintendent's office. We planned out our work. I had promised the trustees faithfully that I would do beginners, first, fifth, six, and seventh grades. Miss Hires was to do second, third, and fourth grades. I thought that would about balance the pupil load, as poor attendance in years gone by had kept the lower grades filled.

Miss Hires and I were met at the train by Mr. Ellis Surrency in his brand-new Ford car and taken to his lovely home. Along the way long-staple cotton was white unto harvest just as far as you could see. He had a lovely wife, Mrs. Ada Bennett Surrency. They had two fine young sons, Luddie, grade seven, Louis, grade four, and a beautiful little daughter, Lesby, grade three. He told us we could stay with them until we could look around and see with whom we wanted to live. We were very happy there, but Mrs. Surrency was rather frail and did not feel like she was able to take care of us. We found a very happy place to live with Mr. Joseph Smith and his good wife, Mrs. Rachel Purcell Smith. They had a nice new two-story home about a mile closer to the school building. They had a large family of boys and girls. There were Lola, Rollie, Alcott, Algernon, Clark, Grady, Willa Mae, and Jewel, all in school (and several younger children).

It was a wonderful place to stay, with good food, good beds, fine fireplaces, plenty of good firewood. It was the first winter I had ever had that. Plenty of mornings in years gone by I had to break the ice in the wash pan in my room to take my sponge bath before going to school. I thought of it as a blessing and gave a prayer of thanksgiving that I would not have to freeze that winter as I had the five previous winters away from home. They had a nice living room, plenty of good chairs and sofas, and a beautiful organ. This was where the family gathered every night to sing before prayers. Friends, cousins, and other family came on Saturday nights and Sunday afternoons to sing. There was a large, beautiful porch, plenty of good handmade hickory cowhide-bottom rockers, where as long as weather was pleasant enough for porch sitting, I could rest or read or plan my work for the next day. In the wintertime, I would sit beside the fireplace with large glass windows on either side. Best of all, the little boys and girls would bring me good oak wood and fat lightwood knots so they could get into my room, look at my school magazines, and use my small scissors and colored crayons. Mrs. Smith was afraid they would worry me. I would laugh and tell her that children were my stock in trade and that I would let her know when they bothered me. It was a long cold winter, and many an evening they would stay with me until bedtime while I was at my worktable. They would sit on the floor and draw or cut or read or just look at my magazines—all of us cozy and warm.

Mrs. Smith often told me in after years that it was the easiest winter she had ever had since she had so many children. She usually did her sewing after supper each evening, using her big dining table to cut on; then she would roll it up and put in her workbasket to take to her room where she kept her sewing machine. Now, with all the younger children except the baby upstairs by my fire, she was able to do her sewing. She had to make clothes for the children, her husband, and herself, everything except overalls for the men. No shirts, dresses, or underclothes were on the market yet. She kept her family well dressed for all occasions.

Miss Hires played the organ well, as did Lola, the oldest daughter. Mr. Smith and all the boys sang well. So they gathered around the organ every night, learning new songs and enjoying the old ones they already knew, until they had to do their lessons for the next day. We both seemed to fit well with the family plan, and the year was happy for all concerned.

I numbered Mr. and Mrs. Smith and their large family of children among the best friends of my life. I never heard a cross word spoken by parent or child or neighbor the whole year I lived with them. Their food was wonderful. They raised practically all of it—beef, pork, chicken, and turkey; rice, potatoes, and corn; milk, butter, and cream; and vegetables and fruits of all kinds. Our board was reasonable. We did our own laundry, cleaned our own room, and walked to school and back. We visited with the family and enjoyed ourselves day by day. On Sundays we went to church with the Smiths in the big family surrey, drawn by two fine mules, or in the bright, shiny top buggy with the older son and daughter. They had no car as yet.

Our workday was bright and fair. I had brought some stout scrub rags from home and a few pieces of my mother's strong lye soap. I asked Mr. Surrency to bring his wash pot, dip gourds, buckets, brooms, and shuck scrub, as well as his tools for making repairs. He and Mrs. Surrency took us over in their car. I knew it would be a long hard day. On the way, a few others joined us as we passed by and told them where we were going and why. They had never heard tell of that before—the teacher coming on ahead to get the building straight. Usually the first day of school was a hullabaloo. Any cleaning or straightening was done after the first day, and usually a week went by before there was time to settle down to work. I knew that all the work could not be done in one day, but we could get it orderly enough to begin classes. The trustees and other patrons could do the remaining jobs day by day as they had time from the cotton fields on rainy days.

First we shoveled and swept, getting rid of all goat droppings and trash that had accumulated over the summer months. Then we scalded and scrubbed the furniture and woodwork with strong, boiling lye-soapy water and sand. We polished windows and counted the panes that were not there for us to polish. Some sashes were too decayed to hold a new pane. We examined the door locks, which didn't, and the window locks, which were not there either. I told the trustees to cut me window props to reach diagonally across the windows so I could prop them up of a day and prop them down of a night. We also checked the furniture, which was in sad repair. I made a list of needed supplies—locks for the two doors, windowpanes, some sashes, a well bucket, material for mending benches, and a stovepipe bolted together at the blacksmith shop so as to not telescope when it got hot. The doorsteps were so poor that they were dangerous to use at all. All were major repairs that would take quite a bit of money for material and labor. The building was sixty-five feet long and forty feet wide. The one heater, in the middle of the room, was in poor condition and insufficient to heat the building. Off to one side was a stage, about ten feet wide. The toilets needed major repairs also. But the workers were able to prop the old ones upright until they could get new ones built nearby. With no money, no labor, and no material, the trustees asked all the patrons to meet Monday morning. They asked each family to give twenty-five cents to help buy materials and asked for a day's labor to do the work. Or the family could hire someone to work in their place.

A blue calico curtain had been hung the full length of the building so two teachers could work at the same time at the same end of the building, one teacher on each side of curtain, sharing the one blackboard all the way across the front of the room. The curtain gave evidence of having caught fire several times from being pulled too near the heater by some frisky boy or girl. I asked for the curtain to be put crossways. Miss Hires would have the back end of building, and I would take the front. The trustees said, "What! With no blackboard?" I told them we would have to manage to get her one. We were there to work, and we had to arrange the building so work could go on. They said she will have no heat, and I said we will reach some plan to get her a heater flue and heater. I did not believe that some one hundred pupils and two teachers could keep warm by that one small Dixie heater (a long-body heater with two caps on top), a very poor heat-producer. When we finished getting the curtain changed and the seats and desks arranged, the trustees wondered why they had not thought of this arrangement before, thinking maybe they could have had school the last four or five years in place of all the trouble and misbehavior.

I looked around, and in one corner of the stage was a large box full of debris—among which were broken desk legs that we could repair and use, and a leather-bound *Webster's Unabridged Dictionary,* a treasure to behold. I was overjoyed and said we must have a strong table for this in the very front center of the room, for it will be in use every day by the 5th-, 6th-, and 7th-grade groups. And we must have comfortable, strong chairs around the table. One of the trustees spoke up and told how much they had paid for the dictionary and said that to the best of his knowledge it had never been used. Its position at the bottom of the trash pile gave evidence of what the trustee said. I told them how much I had always longed for one but had not had access to one since I had left my little log cabin school in 1912. They promised me the table and chairs for Monday morning. So I dusted it and placed it on my desk, ready for it to be put in its place of need and honor. In the trash we also found a Wayne County map showing the lotted and head-right land, a Georgia map showing the geographical details, and a map of the United States, showing all the land cessions of the nation. I was thrice blessed with these good maps, and we placed them on the walls, where they could be easily studied by one group at a time.

Another trustee told me of the awful times they had around the well, which had two buckets on a chain and a pulley; when one bucket was brought up, the other went down. They were both full of holes. I asked for the pulley and chain to be fixed and for two good new buckets. I was sure I could get rid of their troubles at the well. We would drink our water with decency and pleasure and in an orderly way. The fall of the year was fast closing in, and soon wintertime would be with us. I thought that while we were all there together we had better settle the wood question. I mentioned it, and they said they had always depended on the patrons to bring the wood. But sometimes they did not do it. When wood gave out, and the teacher would have to turn school out to keep the children and themselves from suffering from the cold of the winter. I suggested that they tell the patrons of our needs. If each patron brought one load of good wood as we needed it, I would keep an accurate account of who had brought wood and notify the next patron to bring a load. I would never be able to teach a bunch of freezing children, and neither did I like to be cold myself. They seemed to think it fair; they were all landowners and had plenty of wooded land.

The sun was sinking low when the final touches were put on the building, inside and out, and it was a tired bunch of people who left the O'Quinn School building that late September afternoon. I spent Saturday getting my plans, material, and thoughts together for Monday morning. Sunday was a beautiful day, and Miss Hires and I went with Mr. and Mrs. Surrency to church in their shiny new car. There we met a lot of our patrons and pupils—a very enjoyable day.

Monday morning we arose early so as to be the first to see what all had been done Saturday. The old well buckets and chain had been replaced. New panes, sashes, and props for the windows were in place, as were new locks for the doors. The desks, benches, and chairs were in an orderly arrangement. The schoolhouse was nice and clean, and some little girls had brought beautiful pink roses for the teachers' desks. So, all in all, things were looking much improved.

Patrons, pupils, and visitors soon were coming from every direction. There were mules, wagons, buggies, and one or two cars, but most of the children were walking, their books and slates clutched tightly in one hand, their lunch pail in the other. All came in quietly, laid their things down, and went back out to play. The trustees and other men were gathered in the far corner of yard under a clump of oak trees, talking quietly and earnestly. The ladies were all in the schoolhouse with Miss Hires and me, making small talk. I felt that they knew the reason for the talk among the men, but we asked no questions. I wondered in my own mind what they were planning; had they decided to fire us?

Miss Hires and I had our names on the blackboard and also the grades we were to teach. When eight o'clock came I went to the front porch and rang my large brass bell loud and long. Miss Hires stood on one side of porch, and I on the other. We asked the children to get into lines in front of their teacher. The first-grade children were with their mothers and already within the school building. I asked the children to walk in quietly and to find seats. I called to the trustees, who were outside, that the time had come for us to begin our day's work. They soon came in. At the front of the room I picked up my Bible and read from Genesis, where God created the heavens and the earth, and every day when he finished his labors he said it was good. I remarked that I hoped we could say "it was good" each school day when our work was done. I asked all to stand and to say the Lord's Prayer with me. Then I asked them to remain standing while we all sang "America," all four verses. It got kind of feeble in the second, third, and fourth verses. We would sing it better the next time.

Then I asked the trustees to talk. They said some nice things about Miss Hires and me, and how they expected such a good school year. They asked each family to give a quarter to meet the present needs and told them about the firewood schedule. They told of the major repairs that were still needed: a new set of doorsteps, another flue, a heater for the second room, three eight-foot lengths of blackboard for Miss Hires's end of the building, twelve tiny chairs for my first grade, and a moveable partition of wood to replace the curtain.

They had agreed among themselves that as soon as schoolwork got well organized they would ask the community to plan for a major moneymaking entertainment for these major needs. I told them that I did not feel we could put off getting the blackboard for that long. In fact we needed it badly that day. So they decided they would underwrite the blackboard and ask Mr. Surrency to see if he would bring it back in his car when he went to see the county school superintendent Tuesday to get the books. Everyone was to bring their money to me Tuesday morning for the books on the list I was to give out before the close of the day Monday. I further spoke and said we could not wait too long for the flue and heater, for cool weather would soon be upon us, and our work would be hindered and the children's health impaired if we could not be warm and comfortable. One mother spoke up and said that heretofore they had always kept the children home on bad days. I told them that I had given my word of honor to do my best to keep the children in school for the full term so we could meet the requirements to have two teachers. The trustees said they had made the same promise to the school superintendent. Mr. Erastus Jones, a good carpenter and brick mason, said he and his boys would gladly do the repairs on the off days from their farmwork. The trustees asked him to make out the bill of material for the repairs that had been agreed on, and I added a dinner pail rack and coat hanger place for the porch. So here we were on the first day of school, bound together by a moneymaking project and the repair work. There wasn't any PTA then to execute such plans, so the ladies all agreed to plan and carry out a moneymaking project.

It was all moving in the right direction, and now we were about to get down to actual routine work of registration, classification, book lists, and schedules. But then one of the trustees said there were some rules that the trustees and patrons wished to set forth. I asked him to please state them. He began with the terrible trouble they had at the well, the disorder when leaving and entering the building, the continuous courting that had been going on, and the high number of "runaway marriages" that had occurred among the students. He wished the strictest rules set for getting water, leaving and entering the school building, and leaving the building for home. Girls were to be dismissed at one time and to form lines for getting water and entering the building. Boys were to be formed in another line for the same purposes and to be dismissed at another time for home going. No note writing or courting was to be allowed on the way to and from school. I had been seated at my desk all this time praying every minute that I would know what to say and do when he had finished.

When he was through, I asked if there was another trustee who wished to make a statement. They said no; the one trustee had spoken for all three of them. Then I asked if any of the other gentlemen wished to make any remarks, and they heartily agreed with the plans that had been set forth. Then I asked the ladies if they wished to make any remarks. One of my very dearest friends (of later years) spoke up and said that all she could say was that these rules should have been set forth years ago—not much use to lock the stable after the horse had been stolen.

Everything got deathly quiet. I knew my time had come—to sink or swim, to act or submit, to succeed or fail. I prayed silently: "O God give me the courage, power, and knowledge to do and say the right thing; to be the master of my school; to not make foolish promises that I could not keep; to not commit myself to situations that had not yet happened, may never happen, and if they did happen might be circumstances entirely beyond my and Miss Hires's control." I feared that deep open well and all the terrible tales I had heard of how the big bullies had held the little boys by the seat of their pants over it and told them if they did not hush they would drop them to the bottom of it. I arose from my seat and put on the most dignified smile that I had ever tried to produce. I thanked the trustee who had talked for the others. I also thanked the other trustees and patrons for coming and for endorsing the rules he had set forth. I told them Miss Hires and I would always be happy to hear their wishes and plans for the school. I told them about my rule that everyone was to do right, by themselves and by every person they came in contact with. I assured them that I would always do my best with each of the fine boys and girls they had sent to me, that I would teach their children the basic foundations of reading, writing, spelling, arithmetic, and the English language in all its forms. Here I pointed to the dictionary we had found in the pile of debris and my Bible. I said that those two books were the best guides for our tasks and that they both would be used diligently day by day.

I further stated that our hours would be from 8 A.M. until 4 P.M., with the following relief periods: 10:00 A.M. until 10:30 A.M.; noon until 1:00 P.M., for lunch and playtime; and 2:30 P.M. to 2:45 P.M.. But I suggested that they might wish to change the hours to 7 A.M. until 3 P.M. during September and October to help with the cotton-gathering situation, as Miss Hires and I had noticed that quite a few of their fields were yet white unto harvest. I had been born and reared on a farm and knew you could not do much early-morning picking, but children could get home in the early afternoon and pick many pounds before nightfall. They all seemed to thrill at the idea (Daylight Savings Time did not exist in those days). Miss Hires and I urged perfect attendance for their pickers. We were willing to do anything we could to help harvest the bountiful crop. We might even agree to pick some ourselves. That brought a big laugh from everyone. So the trustees put it to a vote and agreed on the earlier hours through the last Sunday of October.

I called on Miss Hires for her talk. She was quite pretty and also very modest in her ways. She arose and said she agreed with me one hundred percent. She said that she, too, had only one rule—the same as mine—to do right all the time and that she would do her best to do right by every lovely child she had. She could hardly wait to find out their names and grades and to begin her work with them. She heartily sanctioned the early time schedule and told those assembled not to be surprised if they saw us in the cotton field after school. She knew from her talks with me that we would be busy for many weeks getting all the work set in order that we had planned for the year. Our first goal was to keep the attendance at ninety or above so we could have two teachers or she would have no job. She asked that students never be kept home on cold or rainy days, as we would keep them good and warm by the nice new stove they were going to give us. Miss Hires thanked them for coming to the school during their busy cotton-picking time and extended her kind invitation to them to return at any time to see how their children were getting along or to give any information they wished concerning their children. After she had finished, I again thanked them for coming and participating on our opening day. I then asked them to excuse us so we could turn our attention to the children, who had waited so patiently for two hours, saying they could stay with us if they wished, but it was time go forward with our schoolwork.

They all said they must go. Each patron with a first-grade child brought him or her to me with a note containing their name, age, and parents' names. I set the children down on the edge of the stage floor and told them we would have pretty new chairs just their size in a few days. I said for them to be sweet, that I would be with them in a few minutes.

The patrons, visitors, and trustees came by and shook hands with me and invited me to come to see them when I could. I told them I surely would, just as soon as I could get caught up with schoolwork. They also invited me to their church. They told me where they worshipped, which Sunday was their church service day, and that Sunday school was held every Sunday. They were mostly Baptist. The O'Quinn Baptist Church was just across the road from school, in a beautiful new building not yet complete. Wesleyan Methodist worshipped at Liberty school district, and the Methodist Episcopal church worshipped at Satilla, in the Empire school district. They told me as they passed out that they knew we would have a good school year and to be sure to have their children behave and do the right thing. I told them I knew we were going to have a great school, with all these fine boys and girls to teach and all you fine patrons to back us up. They should not worry. I had a fine teacher to help me, and we were going to take good care of the children and teach them well. We asked them to not forget about our moneymaking entertainment. After they told me good-bye and made their faithful promises to me, they passed on to Miss Hires at the back of the room. They told her good-bye and invited her to come with me to see them and to come to their church and Sunday school. They were soon out the door, off the porch, down the old rickety steps, and across the schoolyard to their buggies, surreys, wagons, and one car.

I told the students how proud I was of them and how much we had to do before home-going time. But we must also have some rest and relief from our long hours of sitting. With only one set of insecure steps, we would have to be extra careful of our going and coming. Miss Hires and her group would leave first, through the door on the right and down the steps to the play yard in single file. We would leave through the door to the left in same manner. This day I would attend to the water-drawing to see that everyone got a cool drink as quickly as possible so they would have some time to play. We would be happy to use the two new buckets and four dozen brand-new tin cups. The trustees had also brought a big "blue Whistler" barrel sawed in half to make two cypress tubs to hold the wastewater so no slop or mud would be made around the well. There would always be water there for the thirsty cattle, goats, and other stock that passed our way.

We would have thirty minutes for our break, then I would ring one bell, and everyone was to get in their own line and return to their own room. Only my children would go in first so as not to bother Miss Hires's children as we passed by, just like she had moved out of our way as we were going out. I stayed at the well all during recess. They had the whole thirty minutes to drink water if they wished. When I left the well to ring the bell, there would be no more water drinking. All cups were to be hung on the cross boards so the sun would keep them pure and sweet. The well tender would have to bring the cups in each afternoon before we left for home. Everyone was busy talking or drinking water. Some walked down to the back of campus for personal relief. A few of the more forward older boys and girls ventured to speak with Miss Hires and me to tell us how proud they were the way we responded to the trustees' long list of rules. The said they intended to "do right," just as far as they knew how. I told them we were there to guide them the best we knew.

I rang the bell, and all were soon inside and quiet. Our partition was pulled across the room. We began at once to register the children, listing their ages, grades, parents, home, and its distance from school. We also made lists of needed books and their prices. I started with the seventh grade and their spelling books. After getting their information, I gave them an assignment to prepare for their spelling lesson the next morning. I told them to begin studying as soon as they returned to their seats. I gave them plenty of work to do: adding prefixes and suffixes to words and word matching. Then I called the sixth grade and the fifth grade, going through the same routine with each. When my older children were hard at work, I gathered my eleven little beginners around me, got the slips of paper their parents had made out and listed their books, slates, pencils, and other supplies. They all said my name, and I called their names and had them to walk to me one at a time as I called each name. I sat while I was working with them. I gave each a piece of crayon and asked them to go to blackboard and draw me a picture, saying I would look at it after a little while.

I called the seventh-grade English class to the recitation bench. I found out who needed books. Many of them had books from the previous year or from an older brother or sister. I assigned their English work for their first lesson on the morrow and returned them to their seats to prepare. Sixth and fifth grades were called up separately, registered, and given their study assignments the same way. I turned back to my first-graders, looked at their pictures, asked them questions about their pets, babies, or toys. I called the seventh, sixth, and fifth grades again and made book lists for world history and Georgia history. Grade one counted their eyes, toes, and noses. By this time it was noon. They marched out as before.

I attended to the well. Everyone was to get a drink, wash their hands, get lunch, and eat on the lawn. When they finished they put up their lunch bucket and played until I rang a bell ten minutes before coming-in time, enough time for everyone to get another drink. I hardly had time to attend to my own personal needs, between watering everyone, eating my own lunch, ringing the bell, then watering everyone again. I promised the children I would not be that busy every day and would soon be able to play singing games with them. I checked through grades seven and five for geography books, made book lists, and assigned lessons. While they were at work I called grade one and had them tell me where they went to church, where they got their mail, and now where they were going to school.

Following came the work for which they were all waiting, arithmetic. Country children always excel here. I suppose it is because they have so many things to count, measure, and weigh. Again, I started with the seventh grade. Then the first grade and I had a big time counting to one hundred and making the figures on their slates.

Next came reading for grades one through five. I found that very few had read books. I told them we were going to learn to read—if we did not learn anything else—because reading was the basis of all their knowledge, and if they could not read well, they would never be able to learn well. I ordered a wonderful series of prose and poetry books for grades five through seven, delightful and informative reading to help them become comprehensive and masterful readers. My, how the children enjoyed those books throughout the year as they became acquainted with some of the world's finest authors. At 2:30 we rested, got relief for ourselves, and cooling drinks of water. No playtime this period. I attended the well until just before coming-in time. I called Miss Hires to relieve me for a few minutes. When I returned, I rang the bell. We assembled as before. Only one hour and fifteen minutes more of the long, long day. Right to work we both went to finish our book lists. I called grades five through seven for book lists and lesson assignments in health. The whole world was becoming health conscious. I surely was, and I intended to have a strong health program as well as a basic text. Typhoid fever, chills and fever, or malaria fever ran rampant; so did hookworms, measles, mumps, whooping cough, pneumonia, diphtheria, and dysentery. I detained the seventh grade to talk to them about agriculture and civics, which had an added basic text for each subject for grade seven. The state examination, which was given each year to admit our students to high school, carried a section of questions on each subject. I had already made up my mind that I was going to have a large seventh-grade graduation class. They asked me how in the world we could do it, saying they already had more work than they had ever carried before. I told them we would manage somehow. I did not intend for them to be lacking in those two subjects at the end of the year.

We finished our day's work with a few vital instructions that applied to the whole school. So our curtain was pulled back after I had inquired of Miss Hires if she had finished. Everyone had their book slips, and all were charged to bring their slips back the next morning with the correct amount of money because Mr. Surrency was to be there early to get the master list and the money. I also reminded them that we would go to work tomorrow morning at seven. They all liked that. I gave Miss Hires her box of tin cups, and I gave ours to one of my larger boys. On the morrow one of the larger boys would keep the well and bring in the cups at close of day. I would make a list of boys who would keep the well, get wood, and fire the stove day by day, and a like list for girls who would sweep the floor, keep fresh flowers, and various other tasks. Miss Hires would make a similar list for her children. I told them we would also have our class schedule and study periods for each class ready and posted the next morning. One of the girls spoke up and said there were no brooms fit for sweeping. I told them that on the morrow I would have the boys take our new ax and cut me some of those large palmetto fans at the back of the school grounds. I would bring a fork and twine from my boarding place make us four stout palmetto-fan brooms that would last all the year. The same girl said, "Do you know how?" I told her. "Oh yes, I know how to use them also, and I know when they have been used well."

Miss Hires and I would be working far into the night getting our rolls, class schedules, and book lists. We would be back on time in the morning and expected the children to be there on time, ready for eight hours of work. Every child had a lunch pail and shoes, and most of them had their spelling books to do some extra study, as I had told them we wished to keep a record of all the perfect spellers beginning on the morrow for the whole year. We would use those records to make up our grades for the report cards that they would get at the end of each month. At four o'clock, everyone left quietly. I wanted them to see how quickly they could get home and to let me know in the morning how long it took. (There would not be a school bus in county for many years to come.) I also wanted to know how many pounds of cotton they picked before nightfall. Everyone knew their way home, and that is where we expected them to go. We had control over them until they reached their home, just like their parents had control over them of a morning until they reached us at school.

We closed and propped the windows and put away the cups. Miss Hires and I gathered our things and, after locking both doors, checked the toilets, surveyed the schoolyard for any unsightly waste, and went to our boarding place. We had much to do. We had each enrolled some fifty students. I did not see how one person could have had a school with that number enrolled. I think that had been the trouble. There were far more students than one teacher could instruct satisfactorily. So the students just stopped trying to learn. One girl had already told me that Miss Kate just tatted all afternoon. I expect she was tired by the time afternoon came and had to stop and rest. My reply to her was that we would have to work the whole eight hours every day for seven months if we expected to finish seventh grade as we had planned; she replied that she surely was willing to try.

The people of the community were highly cultured, well-off farmers who had come across the river from Liberty and Tatnall counties and settled in Wayne County when it was still Appling County. They came after a treaty was made with the Indians in the early-1800s. The land was taken from the Indians, surveyed and lotted by the state of Georgia, and sold for five dollars in gold for original plot and grant by the secretary of state for 490 acres more or less. There was not a tenant in the whole community. They had cleared their own fields and split the rails to fence them. They had built ample barns to hold their bountiful harvests and well-cared-for animals. Many of them could trace their forebears back to the Midway colony and had belonged to the agricultural society carried on there by the famous scientists the Le Conte brothers. They could tell some hairraising tales about trying to get their flocks and herds across the mighty Altamaha at Beard's Bluff without losing a chick or a child or a lamb or a pig. They always said what made them so strong was praying so to God to guide them across that mighty red water. They were thrifty and intelligent farmers who now produced all their food.

The wonderful Sea Island cotton was "king" and bringing one dollar per pound at the J. H. Walker Company, an outpost of the great Sea Island market established at Blackshear by the Brantleys in 1857. The fertile land bounded by Satilla Creek, Dry Creek, Reedy Creek, and Coleman Creek made up this beautiful countryside. I don't think I ever saw more beautiful or highly favored land in all my life. It is still one of the loveliest communities in the county. There were Surrencys, Longs, Smiths, O'Quinns, Grahams, Burkhalters, Jenkinses, Purvises, Harrises, Hodgeses, Joneses, Yeomans, Tyres, Bells, Crosbys, Westberrys, and Todds from Tatnall and Liberty. In later years an influx from North Georgia found their way to this blessed land, Sharps, Withrows, Gateses, Hills, Millers, and Pences, all intelligent and so proud of the broad rolling acres and warm sunshine after their hard life in Gilmer and other far northeast Georgia counties.

This was a far cry from the swampy and sandy land where I had worked for the past five years. I tell you I felt like I had come to the promised land. But things moved here with a quicker pace and were more demanding of the people and the community as a whole. Their way of life was strictly farming, while on the other side of Wayne County it was timber and cattle. When I think of those handsome young lads and beautiful young girls who faced me that fall morning, I sometimes wish I had been conducting a charm school in place of a hard-core year of study. When I now think of them in my mind's eye as they sat there so well behaved that morning and think of the fine men and women they made, I say a prayer of praise and thanksgiving that I had a chance to help them on their way to manhood and womanhood. I recall them as vividly as if it were yesterday: Paul Bell; Clyde Burkhalter; Vera and Valerie Burkhalter; Duncan, Sam, Leroy, Reuben, and Charlie Crosby; Francis, Leila, Lula Belle, and Luel Crosby; Clyde Gates; Frank, Ernest, and Ivy Graham; Leonard Graham; Beulah, Edith, and Pear Harris; Ida Hill; Clyde, Dock, Leonard, Gordon, D. M., M. E, and Jerome Hodge; Burnham Jenkins; Jimmie, Vernon, and David Jones; Marvin Long; Vera Long; Nola, Winnie, and Frankie Miller; Wayne and Glynn Miller; Charley and Riley O'Quinn; Jesse, Frank, and Dock Purvis; Mamie, Fannie, and Mildred Purvis; Clara Sharpe; Lovie, Reed, Paul, Robbin, and Lee Sharpe; Denny, Rollie, Alcott, Algernon, Clark, and Grady Smith; Lola, Willa Mae, Jewel, and Edith Smith; Ernest, Luddie, and Lois Surrency; Leslie and Letha Surrency; Hershman and Melvin Tootle; Otis and Mayro Westberry; Vada Westberry; Edith Withrow; Morris and Joe Withrow. There were many more that I am not able to recall right now.

Miss Hires and I were there well before seven the next morning. We each had set up the children's desks in five rows—Monday, Tuesday, Wednesday, Thursday, Friday—indicating which row passed out of the building first on which days of the week and the order in which we did our tasks. It was so easy for the teachers and pupils to remember. We continued our Bible reading from Genesis and prayed the Lord's Prayer. We tried to sing "America" again, and I promised to write it on the blackboard before I left for home that day so they could copy it on the morrow. All were seated, and as I called the roll they were to bring me their book list and money. Usually one child had all the money for one family, and I compiled the list then and there, which saved a lot of time. When Mr. Surrency got there we had it all waiting for him. He was soon on his way and hoped to be back before our day was done.

We began our lessons: first recitation, then a study period following the assignment of each lesson. We had two rounds for all four grades—spelling and English—in the half-hour before recess. In the hour and a half between recess and lunch, we had another two rounds—arithmetic and geography—for all four grades. After lunch we had history and reading for an hour and a half, then a short relief period. The subject of our last lessons varied by day of the week: on Monday we had health; Tuesday, writing; Wednesday, agriculture; Thursday, civics. Friday was for class activities. That was our schedule for the week. My first grade was to get their portion of every round, eight in all. We were going to learn to read, write, spell, figure, tell stories, and listen to stories, and we would have two periods a day in which to ask questions and maybe do some extra reading on these rounds. Miss Hires had a similar schedule worked out and posted for her pupils. Everyone would be busy at work or play all day long and, we hoped, happy.

We organized games for eleven groups: for the older boys, baseball; for the next group, catch. The older girls usually watched the boys or played singing games. The next age group of girls played Lady Come to See Me. The little girls played with dolls, and the small boys played marbles, stick frog, Rolly Holey, or barnyard. My first-graders played, five times a day, in the shade right out my window. They kept their toys in a box and would take them out on good days. On cold or rainy days they would play quietly at my feet (and we had plenty of cold wet weather that winter). The little boys would make barnyard animals from cornstalks, feathers, pine burs, and other objects. I wish you could have seen their cows udders and teats made from the pith of cornstalks, very real-looking.

Miss Hires and I were both working hard, behavior was above the ordinary, and punishments were few. It looked like all would be well with us. We had not stopped work since our arrival in early fall. We were both happy with ourselves and our situation. We had to attend a teachers meeting each month, and we were very proud of our report and attendance. Our first venture into community life, beyond attending church with our folks where we boarded, was the singing convention, which was always held at the Wayne County courthouse the third Saturday and Sunday in October. Singing groups from all over the county came and sang for the joy of it. O'Quinn always had several nice singing groups, as the singing master, Mr. Jenkins, lived in our community and always produced outstanding quartets, trios, duets, and solos from our community for the affair. A lot of preparation would go on all summer to get the songs ready.

The whole countryside would prepare bountiful dinners, and everyone—big, little, old, and young—would load up in wagons, surreys, and buggies. All from yonder side of the schoolhouse would meet there at the crack of dawn. The other groups would join us as we passed along toward Jesup. We would be in Jesup in time to hear our singers when the convention began at ten. First we had to secure the horses and mules, then take lunch baskets over to the courthouse. There we met friends old and new. We were ready to spread lunch at noon. At one the singing begin again and lasted another two hours. Afterward we gathered back to our teams, rejoicing because O'Quinn had been voted first place on several numbers and was also recognized for having such a large participation of the whole community. Our going and coming was gay and as enjoyable as the participation in the singing. Back home by late nightfall, everyone was happy and had many tales to tell about the wonderful singing convention trip.

Our next venture into community life was the Wayne County fair held for one week by the Wayne County Fair Association on their grounds in Jesup, where the Farmers Market, Wayne Line, and Veterans of Foreign Wars now stand. The grounds were nicely laid out and provided an exciting midway and good facilities for exhibiting livestock and poultry in a sanitary manner. It was wonderful there for many years. I do not know how or when the Wayne County Fair Association was dissolved or how the property was disposed of. In 1970 the Jaycees said they were holding the first Wayne County fair. They were in great error. All during the teens and early twenties, the Wayne County fair was going strong, and I hold pictures to prove it. Our group was well represented.

Our boys and girls had pigs, chickens, calves, canned goods, fancywork, corn, and potatoes, among other items. The adults exhibited field crops, fancywork, and baked goods—a wonderful exhibit of their way of life. We were proud to be a part of them, and we did not fail to let them know it. We were so happy to have them march in with us under our O'Quinn School banner. This was on Wednesday, "school day" at the fair, and all schools got in free. Most of our people were exhibitors and got in free anyway. They had come down on Monday to place their exhibits, and some of them had come every day to care for the animals. So their marching with us was not to escape the gate price but to do honor to their school and teachers. We were as proud of them as they were of us.

No one prepared lunch, as we had left before daylight that crisp morning. All the children had been saving their money to buy food at the fair, hot dogs, hamburgers, popcorn, and peanuts. We had warned them about the midway shows such as Hoop-a-la, Rooky-Pooky, and other chance games, but some of them got stuck anyway. They enjoyed the Ferris wheel, merry-go-round, and other rides. We encouraged them to enjoy the exhibits of their own community as well as those of the other communities. They would come to tell us of all the blue ribbons O'Quinn received. You could see the pride in their eyes. We helped them find their mothers and fathers when they had strayed too long. In fact Miss Hires and I were on hand all day long to help them enjoy themselves, and we enjoyed seeing our friends and their wonderful exhibits.

My dear friends from Hopewell exhibited their artistic handiwork and fine bakery articles and canned goods, everything that made a home beautiful and comfortable. We were so glad to see them. My good friends from Sandy Hill were there, with their wonderful display of home crafts, farm and garden products, and fine animals. One of the loveliest displays was from Midway, an exhibit of dried fruits and herbs from their garden and orchard as well as farm crops and animals. They had such a wonderful array of potted ferns, geraniums, and begonias as well as cut flowers, roses and chrysanthemums. To see their display was worth the trip to the fair. Misses Claude and Noon Bennett helped create this community exhibit. Eight generations from one family exhibited their handiwork in the Union School display. The D. Hopps Bennett family had the socks knitted by their great-great-grandmother and worn by their great-great-grandfather at Valley Forge in General Washington's encampment. There was not much from the lower end of the county, as their way of life was still mostly timber and cattle, and it was too difficult to bring animals and large exhibits that forty to sixty miles across the Great Satilla on muddy and sandy roads.

The 4-H clubs were well represented, especially with their tomatoes, canned goods, corn exhibits, some poultry, and pigs. Liberty, Piney Grove, Madray, Springs, Oak Grove, Screven, Ritch, and Brentwood Consolidated all had exhibits. Our 4-H club boys and girls and their parents had wonderful exhibits. All in all it had been a great day, and we hoped to get everyone back to O'Quinn without an accident or lost child.

We had laid our plans well, long before the day, arranging for our transportation and instructing our children on procedures. Miss Hires had led the wagon train, driven by Jesse Purvis, my largest and most dependable boy. He had borrowed his father's runabout buggy and fine buggy mule. Mr. Purvis and the rest of his family were in the stout two-mule cotton wagon he had just bought. So we had the head of the line all set. I had arranged with Mr. Joe Smith to bring up the rear with his fine new cotton wagon drawn by two of his finest mules, while his son Rollie and daughter Lola rode in their top buggy up near the front of the line to help keep company with Miss Hires and Jessie. Mrs. Smith and I and all the small children sat in the back of the cotton wagon, and Mr. Smith and the older boys sat on the seat. We had a quilt on the floor of the wagon for the younger children to lie on if they got tired on the way to and from the fair. All the other surreys, buggies, and wagons came into line between Miss Hires and me. We had them numbered in order and made a list of all persons who were to ride in each vehicle. Each driver had a list of the persons he was to carry, and Miss Hires and I each had a master list of the whole wagon train. I was not about to sponsor a trip to the fair and lose any of my school children while doing so. I had worked

[93]

with people long enough to know that some grown folks got so excited on trips like this that they almost forgot their own children, much less some other child they were supposed to keep up with.

We set 4 P.M. as the time to leave the fair grounds, allowing time for Miss Hires and the parents to get everyone out of the fair and onto the right wagon. All our drivers were waiting with the teams. Miss Hires and I checked with every driver to make sure he had his load, and we called the roll of all who were supposed to ride each wagon. We had given strict orders that no one was to ride another's wagon and had instructed the drivers not to permit it if anyone tried to do so. By 4:30 we were ready to ride. Miss Hires and Jessie led the wagon train. Mr. Smith patiently helped get every wagon ready to move. He told Jesse to proceed slowly so no one's team would be overtaxed. All the teams were fine mules, well cared for, and could make good time on the road and in the fields. The stars had begun to twinkle ere we crossed Satilla Creek; by time we crossed Boggy Swamp and Dry Creek, the sky was brilliant; and by the time we had gotten to Reedy Creek, the new moon had gone to sleep. It had been a wonderful day, a good day, a happy day, a tired day, and a blessed day—everyone was home and safe. What chores had to be attended to were soon accomplished, and everyone was off to bed, for the next day was a school day. Of course when we got back to O'Quinn community each team returned to its own home. Mr. Smith's was the last team on the road to Reedy Creek, the school district line, except for the Crosby family—one farm nearer the creek than Mr. Smith's. They passed on by and were soon home with their ten lovely children.

While Miss Hires and I were at the fair, we had attended to a very important piece of business pertaining to our schoolwork. We had contacted our high sheriff, Hon. London Rogers, and asked him to attend the Thanksgiving program and moneymaking entertainment we had set for Thanksgiving evening. In those days we had no holiday on Thanksgiving. It was a school day, the same as any other day. Our trustees were a little afraid to have a public meeting at the schoolhouse, as in the past there had been some intolerable behavior. Harnesses had been slashed, and the horses had been unhitched to go wherever they would. Saddles had been loosened and slung under the horses' bellies with the girth over their backs. The wheels of buggies, surreys, and wagons had been swapped from front to back, and seats were carried off to the creek swamp and slashed. The behavior inside the building was such that no one could enjoy the entertainment. The trustees had not permitted any kind of public entertainment at the schoolhouse for more than five years. We had almost perfect behavior in school, so we were willing to try the entertainment, but we could not run the risk of public misbehavior. So we asked the high sheriff to come and be there unannounced on the inside of the building, and we asked for two strong deputies to be on the outside unannounced. We felt we would thereby find the culprit who had been doing the damage all these years. We could not believe it was any of our students. He graciously agreed to do so.

Mr. Rogers was a good friend of my father. My father had often stopped overnight with Mr. Rogers's parents, Hon. Joseph Rogers and his beloved wife, Martha Harper Rogers, on his way to or from our home. Sometimes he would be on his way to attend a county commissioner's meeting or a county board of education meeting during the years he served on these boards and had to drive some forty miles by horse and buggy to get to Jesup. He would leave home the afternoon before and spend the night at the Rogers home, then drive the thirteen miles on to Jesup the next morning in time for ten o'clock meeting.

We had planned, with our school parents, for an oyster supper, with hot coffee, hot chocolate, and cake for those who might not care for the oyster stew. All our ladies were wonderful cake bakers, and all had great old Home Comfort woodstoves and the know-how to control the temperature to the perfect degree for cake baking, using dried green pinewood, split to measure, for their fires. They had plenty of fresh ingredients to make a perfect cake. They furnished the butter and milk for the oyster stew, and the milk and cream for the coffee and hot chocolate. All I had to buy were the oysters, which I got for a dollar per gallon, the sauce, pepper, coffee, cocoa, sugar, and crackers. We were all set up for our supper. We did not intend to try fried oysters, as we had only my two-eye flattop heater, one eye for the coffee cauldron, the other for the oyster stew, and Miss Hires's one-eye tall heater for the hot chocolate. There were no paper cups, plates, napkins, or throwaway spoons in those distant days. All the eating utensils came from the homes of patrons and were washed and used over and over again during the evening. Everything was planned to the last detail—who was to bring what and how many and how much. I saw to all the material bought at the store. I bought it all from Mr. Hatcher at Screven, who trusted me to pay him the next morning. Mr. Smith was assigned the task of getting the material from the storekeeper and to the schoolhouse. We planned the food, the entertainment, and the decorations, choosing a Thanksgiving theme for program and decorations.

We decorated the front and back of the building with garlands of dried herbs such as sage, thyme, pennyroyal, rosemary; garlands of red and green peppers, popcorn, dried peas in the hull, short lengths of sugarcane, and dried seedpods of okra; kefir pears and purple-top turnips; bunches of collards, mustard, green onions, and scallions—anything the children could bring. Then we made points of interest at two of the support posts, one in the front and one in the back of the building, where we made a great heap of farm products. We had baskets of sweet potatoes and pumpkins; sheaves of rice and oats; stalks of sugarcane; jars of honey and jugs of syrup; cured hams, bacon, sausage, and strips of sun-dried beef; bowls of eggs and cans of lard; pecans, walnuts, and hickory nuts. The posts were entwined with running fall peas that had both green and dried peas on them. The children held ears of their fathers' finest corn, with the shuck stripped back to show the golden grain, as we sang John Greenleaf Whittier's "Corn Song." When the program was over, my children were to march from the stage to their designated places and lay the corn on the heap in a neat upright circle around the post at front of my room. Miss Hires's children were to do the same at the post in her room.

Our program was planned from our daily work and was as perfect a program as I ever produced. It was as follows:

1. "America" sung by whole school and congregation

2. Psalm 100 recited in unison by the whole school

3. A short essay by my best history student telling of America's first Thanksgiving

4. Three songs: "Swing the Shining Sickle," "Over the River and through the Woods," and "The Corn Song"

Colorful garlands decorated the back of the stage; rows of golden corn were at the foot of the stage. The great bounties of harvest products were tagged and were to be returned at the close of the entertainment to those who had provided them. Our blue curtain, once used to divide room lengthwise, was used across the building to be drawn for our stage curtain. Our new movable plank wall had been taken down at close of the school day and stacked neatly in four piles, one on each side against the wall in Miss Hires's room, and one on each side against the wall in my room. When the program was over, these smooth planks were to be laid across the desks and used as tables for the oyster supper.

Miss Hires's desk was to receive cakes, hot chocolate, coffee, sugar, and cream. My desk was to receive oysters, crackers, sauce, salt, pepper, milk, and butter for oyster stew. We had plenty of dishcloths on each desk. Beautiful bouquets of homegrown chrysanthemums, or "Thanksgiving pinks," as our people called them, decorated our desks and the supper tables. The children had been instructed to bring lanterns to hang on the wall between the windows and on the large support post that ran the full length of the building, at every loft space, and in two rows, one each across the front and back end of the building. Miss Hires and I each had a Coleman lamp on our desk. The inside of the building was well lighted. We had lanterns on the porch post, at the steps and each side of the door, and on our lunch shelves between the doors. We were so proud of these that we wanted everyone to see them.

Our children were costumed appropriately with near no cost at all. We had saved white wrapping paper and had cut white Pilgrim collars. The boys wore their regular suits, with their coats belted down with their wide leather belts. They held up their trousers that night with suspenders and borrowed large black wool hats from their fathers, uncles, cousins, and neighbors. These men were the "wool-hat boys" that our great Governor Talmadge talked about so much in later years. Our girls wore long dark dresses with large white paper collars but had to pay ten cents to buy white cloth to make the plain white aprons and caps they were to wear while helping to serve supper. If a girl did not care for her white cap after the entertainment, she could easily undo it and make another apron or serviceable cloth, as the caps were a plain fold all across the front and gathered around back to fit snugly on the head.

We had school that day as usual, and school was dismissed at regular time. All were told to hurry home, milk, dress, and to hurry back, bringing us the milk for our festival. We wanted them back by sundown so we could get them costumed and ready to open the program as soon as the crowd arrived. We did not want to hold up the festival, as moneymaking was our job that night.

We had already had a meeting with the trustees and agreed that at the dinner we would make an announcement of the amount of each of the bills and how near we came to being able to pay them. If any money was left over, we would pay on the trustees' debt on the maps and big dictionary from which each one of my older students was getting so much good. The trustees had to make these payments themselves, as the county did not pay anything toward equipment. There was no tax money for supplies or books and very little for teachers. All the money we made was to be used before sunset the next day, and a public statement had to be made by trustees and teachers about how much we made and what became of it.

Miss Hires and I did not go home after school that day. After the children were gone we rested a wee bit, then refreshed our personal appearance and changed our clothes at the girls' toilet. We were ready to receive the milk, butter, dishes, and other supplies as the children began to return. They were so excited. Some of them could never remember having an entertainment at their school before. We told them all to go relieve themselves and to hurry back. We took them behind the curtain and began to get them into costume. I never remember having seen a more authentic group of Pilgrim children. We were so proud of them. We checked our list. Everyone was there except one boy, Paul; no one could find him. I sent some of the children out to call to him, but there was no answer.

By this time it was dark, lanterns had been hung, and our people began to arrive. The ingredients for the stew were there in abundance on my desk, and Miss Hires's desk was stacked with golden brown pound cakes. In the center of her table was one of the largest and most beautifully decorated cakes I had ever seen. It had been baked in a huge dishpan by Mrs. Cleon Burkhalter. The whole countryside knew of her fame for baking the most delicious cakes that a mortal had ever tasted. The crowd could hardly wait until it was sliced. It was to be a contest prize, given to the young lady voted the most beautiful in the community. Votes would sell for one cent each. The contest would be the last event of the evening. The girls had been instructed that the winner of the cake was to cut it and invite everyone present to have a slice. If the people came and spent their money well for us, this would be their bonus, and it would leave a sweet taste in their mouths for the next time we called on them to help us. By this time the building was filled to capacity. Every seat was filled, and people were standing along the walls. I nodded to the children to get set; then Miss Hires and I pulled the curtain clear and wide so every child could be seen. Our master of ceremonies, Jesse Purvis, stood in the center of the back row. The children turned a wee bit in the middle of the three other rows so he could step out to front and ask the congregation to stand to sing "America" with us and to remain standing while we read the psalm. We sang all four verses without a break. After the fourth verse, we bowed our heads in reverence to the great God our King as we began the psalm, reciting, "Make a joyful noise unto the Lord, all ye lands!"

Just as we finished, two boys came out of the blue and began to pull the long golden peas from the vines wrapped around our harvest display at front of the room. They shelled some of the peas, and just as they raised their hands to throw them among the crowd of people, our high sheriff laid his hand upon the shoulder of one of the boys and said, "Hey! Sorry. How did you get here, and where did you come from?" Paul answered, "I came from home with my father and mother," and Mr. Rogers said, "Where are they now?" Paul answered, "Sitting over there." Then Mr. Rogers said, "You go over there and sit beside them until the program is over with," which he did. Then he asked Lester, the other boy, who he was and where he came from, and he said. "I am Paul's friend, and I came with them." Mr. Rogers then said, "Well you had better go sit by your friend, or you will have to come sit with me." So Lester went and sat with Paul and Paul's father and mother. Lester was from another community and seemed to be Paul's chum in all his misbehavior at all times. Mr. Rogers quietly went back to his place near the front doors.

Jesse had stood quietly during this little disturbance, and he and all the children held their composure well. Then Jesse gave his well-prepared essay on our first Thanksgiving. He gave a short history of our Thanksgiving; then he recited the "Landing of the Pilgrims." He gave his word of thanks for our bountiful harvest and God's blessings on the people in the O'Quinn community. His delivery was excellent. He stepped back in line and announced our next two songs. I then stepped to the center of the stage from behind the curtain and thanked all the people for being there. I told them about supper and the price of each item and about the contest to choose the most beautiful girl in the community. I reminded them that "pretty is as pretty does!" I also told them of our need for money and that I hoped everyone would stay and enjoy the evening with us. We would be ready to serve as quickly as possible after we made a few adjustments to set up our dining tables. They should just enjoy themselves visiting with each other as we made ready.

I nodded my head to signal the children to come off-stage in a nice orderly line. I soon had a pot of stew and a pot of coffee going, and Miss Hires and her helpers had a pot of hot chocolate. In due time our supper was in full swing. Cotton was selling at $1.25 per pound, more than $600 a bale, so money was flowing freely. The food sold as fast as we could prepare it. Everyone was jolly and gay. No one misbehaved indoors or out, as our high sheriff had brought two of his best deputies to see after outside while he attended to the inside. Some folks were surprised when they saw Deputy Jim Tyre and Deputy Gary Rogers walk in for their stew. But there were no harnesses cut that night or saddles fastened under the horses' bellies. Finally everyone had eaten all they wanted, and the voting began. As people voted, I counted the votes and the money and recorded the score. Many were running for the honor, but our beautiful young teacher, Miss Carrie Hires, won the cake. She thanked everyone graciously: Mrs. Burkhalter, who had baked it, and all the people who had voted. She graciously remembered the trustees, who had let us use the building, and all the children, who had brought the beautiful decorations. She also thanked Sheriff Rogers and his two fine deputies for keeping such perfect order, and all the parents and children for taking time to be with us. She invited everyone to come by her table to share her beautiful cake.

While she was serving the cake, the trustees and I were counting money and rejoicing that we would be able to pay our outstanding bills as follows: Mr. Jim

Clark, for lumber for steps, moveable partition, lunch shelves, cloak rack, and toilet repairs; J. H. Walker Co., for nails, lime, bricks, and heater; the county board of education, for blackboard and tiny chairs; Royal Blacksmith shop, for flue hangers, irons, and bolts for stovepipes; Mr. Erastus Jones, for carpenter work and brick mason work; Mr. Quett Hatcher, for oysters, crackers, black pepper, catsup, coffee, chocolate, and sugar. We would have enough money and some to spare. I suggested we make their final payment on the dictionary and maps. They seemed very happy with the suggestion and instructed me to get a money order for that purpose when I went to town Saturday to pay other bills. Everyone by now had a slice of cake, had gathered their things together, and were ready to get their lanterns when I said the word. We checked the stoves, closed all the doors and dampers, and propped all windows. I surveyed every corner of the building, walked up and down every aisle, and locked the doors. We checked both toilets to see that no troublemakers were secreted there, then checked the well and steps. We were so proud of our new steps, all the way around the porch and mitered at the corners. They were one of the most beautiful sets of wooden steps I had ever seen. There was room enough for every child to get on or off the porch simultaneously if they so chose.

Mr. Rogers and his deputies were yet with us. We thanked them profusely and asked their charges. They said there were to be no changes, that they were just performing their bounden duty to keep order wherever needed. If we needed their services again, they would be only too glad to come. He warned us to keep a close check on Paul and Lester. He said those two boys had mischief in their bones.

The next day, Miss Hires and I were at the school by good daylight, and with the help of some of our larger boys we soon had our desks, chairs, tables, and "removable" partition back in place. After our opening song, Bible reading, and prayer, I told them how much money we had taken in and subtracted our items of expense. I gave the net returns and told where every penny had gone, even the amount we gave the trustees for their last payment on the old account. I had it all on the blackboard and pointed to it item by item and told them to make a copy, as they had time. We would do our recitations and study periods in our routine fashion, and we would do our talking at recess and at noontime that day.

At recess everyone wanted to talk at once and tell different facts of the evening's entertainment and our successful moneymaking project. Everyone was so happy that their beautiful young teacher had won the cake, and they applauded that she was so generous to give it all away. They were so excited over the success that they wanted us to have another entertainment right away. Couldn't I think of something for which we needed the money very badly? Yes, I told them, I knew of plenty of things we needed. We needed a new desk for Miss Hires. We needed window shades for the east and west windows. When springtime came again, with all its brilliant sunlight, we would be bothered both morning and afternoon with the direct sunlight across our desks, and that would be bad on our eyes. I would also like to have one more dozen of the next size of little chairs. The way the North Georgia people were moving to our community, on account of such good prices for Sea Island cotton, it looked like we would need those chairs before the term was up.

They wanted to know what could we do. I asked had they ever thought of producing a play? It would require only a few playbooks but plenty of hard work. They were all for it. I told them the trustees would have to give their consent. I told them it could not be until after Christmas, as we had to have our midterm test before the Christmas holidays, and besides I thought practically every child was very much involved in their own church's Christmas program, and we surely did not wish to interfere with that. I thanked everyone and told them how proud we were of their beautiful presentation before the oyster supper. I promised them that I would see the trustees the next week, after I had paid all of our outstanding bills. I wished to take each trustee a copy of how every penny of it was spent and to thank each one of them personally for their support. Then I would ask them to let us have the play to raise the money for our next purchases. The project would provide entertainment to the community and training to our young students in the fine arts of acting, singing, and dramatizing. They all agreed if it would not take school time, and I told them we would practice at night and schedule the performance for early January to be out of the way before the children had much hard fieldwork to do. After I had made my rounds the next week and secured consent from all three trustees, I called the larger boys and girls together and told them upon what conditions I had gotten the trustees' consent. We would learn our lines outside of class time and would practice at night. No student would be permitted have his play material at school or be allowed to skip classroom work to study or work for production of the play. They all agreed to abide by these rules.

The next step was to select the play. I had plenty of catalogs from different publishing houses. We began to check the plays for the number of characters and kinds of scenery needed. We finally settled on *Al Martin's County Store*, with thirty characters and one scene. Only two characters had long contiguous parts, interspersed with the comings and goings of the other characters. Everyone quickly said that Jesse Purvis should have the lead role because he had been so marvelous as the master of ceremonies for our Thanksgiving program. Jesse agreed. Several would have liked to have had the second-most important part, but

Duncan Crosby, a large overgrown boy who was a nonreader, just pleaded for it. Everyone said, "Oh no, Duncan, you cannot read well enough to do that part." His answer was quickly given, "I am not going to read it, I am going to act it." He said, "Miss Mizell, if you will read it over to me one time and tell me what I am to do, I guarantee I will do it and say every word where it should be said. Let me have a book to take home to my mama, and when the time comes to practice I will be ready." Now, who could resist that kind of determination? So I agreed for Duncan to have the part; they all shook their heads. Several boys said they would be his understudies, so if he got sick and did not show up, the show could go on.

He was to play the part of the town whittler, but he quickly asked to let him be peeling and chewing sugarcane. There were twenty-eight characters he had to deal with individually besides carrying on a continuous conversation with the storekeeper Al Martin. Next to be chosen was the village belle, who was setting her cap for the new storekeeper. Everyone said, with a unanimous shout, that must be Miss Hires. They all thought she was so pretty and sweet, clever with her ways, with a winsome smile and sparkling eyes. Now we had all the lead rolls filled. The books were ordered and all parts assigned before the Christmas holidays.

The date of the play was set for the first Friday night at the end of our first week after Christmas, while our country folks were still holidaying. I was to place an announcement of the play in the county papers as I went through Jesup going home for Christmas. I was also to have the program printed with a list of characters, the names of the actors, and the names of those who were to help with costumes, scenery, and props. We drafted a sheet showing time, place, price, and the use to be made of the money taken in. The trustees' and teachers' names were placed there so everyone would know who was sponsoring the affair. I distributed the books among the characters and read one to Duncan, explaining every situation to him and his mother until I felt they thoroughly understood the different characters and their actions. Every one of the thirty was told to know every word of their part by time we returned after the two-week holiday, when we would practice four nights and have the performance on the fifth night.

While I was in Jesup I invited our high sheriff and his deputies to return to us for the holiday entertainment. After our vacation, practice was carried out as scheduled. They knew all their lines at the first practice. All we had to do was get the feel of the play to make it complete. Duncan stole the show. He not only knew his lines but put in many ad-lib comments that carried the show to perfection.

We used the same seating arrangements as we had for our Thanksgiving program, taking down our "removable" partition and making seats around three walls. One brilliant Coleman lamp was on Miss Hires's table; the other one was on the stage in Al Martin's store. Our lunch rack from the front porch served as the shelves for the store, and we made a counter from part of our movable partition. We borrowed an oak flour barrel for Duncan to sit on while he chewed the cane he kept buying from the storekeeper. He would put his chews in the barrel that was holding the long, soft juicy sugarcane. Everything for the play was set up before the end of the school day. There was plenty of wood for both stoves. As I remember, it was a clear, cold, brilliant moonlit night. The actors had been instructed to dress at home before coming to the schoolhouse, as the stage did not have space for a dressing room. There was only standing room for the characters behind the curtain in the little anterooms we had curtained off with a sheet at each end of the stage to make places for the characters to stand before they went onstage. After they had played their parts, they returned to seats against the wall just down from the stage.

We only had one door open at the front of the building, as we had only one table and one brilliant light. I attended to this until it was time to start the program. Every seat was taken, and there was standing room along the three walls. Both stoves had been going steady since early nightfall, and the building was nice and warm. Everyone was happily awaiting O'Quinn's first try at a stage play. I thanked them all for coming and told them I believed we would have enough money to pay for our next purchases. We hoped they would enjoy seeing the play as much as we had producing it.

The curtain rose, and Al Martin's Country Store came alive—with all its buying, selling, and bargaining; visiting, gossiping, courting, and matchmaking; political campaigns, religious fervor, crop conditions, marketing problems, weather, and what have you. The audience was kept in an uproar of laughter for the full two-and-a-half-hour performance. Needless to say, Duncan Crosby stole the show. He was ready with a witty remark on all subjects discussed and could add humor and pathos to any situation.

A long cold winter set in, the most snow I have ever seen in this part of the country. Freezing days and nights lasted for weeks, but we were now comfortable at school with two good heaters, plenty of chairs to circle around each stove until the rooms became well heated in the early morning. Our one-wagon-load of wood from each patron had not been near used up. Everyone had brought their load when I requested it, and everyone always got a note of thanks signed by the children and teacher from each room that had used the wood. They were always thanked generously for the type of wood they brought and on how well they had balanced the oak and gum with the fat lightwood knots and splinter wood. Miss

Hires looked mighty pretty and contented behind her new desk, with its generous drawer space. Our attendance was practically 100 percent. The school began to look like three teachers might be needed.

The war was getting more terrible. Cotton prices had gone higher, and farmers were clearing new ground, getting ready to plant more cotton. Money flowed freely. Our nation needed every dollar they could muster for supplies for our soldiers and our allies. Our trustees asked me to arrange a sale of Liberty Bonds in our community. They said they and their wives would prepare an old-fashioned dinner with plenty of hot coffee. The dinner was both bountiful and delicious. The bond sale was held in the front of the schoolyard, the speakers using the back end of a two-mule cotton wagon to carry out the bond sales. It was a big success. For many of the farmers, the Liberty Bonds were their first financial investments. They continued to buy as long as the sales were conducted locally. I would contact the county Liberty Bond committee, setting dates and getting speakers. I secured the services of Hon. Ben Gibbs, Bill Turner, and Julian Walker, setting the date and time to suit them. When the word got around, people would come with their well-filled baskets, the wash pots nearby with steaming coffee. Although flour and sugar were rationed in the county for the war effort, everyone was served. We were often told that O'Quinn community launched the most successful Liberty Bond sales and made the plan workable for the whole county.

Our schoolwork was going forward at a steady pace. More and more of the old library books were being found, and I added new ones every time I had any money left over from any other projects, from story and picture books for the beginners right on up to the finest of prose and poetry, history, and literature for the upper grades. Our 4-H club work was moving along. Our civic projects took many shapes and forms. Through the mail came bulletins telling us of the terrible cattle tick that was robbing our southern cattlemen of their profits. They told how community dipping-vats could be installed, how cattle could be driven through a chute to the vat and there be treated with the right formula to kill the ticks. In a few seasons the tick would be no more.

One of my fourth-grade pupils, Dock Purvis by name, took his pamphlet home and showed it to his father and asked him to do something so their cattle would not be sucked to death by the poisonous seed ticks. Ticks ruined the milk and that made it not fit for use. His father, Mr. Ashley Purvis, a member of the sitting grand jury, asked permission to borrow the pamphlet to carry with him. He presented the matter to the county grand jury. It was thoroughly discussed and recommended that a compulsory dipping program be set up for the whole county. Vats were built community by community, and cattle drovers were hired and paid by the county to help the farmers get their cattle to the vats and back home in good shape. The federal government came in with assistance to help with the program, and in a few years the tick was eradicated. Fine-blooded cattle could now be raised at a profit without the danger of the terrible tick fever. We had used the cattle dipping as a subject in our Friday afternoon debating class in civics. It was unanimous that the dipping-vat was the way to better cattle raising in Wayne County.

In our civics class, we tried to debate subjects vital to the children's way of life, for instance, what was the best way to mellow all that new land being cleared for growing long-staple cotton. Many plans were set forth, but the one that was debated was to rid the land of trees and stumps. They had to be dug and burned out by hand, as there were no stump pullers or bulldozers yet. They would plow the land as best they could with a mule plow and then harrow in a generous supply of chufa seed in early springtime and let it grow to full maturity. By late fall and winter they would turn loose a herd of piney-wood rooter hogs to root for the nest of chufas under each clump of tall chufa grass (also know as nut grass or ground almond). When the hogs had finished you would have a field of fine fat meat hogs and a well-pulverized field to harrow, plow, and seed with silky long-staple cotton. This plan won the debate not only in the classroom but also in the field.

The small boys whose fathers had been planting a small patch of ground almonds for winter eating soon found that chufas were good for something besides filling your overall pockets with them each morning to take to your playmates at school. They could sell them at one dollar or more a peck to their neighbors who were preparing new ground. I told them how to make a chufa harvester, a large, stout boxlike frame with legs. The bottom was covered with coarse hardware cloth (strong closely woven wire screen), which let the earth fall through but prevented the chufas from going through. I told them to turn up their chufa hills with a pitchfork, let them dry in the sun, and then grasp them by the tall grasses and beat them over the side of their boxes to catch the chufas, shaking the boxes by their four handles (two at each end) to cause the soil to fall away. Two young boys working together could easily gather two bushels (worth eight dollars) after school in the crisp fall weather. One of my students asked, "Miss Mizell, where did you learn how to do all that?" I always told them that I had come from a farm also and learned to do many things there, how to pick geese, sew a fine seam, and bake pound cakes, as well as how to wash chitterlings, make sausage, and boil sugar candy. This always brought a laugh and a merry shout among the group. We were very happy in our year of hard work.

Lessons rolled on. We gave monthly tests, checked work daily, and kept up with the outside projects. I began to think of who was going to get that grade-seven state certificate and what was to become of them when they had finished, since there was not a high school in the whole county. The Baptists had Piedmont, a boarding school in Waycross, where they tried to further the knowledge of their young ministers. It was known as a "preacher factory." The Presbyterians had a boarding school in Blackshear, better known as a finishing school for "select young ladies." The Methodists had a school at McRae for the advancement of missions and church-related work. Jesup was struggling to carry regular graded work for both boys and girls, but they never had gotten above grade ten, and very few students got even that far.

I began thinking of preparing myself to add on grade eight for the next school term to take care of them. I was setting myself the task of entering the University of Georgia for the 1918 summer quarter to brush up on my academic work and prepare myself with some of the best methods to use in teaching boys and girls above the elementary grades. In other words, I was going to aim for a high school license before September.

Our school term would come to a close in early April. We were still far from a nine-month school term. The trustees came and asked for us to prepare an old-time school closing that every child would take part in, and to make it as good as or better than our play had been in January. We had already planned for a seventh-grade graduation to be held at the close of school. So we now set up our practice time each afternoon from noon until little recess, beginning three weeks before school closing. The last week was to be spent with tests in the morning and practice in the afternoon. There would be songs, recitations, pantomimes, drills, dialogs, and the farewell speeches of the graduates, followed by the closing song for the whole school. It was well planned and some three hours long. It was to be given on the front porch of the school building, and we were to use the same type of seating I had used at Sand Hill in 1916. I had the patrons saw wood blocks to measure and mark their name on one end. We used the stout smooth plank from our movable partition across the blocks to make the seating for the congregation. We used our lanterns and powerful Coleman lamps to light the stage, which was decorated beautifully with lovely roses and other garden and wild flowers of the community.

Our story would not be complete if I did not digress a wee bit and tell you of the wedding of our lovely Miss Hires and our star student, Jesse Purvis, a few weeks before school closed. It seems that I started the ball rolling when I asked Jesse to get his father's mule and buggy to head the school wagon train when we went to the county fair in October 1917. Afterward he ventured to visit her at her home in Redland during the Christmas holidays. They had been courting through letters carried back and forth by one of Jesse's sisters. He would take her to church on Sunday, but there was never any show of affection at school. It came as a surprise to all of us. The Reverend W. D. Crosby, just down the road from our boarding place, married them early one evening, and Jesse took her home with him that night to one of his father's new tenant houses. Jesse had it all fixed up and ready for living. They had planned to wait until school was out and have the wedding as a surprise at our closing program (which I think would have been lovely), but they did not know how I would take it, so Jessie decided all of a sudden that evening not to wait any longer. Both families were well pleased, and the whole community was very complimentary of both of them and the choice they each had made. It was quite a gala affair. The whole community was there. The younger children whom she had taught so well were overjoyed. They said that now she could be with them all the time and would not have to go away and leave them as the other good teachers had.

This part of the story would not be complete without telling you of the many fine boys in that school, obedient and brilliant students who developed into stable young men. This was one of the best groups of learners I ever had. They were eager not only to learn but to excel in all their studies. I told them of the work on written communication I had done at Sandy Hill the year before, and they asked that the same task be given to them. I wish you could have seen the beautiful work they turned in, from each a portfolio of an average of 150 letter forms done in their own handwriting and word arrangement. They never tired of their history and geography studies. Every day their spelling and written work improved. In arithmetic they mastered the facts, tables, measures, and rules needed in everyday living. They shouted with glee when they learned they could memorize addition and subtraction tables the same as they could multiplication and division tables. One day a boy said to me, "Miss Mizell, how many hours do you think we have already thrown away by not knowing this?" I told him I expected it would run into the thousands during their school life.

Our civics took us into debates about everyday community problems and had us tracking down evidence of both sides of many questions. Agriculture brought to us the magical knowledge of science through trial and error and taught us to record facts, not guesswork. The broad field of health covered our personal health and extended into our homes, community, county, state, and nation. We had the help of a Red Cross nurse for several weeks to give our girls specific training in the home care of the dangerously ill. That was when the terrible flu epidemic was creeping near us. When it finally struck in the latter part of 1918, and 1919 and 1920, O'Quinn community suffered the least fatalities of any part of the county. I have always believed it was because of the sound training they received in 1917 and 1918.

My boys were happy in their play. I received a lot of help from Leonard Graham, an older student, who was a born leader. I have often thought what a wonderful coach he would have made. He helped get every age group and size of boys organized into their favorite games, all the way from baseball to Rolly Holey. He soon had the boys making perfect baseball bats from pieces of hickory, and good baseballs from the legs of old handmade "Georgia knit socks." You could unravel them and recover the long length of yarn. You could then wind the yarn about a hard object and make a baseball. They made chinning bars from long cypress poles fastened to our strong oak trees, and a jumping pit filled with sawdust. The jumping bar was made of black gum. There was a nice homemade vaulting set— a good job well done with only our school ax, a good pocketknife, and a few strong nails. Our boys far outnumbered the girls. The girls sometimes kept score for the boys in their competitive games. You never had many absentees with a daily program of enjoyable games, no matter what the weather. When there came a rainy day, they played indoors, and there is where I always had to take over and set forth the games that could be played without damage to the books or property. Here is where our girls always shone in helping set up our parlor, or indoor, games. Even though the boys were outstanding, my first-grade class was special as well.

My time in the O'Quinn community was the last chance I ever had to teach a large class of beginners (such delightful work). I have always wished I could have had this as my life's work. They all did well and were ready for grade two. They had learned to read, spell, write, do their numbers to one hundred, add, and subtract. They could tell time, count money, and measure all the way from a teaspoon to a gallon, from a second to a year. They could talk well on many subjects, knew how to listen well, how take messages and bring back an answer. They had learned colors and shapes. I could go on and on about thousands of things they learned, but the two greatest were to listen well and then respond well to what they had heard (two important skills that make a great student).

While we were preparing our outdoor play program, it became clear to the trustees that we badly needed more than the one-acre tract on which the schoolhouse was set. They asked me to visit Mr. Robert Todd, who lived close by and owned land on three sides of the schoolhouse, to ask him about obtaining some of his acreage. He graciously gave us three strips of land adjacent to the school, one each to the south, north, west, provided the deed would say that the land would revert back to his estate when it was no longer needed by the school. The trustees more than rejoiced when I brought them the glad news of the gift. Once the deed was drawn and signed, the trustees fenced the campus with strong wire, placed one large gate at the front entrance, trimmed all the trees, and leveled the grounds. These improvements protected the school and grounds and made a beautiful campus. Years later, Mr. Todd's son, C. L. Todd, told me that the land did eventually revert to the Todd estate.

As time passed, we continued to make improvements. We had a cover made for our open well, with a good lock and key, to keep vandals from filling it with trash. We erected a cypress flagpole; our children sold one gross of lead pencils imprinted with the school name at five cents each ($7.20), and the pencil company gave us a flag. We were the first school in the county to raise an American flag at school. We raised it on January 19, 1918, General Robert E. Lee's birthday. Dr. Colson, a reserve Army officer, came to help us raise it correctly. He fixed the rope for us and showed the children how to raise and lower the flag without abusing it. The school, the community, and the county were proud of us and our flag. With so many of our boys going into military camp and overseas into the war, a flag was especially respected and protected.

With our schoolwork completed, tests given, papers graded, promotions in order, and report cards prepared, we were ready for our school-closing program. The time was set for first dark the last Friday of school. Everything was ready. We had made arrangements for the seating, and our stage was all set. The children were seated in the schoolhouse ready to come out as their part in the program came up. Bouquets were in place by the porch columns at the head of steps and all the way down the steps on either side. The lamps were all lit. It was a beautiful setting. The decorations were put in place, including bouquets of flowers and a welcome sign covered with garden-fresh pink roses. The two front doors opened at once, and the children marched out at each door and joined in the center in line after line. We had seven full lines (representing the seven grades). We had to shift a few from grade to grade to make our lines come out even. My precious first grade was in the front row with a few small ones from second grade. We sang our welcome song, and the best speaker of the year gave the welcome speech. This was all well received by the large crowd in front. Every seat was taken, and even though people had brought their chairs and wagon seats, many were yet standing.

The program continued, with songs, marches, dialogs, and recitations. I never will forget the first grade's performance. The little girls were all mothers and nurses, with their dolls as babies. The little boys were fathers and doctors at the doctor's office. They had every ailment imaginable, from measles with red splotches all over the dolls' faces, to whooping cough, broken bones, scratched feet, and cut fingers. It brought down the house in laughter and surprise at what a first-grade child could do. I never will forget how sweetly Miss Hires (now Mrs. Purvis) sang that night for our girls to pantomime "My Faith Looks Up to Thee." I never heard her sing again after that night. Burnham Jenkins and his father, the singing master, and several of the men and older boys had prepared a medley of songs for an all-male chorus. About the middle of the program they asked me to let them perform before the program was over. So I agreed for them to have time just before our graduation. It was a beautiful chorus, well prepared, and enjoyed by everyone.

The graduation began with a lovely recitation from each graduate. They sang their class song; then the sixth grade sang a song of cheer for them. We had invited the school superintendent, B. D. Purcell, and all the county board of education members; our home agent, Annie Bennett; and our farm agent, J. P. Shedd. Mr. Purcell had been asked to present the seventh-grade certificates to the class, which was to be the last event before the closing song. He stated how proud he was of all of us and how he hoped the community would invite us back. He said that plans were being made for O'Quinn School to have an eighth grade and that every one of those boys and girls would be back in school come September. Following came the closing, or farewell from the whole school, and "Good Night Ladies." The curtains were then closed, but the people called and called until the curtains had to be opened again. The trustees called for the teachers to come to the front, and they told us how much they wanted us back. The whole crowd rose in our honor and to sanction what the trustees had said about our returning for year 1918–19. The curtains were closed again.

All the children had been instructed to put all their costumes in their bundles to take home. They had already taken their books home. All windows would be propped down, all the doors locked. We asked the older boys to help us get our partition planks off the wood blocks and back into our building. The farmers could get their stove-wood blocks into their wagons that night, as plowing time in April was at a premium, and I had promised the farmers only one extra trip to bring me the blocks. They could take them home the night of the closing, as well as the sheets, lanterns, and flower vases we had borrowed. The first-graders had asked for the welcome sign. They thought it so wonderful that they knew how to spell "w-e-l-c-o-m-e." The whole community visited and enjoyed themselves while the dismantling was going on. Soon everything was back in order, and the last good-byes were said. The school year had come to an end.

I went to my boarding place to sleep for a few hours. My trunk was packed, locked, and tied, and my grip was almost packed. My school reports were ready for me to give to the school superintendent as I passed through Jesup early the next morning. I was to leave before day in a two-mule wagon to catch Train No. 58 that came through Screven about six o'clock. So we would have to be up and about by four. When I arrived in Jesup and turned in my records, Mr. Purcell asked if I knew that I had made the average not only for two teachers but for three. I told him, "Yes, sir! I knew that. And that was how I had hoped and planned for grade eight to be allowed." Then he told me that he wanted me to go to the University of Georgia for the summer quarter to try for a high school license. I told him I had already planned to do that, so we talked of courses and methods. Then, of all things, he told me he wanted me to go to Union School to finish out a term there, that the teacher, Miss Grace Worsley, had the flu and was unable to return to finish her term. He said to me, "You will need the extra money for your quarter of study." There were no grants or loans in those days; you had to have the money or you did not go. I told him that before I could go to Union School I would have to go home to see my father and mother, whom I had not seen since Christmas. All my clothes were dirty, and all my winter clothes were in my trunk. So I told him to let me go home, revamp my wardrobe, and see my father and mother. I would be back Monday night on my faithful Bogey.

I left Jesup at noon Saturday on Train No. 85 for Nahunta. As usual, my dear father was waiting for me at the station with faithful Old Bob and the wagon. We were soon loaded up and drove the short distance to our home. Mother was waiting for me. I fell into her arms. There was so much to tell and not much time. They were both anxious to hear about my work and to know I was happy. It seemed like many years had passed since I had bounced around in Henry Mikel's little runabout car to see the trustees of O'Quinn School. But a successful term had come to a close, and here I was at home with my dear parents again—their same darling baby daughter.

CHAPTER 10

Springtime at Union School

Union School was close to the bank of the Altamaha River, on Ellis Creek, about three miles north of Grangerville. I arrived on a Tuesday morning, after a weekend at my home in Nahunta. I had left home on Monday night, spent the night in Jesup at the local hotel, and arose early Tuesday morning. Before catching the ten o'clock train, I had a visit with my superintendent and received my supplies and records for this school.

No one was at Grangerville to meet me. So I went to the office of the large timber company there, and one of the young gentlemen, a Mr. Hill, took me out to Mr. Hopps Bennett's home at Union. Mr. Bennett was the head trustee but did not know I was coming, or he would have met me. I offered to pay the young gentleman, but he would accept no pay. When I arrived at the Bennett home, they invited me to have lunch with them. They also said I could live with them until their three older children came home for the summer. I enjoyed my stay there very much. Mrs. Bennett was a very delightful hostess, as was her mother, Mrs. Surrency, an elderly lady but quite entertaining with her stories of yesteryear.

As soon as we finished lunch, Mr. Bennett took me around the school district in his buggy to tell the pupils to be at school bright and early the next morning and to bring all their books. We did not have a day to lose. To get the term out by June 30, when the school year ended, I would have to teach on Saturdays to make up the two days I had missed that week. Mr. Bennett and I made the rounds to all the homes, then went by the little school house, a nice little building with homemade benches, tables, and chairs. It was in good condition without an inch to spare. The great old Union Baptist Church was right across the way in a beautiful grove of stately yellow pine, magnolias, holly, live oak, and luxuriant palmetto fans. It was one of the oldest churches in the county, built of heart pine and always kept in perfect repair. A snow-white sandy road nearby led toward Barrington's

Ferry and the King's Highway from Savannah to St. Augustine, better known as the Post Road. I enrolled some forty-five students, grades one through seven, among them Browns, Bennetts, Mays, Nicholses, Calhouns, Martins, Richardsons, Walls, Yeomanses, Sylvesters, Hoppses, Scotts, Robersons, and Gardeners. They were all obedient, exceedingly smart, and well-behaved children. That is one school where I never had to mention punishment a single time. They were such happy children. You could hear them every morning, talking, laughing, and singing on their way to school. And they played so well together.

Our three months for school, April, May, and June, were the busiest time of year on a farm. All the people in the community owned their own farms, so they needed their children to help plant, hoe, and set their crops, yet they wanted them to get that three months of school. On the first morning of school the trustees wished to know if I would do them the favor of opening school at seven o'clock and cut recess and the lunch period a little short so that the children could get out about two instead of four. I told them I would be only too glad to do so. We would get to school while the dew was still on the roses, and we could smell the honeysuckle and jasmine that were blooming so profusely in the large cemetery across the road by the church. One of the oldest in Wayne County, this beautiful cemetery is still well kept this good day some sixty years later.

I quickly picked up the studies where their former teacher left them at Christmastime. The parents were anxious for their children to finish their grades, as some planned to enter the higher grades at the Jesup School. In Jesup they would be staying with their kinfolks because there were no school buses to take them back and forth to school. Some large families rented rooms or parts of dwellings and lived in Jesup from Monday morning until Friday afternoon. A few drove in, but not many, as the horses were needed for plowing. A great many walked for many miles around. Any child in the county who qualified could go to Jesup High School free of charge if they could get there. Others had hopes of attending some of the church schools in our part of the state. Others had kin at Brunswick, where there was one of the earliest good high schools in the state. I did my best with all the grades, especially with the seventh, to prepare them for the transition from a small one-teacher school to a larger school.

The first great world war was going on at a terrific pace, with the boys being called up for military duty every day. Everyone was buying a newspaper every time they could get to town to see the casualty list. Troops were being moved in great numbers, and the Red Cross was doing its best to serve wherever it was needed, at home or abroad. War bond sales were being conducted throughout the country. Sugar and flour were rationed. Mules rose in price to $750 each. So many were being bought to send overseas to pull caissons, as there were no trucks or tanks as yet. The cavalry were men on the finest warhorses, and Army mules pulled the artillery. Foot soldiers were actually on foot, except when they moved long distances on troop trains or ships. Our work at school went on.

I stayed with Mr. and Mrs. Bennett for only a few weeks. By May they were getting ready for their "off-children" to come home: Mary Fleming Williams's husband taught in the early schools of Miami, Florida. They were coming home. Constance, the oldest daughter, taught in the local schools of Wayne County, and Lawrence was in Piedmont School in Waycross. From the Bennetts' I went to live in Mr. Salem Yeomans's home nearby. Mr. Yeomans did some kind of work at the courthouse in Jesup. I think he was on the tax assessor's board. He would arise early and walk to Grangerville, catch the early morning train, work all day, return in the afternoon on the four o'clock train, and walk home. Mrs. Yeomans, the two sons, Alvin and Kel, and the daughters, Lottie, Cleta, and Myrtice, ran the farm, tending the cows, hogs, chickens, ducks, geese, and turkeys as well as the four babies who were not yet walking. The oldest of the younger children had been stricken by polio and was bedridden, Herman and Hollis were twins, and W. O. was the youngest. (Later, Herman ran Yeomans shoe store in Jesup; Hollis moved to Washington, D.C., where he did well; and W. O. was our tax collector for a long time.) All the children except the babies were in school with me.

Mrs. Yeomans cooked a big country dinner every day. As soon as we got home in early afternoon we would all eat. The boys would be in the field until nightfall, laying by cotton, corn, and sweet potatoes. One of the girls would tend the babies, and Mrs. Yeomans and the other two girls would do the evening chores. They would gather vegetables for the next day and tend the young poultry and the old sows and pigs, getting them all into their well-built covered pens to keep them safe from the wild cats, river panthers, and other predators. Then they would water and feed the horses, build "smokes" for the cows in the cow pens, and milk the cows if the calves had not been with them all day. Usually, after early morning milking, the calves were allowed to run with the cows all day, growing fat and strong off the juicy grass and rich, sweet milk from their mothers' bags. In the evening the calves and cows were enclosed in separate pens.

Early in the afternoon, the daughter who had been left with the babies would see that their diapers were rinsed and hung out to dry with the other baby clothes, which her mother had washed and boiled sometime during the day in the hundred-gallon kettle. Then she would churn the big old "flip-flop," a three-gallon churn of cream to get sweet butter and an abundant supply of buttermilk for bread-making and drinking; following that, she began preparing the vegetable for the next day's big meal. Each week a different one of the three girls would stay home with the babies; then for two weeks she would do the evening chores with her mother. After the chores were finished and everyone was home, there was a good supper of milk, butter, bread, honey, fruit, Georgia cane syrup, and vegetables again if you wished followed by happy conversation, the news of the day from home, school, and town. Mr. Yeomans usually brought home with him all the local news as well as the *Savannah Morning News*. Then there would be singing around the organ by Coleman lamplight, and off to bed for a good night's rest, for it took early rising to be ready to walk the several miles to school by seven o'clock. It was a well-run home. Everything was done on time. Everyone did their part.

After the first two Saturdays, our Saturdays were usually spent on the beautiful banks of the Altamaha River and in the lovely parklike woods that made up that large acreage known as San Savilla, some of the most beautiful land I ever beheld, long-leaf yellow pine, magnolia, hickory, cedars, chinquapins, and sparkleberry trees, giant huckleberry bushes and grasses so luscious and green. Mr. Yeomans would look over his crops on Friday afternoon, and at supper that night he would say to Mrs. Yeomans, "I believe these boys and their horses have earned a holiday from farmwork until Monday. How would you lady folks like to join us down by the riverside for an old-timey fish fry? We plan to leave at the crack of dawn, and we should have an abundant supply of fish long before noontime. You and the girls take care of the stock, swine, and poultry, get the milking done early, and hitch old Nell to the wagon. Bring the babies and the cooking pots, pans, dishes, the grease, salt, meal, coffee, and your buckets for berry picking. You come on as soon as you wish, and pick berries until me and the boys come with the fish." Everyone would be so happy; they could hardly contain themselves for an early bedtime. Off to bed we would go. No pea shelling tonight, for the morrow it would be good freshwater fish fried to a golden brown, hush puppies, maybe potato salad, and fresh huckleberries washed in the clear cool spring water that ran out of San Savilla Bluff. Quite a change in diet. Mr. Yeomans usually caught far more than we could eat. These were cleaned and salted and saved for another day's cooking back home.

On Saturday morning Mr. Yeomans and the boys were up early and ready for the hearty breakfast Mrs. Yeomans had prepared. Soon after, the rest of us were up and about. We ate breakfast, cleaned up, and assembled what we needed for the fish fry and berry picking. We set everything on the edge of the side porch, where we could later drive old Nell and the wagon alongside to load the supplies and the babies, their pallets, a big box of clean napkins for them and a box to put the soiled ones in. Mrs. Yeomans and two girls were off to the cow pens to milk before the sun was up. They brought in the milk, and we put it away, fixing several jars to take with us for coffee, bread making, and to eat with our huckleberries. We placed those jars in buckets of cool water and set them on the porch. Mrs. Yeomans and the girls put the extra horses to the pasture. The cows were left to roam free, as were the hogs, goats, sheep, and geese. The goslings, young chickens, and turkeys were kept in their covered pens for the day, as the hawks were especially bad when everyone was away.

After the necessary work was completed, we loaded our wagon and secured the babies on their pallets. The oldest daughter, Lottie, drove. Mrs. Yeomans, the two other daughters, and I walked with our berry buckets in our hands, as Mrs. Yeomans said we would pass through acres and acres of blue dangleberries on the rolling grassy plains before we came to the high-bush black huckleberries of the river swamp banks. We were well on our way before the sun was above the treetops. The dangleberry bushes were laden with large sweet fruit. All we had to do was run a hand down each limber twig to have a handful. We soon had our pails overflowing. Mrs. Yeomans regretted that we had not brought the wash. She said Mr. Yeomans and the boys had told her of the abundant crop just as far as the eye could see, but she had no idea it was so great. By and by we were at the river's edge. We set out our pots and pans and knives and began to gather fallen limbs to make a cooking fire. Because we had eaten breakfast so early, we were all anxious for lunchtime to come. Mr. Yeomans and the boys arrived with their long strings of fish. They began to clean them and send them to us by the pans full. Our cooking fires were a bed of red hot coals by this time, with a stout green pole laid on each side to keep the coals from spreading and to protect the pots from sand and trash. We had a row of about six pots on the poles, and we kept adding small limbs to keep the heat at an even temperature. One pot was for coffee water. The others were for frying the fish and hush puppies. Mrs. Yeomans would fry the fish in clear grease until it got real fishy with crumbs; then we would take that pot and fry hush puppies until all the grease was used. All the while, she would be frying fish on down the line, and we would follow with the corn bread. I know that in less than an hour we had plenty of golden-brown fish and a great pan of hush puppies (or corn dodgers), enough to go around our whole party and then some. A large bowl of potato salad, hot coffee, fresh cold spring water, and a large cup of cold dangleberries and sweet milk made our noon day meal. What a feast it was, so different from all those good vegetables, cured meats, and hot breads, cakes, and pies that we usually ate. I will never forget the joy and happiness of everyone there.

After we ate, we talked and laughed and joked, enjoying the beauty of the giant forest, the soft carpet of fallen leaves and pine needles, the clear blue sky above, the bright May sunshine filtering through the green leaves, and the gentle breeze. Mr. and Mrs. Yeomans planned the afternoon activities. Mr. Yeomans said that if Mrs. Yeomans and the girls could manage the chores, he and the boys would take the rowboat back to the sloughs where they had found mayhaws in about the same abundance as we had found the dangleberries. They would do some fishing as they went and came, as some fish bite better in the late afternoon. Mrs. Yeomans told him she also wanted to pick some of the high-bush huckleberries before we left the swamp hammock on the way out. So plans were made that fit everyone. Mr. Yeomans and the boys soon had a skimmer and clean sacks for the mayhaws, their fish strings, and a cask of cold spring water and were in their boat and away. Mrs. Yeomans, Cleta, and Myrtice emptied the dangleberries in the large pans we had washed and dried after lunch. Now they had the buckets empty and ready to be filled with huckleberries from the hammock. Lottie and I cared for the babies and finished cleaning the pots. We put the leftover fish and hush puppies in a large pan and covered it securely to take home for supper, if any one was to be hungry. We made sure that every spark of fire was out, the coals covered with wet earth as an extra precaution, and our green poles rolled away and covered with earth too. We spent the rest of our time picking sticks from the dangleberries so Mrs. Yeomans could make a deep pan of blueberry pie with golden flat cream (not whipped) for our Sunday dinner and a supply of berry muffins for our lunch buckets for the next week. (It would be twenty years before schools would have lunchrooms.) We worked as rapidly as we could as we knew they would not be gone too long.

We finished our work, loaded the wagon, and hitched up the horses. Just as Lottie was putting her hands to her mouth to make the Ya! Ho! we saw them coming, their buckets heaped, one in each hand. They set the buckets in the wagon, and we were on our way home. There was no stopping for berry picking, as we had no empty buckets, and besides there was so much work to be done to get ready for the sing at Union Church that night. Company was coming tomorrow, and a big dinner was to be cooked. As soon as we arrived home—with Old Nell, the wagon, and babies safe in the yard by the two big back porches—Mrs. Yeomans, Cleta, and Myrtice, with their baskets, tubs, and buckets, hurried away to the garden to pick tomatoes, squash, okra, cucumbers, corn, butter beans, and peas. Lottie and I were left to unload. Mrs. Yeomans expected her husband and sons to bring in quite a catch by the setting of the sun, so while she was in the garden, she gathered a double handful of bear grass with which to make thongs to hang the fish fillets to dry in the hot sun.

Lottie and I put everything to its place; then Lottie went to put up the wagon and Old Nell. Lottie gave her an extra portion when she fed the horses, as Old Nell had not had the day at pasture as the others had. Lottie brought a basket of eggs back from the barn as she returned, ne'er a lost step on this well-organized farmstead. Then she and I put cream in the flip-flop to make fresh butter and buttermilk for the morrow. The churn got its name from the sound the dasher made as it passed through the cream. I went to churning, and Lottie went to get the baby clothes that had been hung early that morning. She carried great buckets of home-ground yellow cornmeal mixed with clabber and an abundant supply of fresh green onion tops, chopped fine, to feed the goslings and young turkeys.

By this time Mrs. Yeomans and the girls were back from the garden with their baskets overflowing—cucumbers, squash, okra, tomatoes, peas and butter beans. They set them on the shelf of the east porch to catch the dew and coolness of the night, each product in its own basket. Irish potatoes and most of the onions had been harvested some weeks before and were on the cool earth under the house to dry and cure and be ready for use during all the summer and fall. Mrs. Yeomans laid her bear grass down by the boiler shelter, where racks were kept for drying fish and beef. The racks were placed in the sun each morning and brought back each evening and stuck securely on the high plate of the boiler shelter away from the reach of dogs, cats, and varmints. The dew of the night was not good for the drying process. Mrs. Yeomans and her helpers tended to the pigs and horses, feeding them and securing them for the night.

I churned the butter; washed, salted, and molded some; and put the buttermilk into gallon glass jugs with handles and good cork stoppers. The buttermilk was ready for her to put in the well to keep cool. She did this by tying a plow line through the handle of the buttermilk jugs, letting them down to the bottom of the well, and fastening the lines securely around the post of the well curbing. The sweet milk would be done the same way. Many flat pans would be set for cream and placed in the securely screened little dairy house out under the shade of the big oak tree. Then several gallon jugs would be filled to go down into the well to stay cool until suppertime and for breakfast the next morning. I folded the baby clothes while Lottie hurried to the stacks of split green pinewood, sawed to measure to fit the Home Comfort stove. She filled her wheelbarrow with logs and several handfuls of finely split fat pine from the splinter stack. She then filled the wood bin on the back porch so there would be no wood-gathering for that big Sunday dinner on the morrow. As soon as I finished folding the baby clothes, I began shelling the butter beans and then the peas for the morrow's dinner.

As Lottie finished with the wood, we heard Mr. Yeomans, Alvin, and Kel, as well as Mrs. Yeomans, Cleta, and Myrtice, all coming from the turn up the lane. Lottie hurried to feed the babies and to bathe and dress them, all nice, cool, and clean for bed. Cleta and Myrtice were just in time to help her. While Mrs. Yeomans fixed the milk and washed and scalded the milking buckets, Mr. Yeomans and the boys stopped at the boiler shelter to clean, slice or fillet, and string their enormous catch of beautiful fish for the drying racks. Kel used the wheelbarrow to bring sacks of mayhaws to the house. They would go on the scaffold of stove wood he had made under the house to keep them off the ground and cool until Mrs. Yeomans used them the next week to make her winter's supply of mayhaw jelly. Mayhaw fruit makes the best jelly I ever tasted; its flavor, aroma, and color are beyond comparison. We were all so happy over the large amount they had gathered. Mr. Yeomans said, "That will take another hundred pounds of sugar next week."

Mrs. Yeomans had called for supper and asked us to tell her what we wanted. I told her, "Just a glass of good cold buttermilk and some of that good leftover corn bread for me." Others chose dangleberries and sweet milk. A few wanted the leftover fish and hush puppies warmed up and some coffee. We were all soon fed, and everyone was busily dressing for the Saturday night sing, when Mrs. Yeomans said to me, "If you will, go with the girls." You see the boys, Alvin and Kel, had to go for their girlfriends. Everyone walked. The horses had plowed all week long and it was just a short distance to walk anyway. Everyone had rather walk than get in and out of a wagon or buggy, hitch up and unhitch a horse and put it up afterwards. Mrs. Yeomans continued, "I will stay home and keep the babies and save hitching up the horse and wagon again, and also, I have not yet gotten my two big fat hens butchered for the morrow. I must have them early so as to get them cooked before church-going time." I said to her, "Why did you not tell me you wanted two big hens butchered? I would have gladly done it for you." She said to me, "You have done enough for one day, and besides I think the babies and I had better stay home tonight. They are already asleep."

So, Alvin and Kel went across the way to get the girls, and Alvin and Mozena, Kel and Anna, Lottie, Cleta, Myrtice, and I walked to the bend in the road and were met by the Martin, Sylvester, Gardner, Wall, and Bennett young people. The Browns, Calhouns, Roberts, Richardsons, Nichols, and Hopes came from the other side of the church. We were all soon at the church. The good singing, laughing, and songs were soon going strong; the fine old organ was giving forth its melodious music. Everyone sang with joy and gusto until quite a late hour. All around received invitations for Sunday dinner after preaching the next day. I think I was asked by every family group there. I told them Mrs. Yeomans was planning a big dinner, and I had promised her I would surely be there, but I could go with them some other time. Some of them said there were not too many Sundays until school would be out, and how was I going to get all around. I said, well I would surely try, which I did manage to do somehow. When we returned home, Mrs. Yeomans had not only butchered two Plymouth Rock hens from her fattening pen, where she always kept at least eight or ten big fat hens ready to be butchered, but she had baked a great big dangleberry pound cake and had cooked dozens and dozens of blueberry muffins for our lunch buckets the next week. I asked her if that meant we wouldn't have the deep-pan dangleberry pie with flat cream for the morrow, and she said, "Oh, no! The cake is for Sunday night supper, and the pie will be for tomorrow's dinner."

While Mrs. Yeomans was doing all this wonderful preparation for tomorrow's dinner, Mr. Yeomans had been planning the farmwork for the next week. He would have Alvin and Kel lay by the two big fields of corn and have them side each row on both sides. The two girls, Lottie and Myrtice, would drop field peas by each hill of corn, three peas to the hill, to make all those good late green peas for table-eating and dried peas for winter table-eating use. Then they would take a buzzard-wing, a wide-sweep plow, to run the row middles clean and cover up the peas. The girls would then finish the two fields of cotton, try to get to the Irish potato and onion ground to break, harrow it thoroughly, and lay off in rows for the planting of the last crop of speckled butter beans come the full moon in June. You know, if you plant butter beans every full moon from March through June, you can have fresh butter beans until Christmastime. You pull the late bushes up when they are loaded with green beans before the first killing frost and hang them in a dark, cool place—like the smokehouse on the empty meat sticks—and they will keep fresh for weeks. Cleta was to help her mother the next week with the babies.

Mrs. Yeomans said, "Oh, it is so hot and dusty for them to have to plow so hard each afternoon when they get home from school." And Mr. Yeomans said, "Always remember that 'May dust is Gold dust' to the farmer. The good Lord sends the dry season for him to clean his crops and do his last planting of the springtime."

Then Mr. Yeomans proceeded with his planning. "Send Mr. Hopps Bennett word that Alvin will be there early Saturday morning to help him butcher the beef, and we will take a hindquarter. I am sure we will be needing it, with your sister Mrs. Richardson and her four children, Earl, Otis, Arnold, and Bernice, coming to pick and can huckleberries and help you make up all those bags of mayhaws into jelly. You remember she said that she and the children would be here for several weeks as soon as their school was out and that Mr. E. A. would come with them to help bring all the canning things and then come back for them when she had finished. Also I want you to strip out some of the nice long rounds of beef muscle to dry for later. The fish will be dry in a few days, and the sticks will be ready for the drying of the beef. While Alvin is gone to help with the butchering, Kel and I will move the cow and calf pens further down the line, as I believe we have the field rich enough for our last potato planting. Have we not already turned it under twice? This will make the third time, as we will break it after we get the pens moved. Then it will be ready to catch the first June rains that come so we can set the sweet potato vines to make our seed for next year. I am going to let Kel try his hand at laying the 'worm' for the fence." For hedge and rail fences, to "lay the worm" means to lay the course of the fence. Mrs. Yeomans said, "Aren't you afraid the cows can butt it right over?" Mr. Yeomans reply was, "Kel will have to learn how sometime, and I believe he is capable now of putting us up a fence that will stand the test. You know this will be the last set of pens for this year, as we will cow pen it double-time to make it double fertile for our winter garden. And don't forget to clip and set about four rows of bearing tomato limbs, so if the June rains come we will have our fall tomatoes to go with the peas and speckled butter beans. Let's try a few rows of late okra along beside the potatoes also."

I had already known about the beef butchering at Mr. Bennett's the next Saturday, as the schoolchildren had been telling me about the "beef club" all their parents belonged to. It was Mr. Bennett's turn to butcher this time. You bargained with Mr. Bennett to take a certain portion, and when it was your time to butcher you paid back that portion to Mr. Bennett. If Mr. Yeomans was to butcher in August, then he would return one hindquarter to Mr. Bennett pound for pound. Because there was no ice or electric refrigeration or even canning of meats, the only way to preserve what you did not use fresh was to salt cure or sun cure (dried). Some would take tripe, liver, head, or a portion of or whole front- or hindquarter. It took twelve members to make a club, or six to make a half club, or twenty-four to make a double club. Most communities tried for the twelve-member club. By butchering one cow per year you had access to fresh beef thirteen times per year; in a double club, twice a month; if a half club, every two months. This was "cattle country," but there was no stock market then. You received benefits from your cattle herd from your milk, butter, and cream and from whatever meat you were able to consume at your table. The meat was sweet, tender, and nutritious, not at all fat. The herd's waste products were used to fertilize the fields.

I had a special invitation from Mr. Bennett to come have Saturday dinner with them, as they had planned to have fresh beef liver and sweet potatoes plus the regular fresh vegetables, fruits, berries, milk, butter, and cream. He knew how well I liked fresh liver smothered in juicy sweet onions, just as he liked it. He invited me to spend the afternoon because all their children would be home, and he thought I would enjoy them. Mary Fleming and her husband were to be up from Miami. I also knew that as Mr. and Mrs. Yeomans's oldest daughter, Vonnie, and her husband, Mr. Willie Dukes, and family, who worked down there were coming up with them. Constance would be home from her school at Oglethorpe, and Lawrence would be home from Piedmont. So when the next Saturday came, I went as promised, after I had finished my personal laundry and what other necessities I had to do.

I could smell the delicious food quite a distance before I reached the Bennett home. The meal was wonderful, the family was so happy to be together, and conversation flowed freely and joyously among this great family of four daughters, two sons, mother, grandmother, and father. After the bounteous noonday meal, we retired to the long wisteria-clad front porch, and Mr. Bennett began to tell me what all he wished me to do. The first thing he wanted to know was if his son Lawrence, later Dr. L. R. Bennett Sr. of Jesup, could enter school. His daughter Adelaide had told Lawrence in her letters how much she was enjoying her history, English, geography, arithmetic, and literature, and Lawrence had asked to attend also. I told him sure, if Lawrence would take hold of where we were in grade seven and have lessons of the rest of the class. It seems that Lawrence was having problems with some of his subjects at Piedmont, and Mr. Bennett was sure I could help him overcome his difficulties. Lawrence often told me afterward how much he learned in those few weeks he had me for a teacher. He said it was of great benefit to him all down through the years, in his college years, and in his profession.

Then Mr. Bennett told me he had heard of the wonderful Liberty Bond sale and school closing I had had at O'Quinn. He wanted us to have a bond sale and old-time school closing at Union, which used to be known far and wide for its exhibitions at closing time, but they had not had one for years and years. I told him I would be glad to cooperate in any way I could. So we set to lay the plans and to get them sanctioned by the rest of the trustees and patrons. If they agreed, we would carry out the plan for the last day of school as follows: We would have roll call at seven, the usual time. Then we would get all the books stacked up ready to take home that afternoon. We would prepare a display of copybooks; folders of letterforms, maps, and sentence diagramming; history charts, and arithmetic rules. Following that we would have an old-fashioned spelling match, an arithmetic match, and a geography recital of "states and capitals," foreign countries and their capitals, the great rivers of the world, their ports, and the sea or ocean they flowed into. After recess, public speaking and the bond sale would start at ten. An old-time picnic dinner for school and community was to begin at one. After the picnic, everyone was to go home to do their evening barnyard chores, then to return for the school-closing program, including the seventh-grade graduation. Mr. Bennett wished for Congressman Lankford of the then Eleventh Congressional District to be invited; Mr. Bennett's brother, Col. R. L. Bennett, the county attorney, was to introduce him. Of course, the county Liberty Bond sales committee would be there to speak and sell bonds.

I told him of the wonderful seating plan at O'Quinn that I had borrowed from Sandy Hill, where I had taught in the Uncle Enoch Bennett community. Mr. Bennett laughed and said Uncle Enoch had carried the idea with him to his new home at Sandy Hill when he left the Union Church community to settle up there at the headwaters of Penholloway Creek. The seating arrangement had been brought to Union by some of the oldest settlers when they came to settle Wayne County. It was known as camp-meeting seats. Mr. Bennett said he would furnish the lumber for as many seats as I could get blocks for. I told him how it worked to have everyone saw the blocks to fit their stoves and then write their name on the end of their blocks so they could readily gather them to take home after the program. Mr. Bennett could gather his lumber to take back home to help repair his turpentine quarters.

I also told Mr. Bennett that I would want time during the school day to practice for the program. The nights were too short, and the children were working too hard and late to expect them to come to night practice. I told him I wanted the period after lunch each day until little recess for the last four weeks of the term. It would take me one week to get my material together and to plan a program. He said he would get permission for this from the trustees and patrons as he went around to get their approval for the school-closing program. He would try to let me know by the Monday next.

Then he asked me to return come September to teach their school for the next term. I told him I had promised them faithfully at O'Quinn that I would return there, but I thanked him kindly for giving me the opportunity to teach in the Union community and told how much I had enjoyed every minute of it, the children, the sings at the church, the fishing, canning, berry picking, swimming, and the school library, the best one I had ever had. I just wish I could have had time to read all the books. The friendship of the patrons and the other people of the community was wonderful. I appreciated having known his father, Hon. John

T. Bennett, who was with General Lee when he surrendered at Appomattox Courthouse.

I told him of the day his father had come riding up to the schoolhouse to inquire after his flock of sheep. As he rode away one of the seventh-graders said he looks just like Robert E. Lee setting on that horse, and I said, "Why not? He had four hard years training under General Lee every day in that awful struggle between the states." John T. Bennett was the father of Hon. Blue John Bennett, a fine lawyer, of Waycross; Oscar Bennett, of Eastman; Dock Bennett, our county school superintendent for some time who died in young manhood of typhoid fever; Robert L. Bennett, the Wayne County attorney; our own Hopps Bennett; Mary Bennett Brinson and Lilla Bennett Parker-Brown; and, I think, some other sons I never knew.

Later in the afternoon, when I returned to Mr. Yeomans's, I found that the older daughter, Vonnie, had gotten home, and Mrs. Yeomans's sister, Mrs. Richardson, had arrived with her children. I knew Mrs. Yeomans could cook enough good food, as she was used to preparing large quantities, but I wondered about the sleeping arrangements. I soon found how it was to be. Mrs. Richardson and Vonnie were to have the bed in the girls' room. Old sheets were put on the floor, and on top of them were placed good cotton mattresses and pillows. They were made up just like the beds on the bedsteads and were not wallowed on either. They were there for the duration of the visit. The boys' room was arranged likewise, and everyone knew where they were to sleep. Mr. and Mrs. Yeomans and the babies had their regular sleeping room, and I had mine all by myself, where I could do my schoolwork as usual. I never would stay at a schoolhouse in a densely wooded area alone. It was too dangerous. I could prepare my work just as well in my own room at my boarding place. I have often thought how well Mrs. Yeomans adjusted to any situation. She was one of the greatest souls I ever knew, always able to carry on happily under any circumstances.

On Monday Mrs. Richardson and her children took a bucket in each of their hands and hied away to the huckleberry woods. They came with us as we walked to school in the early morning, going on beyond the schoolhouse quite a distance to get to their berries. We turned up to the school and to our lessons. We saw no more of them until after we got back home. They had filled their buckets and returned before the heat of the day, cleaned the berries, washed them good, and had them ready to can as soon as the big dinner was over. They and Mrs. Yeomans had their dinner before we got home, so we would not be too crowded at the table. Before supper Alvin and Kel plowed until dusk; Lottie and Myrtice dropped (planted) the peas; Cleta helped with the babies; I churned so we would have fresh buttermilk and sweet milk for supper. I never did want anything more than a glass of buttermilk and a piece of corn bread for supper after that wonderful late noonday meal. The next morning it would be the same plan over again. Mrs. Richardson was getting her berry jars filled in scheduled time and would be ready the next week to help Mrs. Yeomans make mayhaw jelly.

Mr. Bennett came by the schoolhouse to tell me that the trustees and patrons agreed to the old-time school closing, bond sale, and noontime picnic. They wanted the school closing to be real good and were willing for us to have the practice period for which I had asked. They were also willing to bring the stove-wood blocks for the seats and to bring a picnic dinner. The church had said we could use their long outdoor table to spread the dinner, if we would be sure to leave everything nice and orderly. Although the church was just across the road from the schoolhouse, we never did go over there to play or anything. In other words it was off limits. When Mr. Bennett looked around at our grounds he saw how badly the trees needed pruning and how much debris there was from storms of many seasons, even around the church's outdoor table. So he asked the boys to come the next Saturday to help clear it away. He would bring two of his strong workmen to trim the beautiful trees—oak, magnolia, holly, cedar, and maple—so we could walk among them and people could drive up with their horses and buggies and wagons. Of course they all wanted to help. He told them to ask their parents if they could come and if their parents would also, so maybe they could get through by noontime. He would have some fish caught and bring some of the women over to cook fish and hush puppies down by the creek. They would have a fish fry after they finished their work, and all the men and boys could go in swimming before going home. He told them it would be a hard morning's work, but surely wanted it to be a pleasant place for people to be. He said he did not want any ladies to come and catch the ribbons and blossoms on their hats in the scraggly limbs of the trees, or to tear their skirts or hose on the fallen limbs or briers.

After he was gone I told the children we were in for a lot of hard work to get the place all cleaned up and beautiful. We needed wood blocks to hold up the seats out in front, some sheets to make curtains for our stage on the front porch, and some large containers to hold sprays of our native flowers to decorate the steps and edge of porch. They would have all their costume material in a box on their seats inside the building the night of the program, as that would be our dressing room, and we must not be late for the different acts. We talked of the program and what all we wished to present for our parents and friends. We planned as follows:

1. An opening song for everyone and a welcome by our best speaker.

2. A funny play for the older boys and girls. We selected *The Tramp at the Picnic.*

3. A motion song for the younger boys and girls.

4. A "Lady Come to See Me" play for the middle girls, where they were make-believe ladies sending their children to school and church at Union.

5. A health play about malaria fever. It took a doctor and several people having chills and fever. It took both boys and girls.

6. A medley of patriotic songs. Girls with red, white, and blue badges and caps. They sang "The Star-Spangled Banner," "O, Columbia! The Gem of the Ocean," "Dixie," "Over There," and "Au Revoir but Not Goodbye."

7. A precision flag drill by a group of boys and girls.

8. A selection of patriotic poems by a group of children, each child standing when his time came to give his poem.

9. A group of middle-sized boys and I made up a play to suit the occasion. It covered schoolwork, home duties, church going, going to town, visiting neighbors, and fishing.

10. The seventh-grade graduation. That was an important event in a child's life in that day and time. There was not a high school in the whole county. Jesup was struggling toward one but had not advanced any further than grade ten as yet. So a good topic was selected for each of the graduates, and they also would sing the class song. Mr. B. D. Purcell had agreed to give them their certificates.

11. Then we would have our closing song by the whole school and would sing "Goodnight Ladies." Thus would end the all-day and half-night Union School closing for the year 1918.

We sent invitations to Hopewell, Mt. Pleasant, Midway, Gardi, and Bethlehem, among other communities, asking them to come and enjoy the occasion with us. Special letters were sent to Congressman Lankford, B. L. Bennett, and others from Jesup who were to help us with our bond sales and also to enjoy the event.

The first Saturday in June was our last teachers meeting for the year with our superintendent. Most of the teachers were through and ready to turn in their records for the year and to get their instructions for the opening of school in the fall, but not so with me. I had to teach to the very last Friday in June to get the time in for that school year. I gave Mr. Purcell the list of my seventh-grade graduates and asked that he prepare certificates for each of them. I then did my shopping for the materials for our program. I wanted red, white, and blue bunting for banners and for my students to wear when they sang the medley of patriotic songs. But alas, I could not get the bunting and had to settle for crepe paper. I also bought the many flags for my flag drill. When I had secured all my supplies, I went home with my sister Lula to where she was teaching in the New Hope Community, away up the river on the Lanes Bridge Road. The teacher there had had a severe case of flu and was never able to return to finish out her school term. So when Lula finished her school term at Nahunta, our superintendent had gotten her to finish the term at New Hope. She was living in the home of Mr. and Mrs. Millard Pye. While I was there, they had a sing for us at the home of his father, Mr. Jim Pye, where his sister Miss Laura Pye played the organ very nicely. I enjoyed my stay very much, but I had to return to Union Sunday afternoon. I had to catch the Atlanta-Brunswick train at Odum and get off at Grangerville, where my people would meet me. I had twenty hard days' work to do before my school closing.

I had not forgotten my promise to visit in the homes of my students. I spent one weekend in the Calvin Brown home, with Mr. Brown, his charming wife, Mrs. Georgia, and their children, Ruth, Sadie, Lovie, and Harry. It was a delightful weekend. They had a sing for me on Saturday night, and we enjoyed all the neighbors and kinfolks who came to make merry. Then I spent one weekend with the Sam Nichols family. There I enjoyed Rachel, Macie, Callie, Allen, and the other children. It was there, too, that I found the Sacred Harp songbooks, the ones with the four shaped notes. This was the kind we used to study when I went to singing school with a singing master when I was a child. I got to spend just one night with the families of the other pupils. There were not enough weekends to go around, and I did the best I could. I enjoyed all my visits.

At last the great day arrived, Friday, June 28, 1918. The children stacked their books and put their costumes on the proper benches. This done, we then put up wires around the porch to hold the borrowed bedsheets we would use for curtains. The curtains were securely fastened and pulled back against the wall. Then we arranged the large urns (flip-flop churns), filled with beautiful flowers. They were a beautiful sight, and the aroma of cape jasmine, roses, clematis, and tupelo filled the air. We wiped the dew and dust off our plank seats, and now they were ready for occupancy. All was in readiness. I gave recess as usual at 9:00 A.M., enough time for the children to get water and relieve themselves. By then the crowd began to gather—horses, buggies, surreys, saddle-back, and single and double wagons. The picnic baskets were secure in their places until noontime, when they would be brought out and spread on the great old outdoor table. I rang the bell at 9:30 as always. We already had a house overflowing with appreciative parents, kind friends, and honorable and interested visitors. I told them of our schedule and that the exhibits would stay up until 3:00, when the children would take their work down to take home with them.

The program started with the arithmetic matches. I began with grade one. They counted to one hundred. Grades two and three added to one hundred and also subtracted. Grades four and five did their multiplication tables and division. Grades six and seven did common and decimal fractions, percentages, and measurements. Then came the spelling matches. Congressman Lankford and Mr. Bob Bennett gave out the words. The children spelled well. Everyone seemed to enjoy it. The history and geography were also enjoyed. By 11:30 we were ready for another rest period. This concluded our indoor exercises. The patrons and visitors were welcome to look over the exhibits if they chose to do so. Our bond sales were to begin at 11:45 and last until 1:00. Congressman Lankford spoke and brought the people up to date on the affairs of the nation. Everyone was attentive and seemed to enjoy his talk. The sale went well. It was the first time many of the people had ever invested in support of the war effort. Soon after, the bountiful dinner was spread on the table, which was graced with the aged and beloved John T. Bennett. Everyone was invited to come and eat. All seemed to enjoy the summertime vegetables, fat chickens, dumplings, dressing, fine pieces of beef, cured hams, and fresh fish in abundance. There were cakes, salads, pickles, and pies to fit any taste or appetite. When the meal was over and the table was cleared, our patrons and visitors began to depart.

Quite a few of the visitors went home with their kinfolks so as to be back for the closing exercises that night. Most of the children had to hurry home to get their evening chores done early. They had been admonished to be back and in their places on time. Our program was to begin right at eight and run for three hours. I did not go back to my boarding place, as I had to see that the grounds were in readiness for the evening and that the school building was in order for our dressing room. My six middle-grade boys, who had gotten permission from their parents beforehand, stayed to help me get everything in order. We gave the flowers fresh water, trimmed and burred the lamps and lanterns, and put them in their places. We dusted, counted, and arranged the seats and made sure the curtains were in perfect order for pulling. We saw that nothing had been left behind in the schoolroom, that everyone's things were gone. All mine were in a box ready for me to pick up when my day was done about midnight, as I was scheduled to leave on the early morning train for my journey homeward. Mr. Hopps Bennett had promised faithfully to have a team and two men there that night to gather up his seat supports and the lumber we had borrowed for seats. All the other patrons were supposed to get their own blocks. Of course the sheets, lamps, and lanterns were all to be returned to their owners at the close of the program.

Eight o'clock came, and the seats were soon filled. The children were there, and the program was ready to begin. The stage was well lighted and decorated beautifully. I announced the numbers and the performers: printed programs were too expensive, and typewriters were yet scarce. Our songs, drills, marches, dialogs, and recitations were well learned, and each group was well received by the audience. The patriotic numbers were appropriate, and the audience made no bones about where its support for the national cause now lay—the same as they did in the days of yore when they laid down their life, health, and wealth for the cause of Dixie. It still brought a flow of pride to their hearts. We had standing ovations after the "Star-Spangled Banner" and "Dixie." The next part of the program was to be a play by my sixth-grade boys and me. They were good boys but were slow learners and nonreaders. They had not fit into the program well, so we made us up a play. I was the "mama," and they were my six sons. We built our play around the everyday things I knew they could do well. They were the six who had come to help Mr. Bennett clean up the grounds and the ones who knew where to find Uncle John Bennett's flock of sheep. They knew where to find acres and acres of dangleberries and how to fix a bee sting with a chew of tobacco. But, alas, when the stage was ready for us to appear, only two of my boys could be found. The show had to go on.

So I began to call as loud as I could, and one of the two who were in the building came running to me from his seat on the far corner of the porch and whispered that the missing boys had gone to the swimming hole in Ellis Creek, right down the big road a few hundred yards. I told this to the audience and sent the two boys just as fast as they could run to tell the others to come quick. While they were gone I kept the audience in peals of laughter telling them what a time those six shy boys and I had that school term and how much I had learned from them of the Union community's history, church meetings, weddings, funerals, parties, crop failures, and successes. Now on this beautiful moonlight night they had escaped the school-breaking. Then the two boys came back from the swimming hole, telling in a whisper that Harry Brown and Allen Nichols had stolen the other boys' clothes and would not let them have them back. So I had to tell that to the audience. I asked out into the crowd if Mr. Hopps was going to let Harry and Allen stay in his townhouse with Mrs. Bennett, Adelaide, and Grace while they went to the Jesup School, and Mr. Bennett stood up and said no, and to go quickly and tell the boys so. Soon my four missing boys were there, all nice and clean and cool, but out of breath. First I corrected them about going to swimming hole from school and told them they would surely be remembered tomorrow if it were a school day for us. As it was not, we would have to forget all about it. We had our play to do.

The play was conversation about everyday happenings among us at school and at home. So we began. I asked Robert just what did he mean when he asked Mr. Hopps Bennett to put all those limbs they had trimmed in a "lazy-man's woodpile" in place of a "brush-burning heap." What was his reason for requesting that it be done that way? He explained that you start a circle and put the butts of every load of limbs on the inner ring of the circle until you had all your limbs so piled and the circle complete. You let them stay there until they were dried; then you get a good chopping block, a sharp ax, another block to sit upon; and boxes, baskets, and bags to contain the chopped wood. Then you go into the circle and start pulling the limbs to you, chopping them as you came to them—big and little, all in the right lengths for your heater, fireplace, or what have you. Do that day after day, and by and by you would have the brush all gone, no fire hazard, just leaves left to decay and go back to mother earth. You would have yourself a good supply of hardwood for the winter without cutting down a single beautiful tree, and no tired aching back from heavy cutting.

Then I told Tommy I would like for that whole crowd to know why he always kept that little square of apple sun-cured tobacco so neatly wrapped in a white cloth in the bottom of his pocket. He told them he kept it wrapped so it would be nice and clean when he had to chew it to go on a bee sting or centipede bite for someone at school. Then I told how many times I had had to call on him to do just that and how quickly the injured one got relief. He reached into his pocket and brought out his square and said, "I never go anywhere without it." The crowd just hee-hawed. Everyone knew about his tobacco-chewing habit. We went on and on about such homely knowledge for some time. All six told of different things they knew and could do well. I told them how proud I was of them and how I knew that each one would make a fine man. I was proud of them, even though they had made us late by going to the swimming hole. The fact was they stole the show.

Now the curtain came up on our sweet seventh-grade graduates, seated on the well-lighted stage in all their young beauty. The girls wore white organdy dresses, pretty slippers, lovely ribbons, and beautiful gardenias, so snowy white and fragrant, tucked in their hair. The boys wore white duck trousers, white broadcloth shirts, black bow ties, and black oxford slippers. Mr. Purcell came up from the audience to his chair and a small table, on which were a good Coleman lamp, a lovely bouquet, and a tray holding the seventh-grade certificates. He began by addressing the audience. He commented that Union was one of the oldest settlements in Wayne County—probably older than Waynesville or Jack's little three-cornered piece of brick that he carried in his pocket all the time. Jack was one of my six middle boys. He had found the piece of brick at the beautiful bluff at San Savilla, and I had gotten after him about it in our play, just a little while before, and about having to continuously darn his pockets on account of that piece of brick. He told me he planned to carry it until someone told him why all those lovely bricks were buried so deep down in the bank at San Savilla. Mr. Purcell commended Jack and told him to keep searching, that someday we would know why they were there.

Then he told the beautiful story of our little school building. How Mr. Dock Bennett was courting Miss Annie Brinson, who had come to Wayne County from Hephzibah, near Augusta, to teach public school. She had an aunt, Mrs. Sallie Brinson Clary, who had been one of Wayne County's earliest teachers and was rated one of the best for her day and time. Miss Annie told Mr. Bennett she cared for him very deeply, but she had dedicated her life to teaching. He told her she could continue to teach after she married him if she so desired, and he built that lovely building with his own hands and presented it to her as a bridal present. When Mr. Bennett died of typhoid, he left Mrs. Annie with one little daughter, Marie. Mrs. Annie taught for many years. She was one of the best teachers and home agents in the nation. She passed away on April 5, 1928, of pneumonia.

Mr. Purcell continued telling of the many fine teachers who went forth from Union community to teach at other schools in Wayne County and in faraway places: Sallie Richardson Crawford, Georgia Gardner Owens, Lula Sheppard Hopkins, Ethel Sheppard Hopkins, Constance Bennett Roberson, and many others down through the years. Then he added the long list of prominent lawyers, including Blue John Bennett and Robert L. Bennett. He did not leave out the ministers, farmers, cattlemen, foresters, loggers, and fishermen who were there with us that night. Then he spoke of the wonderful library Union had, probably better than Jesup's at that time. He told how he was struggling to make Jesup the Wayne County High School. It was still a city school but had never been able to become an accredited high school. In January 1919 the Jesup School became the Wayne County High School, but it was not yet accredited. Although Mr. Purcell passed away in the winter of 1971, he lived long enough to see "Jesup High School" really become Wayne County High School in 1970, when every child in the county—no differentiation by color, creed, or religion—was allowed to enter.

After his well-delivered address to the boys and girls and the audience, I turned the seventh grade over to Mr. Purcell, well prepared and having faithfully completed the work of seventh grade prescribed by the state of Georgia. He granted them their certificates. Not many boys and girls in that day and time ever completed that much schooling. The audience rose to honor the whole class. Next came the closing song and "Good Night Ladies," with the whole student body joining the graduates in the closing number. The day was done, and my wonderful three-month stay was over.

After the crowd had gone, and the children told good-bye again and again, I locked the lovely little school building and left for my boarding place for a few hours' sleep. Then before daybreak, I was up and away to catch the early morning train for my journey home. I stopped in Jesup to turn in my records, get my pay, and do a little shopping before I caught the noonday Train No. 85 for Nahunta. I was scheduled to leave Monday night for Athens, for the summer quarter at the University of Georgia.

Ellen, Martha, and Lula Mizell, sisters, look at Martha's newly acquired teaching certificate, 1912.

*The Honorable B. D. Purcell,
Wayne County school
superintendent 1906–26.*

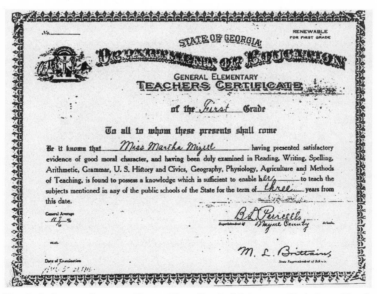

*Martha's first teachers certificate, First Grade (highest quality), issued by the
Wayne County, Georgia, school superintendent in 1912. The certificate was
revalidated every three years.*

Martha's first teaching job was at Burnt Bay School, on the fringe of the Okefenokee Swamp. The school was in session for four months, January through April 1913.

Martha Isabella Mizell, a freshman at the University of Georgia, Athens, summer of 1915.

Martha Isabella Mizell,
a young public school teacher in
Wayne County, Georgia, circa 1919.

O'Quinn School, Wayne County, Georgia. Martha taught here 1917–18
and 1919–20 and worked to help pass the first school bond issue to improve
the local school.

Martha Mizell and Lawrence P. Puckett Sr. were married
December 29, 1920, in Nahunta, Georgia.

*Jesup High School building, 1906–26. Martha organized the
first Parent Teacher Association in the high school in 1923.*

*Lawrence Parham Puckett Sr.,
a charter member of the Jesup,
Georgia, Kiwanis Club, 1926.*

Empire School, Wayne County, Georgia. This school was formed by consolidating several smaller schools into this building. Martha taught a total of eleven terms in this school, 1932–38, 1942–46, and 1952–53. One year, during the Great Depression, she received only six dollars for a whole term's work.

Gardi School, Wayne County, Georgia. Martha taught school here five terms, 1938–42 and 1951–52. The first hot-lunch program for school children in Wayne County was started here by Martha.

Jesup Junior High School, Wayne County, Georgia. Martha Mizell Puckett taught four terms here 1958–62 and completed her fifty-year career on Wayne County's education program here on December 19, 1962.

Martha Mizell Puckett, a teacher at Patterson High School, 1955

CHAPTER 11

Summer School at the University of Georgia

I arrived home on Saturday, June 29, 1918. My sister Lula had closed out her school at New Hope a few days before me and was already home when I arrived. She was tired, given out. She had not gotten much done and had almost given up the idea of going to the university. But I was pledged to go. We knew there was no time for sewing a new wardrobe. We would have to do with what we had. We visited with our father and mother on Saturday afternoon and Sunday after church hour. On Monday morning we arose to launder our clothes. We unpacked our winter clothes and got our trunks ready for our bedclothes; we had to take pillows, towels, sheets, blankets, and a full summer wardrobe of shoes, clothes, and toilet articles. By Monday night we were packed and ready to leave on a late train for Jesup, where we changed to a midnight Southern train (that came right by Nahunta but was not allowed to pick up passengers from Atlantic Coastline stations). We changed again at Macon to the Georgia Railroad that took us to Athens. When we got settled on the Southern train I went to sleep and slept all the way to Macon.

Once in Athens, we registered for our classes, bought books, and paid fees for lodging, board, infirmary, and entertainment. We stayed in Chandler Hall and had our meals at Denmark Hall. Our schedules were made out, and we were ready to begin classes the next day. I had United States history from Dr. McPherson; geography from Dr. Sell; English from Dr. Peter S. Brown; and general science and physics from Dr. Hendren. Dean Woofter taught school management and rural school problems, and Dr. Payne taught world history. My load was heavy, and I knew I would have to burn the midnight oil. I had to deny myself many things to have the money to attend this quarter. I had come to learn.

Lula and I went to lunch. My sister felt bad and ate scarcely any lunch. On the way back to Chandler Hall, I suggested we stop at Crawford W. Long Infirmary, right by the sidewalk. We went in; the nurse checked Lula over and found her with a burning fever of 104 degrees Fahrenheit. She suggested that my sister stay for the night and let her check her further. I left and brought back a gown, slippers, bathrobe, and toilet articles. The next morning the nurse told me she wanted Lula to see the doctor when he came at ten. So my sister stayed in the infirmary, and I went on to classes. At noontime, her fever had not abated. I brought her more gowns. After the doctor's second round, he pronounced Lula's illness a serious case of typhoid fever; it was too dangerous to move her. She was isolated. No one was allowed to go in her room, only the nurse and the doctor. I could only go as far as the door. The fever raged on, forty-two days come and gone, and still the fever raged on. I did the best I could with my classes. I went on no excursions or picnic trips as we had when there in 1915. I went to see Lula three times a day: morning, noon, and night, never knowing whether she would be dead or alive when I came by the next time.

The summer quarter was about over. I had made my grades, taken my tests, and now had my high school license, permitting me to teach eighth grade and above. My money was all but gone. I did not know what to do or where to turn. I wrote to one of my older brothers, William F. Brown (my mother's only child by her first husband, Benjamin F. Brown, a returned Confederate veteran who died when William was a small baby). He sent me twenty-five dollars with which to get home, but I could not go home and leave Lula. I wrote to my other older brother, Frank (F. M. Mizell, my father's oldest son by his first marriage). He came to Athens and asked me to take him to see the doctor. The doctor told him it would mean death for my sister to be moved at that time, and it would be weeks and weeks before he would give his permission for her to be moved. Then my brother asked me to take him to the director of the summer quarter, Dr. Howard C. Odum. They talked at length and finally came up with these facts.

The Great War was still raging. The University of Georgia was overflowing with officer-training candidates. The infirmary would not be closed in September. Therefore it was proposed that I move from Chandler Hall to the infirmary, as Chandler Hall would be closed. To pay for my board, lodging, and laundry, I would help the trained nurse, Miss Mary Donaldson, with her overload of work with the officer candidates. It was a happy arrangement. Dr. Howard sent some of the campus workers to take our trunks and suitcases by wheelbarrows to the infirmary with no cost.

I went to work as a nurse's aide, busy from morning until far into the night every day. The fever slowly left my sister. She was nothing but skin and bones and could not walk a step. Slowly her temperature returned to normal, and she began to rebuild her ravished body and mind. It was a slow, long job. September came and was almost gone. Finally the doctor said I could take her home if I could manage to change trains with her. He called the Red Cross to help me change trains in Macon. Then I had to change in Jesup. Our father was to meet us at Nahunta with help to get her on the wagon and into the house at home. My dear friend Annie Bennett made all the arrangements at Jesup for me to change from the Southern train to the Atlantic Coastline train. The trip was made safely and with ease.

I had previously written to Mr. Purcell to let him know of the circumstances we were facing. Lula had been elected principal of Screven Public School, with some ten teachers at that time. I had to resign for her so they could proceed with hiring another principal. I knew that I would have to work near home, if I would be able to work at all. I tendered my resignation at O'Quinn. It just broke my heart, but I knew there was no other way. My duty was to my sister and to helping her regain her health and happiness if possible.

To keep Lula from becoming a wheelchair invalid, the doctor and nurse had given me complete instructions on her feeding and care. I began by feeding her rice water, then beans and pea broth, chicken broth, then gruels, and then soups. Weeks afterward she was able to eat semisoft foods, by and by, soft solids, and several months later, a regular diet. Day by day, she improved. I began to get her to walk. I put her food a little farther from her each day and helped her get to it. Finally she took a step by herself. It took months to get those leg muscles working again. Also the thinking part of her mind had to be trained to work again. I used all the knowledge I had about getting a body's mind into action after having lain dormant and in a stupor for many long weeks from a burning fever.

By late fall I was able to go to work at nearby Raybon School, about five miles from my home. Until the weather became too cold, wet, and bitter in midwinter, I drove Old Bob hitched to the buggy each night and morning. By late December, my sister had built herself up enough to return to teaching. She returned to Liberty School out from Screven, where she had previously taught two very successful terms.

I have often wondered how my brother and Doctor Odum managed to make such wonderful arrangements for me and my very sick sister. But they did, and all her money paid for college work of course went on her sick expense, but that was just a small amount of what that spell of sickness would have cost elsewhere. And then there was my being allowed to work out my board and keep to be able to stay with her. I consider we were thrice blessed. We left in late September with no bills due.

CHAPTER 12

Raybon School and a War Ends

After our hectic summer with Lula's illness and convalescence, I began teaching at Raybon School. It was one of the first nice frame school buildings in that part of the county. Three small log-cabin schools—Willis, Green Head, and Cross Swamp—had been combined to make up this school. The building was sixty-five feet long and forty feet wide, with one heater in the center. One teacher taught at the front end and one in the back end of the long building. It was ceiled, and painted on the outside. There was a side door and a large front door that opened onto the porch. Some desks, many chairs, benches, and tables made up the furniture. There were few maps, only painted boards for a blackboard, and no library, charts, or any other teaching aids. Many children were without books. There was no lunchroom and no school buses; everyone walked. The farthest distance to walk was less than three miles. Cotton, cattle, turpentine, saw-milling, timber, and general farming supported the economy of the community. Though there was not much money, some mighty good living went on in the community. Slow, steady, and easy was the pace, plenty of time to do everything perfectly and time left to enjoy yourself hunting, fishing, and visiting. They were hospitable people—plenty to eat, good beds, still mostly log homes and barns, horses to pull a plow or wagon or buggy. Money was scarce; debts were not incurred. You had abundance if you produced it; otherwise you lived a hard life.

There were more than a hundred students in this district, but cotton-picking in the fall and cotton-chopping and other farmwork interfered with the children's attendance. My main effort was to try to improve the average daily attendance. Miss Clara Strickland was to be my assistant teacher. I taught one, five, six, and seven. She carried grades two through four. Our pupil load was about equal. But I had to struggle to do four grades while she did three. We began in the late fall, starting late because of cotton-picking. We had bright prospects for a good term, but the terrible flu epidemic of 1918–19 was soon upon us.

Our school building was near the ancient Lewis Cemetery, which was extensively used as a burying ground for the neighborhood as well as for those who had gone afar and always had a desire to be brought back home to be buried. All during the fall and winter scarcely a day went by that someone was not buried at this beautiful old cemetery. The school building was also close to the small railway station at Raybon, where only the faithful old Bogey stopped regularly. The many faster trains just flew right on by. When we heard one coming to a screeching stop, we wondered who it was that the train was bringing home for their "long sleep." Someone would soon tell us, and all those near of kin would be permitted to leave school to attend the funeral and burial. It usually took a large portion of those in attendance at school, for the community was very closely connected in kinship, with marriage and intermarriage. The following families made up the majority of the families: Lewis, Morgan, Harris, Herrin, Purdom, Smith, Willis, Wilson, Hendrix, Cross, McDonald, McClelland, Lyons, and Highsmith. It was the doctor's orders that a corpse be buried at once, especially if it had been shipped in from a long distance. I went to many a funeral in the late evening and even in the nighttime, as I remember one body coming in on a later train than the relatives had thought, and they kept waiting until the train that had the corpse came to a roaring halt. The casket was loaded on the wagon and taken to the cemetery. Lanterns and fat-pine torches were always ready for occasions like this, and we all followed the bereaved family. Funeral rites were conducted, and the body was lowered to its final resting place by the light of the torches and lanterns, eerie shadows of trees and tombstones falling near us. I can tell you it was a very sad situation. The Great War was still raging, and many of our local boys were at nearby Camp Wheeler, in Macon. Camp McPherson, in Atlanta, and other training sites in our region sent us the bodies of many who had fallen victim to the epidemic. It spread rapidly and was fatal to doctors and nurses as well as to the ordinary person.

We carried on our academic work as best we could under the circumstances, but no one had time for pleasure or merrymaking, with waiting on the sick and burying the dead. Raybon had long been famous for its all-out community activities, such as debating, singing schools, community drama, and little-theater plays, but there was none such now. Most of our able-bodied young men were in the service—overseas or in training camps—so there was no one to promote the plays or to be in them. There was scarcely a day that I did not have to send a child home with the flu for a long period of serious illness. It is sad to tell that some did not live to return to us.

I finally succumbed to the terrible disease. My fever went so high that my sight was impaired. I got on the Bogey and went home. The train stopped at the crossing near our home to let me get off and to help me to my father, who had watched the train stop and came to meet me. I had sent my schoolchildren home and told them to stay there until I sent them word that I was able to return, for there was no one to take my place. My assistant teacher was stricken later, and the school was closed down for many weeks. My case was severe, and I was out of school for many weeks. A few weeks later I came down with the big red measles. They surely did me badly. My eyes and whole system were generally in a weakened condition. But with good care, medication, and the blessed springtime, I finally got to where I could go to school again. I surely had taken a severe setback in my general health.

The whole community participated in one of our activities in support of the war effort. We gathered hickory nuts, cracked them open to get the meats, and then charred the shells until they were solid charcoal. We cooled them with water, dried them, and put them in stout crocus sacks, sewing them up tightly with strong twine. We delivered them to the nearest Red Cross station to be shipped to the correct office of the War Department. The shells were processed into the purest form of carbon, which was used in gas masks for our troops. November 11 was set as the day for us to do this project. All the school children brought their lunches as usual, a jug for water, many horses and wagons, and sacks, buckets, and baskets. We rang the bell at the usual time. I called roll and told them of the great need for these nut hulls. Our community had such an abundance of hickory nuts in the nearby hammocks of the Great Satilla Swamp, which came to the very edge of our school campus. I asked each child to do his best. Many of the patrons were present to go along with us. We were soon on our way, laughing and talking about who maybe would be able to breathe better, helped by the carbon we were planning to provide.

We were to be back at the schoolhouse, ready to dismiss school at the regular time, four o'clock, so children could go home and do their chores, eat their supper, and feed the horses we had used. The children and all their parents together were to return to the school building to help crack nuts and roast the hulls. Neither I nor my assistant teacher went home. We stayed at the school building getting everything ready for the nut-cracking and hull-roasting. By the setting of the sun, our pupils and their parents were coming in from every direction. Every parent in the district was there. We set up many roasting fires, each one having its own large tub of water to cool the charred hull so we could sack it. We worked diligently from first dark until around ten. By this time we had practically every hickory nut cracked, with large pans of rich, sweet kernels ready for fruit and nut cakes, cookies, and Christmas candies. Some one hundred sacks of charred, cooled hulls were sacked and sewed up with bear grass, ready to be shipped when all the communities of our section were ready with theirs. We were very proud of our day's work. There were some thirty-three young men in the service from among the families that were gathered there that evening. Our sacks were spread out over the campus some distance way from the building for fear there might yet be some spark of fire left in some of the hulls.

We all went home feeling we had done a greatly needed project and prayed for peace to come. Alas! Train No. 85 sped by our little village, grabbed the mail sack from the stand, and threw off the sack containing the *Savannah Morning News*. There on the front page of that daily paper was the great news that the war had ended at 11 A.M., November 11, 1918. And the armistice had been signed by all nations concerned. No more battles or bloodshed. Peace! Peace! Peace! So our sacks of charred nut hulls lay there, never reaching their destinations. I had them put under the edge of the building to keep them out of the way until we got the word about what to do with them. Finally the message came. It was short, but oh how sweet: The Red Cross was proud to announce that since the treaty of peace was signed, the War Department would have no need for the carbon. We were free to dispose of our nut hulls as we saw fit—to some blacksmith for use in his shop or to anyone who wished a real hot fire without any blaze. By and by we used ours in our heater at school for our winter fuel.

Servicemen were now slowly trickling back home, but many never returned. The flu epidemic raged on. We tried as best we could to carry on our schoolwork. This was the saddest school I ever taught in all of my fifty years of teaching. Right there among my own people; practically every child in the school was my near kin. I had always been taught to do whatever my hands found to do, and I suppose I did the same here: I helped bury the dead. Springtime finally came, after a long, cold, wet winter, with death and serious illness knocking on every door in the school district. We finally took courage and planned for an old-time school closing and late evening supper, as everyone was busy trying to get late crops planted.

The program included every child in the school. They all seemed to enjoy their parts, and the whole community was appreciative of our efforts. The evening meal was abundant, delicious, and beautiful. The fellowship was kind and enjoyable, but very sad at many a turn, when we thought of the dead ones who were not with us anymore—how much we missed them and always would. Raybon School would never be the same again. Great community debating teams developed here, debating political questions, agricultural facts and fancies, timber-growing policies, and cattle-raising for profit and investment. Even the great fishing pleasures of the mighty Satilla were debated, and several fishing camps were developed after these heated discussions. All was at a standstill now. I was invited back to try the next term, with the hope of better health conditions to work under. I thanked them for their offer, but I made no promise. I knew I was pledged to return to O'Quinn School if it was at all possible for me to do so.

Many were the soldiers and sailors returning home every day now, trying to readjust to our peaceful way of life. My brother A. J. Mizell got home in February 1919, after seven years of service on the high seas. He was on convoy duty during the war, working as much as twenty hours out of the twenty-four, on lookout duty for submarines and other dangers of that day and time. He soon found work on the track maintenance force of the Atlantic Coastline railway and began to make his return to civilian life. He lived with us in Nahunta, but he missed the old homeplace farm, as I always missed it, and mourned for it even to this good day.

This story would not be complete if I did not tell you of some very "stinking" trouble I had at this school. I have often laughed about it; even today I can smell it. One cold morning in the early winter I could hardly call the roll for the strong offensive odor in the room. As soon as I had finished I arose from my desk and began to walk among the students to sniff out the culprit. In a flash, almost, I located the culprit, Oliver. I asked him if he had difficulty in securing his pelts the night before. He would not talk. I told him he would have to try to get rid of the odor, that we could not endure it in the classroom. I asked him to take off his coat. One of his sisters had told me that it was saturated with the musk of a polecat. All the rest of his clothes were fresh and clean that morning, and his mother had told him to wear another jacket, that she would bury his coat and smoke it with green pine tops and sulfur and get the odor out of it. But he slipped off wearing it unbeknown to her. I told him he could sit by the heater all day and hang his coat on the fence until home-going time. Then he could take it back to his mother to get rid of the odor. I knew that her method would get rid of the skunk odor. He would say nothing, neither would he budge one inch. The warmer the room got, the more overcoming the air became. So I finally told him if he would not go, I would have to take him out. I proceeded to take him to the door and down the steps. I took the coat off him and hung it on the fence. I had held him all this time. I took him back to the room and carried him to a seat near the heater. He was rather sullen all day, but we had a better-smelling room. Closing time came and home-going time, but Oliver did not get his coat off the fence. So when I came out to go to my boarding place, I saw it there, and I told the other teacher I would have to get the coat to the mother. Good winter coats did not come easy in that day and time on farms. So I secured a long, stout stick, put the coat on it, put it over my shoulder, and went to his home some three miles across the Indian swamp. The mother was so sorry it had happened and that Oliver had been so stubborn. When his father came in he just laughed about it and said that maybe he could keep Oliver home at nights now so he would not be going over to his uncle's every night to go hunting with him in his own private hunting hammock. If Oliver did go, maybe he would know better than to wear his best and newest winter school coat. He wanted to know of me what I wanted done about it. I laughed also and told him not a thing, but for Oliver to be to school the next day, and every day thereafter, smelling nice and clean and sweet as a schoolboy should. We all had a big laugh, even Oliver. Of course I had to stay all night.

I had gotten really interested in why Oliver would walk night after night some three miles to his uncle's to hunt, in place of going hunting in his father's nearby woods, where he would not have to walk that long way over and back in the wee small hours. I asked him why he was always so sure of a payoff for his many miles of walking. He said because the fur-bearing animals were always there waiting for him and his uncle Joe. I got so interested that I decided I would go one night right away to see Joe Lewis and get the secret for my own knowledge. Joe Lewis and Oliver's father, Riley Lewis, were my mother's first cousins, sons of my great-uncle William Lewis, who raised my aunt Ruth Purdom Craven and my uncle Thomas Purdom when they were left orphans in the 1860s. So I sent word to Cousin Joe by his children in school that I wanted to come spend the night with them if he could spare a night off from hunting. He sent me word when to come. So I went home with the children at the appointed time. That night after supper we got to talking about my episode with Oliver and his polecat-scented coat. They all had a big laugh. I laughed also, but I told them if they had been shut up in that well-heated schoolroom with some seventy-five children that cold winter morning and had that scent up their noses they would not have thought it so funny. It became a joke around school and the whole community, with folks telling their children that they had better mind me or I would give them the polecat-coat treatment. We discussed the hunting preserve at length and its abundance of fur-bearing animals year after year. Cousin Joe told me the story of it.

When his father gave him this land when he became age twenty-one, this lovely hammock was a big portion of the acreage. When Joe built the spacious log cabin for his bride-to-be, he wanted an avenue from the high road from Little

Snake Bridge to Ammons Ferry to come right up to his cabin door. But this dense hammock of tall yellow pine, hickory, nut trees, chinquapins, and many types of oak was between him and the high road. So he put in to hew a broad avenue to the high road all by himself. After many days of back-breaking work he had the avenue broad, wide, and straight from his front door to the high road. But when he had it finished, and the stumps dug out of the road bed, he had a little talk between himself and the hammock, telling it how it was a gift from his father to him and how he never intended to clear another foot of it. He said he talked on and on to the hammock, but it never said a word; it just stood there in all its luxuriant glory. He told it he would clear the open grassy land right up to it and try to make his living off those acres, and he reckoned he would keep it to remember what his father gave him on his twenty-first birthday. But when autumn came, the animal tracks were all over his new-cleared broad avenue. He thought, well, he would have plenty of neighbors, even if they were the smaller fur-bearing animals. His father let him take his favorite blue-speckled hound dog to keep him company even before he was married. He had his new home about ready and was working on the rails to fence his cleared acres. Every morning he would count the animal tracks. So he finally took off enough time from building his home and went hunting. His kill was soon as much as he could take care of until the wee small hours of morning, just giving himself time for a little napping before another hard day's work. Night after night the kill was abundant, and before the winter season was over, his furs were accumulated into a great heap to be floated down the Great Satilla to a faraway market. It was that way every night he hunted there. He often thought of what his father had said to him when he complained about his piece of land with that terrible hammock "right in the middle" of the acreage, while Riley's gift of land was so broad and open. His father had replied that it was the most valuable piece of land he had given to any of his children. And Joe had found it to be so. He owned some of the finest Sea Island cotton land in the basin of the Big Indian Swamp and the south basin of the Great Satilla, but without labor or expense, the dense hammock had brought greater returns in furs year by year than had the Sea Island cotton acres. Just the pleasure and excitement of the hunt on a bright winter night after a hard day's work in the crisp fall weather made it all worthwhile.

He never allowed the land to be burned. Every tree was a perfect nesting place for the young of all animals of the woods; the fork of every tree, a bin for the many nuts produced from the well-nourished trees of this rich hammock land. The trees provided cooling shade from the noonday sun for his large herd of cattle that usually stayed in the outback or the grassy meadows. They came to the

Great Satilla River to drink the pure, sweet water and then would return to the cool shade of the hammock to chew their cuds until milking time. Joe would come get them and drive them to their pens, separating them from the calves in another pen. After they had been milked the next morning, the herd would be turned out to go free together until the close of day. Anytime he needed a good load of cattle droppings for his garden crops or fruit trees, or his wife's beautiful flowers and herbs, Joe always knew right where to go to find an abundance of it. It was free from harmful weed or grass seeds, just pure droppings from the sweet grasses they had grazed day after day. He said that the hammock had had many visitors through the more than fifty years since he had cut the broad avenue through its heart. They just left the high road to drive up the beautiful broad avenue to enjoy the beauty of the hammock, especially in the glory of the fall months or in the lacy beauty of the springtime. Some, just to be free from the noonday sun in the hot summertime, probably expecting to find a magnificent castle at the avenue's end, would stay to enjoy the beauty, love, and abundance of the little log cabin home at the end of the broad avenue. And now I knew why Oliver walked all that way, night after night, to go hunting with his uncle Joe and his boys in their own private hunting hammock. Oliver grew up to make a fine man and became a beloved minister in the church of his youth, the Oak Grove Primitive Baptist Church.

Of the many lovely places I became devoted to down through the years, I think of this avenue most often. Especially in the crisp autumn days, I see in my mind's eye the beautiful hues of this hammock. I envision the green needles of the tall pines, the purple of the sweet gum and black gum, the yellow of the poplar and chinquapin, and the many reds and purples of the maples and oaks. I can smell the sweet odor of the myrtles, the pines, and the roots of the many lesser plants.

CHAPTER 13

At Goose Creek

I closed out Raybon School in April 1919. The very day I got home I had a letter from my school superintendent, Mr. B. D. Purcell, asking me to go to Goose Creek, a new school that had been built on the established highway between Odum and Madray Springs community. The gentleman who began the school had come down with the flu and was never able to return. I do not know whether he died or not. I wrote to Mr. Purcell that I would need a few days to get my wardrobe ready for summer work and that I would do my best to leave home on Friday night. I asked him to let the trustees know that I would arrive at Odum around eleven Saturday morning on the Southern train. I planned to leave home Friday night, to spend the night in Jesup, and to be in his office early Saturday morning to get my supplies and instructions. I also asked him to notify the trustees that I would work on Saturdays to make up the days I had lost by my late arrival. I had just gone as far as I could without some work on my clothes. Ladies clothes still had to be made from bottom to top. You could buy a woolen suit or coat for a price.

I had an enjoyable week with my father and mother. My mother and I got my clothes all ready by fresh laundering, mending, and darning and by making a few new garments. Father helped with the household tasks by shelling peas or beans, scraping new potatoes, stemming strawberries, churning cream, or plucking chickens, talking with us all the while and giving me great quantities of his knowledge of human nature, particularly of the children and adults with whom I would have to deal.

I was met at Odum by Mr. and Mrs. Silas Griffis and carried to their lovely home overrun with many sons and daughters. Cleo, Lottie, and Pearl would go to school to me. Lena and Gertie did not enter school, because they both were needed very much for the farmwork at home. Curtis and Arthur had been in the

Great War but were expected home at any time, as were many other boys of the community. Lula and Lizzie were married: Lula, to Mr. Bob Hilliard, who lived nearby; Lizzie, to Mr. Westberry, in Savannah. Walter, the oldest son, was married to the lovely Maggie Copeland. Marion and Lawrence were both busy with the farmwork. The Griffis family had a large farm and produced long-staple cotton for cash, and corn, sweet potatoes, peas, peanuts, and velvet beans as supply crops and for home consumption, as well as sugarcane, hogs, cattle, chickens, and a thriving truck patch. They made two trips to Brunswick each week to sell whatever vegetables were ready then—green onions, new Irish potatoes, garden peas, cabbage, fresh turnips, mustard, and snap beans. They also included butter, buttermilk, fresh eggs, hams, sausage, bacon, fryers on foot, fat hens, syrup, and lard. They always had the back of the car loaded down and left before day. They would have a good day's sale and be back home before nightfall. Their home was a busy place. I was there only temporarily, as they were expecting their two older sons any day and would need the room I was using. So Mr. Lester Hires and his good wife agreed for me to live with them. I enjoyed my three months' stay with them very much. They had only two children, Tifton, grade seven, and Myrtice, grade four. They were lovely children, well behaved, and smart in school. They worshipped at Red Hill Baptist Church. We attended Sunday school there each Sunday and preaching day once a month. Mr. and Mrs. Griffis were devout Wesleyan Methodists and worshipped at Bethlehem. They were anxious for me to attend church with them, but after I moved to Mr. Hires I had no way to get back on the Griffis's side of the creek on Sunday morning. I would go home with the Hires girls sometimes on Wednesday afternoons and go with them to prayer meeting on Wednesday night.

The first morning of school I had some fifty students in grades one through seven, all by myself. I would work the full eight hours just as hard as I could go, trying to get to everyone on time. I used my same plan of assigning work to be done by each class in each of their studies right after I had their recitation for the day in that subject. They would thereby know what books they needed to take home with them according to how much of their assignment they had prepared by the time their study period was up. Farmwork was in full swing, and all children helped their parents. The first morning of school we set the same schedule as I had at Union. Taking in at 7 A.M., cutting on recesses and noontime a wee bit and dismissing at 2:30 P.M. The children worked in the fields until nightfall. Their nights were so short, and they were so tired and growing fast; I did not expect much study at home, and I tried to arrange for most of the studying to be done during school each day. I always found this to be a mighty good plan. The trustees

[145]

liked the plan very much and commended me highly for the amount of work we covered during my three months there. I persuaded them to get a new set of readers all the way from first through seventh grade. That gave each child two readers and broadened their knowledge to some extent.

The schoolhouse was a nice new building, the same design as the one I had at Bamboo. The schoolyard was well shaded with native oak and pine. All the trees had been well pruned, and the grounds were cleared of underbrush. We had a good water pump and very good outdoor toilets. The furniture inside was better than usual. I had a good desk. The children all had desks or tables and chairs and a nice little room on one end of the porch for hanging their coats, wraps, hats, and shoes. In it was also a shelf for lunch pails. There was also a good heater, but we did not have to use that but very little at this time of year, starting the second week in April. We completed three months of school, with me teaching on several Saturdays as I had promised them.

My students were from the following families: Waters, Boyd, Odum, Sports, Griffis, Sapp, Murray, Hires, Withrow, and Hilliard. They were well-behaved, very bright, and smart students. No discipline problems arose at all while I was there. We worked hard and tried to overcome the breakdown of that school term. I tried to spend one night in the home of each of my patrons. I found them all to be honest, hard-working people, striving for an honest living. They all owned their own homes and did their own farmwork, as there were no tractors yet. There were very few cars; horses and mules provided power as well as the transportation on the farm. Everybody seemed to be well fed, well clothed, and comfortably sheltered with a few luxuries along the way. The Home Comfort stove still held sway in the kitchen. The Singer sewing machine was used to make the clothing for the family. The old-time organ made the music. Featherbeds, cotton mattresses, homemade quilts, and pillows all made beds fit for a king to sleep therein. We planned no entertainment or class trips, as it was the busy season on the farm. With so many of our boys trickling back from overseas, everyone wanted to see them and hear them talk. The trustees came to me and wanted me to help them plan an ingathering in honor of the returning boys, as there was no central church of the community. I suggested to them that we plan and old-time school-breaking for the last day of school, Friday, June 27, 1919.

I never shall forget that day and the joyous occasion. They were powerfully pleased and wanted to know what they could do to help. I told them to clean up an extra width of the schoolyard by trimming the scraggly lower branches of the large oaks and cutting the underbrush and briers. I suggested that they take the leftover lumber from their new building and build a nice, long, well-braced table in sections; then it could easily be put up and taken down and stored for use again and again for big school dinners or for other community functions. I had found this lumber on the front porch when I arrived and had my boys stack it carefully beneath the building off the ground and out of the weather. I said we should get the parents interested in the project and ask them to bring the finest dinner they had ever prepared, to come early to enjoy the exercises, and to help entertain the returning heroes of which we were all so proud. Last, but not least, I asked the trustees to permit me time from the regular lessons to prepare the program. There would be no night practice. Everyone was working hard in the fields, from when they got home until nightfall. I could not think of asking these young, growing children to come at night. Some would have to walk two to three miles to get there through the woods, over foot logs across Goose Creek, which was always deep and sometimes very swollen and turbulent.

I knew how to prepare a good program, but it took time, and I would not try it if they did not wish to provide the time. We had one more month of school. It would take me a week to plan a program that would include every child. I told them schoolwork must go on—classes finished, tests given, promotions made, and cards prepared for the children to receive the last day of school. I would do my best to get the program ready with the time after lunch until two o'clock each day for the last three weeks of school. That would only give us fourteen days, as we would have to present it on the fifteenth day. I assured them that we would work as hard preparing our program as we did our lessons, and I would go from one group to the other day by day during the two hours we were to work on the program. I would ask the children to put some extra study on their lines at home so we could put our whole time on presenting the program beautifully and entertainingly. I also told them I would be glad to prepare a display of written work from grades one through seven. We had saved it all for such a chance to display it. I would be glad to schedule matches in spelling, history, arithmetic, and geography for the morning program. They heartily agreed. I told them my seventh grade would have to be recognized and given their certificates so they could go on to high school the next year. If you will remember the Jesup School was named the Wayne County High School in 1919.

I asked the trustees to go among the patrons to see if they agreed with us and would be willing to make it a 100 percent success. I did not want it any other way. I wanted every child to be in the program, and I wanted all the patrons there to see and hear their children performing and also to help welcome our boys home.

The servicemen should be invited to the festivities. If I could have their names and addresses, the children and I would write to each returning veteran and invite him to our welcome home celebration for them and to our school-breaking.

I asked them to contact the patrons, and if they succeeded, to please let me know. If the trustees wanted to come the next Saturday to clean the grounds and prepare, the tables, I could let them have my three or four largest boys to help, as we were to have school the next Saturday. All went well, everyone wanted the school-breaking and the welcoming-home of our returned "service boys." The grounds were cleaned and prepared beautifully. The table was built, readied for quick assembly, and placed back beneath the schoolhouse until the day of the festivities. The children were more than delighted to know we were going to have a lovely program in honor of our returning heroes.

School went on as usual. Beginning at seven, we had classes until noontime. After lunch, until little recess, we had practice and study time for the program. From little recess until going-home time, we planned our behavior for the closing day, how we must act and do to make everyone welcome and proud because they had taken the time to spend the day at our school.

No more visiting for me. I had my schoolwork to plan and the program to assemble to suit the children and the audience. We would have a Mother Goose play for all of the younger children, "The Old Woman Who Lived in a Shoe"; some recitations, several little plays for the middle age groups, and one play for the older boys and girls; a welcome song and a farewell song; a medley of war songs, "Over There," "Au Revoir but Not Goodbye," "Katie, Beautiful Katie"; and a medley of patriotic songs, "America," "The Star-Spangled Banner," "O, Columbia! The Gem of the Ocean," "America the Beautiful." Our children could sing well. The seventh grade would have a nice little program of a recitation for each one, a farewell class song and then the talk by Mr. Purcell, who would present the seventh grade certificates. A farewell song by all the school would close the ceremony. I then would give out their report cards. I delayed giving the cards 'til the end so they would not have to keep up with them all day and probably lose or damage them in the melee of the long drawn-out day.

The day finally arrived. After roll call, I called the grades, beginning with first grade, to display their written work. We had made lovely folders to arrange it in, with their name, age, and grade in bold letters. So any patron could easily find his child's display. I was very proud of our showing, from grade one all the way through grade seven. Our costumes and props had been arranged in our cloakroom the day before. We had no stage or curtain. We had to dress in our little anteroom, walk out to perform, and walk back for the next group to appear. All the children were up at the front on benches with me so as to be ready when their time came. The audience had the main body of the schoolroom. They had used all our seats and windowsills and had brought in chairs and wagon seats.

By nine, we were ready. The tables were in place on the school grounds. We took a relief period, for the next two hours would be hard on all of us, difficult for us to give ourselves as good a showing as possible in our spelling, history, geography, and arithmetic matches, which were to come up next. By this time our schoolhouse and grounds were filled to overflowing. The oak grove across the way was filled with horses, wagons, buggies, and a few cars. We knew that well-filled baskets, boxes, pans, and pots were waiting to be spread at eleven, when our break for noontime came.

Our academic matches went off well. The first grade counted from one to a hundred by ones, twos, fives, and tens. The second and third grades said their addition tables from one to nine and their multiplication tables up to threes. The fourth and fifth grades said tables for both division and multiplication. Six and seventh grades showed their skill in handling common and decimal fractions and percentages, as well as in giving equivalent tables of common fractions, decimal fractions, and percentages. They all made a good showing.

In history, the first grade gave the name of their school, post office, railroad, and church. The second grade gave county information, right on up to the seventh grade, where they gave national and worldwide historical facts. Geography was conducted in like manner. Everyone seemed pleased that their children had gleaned so many facts about their community, county, state, nation, and world. We had an attentive audience throughout the whole matching program up to eleven o'clock, when I announced that we were in the habit of taking our lunch period at that time each day. Everyone was like us. They had eaten breakfast so early, they were ready for lunch. I invited all the servicemen to come and stand with me under the big oak tree by the pump. The children were to wash their hands well so as to be ready for lunch. The larger boys and girls helped their mothers spread the baskets if they were needed. The younger children played near me at the big oak tree. We had planned two hours for lunchtime so as to give everyone plenty of time to eat, talk, clean up, and be back right at one, when our closing exercises were to begin.

Soon the table was loaded until it almost groaned with the finest of home-cooked foods, chicken and dumpling, fried chicken, chicken and rice, and chicken and dressing; pan after pan of the finest fried fish, right out of Goose Creek, with corn dodgers; sugar-cured hams, meat loaf, roast beef. Salad, baked sweet potatoes, and all manner of fresh vegetables were before us. There were breads, cakes, pies, and puddings of every kind and description, and plenty of tea, coffee, and milk. You name it and it was there. Anything they thought these soldier boys would like to eat.

Three weeks earlier we had written special invitations to our returned servicemen, inviting them to our school-breaking and dinner in their honor. We asked them to be sure to come and to bring their families. You see some of them had no close kin in school. We had told them the time of day of the different events.

When lunch was all spread, a public invitation was given for everyone to draw nigh to the table, where Mr. Hires, our head trustee, would grace the table, after which everyone had all from the table that they wished to have. It was one of the happiest meals I ever remember attending in my whole life. The boys were happy to be home, and everyone was glad to see them. I don't know when I ever felt more proud of myself than I did at this time, standing in their midst and doing honor to those boys who had done so much for all of us. The meal was long and enjoyable. Two hours went by on the wings of the wind. There was food in abundance and some to spare.

As one o'clock drew nigh I had to gather my children and hustle them off to the toilets to relieve themselves. Our two most important hours of the day were in front of us, and we must all be at our peak. The gentlemen and ladies cleared the table, packed the baskets, and stowed them in their wagons, buggies, and cars. The nicely built tables were dismantled and stacked beneath the building for the next time they were needed. All the grounds were cleaned. There was not much trash.

By one o'clock I had the younger children all ready. First we had the welcome song and then the Mother Goose play. We had a big, big shoe drawn for the old woman's house, and all the children acted their parts well. Everyone seemed to enjoy it very much. The little ones were just darling. It was all so real to them. The audience was appreciative. The service boys had come in and were standing in a body at the back of the room. Next we had our comedy plays by our middle grades. They received a lot of laughs and hand-clapping for their interesting little plays. Now we had our two medleys. The veterans seemed to enjoy these very much and realized we were doing singing in their honor. Our upper grades then did their very nice play. They carried out their characters well and gave an almost perfect performance. I was well pleased with them, and I did not forget to tell them so, for they had worked long and hard on their play.

Now came the time of the seventh-grade graduation. Each member of the class gave their recitation and thanks to their parents, the trustees and the community in general for providing them with their first seven years of schooling. I then presented them to Mr. Purcell as being proficient in grammar school work and ready for their certificates. He made his address to each of them, the trustees, parents and community, and to me for having prepared them so well and thereby enabling them to pass with such a high rating in their state examination.

Last came our farewell song, as the whole school, classes first through seventh grades, stood in their correct places so proud and pretty. I handed the children their report cards. Then I thanked the trustees, the patrons, and the whole community for a wonderful three months among them, telling them how much I appreciated each of them and their children. I would always hold them as my dearest friends. Although I would be gone by four the next morning, I wanted them to come to my own home to see me. I did not forget to tell all our servicemen how proud we all were of them and how much we appreciated them for honoring us with their presence. After the farewell song, we had the benediction by our school superintendent. Thus ended our three-month school at Goose Creek.

Of course there were many personal farewells, gentle and rough hugs, from my smaller boys and little girls, and thank-yous from my many parents, trustees, and young servicemen. The children got their costumes, and by and by the crowd moved out and away. I propped the windows and put the schoolroom in order, locked the door, and gave the key to Mr. Hires. With my schoolwork completed, I was on my way to my boarding place to get my trunk locked, strapped, and into the wagon to be taken to Odum and checked for shipment, as I had to leave on an early Southern train at four o'clock Saturday morning for Jesup. I would turn in my final records to my superintendent and leave on the noon train for my home at Nahunta.

I often think of the many wonderful friends I made during those three months: Walter Griffis and his good wife, Maggie Copeland Griffis, who were my dear friends throughout their lives. Walter was Mr. Silas Griffis's oldest son, and they were a young married couple when I was at Goose Creek. My sweetest memory is of Mrs. Nellie Sports Walker Hopps, who was a young lady just out of school and starting out on a career as a public school teacher. She told me how much she would like to teach with me. I told her I would be so glad to have her go with me to O'Quinn that fall. She did, and we taught together until I married in 1920 and we were dear friends until she passed away.[1]

CHAPTER 14

Summer 1919

My sister Lula had finished out her school at Liberty and was home some time. She made plans to attend the summer quarter at the University of Georgia, trying to take the work she had missed in 1918 on account of the typhoid fever she had that summer, and was now on her way there. I was home with my mother and father.

My sister Mary Ellen, just two years my senior, was married to Mr. Benjamin Clifton Lang and lived at the old Lang homeplace, Wayside, in Camden County. She had two lovely children, Waldo Emerson Lang and Matilda Augusta Lang. I had hardly seen the darling little daughter. My sister had written and invited me to visit with her. She said to bring my dress material and patterns, and she would help me prepare my wardrobe for my next year's work. So I had made my plans accordingly. While in Jesup, on my way home, I bought several pieces of nice dress material, muslin, cambric cloth for underclothes, thread, laces, braid, tape, buttons, hooks, and eyes.

I was soon on my way to Camden County for this much needed sewing. I could not make my stay long, as my father and mother had begged me too hard to hurry back. In the two weeks, we got a lot of sewing done and several more dresses cut out and fitted for me to finish after I got home.

The two summer months went by quickly. Daddy, Mother, and I would gather the vegetables, milk the cows, work in the garden, cook, and talk all the time. I had so much to talk with them about, and they both had so much they wanted to tell me. Every time I would get a dress finished, being ready for buttonholes, hook eyes, and finger work of any kind, Mother would take it and finish it for me. And when we got it all complete and pressed, ready for packing in my trunk, Mother would say, "One dress nearer to being gone from us." Seems they neither one could bear to think of their baby child leaving them for several months again. You see, the transportation was still trains with poor connections, horses, buggies, and wagons. We enjoyed every minute of my visit, little knowing this would be our last summer on earth together, and the last summer I would ever spend in our newly built home. That was the way it turned out to be. It will be a summer that I will hold dear to my memory until the last day I live. September came too quickly and I was off to O'Quinn Community School.

O'Quinn School Revisited

Wednesday, August 27, 1919. I was on my way to O'Quinn School again, a year late fulfilling my promise to return to them. I left home on the Bogey, spent the night in Jesup, and arose early the next morning to go to our school superintendent's office for school supplies and final instructions and to sign my contract. My salary was to be one hundred dollars per month. There I was joined by Miss Nellie Sports, my young teacher friend from Goose Creek, who was to teach the second, third, and fourth grades, and Miss Nettie Dart, who was to teach the first grade—leaving me with the fifth, sixth, and seventh grades. We all left on the noonday train for Screven, where we were met by Mr. John Franklin with his new Ford car. We were to live at his home. He had bought the beautiful Joe Smith home, where Carrie Hires and I had lived in 1917–18. Mr. Smith had sold his home and highly developed farm for a handsome profit. He had gone to County Line community, investing heavily in a large acreage of undeveloped land (as he had planned) so he could broaden his acres for his ever-growing household of young boys. All three of us were to live there in the same room I had occupied before. Mrs. Franklin was a lovely lady with a large group of children, among them Leafy, Hilda, Emory, Bennett, Blanche, Perry, and Germaine. I do not remember the names of others.

We used Friday to get the schoolhouse cleaned and in order. We put the desks in place, examined the water well, checked the toilets, noted the condition of the heaters, and counted the windowpanes that were out. We had asked to use the church for first grade. There was no heater in the church; we would have to have that fixed so as to have heat in a few weeks. We had to see the church deacons about that. They agreed for us to use the church if we would bear the expense of installing the heater and building flue. They asked if we would have the children play, eat, get water, and be relieved on school grounds and stack all books, pencils, slates, and papers in boxes every Friday afternoon so they would not be in the way at Sunday school and church. We were to use our little chairs for seats and the church benches for tables. We would have to add another dozen chairs to the two dozen we had bought in 1917. We felt that thirty-six would be a safe count for our first grade.

The other two rooms in the school building were arranged on the same plan we had used two years before. We had plenty of help and had everything in order before the setting of the sun on that day. The bond issue we had talked of for a new school building had lain dormant all the time we were gone. Grade eight, which I had been so hopeful of establishing, seemed to be out of reach (although I had returned to them with my high school license and all qualifications for doing the work). But alas, the First World War had come and gone, and the terrible flu epidemic had taken a heavy toll. Wedding bells had rung incessantly since the return of our servicemen, so there was no prospect of having grade eight at O'Quinn until we raised up another grade. So my hopes were gone there, but I determined not to let my disappointment interfere with moving forward in our building plans.

Our schoolwork moved off quickly and efficiently, and we three teachers soon had a well-rounded program going. So many deaths in the past year left a sadness over the whole community. The gaiety of yesteryear seemed to be gone. Quite a few more North Georgia families had moved into the O'Quinn community, and that added to our pupil load and the need for better housing facilities. We had the land; I had secured that from Mr. Robert Todd in 1917–18. In early October I was on my way to A. E. Sharpe's to spend the night and attend a trustee meeting that had been called at his home, when I was overtaken by Emory Franklin, galloping toward me as fast as he could, waving a letter. I stopped. I was walking with the Sharpe children, some three miles east of the schoolhouse, and was almost there. Emory had walked from school to his home, some two miles south of the schoolhouse. When I had not come home with the children, they told their mother where I had gone for the night. She told Emory of the letter marked "important" and "special delivery" that had come for me. She told him to saddle the horse and try to overtake me. The letter was from my dear friend Mrs. Rosa T. Peek of Nahunta. She told me of the serious illness of my father and advised that I come home at once and that I let my sisters know, for she felt my father was sick unto death. I knew that Mrs. Rosa was a very stable woman and would not have written to me if it had not been a serious matter. Emory told me his father was in Jesup attending to some business and would not be home until after night-fall. I knew there was a fast train from Jesup, No. 83, about 6 P.M. if I could get there by then; otherwise I could not go before morning. So I asked him to go by our good friend and school patron Mr. Cleon Burkhalter and ask him would he come and take me to Jesup to try to catch that train. I told the Sharpe children what news I had received. I asked them to tell their father I was sorry I could not be at the meeting and to ask their sister, Miss Pauline—who had taught some before they moved from North Georgia—would she go and take Miss Sports's work and let Miss Sports do mine until I returned. With that attended to I began walking as fast as I could back to my boarding place. I packed a bag and dressed as quickly as I could, talking to Miss Sports and Miss Dart all the while of how to carry on the schoolwork, with regular classes and recesses, until my return. I did not know how long I would be gone.

Mr. Burkhalter was there in a short time, and we were on our way some fif-teen miles over sandy, rutted roads. Needless to say, the train had come and gone before I arrived. I tried to pay him, but he would not accept any fee at all. I told him I would just sit and wait until next train, and for him to not worry about me. So he returned home. I knew there was no train to Nahunta until about four the next morning. I had two sisters at Ludowici. I would have called them, but there was no phone near. There was a train that way about seven, No. 22, so I boarded it, not knowing if I could get to Ludowici to give them word. My sister Bessie was married to Mr. Roland Smith, a foreman for Hilton Dodge Lumber Co., and my sister Lula was a teacher at Jones Creek School nearby the lumber camp. When I got to Ludowici, about 3 A.M., I soon had someone on the way to meet me at the depot. I sent the letter I had received, along with a note from me telling my sis-ters that I would spend the night with Mrs. Laura Smith, Roland's mother, and for them to meet me the next morning, when we would all go home to Nahunta to see after Father. They met me at the depot as I asked them to, and we were soon on our way. This fast train was stopping only at Jesup, then at Nahunta.

When we arrived home before day on this chilly October morning, we found our father a very, very sick man and our mother so worried, weary, and worn that she could hardly go. We soon took over and had her to go to bed in another room. But there was not much rest for her, as she constantly wanted to know how Jasper (our father) was, and was there anything he needed. Dr. D. L. Moore was the fam-ily physician. He did not give us much hope. I remember my sister Bessie saying as we arrived at home, before we entered, "I smell death." I had hopes. I had left him just a few weeks before getting on so well. He very much hated for me to leave, telling me how he would miss me at the barn and in the garden, and all those good meals I had cooked for him and Mother all summer, and all that good sitting and talking on the porch after supper every evening. He knew us, but he was not able to laugh and talk anymore. I had never seen him like that. It just broke my heart. I put school teaching out of my head and tried to nurse him back to his usual self. He did not respond, but became weaker as the days went by.

My sister Lula had been at Jones Creek teaching ever since she had finished her summer quarter at the University of Georgia, but she was scheduled to teach at Farm Life, out from Screven, beginning in late October. When time came for her school to open, she felt she had to go. She was to be the principal, and the other teachers would be needing her, so she went on to her school. My sister Bessie thought she would have to return to her husband, so it would be just me at home with my mother and father. The doctor still gave us no encouragement. He said that my father was not responding to the medicine at all. There was not much medicine in those days for the aged to strengthen them along the way. We had three brothers in Savannah. I wrote them of Father's serious illness. I also wrote my sister Mary Ellen. With two small children there was not much she could do, but she could come.

Our two older brothers, Frank and Bob (R. J. Mizell), came from Savannah, and our sister Mary Ellen came with her two babies. Frank and Bob came and stayed about two or three days. They talked with the doctor, and he told them he did not see much hope, as our father had steadily grown weaker ever since he was taken so ill one night. He did not see how I was going to hold out to nurse him day and night. Mother had already given out. He did not feel she would be able to nurse him any more. So they talked among themselves and decided to get him to St. Joseph's Hospital in Savannah. The arrangements were made. My mother went home with Mary Ellen. My brother Jeff came and got the faithful horse, Old Bob, and the wagon. Mrs. Rosa was to milk the two cows and tend the chickens and pigs. I was to return to my school at O'Quinn. Father did not want to go. He said there was no better place for him to stay and pass away than home. But my brothers took him to Savannah.

I locked the house, put the key in my pocket, and left on Train No. 82 with them. I got off in Jesup. I went to the baggage car to tell my father good-bye. It was the last time I ever saw him alive. I told him good-bye, to hurry and get well, then come home, and I would meet him there. He said he would soon be back home but not well. I hired Meldrin Knight to take me to my school. We arrived at noontime. Miss Sharpe had been faithful, and the school had been kept going. All were glad to see me. I was planning to go to Savannah over the weekend to see my father, when the word came that he had passed away. It was October 29, 1919. We were all gathered in for the funeral. I secured Miss Pauline Sharpe again to relieve me until I could get back from my father's funeral.

We were all at home and then on to Smyrna Church, where my father was laid to rest next to his second-oldest daughter. Beautiful Sally had died with typhoid fever in her young womanhood in the early 1900s. Jeff kept Old Bob and the wagon. Mrs. Peek promised to attend the cow, pigs, and chickens until we could make permanent arrangements. We all had dinner at home after the funeral. No father was there to grace the table. The hour was sad, but we got through the meal somehow. We were sitting on the porch beside the dining room when our good friend Fred Knox came up with two fine-looking gentlemen and said he felt a bit indelicate in talking business at such a sad time. Mr. Knox had met the early morning train, No. 89, around 4:30 to take Father's body to the cemetery at Smyrna, some ten miles away, in time for an eleven o'clock funeral. The two men were looking for a location to establish their turpentine business, for a piece of land large enough for quarters for his workers, barnyards for his teams, a dwelling house for themselves, and a storehouse for supplies for his workers and teams. They were willing to pay a good price for our property, as the location suited them exactly. It was on the highway and railroad track where they could have a sidetrack installed to take away their products as they made them ready for market. Our brothers urged us to sell. The men offered us spot cash, more than double what we had in it.

We had five acres of land, a nice eight-room, two-story house, a good barn and outbuildings. All five acres were cleared and fenced. There was a well-fenced garden place, a young orchard of plum, pears, peaches, apples, quinces, and pecans, a vineyard all set and growing nicely. The yards were all laid off and set to our favorite flowers and shrubs. Mother's beautiful, delicate pink tea roses were at the kitchen door, the seven-sister roses were on the fence nearby, cape jasmine and sweet-shrub bushes grew by her bedroom window, and clematis, moon vine, and wisteria climbed on the porch. Crepe myrtle and althea shaded the pathway from the gate to the front door, and of course, spirea, hydrangea, and almond rose were in their rightful places. They were the last flowers and orchards my father and mother helped to set out.

I would have said no flatly to the offer, but my sister Lula told them the deal was so sudden, the time so short, and there was only about one hour until the train on which we were all to leave. She and I would return there the following Saturday morning to talk to them further if they cared for us to do that. So we all left, locking the door behind us. Our brothers were telling us to sell, that we now had no need for a home, there would be no one to take care of it, and that we could spend our holidays with them.

I did not care to sell at any price, but I could see that my sister Lula had given a listening ear to what my brothers had been saying. We returned to our schools, finished out the week, and returned to Nahunta the following Saturday. The deal was made to sell our entire holdings for the first price they offered. They were to let us claim one room to store all our things in until our school was out and we could make arrangements for them. I was never satisfied about the sale. I had worked too long and too hard paying for it to see it gone so soon.

November came and went. Then December and Christmas, with no home to go to, no Christmas planning for the homecoming of our brothers and sisters. We went to Savannah to spend part of our Christmas holiday with our brothers. But all the bright lights and merriment did not suffice for the hurry and bustle and cooking preparations, the gift wrapping, Christmas greenery, and tree decorating that I had known all my life. We soon moved on down the Seaboard line to Waverly, and out to our sister Mary Ellen's, where our mother was, and there we stayed until time to return to our schools the first of the year. We did not go to Nahunta at all; we only passed through on the train on our way back to work. This was the only Christmas I ever spent without a home.

Time passed at school. The trustees gave me the job of informing the people about how bonds worked and how money for the new building would come therefrom. They were anxious for a 100 percent approval when Election Day came. So now came the work of getting the community informed on the workings of a bond issue. I made my rounds among the patrons. Night after night I spent with this one, that one, and the other, explaining about the bond issue, about millage, taxation, and interest rates. It would take a long time to pay off the debt; some of the children receiving the benefit of the adequate facilities would be through school and be working men and women, helping to pay for the building where they went to school. All this was so they could understand better how much the bond issue would add to their tax bill each year until it was paid off. You see, this was all new to them. There had never been a bond issue in the county before for a school building. State workers came with plans for the building, for our needs now and for future expansion. I remember well how patiently Miss Elizabeth Holt, with the state school building program, would show and tell every minute detail from the blueprints we were using. The ordinary patron could not do much reading then; yet it was their property that was going to be bonded to get the money to do the work, so it was necessary for everyone to know what the plans were about before they were satisfied to vote more taxes upon themselves.

Beside all my private troubles and sorrows, I had never gone through such a terrible epidemic of big red measles and German measles (now they call it rubella); it seemed every day there would be another case. I had had the big red ones, but this time I came down with the German measles, and the back of my ears hurt ɛ badly, and my mastoids swelled so terribly, but I kept trying to work. The wint was long, cold, dark, and rainy. Sickness was everywhere. There was still son flu about. When Mrs. Franklin got so poorly that she could keep us no longer, ʋ moved to Mr. Burkhalter's. They had sickness also, but we managed to stay ɛ there and to help out when needed.

The work on the bond issue had gone forward. There had been no di agreement as to the site or placement of the building. The present site was almoɪ to the inch in the center of the district from east to west—Boggy Swamp, tʰ boundary to the east, where Liberty school district began; to the west to Reeɛ Creek, where Oak Ridge school district began; and to the south across Reeɛ Creek, where Farm Life school district began. Farm Life School had a fine ne building and ample acres of agricultural testing plots. Mr. Thompson, the pri cipal, had been hired to set up a new program in agricultural subjects for the boɪ and in home economics for the girls. Before he had hardly begun, he came dov with a severe case of typhoid fever, as did his head trustee, Mr. Walton Long, ar many more of his most prominent patrons. Mr. Mikell and Mr. Yeomans, who su vived, were so emaciated that it took them many months to get their strength bac Others were never able to maintain an active life again. It was a widespread eɪ demic.

Reddishville lay to the north of us, a small but well-to-do community aboɪ the headwaters of Dry and Reedy Creek down to the borderline of Satilla Creɛ near Odum. This community was made up mostly of Harris and Reddish fan lies. They had recently built themselves a brand-new schoolhouse by the san plan as Goose Creek and Bamboo and had furnished it well. They did it with the own private money and their own labor, with no taxation at all. Our state surv board said it looked like it could add to the north side of the O'Quinn comm nity more children less than three miles away. So we had a meeting and inviti the parents of these children. They came, 100 percent, and listened to the plan a new building for O'Quinn, to hold five teachers, adding grade eight for ne term, and going on up with the grades as the students' need called for them. Th had been sending their children away for special study in higher learning aft they finished grade seven. I know quite a few of the Harris, Reddish, and Mik young people went to Douglas, to Professors Little and Khul's Normal Colleɟ and Business Institute. After the meeting, they were asked to give their view, ar their spokesman said they would like to have some time to think over it private and report back to us. They asked for two weeks' time, which we graciousɪ granted them. They reported back as promised and said their building was wɛ built, furnished well, and completely paid for. They felt it would be adequate f many years to come. They did not feel it would be the right thing for them to burden themselves with an increased tax upon their property at this time and throw away what they had worked so hard to provide for their children. They commended us highly for what we were trying to do. They said that when they had students who would profit by attending our higher grades, should we get them established, they would be glad to pay us a fee for their attendance. They wished us much luck with our endeavor. So all ended well. Many of them worhipped at O'Quinn Baptist Church and at Liberty Wesleyan Methodist Church, as Reddishville had no church. So we lost no friends; neither did we gain any support.

I had covered the district of O'Quinn, explaining the bond issue, as requested of me by the trustees. Our program of letting the people know what they were entering into was over. Our superintendent, Mr. Purcell, had worked closely with us, and he felt we had done the job well. He and the trustees set the time to advertise the election for the bonds, and the vote was almost 100 percent (I wish I could say 100 percent, but you know there are usually some dissenters in anything you try to do). But the issue passed, with well over the two-thirds majority that was needed to carry the issue.

The school closed early in the springtime, as we had begun early in September and no time had been lost, although I had missed a great deal of time myself. The schooltime had rolled on, owing to the generous help of Miss Pauline Sharpe, Miss Nellie Sports, and Miss Nettie Dart.

My sister Lula and I had not been to our home since early November, and she thought we should go and see about our things. So in early February we returned to Nahunta and called on the people who had bought our home, the Bennett brothers of Millwood. When we arrived, the lady of the house told us that she had been so crowded for space that she did not have room to take care of the carpenters and other workers who were constructing the new turpentine village. So she had to use the room we had reserved for our things, and she had also used our bedding and furniture. She hoped we did not mind what she had to do.

We went to our good friends Mr. and Mrs. Bill Roberson, the ones from whom we had bought the land to build our home, to talk over our troubles. He told us at once of a Mr. Young, who had started a nice home in Nahunta and then decided he would like to sell it and return to the north whence he came. Mr. Roberson wanted us to see it. So they asked us to stay with them for lunch, and afterward he would take us to see it. I cared nothing about going. I wanted to go to school with my half of the money, but Lula was anxious to see it, so we went.

Mr. Young was working on the pantry when we arrived. The bathroom was not yet installed and neither was it painted. He stopped work, and the trading talk was begun. He asked exactly to the penny the amount of money we had in the bank. I did not care to trade, but my sister was anxious to do so. I thought surely the price included finishing the pantry, installing the bathroom, and painting the house. I never knew anything about Yankee chicanery until after that day. He never even hung the doors to the pantry shelves. Neither did he install the bathrooms or paint the building. He never did another lick, but he got all of our money—the very last penny we had—everything we had received for five acres of land and a well-built, two-story eight-room home with broad porches. Thus we became the owners of a small, unfinished five-room bungalow and a few small town lots. And all our money was gone.

Although that was fifty-three years ago, it is still not finished. The doors to the pantry have never been hung, and the bathroom plumbing has never been put in the home. Lula was home before I was, and she borrowed three hundred dollars jointly to finish the house, but it was only enough to paint. She told me I would have to repay the total loan, as she had the burden of having the moving done and also getting the bungalow finished. I told her that was my last loan. I had taught for more than seven years, and my nose had been to a grinding rock every month of my life, trying to buy land and build a home in town for our mother and father, when we had a good home on the farm, where they would have been much happier in their declining years. Now it was all over; I would try to work out that three-hundred-dollar note at 8 percent interest but would never put my name to another one. So the painting was done, and that ended the terrible deal.

I had spent what time I had trying to help our trustees get the bond issue ready. The children who were well enough wanted a school-breaking. It was the coldest March, just freezing weather right on. But we tried to have a nice program. More children came down with measles and rubella and were not able to participate. We did the best we could. All the patrons who were able came, and we had a very nice closing and a large seventh-grade graduation. I was so in hopes that the new school would be ready for them in the fall before they became scattered hither and yon. But I feared it would not be, and it was not. For it takes time to vote bonds, sell them, then have the building erected.

I have often thought of the wonderful class I left there in 1917–18. Jesse Purvis married Miss Carrie Hires, our primary teacher. He stood the test for mail carrier at Atkinson. He often told me about the way he answered the question on what value mail was to the community, and the care you should exert to see that every piece was placed in the right box. He used as his example the bulletins about the cattle ticks that had come through the mail to every box holder on our route. The county was rid of that terrible pest all because a mail carrier was faithful and careful enough to see that every box holder received a pamphlet. Jesse said he would always remember that incident when sorting and arranging his mail for delivery. Handle every piece with care whether it be first, second, third, or fourth class. He got the job and held top positions until his retirement.

Then I remember Clyde Burkhalter and his wonderful work with the J. C. Penney retirement home in Florida. In his application for the job as the superintendent there after his return from the First World War, he was asked to give some plan of cooperation within the community that the people could use to help themselves to better and richer living. He used our plan from O'Quinn School, in which everyone donated one good book to help build a reading library for the schoolchildren. He applied this plan to the elderly people he was to guide into a life of full enjoyment in their sunset years. The last I heard he was yet in that work.

There were the three Graham brothers, Frank, Ernest, and Ivy, the sons of Rev. and Mrs. Johnny Graham, who always became so thrilled every time they looked at a picture of one of the great steam plows on the wheat fields of the Dakotas. One would say, "I intend to be there one day and be driving one of these plows, thirty-two rows wide." They all three made it, but by then there were gasoline tractors, not quite so cumbersome to get around and over the wheat fields.

The five happy-go-lucky Crosby brothers chose to stay home and plow with mules until the mules were replaced by tractors. They became and still are some of the most highly respected men of the school and church community. Then there were the five sons of Mr. Joe and Mrs. Lois Smith, and Mr. Long, who all went away to Sea Island seeking work in the Cloister hotel after the boll weevil struck the great Sea Island cotton industry in the early 1920s. I still see Mr. Marvin Long's name connected with the Cloister as master of their fine stable of horses now more than fifty years gone by. Many of them became county officers, Jimmy Jones, Paul Sharpe, and Lovick Sharpe. Clyde Gates is an auto salesman. I could go on and on and name them from that wonderful group of young men, but there are other things that must be told.

All my girls married well and became wonderful wives and mothers to continue one of the finest communities in our county, state, and nation.

I closed out my work at O'Quinn the last of February 1920 and went to Red Hill community to finish that school, where the teacher, Miss Ruth Dean, had been taken ill with flu and was never able to return.

CHAPTER 16

Red Hill School

When I closed my school at O'Quinn I did not go home to Nahunta, as Lula was still teaching at Farm Life. She began her school much later than I had begun at O'Quinn, so she had quite a bit of time yet to teach. I did not care to stay there by myself. I had a note to pay at the Merchants and Farmers Bank in Jesup. I thought I had better be about trying to work it out. When I went to Jesup to turn in my records from O'Quinn School, on February 28, Mr. Purcell asked me would I go and finish out Red Hill School, a term of three months. Miss Ruth Dean, the principal, had a terrible case of the flu and had not been able to return after Christmas. I told him I would be glad to go and could be ready to start March 1. So he quickly put my supplies in a bundle and hastened me to the depot, where I caught the 11 A.M. Southern train to Redland, five miles up the road toward Odum. He hastily gave me a note to Mr. C. H. Ellis, the postmaster at Redland. In the note, Mr. Purcell asked Mr. Ellis to take me to Mr. Dan Hires, Mr. Purcell's father-in-law (Mr. Purcell had married Mr. Hires's oldest daughter, Miss Mollie Hires). He asked them to board me and to get the word around that school would open Monday morning, with me as the principal. Miss Dean was not yet able to go to work, and time was running out. Superintendent Purcell said he would get word to Miss Ruby Hill to be there Monday morning. She was the primary teacher who had helped Miss Dean.

Mr. Ellis did as he had been asked. Not only the postmaster at Redland, Mr. Ellis was also the superintendent of Redland Farms for the Coker Brothers of Hartsville, South Carolina, and had some twenty families working on his farm, which made up the majority of the students at Red Hill School. Of course, it did not take long to get word to the families that school would open Monday morning and that they were to have all their children there with lunch pails, books, slates, pencils, and paper. He also took me on to see Mr. Jim Poppell, one of the trustees, to ask him to get word to the people on that side of the creek. My students were Hireses, Poppells, Reddishes, Tyres, Chadwicks, Jacksons, Robersons, Rogerses, Herrins, Stricklands, and Elliotts. All were nice pupils, highly intelligent, well behaved, and well taken care of at home.

The older families owned their own farms. The families on the Redland farms were day laborers and received a good wage for that day and time. They grew truck and horticultural crops as well as cotton and supply crops for stock and home use. Like others where I had taught, this school building was sixty-five feet long and forty feet wide, with a heater in the center. The blackboard was ample. The furniture and equipment were adequate. The school grounds were spacious, and the water supply was good. There were two very good outdoor toilets. Many patrons were out for the first morning. The school day was shortened to 7 A.M. to 2:30 P.M. by cutting a few minutes each from noontime and the two recess periods, because the children were needed to work in the cotton fields. The trustees asked that I set my schedule to try to overcome the breakdown at midterm and to plan my work so all grades would be able to be promoted at the end of the term. In other words, they wanted a full day's teaching done every day school was in session. I told them that was my policy exactly, and we would be ready that very morning to begin work where Miss Dean had left off and go forward from there. We had our opening, set the schedule, and assigned grades. Miss Hill had first, second, and third. I had fourth, fifth, sixth, and seventh grades. As soon as the parents had their say, they invited us to come to see them, and admonished us to keep their children busy with their lessons. They all left.

We began to call our classes and to get our enrollment for each class. There were no books to order, as that had all been done by Miss Dean at the opening of term in fall. We had been there some two hours, so it was time for relief, and for Miss Hill and me to do a little private talking. Her father, Mr. Charley Hill, had brought her and her suitcases over in the buggy. I had told Mr. Hill we were to stay at the Dan Hires home. It seemed like a mighty fine place to stay, and the board was reasonable. He drove on over to Mr. Hires's to leave her grips there.

We rang the bell, and all the children came in quietly and chose their own seats by classes—my pupils facing me at the front of the schoolroom, and Miss Hill's facing her at the back of the schoolroom. We called classes and assigned work for the morrow. Some students did not seem to know what to do. I told them to do the assignment that I had just given them. They said, "Oh, but that is for tomorrow; we want to know what to do for today." I still insisted that they do the work I had just assigned them, while I was assigning work to the other three classes in rotation. They soon understood what I meant and liked the plan very much. That was my method for the whole fifty years I taught, and children thrived under it.

They would listen attentively and ask questions if there was anything they did not thoroughly understand. They would study quietly as I worked with the other three grades in rotation, then back to the same group where I had begun. I never permitted one group to interfere with the another group's time. Four groups, and I always did my best to get to each group every hour, fifteen minutes for each group. They had forty-five minutes to prepare work, and if they did not finish their assignment, they were to take the work home to finish. Most of them had to work until nightfall when they reached home, so I did not expect much night work. But I did expect studying to be done in school and usually got it. They soon learned that school was the best place to study, forty-five minutes of concentrated study six times per day. If they waited until after supper at night to do that much studying, they would be up until after midnight getting it done each day. If everyone was working as hard as they could at school, there was no time for misconduct, which made it so much easier on me to keep good order. If everyone was well behaved and happy, with well-prepared lessons, then all of the parents were happy also.

School moved off to a good start. Spring came, in all its glory, with beautiful sweet roadside and deep-woodsy flowers being brought to me by the children every morning. Our schoolroom was a bower of beauty, filled with the delicate odors of the different flowers—violets, buttercups, wild azaleas, ty ty, red maple, tupelo, magnolia, spirea, almond rose, daffodils, and narcissus. We visited among our students' parents and enjoyed knowing and talking with them, eating their good cooking, and sleeping in their downy-soft featherbeds with beautiful handmade quilts, the scent of the sweet shrub, clematis vine, and tea rose wafting through the open window on balmy night air. The cotton, corn, potatoes, melons, and garden crops were growing well, as the whippoorwill told the news far and wide that springtime had come to Dixieland. I had worked so hard all winter over at O'Quinn getting the bond issue ready; I was very happy to find my workload much easier here. No outside work was expected or planned; I was just to do a good job of classroom activities.

We were only a mile away from the railroad station and could easily walk over on Friday afternoon or Saturday morning and ride one of the four daily trains to or from Jesup; they made connections for places we needed to go. I had never had it so convenient before.

I spent one weekend with Miss Hill. Her folks came for her every weekend unless she told them otherwise, and she returned on Monday morning. I told her I preferred to return on Sunday afternoon so as to have all my plans and supplies at hand and in order come Monday.

Preparing for the School I Never Taught

I reached home at a little after noon Saturday, May 22, 1920, from Jesup. I gave the local drayman the checks to my well-laden suitcase and my locked and roped trunk. I hurried on uptown to the local grocery store, where I bought some sugar, cornflakes, a loaf of bread, a pound of butter, a quart of milk, a dozen eggs, five pounds of grits, some peanut butter, and jelly. I went quickly, as I saw the drayman had arrived at my home. I had him put the trunk and suitcase in my bedroom. I gave him his price of twenty-five cents for the trunk and ten cents for the grip and thanked him. I told him I would be needing him again in a few weeks to take my luggage back to the depot when I would be leaving to start summer school. He said to just let him know the date and the hour, and he would be there.

I prepared myself a light lunch of cornflakes, milk, and peanut butter and jelly sandwiches. I had barely finished eating when I heard a knock at the front porch; there were the three trustees from Hickox. I asked them to be seated on the front porch and said I would be with them in a few minutes.

We wasted no time, but got right into our plans for the modern course of study for grade eight in their program for the coming fall. I could not tell which of the three, Mr. Ivy Dowling, Mr. Levi Herrin, or Mr. Allen Courson, was the most enthusiastic on the subject. They had waited for this hour for so long. We began on the time schedule first. School was to open at 8:00 A.M. September 6. There would be two hours of study and recitation followed by a thirty-minute recess for relief and play. Then an hour and a half of study and recitation. Next, a one-hour lunch and play period (everyone was to stay at school during the noontime). The period from 1:00 P.M. to 2:30 P.M. was for study and recitation, followed by a fifteen-minute relief period. The period from 2:45 P.M. to 3:45 P.M. was for study and recitation; it was followed by a fifteen-minute period to prepare for home going. School was to close promptly at 4:00 P.M. for all grades. All teachers were to be on duty with their children for eight full hours. Work would be divided as follows:

Grade 1: teacher following the program of study and some music if possible.

Grades 2 and 3: teacher following the program of study.

Grades 4 and 5: teacher following the program of study.

Grades 6 and 7: teacher following the program of study

Grade 8: teacher and principal (myself) to coordinate all phases of the work—time element, course of study, community involvement, rules and regulations of conduct, plans for expansion as needed.

We took these topics one at a time; the trustees discussed them at length and my position on each one. We settled the time element first, keeping to the schedule set by law and what the community had been use to for many years, that is, eight hours per day, three breaks per day amounting to one and three-quarter hours, which left six and one-quarter hours for study and recitation. This seemed satisfactory to all concerned. Every teacher would know to plan their work accordingly. I especially asked that the first grade be permitted five relief periods per day, and the second and third grades, four relief periods per day. This they agreed to after I told them how it would eliminate so much confusion in children being excused continually. Next we discussed public assemblage or chapel for the whole school to come together. I asked for one hour at least twice per week, on Tuesday and Friday. Responsibility would revolve to each teacher for the whole week, beginning with me and down to the first-grade teacher, then around again. Every teacher would develop a worthwhile and enjoyable program. All school announcements would be made at this time in an orderly and understandable way, so all students would know the necessary workings of the school.

When we came to the rules and regulations of conduct, I told them I had but one rule and that was to do right at all times, in all places, and to all people; and I would expect every teacher to do her best to make fine, trustworthy ladies of the girls, and honest, honorable gentlemen of the boys who came under their care. They should always remember that each day is sufficient for the evil thereof and say to themselves and their children each morning, "This is the day the Lord has made. We will rejoice and be glad in it" (Psalms 118:24). I never committed myself to specific punishment before trouble ever happened, for ofttimes to do so caused trouble to happen to try you out, to see if you would inflict the penalty you had declared. I never committed myself but dealt with each situation as it arose and got rid of it then and there.

They all laughed at how I had had handled two situations at Burnt Bay when I taught there, not yet sixteen years old, and with no experience except my mother wit. When Mr. Miller Crews had come to school at midmorning and sat down with a gun across his lap by the only door and told me he was a trustee of the school and had come to hear his two daughters read and spell, I quickly told him, "Yes, sir!" and called them up to my table.

Then there was the gentleman who came to the school so very angry. He showed me an indecent letter that had been given to his daughter by someone she knew, but she would not say who. I asked him to let me see the letter. I read it over. Every child enrolled in the school was there that day. Everybody had heard that the man was coming and what all he was going to do to me if I did not do something about the one who was doing the filthy writing to his daughter.

After I had finished reading the letter, I checked the pupils again to see surely if everyone I had enrolled was there that morning, and they were. I stepped to the blackboard and wrote the following little jingle: "Kind hearts are the gardens, / Kind thoughts are the roots, / Kind words are the blossoms, / Kind deeds are the fruits." I asked everyone in the schoolroom to copy it, please, and to sign it. The children asked did I mean the daughter and her father too? And I said, "Aren't they in the room?" So everyone wrote it. Then I collected the papers and laid them down in a row; I put the letter down next to them. I asked the gentleman to come look them over and pick out the one that looked like the letter and show it to me. He would never say.

He asked me to select the correct one, and I told him I was no expert at comparing handwriting, and I would not dare do it. But I told them that there were people licensed to do that kind of work, just like I was licensed to teach school. I had heard my father talk about the superior court judge having to hire one in some forgery case in the big court. They were quite expensive to hire, as they were professional people, and their fees were in line with those of doctors and lawyers. I did not have that kind of money. I offered him the papers. He told me no, and said for me to keep them until he could make further arrangements.

I started to compile them, when one of my larger girls asked might they all see the writings. I told them I had no objections if the gentleman did not. He said, "Sure, let them see them. Maybe they could tell whose writing the letter looked alike." They all walked by and looked, but all shook their heads, indicating they could not tell. Then I gathered them up and put them in my tote bag and told him I would put them in my trunk under lock and key until he called for them. So he got in his buggy and left, and we all went back to work as usual.

No more was said at school about it. On the way home that afternoon, one of the girls said the same thing had happened the year before, only the teacher did not have the father and daughter write the copy from the board. There was no similar writing then like there was this time. I did not question her there, as I had noted this identical writing also, but I replied that it would not have been nice for me to say "everyone in the building" and not include them. I never did hear any more about the matter, and there never did appear another obscene letter. The gentleman never did call for the papers, and I kept them locked in the bottom of my trunk until after school was closed and I had returned to my own home.

I told the trustees that I always treated every boy and girl like a perfect lady and gentleman and expected them to respond likewise. I never punished in the dark. All investigations were in the open, before everyone. The corrections were made as the case and evidence demanded, and the punishment was administered. Every child knew why they were punished, and I was always glad for the parents to know and would talk with them concerning the same if they cared to investigate the matter. I had no set time for punishment. It always took time away from class study and recitation. It was hard-earned tax money being thus used, and I did not feel that children should be permitted day after day to so deprive other students of their right and time to study and recite. If they did not care to follow the regulations of the school, they had no business there. I had never turned my back on one yet, in my eight years of teaching, but I had to tell several that if they were not coming there to study and learn, we had no need for them. We were operating a school of joy, pleasure, learning, and happiness—not a reformatory and place of punishment.

I did my best to keep everything pleasant and happy from early morning until the last bell sounded in the evening. And by the way, I always rang my own bells to announce the periods of the day, and I tried to be on the minute. Time was not to be trifled with. I had taught at one school where I never had to mention the word "punishment"; that was Union. You could hear the children coming of a morning, singing in their clear, sweet young voices, and you could hear the same as they wound their way home after a happy, merry day at school. That was one reason why I was so anxious for music to be taught in the school from grades one through eight, as a singing school is a happy school. I would expect every teacher to control her own room and to keep order and decency at all times with her children. But if she needed help, I always stood ready to help her. Every time a teacher has to call for help, it weakens her own powers of discipline.

We came to the community involvement next. I told them I liked public programs when we had something worthwhile to offer the public. I asked them had there ever been a "thank you" program for the donors to the school building fund, and they said no. I told them I felt that it should be done, and I thought that by Christmas we should have things in line enough to be able to present a worthwhile program. We would have our most-advanced English classes write invitations to every donor in their very best hand. Whether the gift was five cents or five thousand, they would all be welcome. I had a program, using lines from the Bible that told the beautiful Christmas story, that would have the whole school sing the correct song for the lines given. It could be prepared with very little time and practice and would make a lovely Christmas celebration. I would involve every child in the school, and we would have the schoolhouse all decorated up for Christmas, tree and all. Refreshments, such as cookies and Christmas punch, could be served. If they were expecting any more donors, the funds could be applied to getting a piano for the auditorium, and strong, sturdy oak chairs for stage—not folding chairs like they had planned. The school children and patrons might be able to contribute to this fund through a Halloween carnival, where everyone could have an evening of fun as well as help pay for the piano.

Here they stopped and wanted to know my religious connection. I told them that they and everyone knew my father, the Reverend J. P. Mizell, and had heard him preach and knew the faith he lived by. I was raised into that same faith. I was taught to respect all faiths, that others had as much right to their religion as I had to mine, and I had taught all faiths and orders and had never had any trouble with anyone about their beliefs. The King James Version of the Bible was my guideline to my life, and I never used any other religious book, not even a Bible story book. I read from the Bible every day and offered a prayer in my humble way for all the children to hear. I never questioned them on their beliefs. I did my best to live mine before them day by day and it was my every prayer that I would never do, say, act, or think anything that was not a help or an ornament to their young, growing minds.

While talking about community involvement, we came on down to close of year, and I said I felt that the public should know what we were about and how far along we had gotten. If we strove for a four-year high school, it would be four years before we had a graduation class, and before four years rolled around, the public would surely desire a report on how much good their donations were doing. We could arrange to make this report by showing off the eighth grade, telling how many we had begun with in September, and then showing how many we had held to completion in June by having them seated on the stage. We could have all the seventh-grade graduates seated in the front row and have the evening speaker speak to them about the completion of their grammar-grade work. Then at the close of the speech, they could come forward, get their certificates from me, pass up to the stage, and take the empty chairs waiting for them. The whole community would see the potential of the high school building and would realize the pace they would have to set themselves to make their "dream school" a reality.

I also mentioned the opportunity that the 4-H club offered their sons and daughters. The county 4-H workers were paid with our own tax money, and we were cheating ourselves and our students if we did not use them to the limit. Their teachings were the latest in scientific knowledge. Their meetings were orderly and gave the best training in parliamentary procedure, public speaking, voting procedures, and record keeping. It was the largest youth organization in the world, a great source of energy, adventure, and learning. The organization allowed boys and girls to communicate with others of their own age in other parts of the county, state, and nation. There was even a worldwide exchange of ideas.

Here they stopped me and wanted to know how I stood on women voting. I told them that I had never sought the vote, but now that it was coming to us as a gift and privilege, it was not only our right to vote but our bounden duty to do so. I had promised my father that I would always remember to cast my ballot. For the more than fifty years since suffrage was given to us, I have never missed an election. I feel that I am well qualified to vote, as I have made a close study of local, county, state, and national governments and their people. I feel like I know in part what is best for us. As we proceeded further in community involvement, I brought up the subject of fuel for heating the building. I told them it would take quite a large amount of wood to keep the building well heated, with six large wood-burning upright heaters going all day long. Because children can easily get sick sitting still in a damp, chilly schoolroom, I have always been noted for keeping warm, comfortable schoolrooms and for having perfect attendance on rainy days. These were "special days," when we ate in the schoolroom picnic-style, sharing our food and playing indoor games. It almost turned out to be a party at the noon-day play period. You can build your average up quickly during a cold, wet winter if you plan for and have a 100 percent attendance on every bad rainy day. Mothers are glad for their children to be in school if they know they are warm, dry, happy, and having their lessons as usual. The trustees told me that getting the wood would be an easy job, as the P. S. Knox Lumber Co. would give us all the waste slabs we desired. So I asked them to get a good crosscut saw and a good five-pound ax, and whoever was the "boy of the day" to see after our needs would prepare the wood for the day. I also asked for a shovel, hoe, and rake to help keep our campus in order. Here, we talked about the care of building. There were no janitors in that day and time; I had to do my own fire-building and room-cleaning. I asked for one good mop for each room and for a cupboard to be built in back of the room in which to store them as well as cleaning cloths, soap powder, and other cleaning supplies.

Next we tackled the water supply. They said they had an excellent hand pump. I asked them about the drinking facilities, and they said no provision had been made. I asked them to make a strong, easily carried rack to hold thirty-five tin cups on hangers for each teacher and to let each teacher be responsible for their care and to see that her children were well watered. We were past the dip gourd and cypress copper-bound buckets, but we were a far cry from flowing water and electricity. We still needed to have water several times a day.

Then we came to the toilet facilities. They said they had planned for two large pit toilets, but they had not gotten that done yet. I asked them to make it four separate ones. One large building with low seats and small openings for small boys, grades one through three, and then one large-sized building for larger-sized boys, accordingly, the same plan for girls. We often found that toilet facilities were a bottleneck when we were trying to get all the children relieved in the space of fifteen minutes. The more children you brought together, the more attention you had to pay to such matters as drinking water, toilet facilities, and heat and air.

Next I mentioned to them a lunch shelf, a coat and shoe rack, and a large cupboard for supplies in the back of each room so the teacher's desk would not have to be always loaded down with the material she would bring in from day to day. Above all, there should be at least one strong worktable for the back of each room; two if possible, so they would have a large, flat work surface. Also there was a need for well-braced shelves under the windows on each side of the auditorium on which to place reading and reference books. We hoped that some day we would have enough books to have a good library and a librarian. You know, a well-read child is a knowing child, and when a child is reading a good book, he or she is always in good company. The donation of good books would be a total community involvement activity.

At last we came to the course of study. For the first seven grades, we would use the state-adopted texts, and I said I would like to see more readers added as rapidly as we could, so as to broaden the students' vision in many fields of study. They should be accomplished in reading, spelling, writing, arithmetic, conversation, communication, pronunciation, enunciation of their English, and be well-read in health, history, and geography from first grade through seventh. We must do our best to get some music in at least one day per week for all students.

We were to build an eighth grade as the cornerstone of a well-founded rural high school. They asked me to state my views on the matter, and they would make their points after they had heard me all the way through. I told them there were so many worthwhile subjects to teach boys and girls that age that it had been hard for me to decide. I had come to the following plan:

1. Georgia history and government.

2. Arithmetic: A general review of common and decimal fractions, measurements, percentage, banking, accounting, tables of comparison of decimals, common fractions, percentage, and all measures in estimates.

3. Health: Both personal and community. A strong course here, as the great flu epidemic was still strong in people's minds, as were the terrible scourge of malaria fever, typhoid fever, hookworms, and the dreaded pellagra. Folks could remember the Red Cross sending nurses to Wayne County to try to take care of the sick and the dying, and men taking hold and trying to nurse the sick as well as women. So all felt the great need there.

4. General Science: A panorama of scientific knowledge in many fields.

5. English: Including spelling, writing, composition, pronunciation, conversation, public speaking, grammar, parsing, diagramming, analyzing, and rhetoric.

6. Reading: Biography, science, dramatic adventure, and other subjects.

7. Music at least once a week.

I told them I thought this would make up a full year of exciting and happy study and lay a firm foundation for higher learning in grade nine. This would be an exploratory course, introducing them to higher learning and the great avenues of advanced study waiting for them if they cared to proceed. The trustees agreed with it all; only they asked that spelling be set up as a study all by itself, every day throughout the year, to overcome a weakness in spelling among their children. I told them that suited me completely. I asked if they had a *Webster's Unabridged Dictionary*. If not, I wanted one to be bought and placed on my worktable at the back of the room before the first day of school. I assured them the dictionary would be used many times every day to look up pronunciation, syllabication, definitions, formation, or root words. I would like to see good maps to suit the grades from first through eighth. I would need a Georgia map and a Wayne County map. The Georgia map was to contain a historical map showing the Indian Cessions; a political map showing counties, congressional districts, and state senatorial districts; and a geodetic map. They were pleased with the other courses chosen. I told them that I was well prepared academically to teach all the courses chosen, that I planned to go to the full summer quarter at the University of Georgia that summer to do further study in child growth and development, high school development, and school administration. It was the best course of study offered. I expected to do further study in some academic subject that could be fitted in the course of study I had chosen.

Our next topic was grading, reporting to parents, study guides, daily assignments, tests, and length of time for each reporting period. Here they asked me to give my ideas for this phase of the schoolwork. I went at it as follows:

1. Each teacher will know what she is going to try to teach her group for the year. She should lay her plans accordingly, giving herself time to do each task efficiently.

2. Inform the children and their parents what the children are supposed to master over each period of study. In other words, provide a study guide for that period. Plan your work accordingly.

3. Tell the students what work you expect them to know and when they are to hand it in. Spread the work out over the period, take it up on time, and add it together to make up that period's grade.

4. File the work in routine form so parents can see whence your grades for their children came and why you gave those grades. With this method there will never be any quibbling that you graded unfairly. All your grades will be right there before the parents' eyes day by day for the whole period.

5. I asked for six-week periods, twenty-nine days to teach, one for testing. We were still having to grade, record, and file at night then, although I begged for time during the day to do it. (That came after I had made my fifty years of working night and day.)

They heartily agreed with my plan for six-week periods and my plan for proof of every grade for every child.

The sun was getting low behind the treetops by now. The trustees seemed to be happy with my viewpoints. They said they wished they had me helping them plan their building program. I told them maybe I would be there in their expansion if we could make our program attractive enough to bring in Wainwright, Knox, Pinebloom, and Buffalo. Wayne County's part of Tiger Bay and Burnt Bay had already asked to come in. I told them that in a few weeks I would be on my way to my summer quarter of study, and I hoped we could meet at their convenience upon my return in August. I told them that I intended to go to Camden County Tuesday morning to my sister Mary Ellen to see my mother and visit with her and my sister as long as I could. Mary Ellen was to help me sew my summer wardrobe. I would come back home only long enough to pack my trunk and grips for my summer of work at the university. I would plan to meet with them upon my return. Mr. Purcell had stated to me that he wished to meet with all of us when I returned.

I told them that I hoped to be as well favored in their community as my oldest sister, Julia, who had married Mr. Frank Highsmith. They had reared a lovely family and had been the trustees' beloved friends and neighbors until she passed away in 1915. My third-oldest brother, Jeff Mizell, had surveyed land, checked timber for cutting, and watched the treatment of dozens of mighty ox teams for the P. S. Knox Lumber Co. My youngest brother, Jerry Mizell, had scaled the logs for perfect measurement for the men who sold their own timber to the same company. If I could do my work for the trustees as well as my family had, I would be more than happy. Each one of the trustees assured me that I would, and that concluded our school board meeting, Saturday May 22, 1920.

I went to my sister's as planned. Mother had been there since my father passed away. I had not been with her since Christmas. She was failing fast and missed my father so very much. We were so happy to be together, but we missed Father and missed being home. We soon got on with my sewing. Of course the daily homemaking tasks went forward, cooking, milking, churning, tending the baby, that darling daughter, Miss Matilda Augusta Lang, named for her two grandmothers. I had hardly seen her since she was born in July 1918. There were bees to rob and honey to squeeze and tomatoes, peaches, pears, and other fruits and vegetables to can. We did all this and sewed some every day. In the course of two weeks I had an ample supply of undergarments, gowns, panties, petticoats, brassieres, and slips. All sewed, nicely finished, pressed, ready for wearing, and packed in my grip. We had also made a lovely brown georgette dress and brown taffeta slip as well as a rose and blue slip, but I never cared for them and did not use them. We made two cool batiste dresses and several pretty dress blouses to go with the black coat suit I would travel in and wear on the cool days we sometimes had in Athens after a summer storm. My Indian Head dress had been made up in a plain, well-fitted style, with an embroidered monogram. All my other clothes had been checked for needed repairs, cleaned, laundered, and packed in my grips and bundles. Everything was finished but one piece of exquisite dress material. My sister did not think I had a pattern, a hat, or shoes that would match its lovely texture, and she would not venture to sew it until we had the necessary accessories. So it was wrapped in tissue paper and carefully packed away with my finished garments to wait for another sewing time. My sister said I had enough, and with all the lovely spring clothes I had made before I left Red Hill, I suppose I did.

My sister, Mother, and I, with the two small children, Waldo and Matilda, did some visiting among Mary Ellen's neighbors. We went to Incachee Plantation. There we visited with the aged Dr. Atkinson, his second wife, Mrs. Rosa King Atkinson, and his daughter Miss Mary Atkinson, who was not married at the time (later she married a Mr. Russell). The doctor had been my mother's physician some forty years. We enjoyed this visit immensely. Then we visited the Jim Strickland family. My mother had helped nurse him through a terrible siege of typhoid fever when he was a small lad, and now here he was a fine-looking man with a lovely family. He had always loved my mother dearly, and she was so glad to see him doing well on his farm with his sons, daughters, and good wife. Another afternoon we went to visit the General Strickland family. His wife, Mamie Lewis Strickland, was the daughter of one of Mother's favorite cousins, Charles Lewis, and his wife Nancy Kelly Lewis. We enjoyed that visit very much. We visited quite a number of the Kelly boys, whose mother was Charity Willis Kelly, another of Mother's favorite cousins, the daughter of Uncle Jim Willis and Gatsy Lewis Willis. My mother and aunt Margaret Purdom were reared in the Willis home after they became orphans.

As we were visiting around and about each afternoon, we would stop and chitchat with my sister's Negro friends and neighbors. Remember there were more Negroes in Camden County than there were whites. My sister had some fine Negro neighbors. One we visited with was Uncle London, who was an aged man who had been Dr. Atkinson's orderly throughout the four years of the terrible struggle of the War between the States. My mother had always heard that Uncle London had seen her father, Archibald Purdom, fall mortally wounded in the first battle of Manassas. So she was glad of the opportunity to talk with him about the matter and asked him did her father suffer much. He said no, it was so quick he did not know what hit him, and the angels were right there to receive him. He was

[177]

wrapped in an army blanket, carried to Arlington Cemetery, and buried in one large grave with hundreds and hundreds of others. He finally said he knew why Miss Ellie was so good to all of his people; she was "Marse Archie's grand-daughter." The Negroes always had great respect for the Purdom men. They had never been known to buy or sell a one of their black people. They had all inherited them somewhere back down the line and were trying as best they could to take care of, educate, train, and fit them for life in a civilized society. They taught them honest work and honest relationships with all those around them, and fitted them with a trade whereby they could earn a living, both men and women. The Purdom men were loved and respected by the Negro people for miles and miles around. They had never been known to whip a Negro, but they seemed to have industrious, happy, obedient, and well-behaved black people on their plantations.

One afternoon we stopped by to visit with Maum Justine, the Queen of the Negro community. She was the midwife to both black and white and was highly respected wherever she was called upon to go. My mother told her of Black Sarah, a field hand who had nursed her from her bosom when grandmother Eliza Lewis Purdom was sick with childbed fever and unable to nurse my mother when she was born. Black Sarah had a baby who was born the same night. She was brought to Grandmother's room, and a cot and cradle were placed nearby for her and her baby. She gave her child one breast and my mother the other one, and she lived there until Mother could begin to take food. Although she was a field hand, she soon learned the ways of a house servant and became indispensable as the head nurse of the plantation. Everyone, both black and white, loved her, but best of all, my mother, to whom she had given the strength of her life to raise. My mother told Maum Justine that neither she nor her children could ever do enough for the Negro race to repay that debt. We stopped by one afternoon to visit with Plucker, one of the younger Negroes. He told my mother what a wonderful daughter she had, and how Mary Ellen had saved his life when he sliced his leg with a broadax as he was hewing crossties and almost severed the large artery in his leg. She took off her apron and made a tourniquet for his leg. She had his father get in the back-seat of her car and hold his leg straight up. She took her two babies, and away she drove as fast as she could to the doctor with him. There his leg was repaired, and he was a well man. Otherwise he would be "crossed over Jordan." He said he and his would sing her praises forever more.

We had a wonderful two weeks sewing, working, and visiting, but time was flying. My sister Lula was to be home the next week from her duties with the Puckett children in Jesup, and I had to meet her at home, as we would have only a few days to make ourselves ready for our journey to Athens. So I finished packing my clothes, all the sewing accessories I had not used, and the exquisite piece of material wrapped in tissue paper so no harm would come to it until we had time to make it into a beautiful garment. We had our last Sunday together, and, my, what a good time we had. My last long visit with my mother upon this earth.

Monday morning my sister began gathering things together for me to take home: fresh vegetables, jars of fresh butter and buttermilk, two quarts of sweet milk, some honey in the comb, pieces of bacon and cured ham, a dozen eggs, fresh sweet corn meal, and some hominy grits. I had four large baskets and boxes full of goodies, and she had slipped in a few jars of canned fruit, some jellies and jams, and enough fresh black berries for a pie or morning fruit for breakfast. As soon as an early noonday meal was over, I was loaded up and transported the nine miles to Atkinson station to catch the four o'clock train to take me across the Big Satilla River and some ten miles to Nahunta. My brother-in-law, Benjamin C. Lang, drove his car to bring me to the station and helped me on the train with all my bundles, baskets, boxes, and heavily packed suitcase. I had to tell my mother, my sister, and the two babies good-bye. I was soon home. The porter and conductor helped me off the train with my bundles. They set them on the ground, and the train was soon loaded and gone on toward Waycross. I looked around, and there was my faithful drayman, Edwin Roberson, and his little gray mare and wagon. I told him to load up but not to leave just yet, as I was looking for my sister Lula on the fast southbound train, No. 83, from Jesup. It was due in a few minutes. I soon heard its whistle blow and saw it slowing for a stop. (It did not stop unless it had a passenger to get off or unless you waved it to get on.) So sure enough, she was on there, and soon off with her heavy grips from her stay in Jesup. The drayboy got her grips also. He had to go to the crossing to get across the railroad tracks, and we took a pathway across the tracks and were soon home. We soon had our things put in their correct places, all my goodies put in the pantry, and my clothes taken out of the grip. I cleaned out my trunk from a year of teaching and made it ready for our pillows, blankets, sheets, and clothes for the summer's study, now ready to be repacked.

Our friends and neighbors came to see us and welcome us home. Of course they wanted to see our new clothes. My friend Rosa Peek saw the beautiful piece of material and asked why I had not used it. I told her. So she looked at it more closely and said it needed no trimming, that it was beautiful enough in its own design that self-covered buttons and belt buckle, a well-designed pattern, and correct stitching were all that was needed to make a beautiful dress. Her daughter, Gladys, was preparing to be married the last of June. Mrs. Rosa said that

Gladys already had a beautiful hat and slippers, but she had not yet been able to find the dress material to go with them. She asked, "Would you sell me the piece of material?" I quickly remembered how she had tended to our farm chores after my father became ill and how she had written to us when he seemed to get no better, and said for us to come to him. So I quickly said that she might have it. She asked me the cost. I told her one dollar per yard, six yards of it and the thread that matched. She told me she had no cash. She had already spent out on her daughter's trousseau, but she said she had an abundance of the best home-cured bacon you ever saw and plenty of good milk, butter, and cream that she could supply us to pay for the material. So I said okay, and she took the piece of material and was soon back with the side of nicely streaked, sugar-cured smoked bacon and some fresh milk, butter, and buttermilk and told me to let her know when I needed more. She was so happy to get the material, and it made a beautiful dress for her daughter. I saw her wear it many times.

We were quite busy getting everything in order, getting our visiting done, and relaxing a little after our hard year's work. One day I went to the post office, and there was a letter for me from the Mr. Puckett where my sister Lula had been staying. It was a nice interesting letter, and he asked to correspond with me. I talked it over with Lula, and she said she thought him to be a very fine man in every way and for me to use my pleasure about corresponding with him. But she thought I should surely answer the letter one way or the other, that he was due that much respect. So I answered it. Then he wanted to come to see me one Sunday afternoon, coming on Train No. 83 and leaving on Train No. 80 for his work in South Carolina. So I let him come. We kept corresponding. He wrote letters about his work, his children and friends, business in general, and happenings here and there.

Lula and I went off to summer school. I had some difficulty getting the course on rural high school development and administration. The class was filled to overflowing, and the enrollment had to be cut somewhere. We each had to fill out a questionnaire telling why we desired the course. I told them that my superintendent requested that I take the course to prepare for my work for the incoming school year and that I was to develop the curriculum for a course of study for grade eight in the school I was to head in the fall. I gave Mr. Purcell's full name, title, and address. I don't know whether they called him or not, but they permitted me to stay in the class. There were not many ladies in the class. Seems there was quite a demand throughout the state for the development of high schools. The old-fashioned village was fast falling by the wayside, and the distant church schools were not meeting the needs of the boys and girls demanding higher learning. So state-supported secondary schools were coming to the forefront. It proved to be a very interesting class. I felt it was just what I needed along with the course in curriculum planning. I filled in the rest of my time with academic work, taking a graduate course in Georgia history and government and another in biology. I took the strongest English course I could find. It went deep into the following: composition, communication, class reports, oral English, conversation, public speaking, meeting procedures, book reviews, and oral reports on any subject that needed to be discussed from the student's daily course of study. It was a marvelous course, taught by Dr. Camp, and I enjoyed it very much. It made me be a great believer in a strong English course for all students, no matter what their field of study. I really burned the midnight oil in that quarter, taking five heavy courses. I always liked to take in all the extra entertainment provided for us, such as theatrical plays, special music, lectures, and art displays. So my time was filled. I have always considered it as one of my finest quarters of study. I took my final tests and finished late one Saturday afternoon in late August.

Mr. Puckett had written to me every day I had been at summer school and had frequently sent me flowers, always long-stemmed red roses. He often asked in his letters why I had chosen a school so out of the way and so hard to get to and from. He requested that I arrange my homecoming on the weekend so he might see me as I passed through Jesup. This was not hard to do, as my last test was finished just in time for me to catch the late evening train to Macon, where I would change to the midnight Southern train that would put me in Jesup about five o'clock on Sunday morning. So I wrote him my planned schedule, telling him I would leave for my home around noontime.

Lula had finished all her work and had left for home three days ahead of me. She had not taken the hard academic and school-planning course that I had taken. She had many more higher academic courses than I had ever had, as she had attended several terms at the Georgia Normal College and Business Institute of Professors Little and Khul, at Douglas, a private institution. She had taken mostly arts and crafts, drama, and pageantry to add a spice of life to her everyday teaching in Georgia's rural schools. Her test at the end of the quarter had been work assignments that could be finished and turned in; then she was through with the course. I was left there all alone in our room, but I got everything packed, my luggage to the depot, and my ticket bought. All I had to do was finish that last test, and hie away to the depot. I remember it was English, a long and particular work, but I took my time trying to make a perfect score, for I was struggling for a high mark. I had made my high school license to teach English, social studies, and science, and I surely did not want any low grades to appear anywhere down the line.

All went well, and I made my train in due time. I arrived in Jesup just after sunup on a Sunday morning. It had been one of the hottest August nights I ever remember. Everyone on the train had their windows open, and the cinders, dust, and smoke came in by the handfuls. I felt as if I had been drug down a chimney, no fans or screens, and at that time, I had never heard of air-conditioning. When I stepped off the train, there stood Mr. Puckett, looking as though he had just stepped out of a bandbox. He wanted me to go to his home with him for breakfast. I declined. Then he wanted to take me to a nearby restaurant for breakfast. I declined again, telling him I could not go anywhere or do anything until I got some of the dust, cinders, and soot off of me. Then he looked so put out about it. He asked might he return around eight, and we would go for a ride before I had to catch my train for home. I told him yes. So he went back to his home for breakfast. I went into the ladies restroom, washed off as best I could, and got a fresh changing of clothes out of my grip so I would not smell like the train smoke. Train No. 85, which I was to ride to my home, was a very nice, well-screened train, and you could ride in decency and comfort. Not so that Southern train out of Macon.

When Mr. Puckett returned, I was dressed, my grip was packed, locked, and checked, and I had bought my ticket to Nahunta. He wanted to know where I wished to ride. I told him that it was his choice to make. So he said let's ride down to Doctortown and look at the Great Altamaha River flowing by so gently and yet so powerfully. I told him I would be delighted, that I had never been closer to it than on the train crossing its flow, when I would be going to Ludowici to see my sister Bessie or going to Savannah to see my two older brothers. I had always wanted to get nearer to it than that. I had always loved the Great Satilla, with deep devotion, but it was just a trickle compared with this mighty stream. So we drove over the bumps and sand ruts to Doctortown, to the old loading wharf, and stopped there on the high bluff under the giant live oaks. The trees were so graceful, with their great outspreading limbs hung with long streamers of gray Spanish moss gently swaying in the light August breeze.

We sat and talked for some time of many things and places. He told me of his work building railroad tracks to the flourishing truck crops on the rich coastal islands off Charleston. He said they were making great strides getting fresh vegetables to New York and to all the big eastern markets, just one night out on the growers' express trains. The trains even had precedence over the fastest mail and passenger service. Vegetables could be picked, packaged, loaded, and iced today and could be to the distant markets tomorrow morning, just as fresh and tender as when gathered. His work was rolling in faster than he could get the contracts completed. He was working hard during the summer so by the coming winter, more and more producers would be able to meet the enormous demands of the trade. I told him of my hard quarter of study, that I believed I had made good in all my classes, and that I hoped for a few days' rest before I began my job for another year.

We got out of the car, walked down to the bluff to the water's edge, and watched the red waters flowing toward the sea. I told him of the courses I had just finished in Georgia history and of studying the terrible problem of Georgia soil erosion. I had learned that the mighty Altamaha had once flowed clear and bright. But when white settlers came, they scarred and gutted the red clay soil deeply to grow cotton and other crops. Much rich clay soil had washed away until they could scarcely grow cotton, corn, or any row crop. Now grass and trees were being advocated for the eroded land. I was a great believer in such a plan and hoped to be able to put some of those ideas across in my work in the fall. There we stood, looking at the great expanse of the water, and, behold, he proposed marriage to me. He said his love for me was as great as that mighty stream, and it would flow on to eternity and never run dry. He was quite poetic and lengthy in his proposal. I said, "Well, I hardly know you, and I am sure I will have to become better acquainted with you before I could even discuss such an important matter." He said, well, he knew me, that he had looked at me many times in the past one and one-half years as he had got off and on trains in Jesup, going to and from his work, and had seen me changing trains going to and from my teaching positions. He had admired my behavior as I went and came.

He wanted to know when he could see me again. I told him I had such a short time before my year's work began in September. My sister Lula had promised some friends at Hortense to visit them during the Big Camp Meeting the fourth Sunday in August, and we were to go from there to see our two older brothers in Savannah before we started to work September 6. He said he would try to arrange to see me somewhere during that time. He asked if I cared to correspond with him further. I told him I had enjoyed his letters very much and found them quite interesting. So we then returned to the car. He looked at his watch and said we would have time to go by his home and let all his children see me before my train came. I told him I would be delighted to go.

They were all back home now from vacationing with their kin in South Carolina and Eastman, Georgia. They were beginning to think about school and wondering who their teacher would be. We drove up and went into the house. He remembered I did not drink Coca-Cola and had ice water served me. He asked me to stay for the noonday meal and take the afternoon train home. I declined and told him my sister would be expecting me on the noonday train. I had been up all night and was beginning to feel like I needed some rest. Several of the children got in the car with us, and we hurried to the depot. I was soon on the train and gone, not knowing whether I would ever see or hear from him again.

I had not contacted my superintendent in any way as I came through Jesup, it being Sunday. He had written that he would try to have a joint meeting with me and the trustees as soon as I got home and had time to set a date for such a meeting. I was to let him know, and he would try to comply with the time and place. I arrived home in a few minutes, as the train did not stop between Jesup and Nahunta and always ran on fast schedule, being a fast mail train. I found my sister well and happy. She was two days ahead of me in gathering news, and she was like Elijah in the book of Job. She was bursting to tell me of all the important happenings, never giving me a minute to tell her anything. She told me that come January 1, 1921, we would not live in Wayne County anymore. A new county, Brantley, had been made while we were away at summer school. The legislature had created nine new counties. Politics were running riot. Hoboken, Hickox, and Nahunta were all vying to become the county seat, which would be developed as the governmental and educational center of the new county. Everyone believed it was the time to run for a county office and to help make up the court ring.

It seems that the need for new roads, bridges, and schools was in the forefront; there had not been a new bridge since my father led the way for the Ammons Ferry bridge to be built across the Great Satilla in the early 1900s. It was the only bridge in the county despite its many deep streams in every direction. So the talk was of a good bridge over Big Satilla and Little Satilla at Trudie, over the Big Satilla at Atkinson, over deep-running Big Buffalo Creek at Hickox, and over the Big Satilla between Hoboken and Blackshear. There was not a mile of paving in the whole county.

They had planned for all schools to start as early as possible and run to December 31. They had hoped to begin July 1, but that did not happen. If it had, they would have had six months of school in Wayne County, and then not had any more school until after taxes were paid in the fall of 1921, allowing them to run on a cash basis. Encouraging their teachers to enter a good teacher-training school in January, and to go through the summer quarter, would enable the teachers to get a full year of extra training. Everyone had plans upon plans for development of the area, but all of this would take more than just talk.

Early Monday afternoon Lula went for the mail, which had arrived on the noonday train. When she returned she said she had two letters for me. Which would I rather have: the long businesslike letter or the short fancy letter? I told her I would prefer both of them. So after she had teased me a spell, she gave them both over to me. The long letter was from Mr. Purcell, telling me of the new county formation and that after January 1 he would have no further control of Hickox School or any other of the forty Wayne County schools that would become Brantley County schools. He regretted having to give them up, as he had always counted Nahunta as the Athens of Wayne County, and some of his best schoolteachers lived in that area south of the Big Satilla River: Mrs. Lizzie Knox Callaway; Miss Lilla Herrin; Miss Verdie Hickox; Misses Verdie, Emie, and Sally Jones; Misses Kate, Lizzie, and Mary Knox; Mrs. S. B. Lary; Mrs. J. B. Lewis; Misses Verdie, Myrtice, and Agnes Middleton; Misses Lula, Mary Ellen, and Martha Mizell; Mrs. Rosa Peek; Misses Sara Jane, Nora, Belle, Cora, Clara, and Ella Strickland; Misses Leila and Beulah Wainright; and Messrs. Morris Highsmith, Perry Knox, Avery Wainright, and Elbert Wainright. Some of these would transfer to upper Wayne County, but most of them remained in the new county and took the four-month work and plan for the one year of college work (three quarters). They were to start teaching in Brantley County schools in September 1921, assured of prompt payment at end of each month.

Mr. Purcell stated that he did not know how the plans would go forward for a new high school at Hickox. The Hickox trustees and many of the other schools were sore with him because he would not concede to the earlier starting date for their schools so they could draw more months of school support from Wayne County before the year was up. He had written to the Hickox trustees that he would come for a meeting with them and me as soon as I arrived, but he had not heard from them and feared he would not, as they were at variance with him on the starting date. If I preferred a full term of work, he had a school waiting for me. The trustees of Farm Life School, of Screven, had been in to see him and inquired about me. They already had their other teachers and were only in need of a principal to be ready to start Monday, September 6, for a full term. He told them that I was due any day from summer school. He would let them know as soon as he could contact me after my return.

The short fancy envelope was from Mr. Puckett, wanting to know if he could come see me Sunday afternoon, arriving at six and leaving at ten for South Carolina, and to please let him know in time to make his plans accordingly. I wrote to him that I would be delighted to have him visit, and I would have supper ready for him.

The whole week long, all conversation seemed to be about the new county, the battle royal going on for the county seat, new roads, bridges, and high schools. News began to come about a young man just returned home after graduating from the Georgia Normal College and Business Institute. It was said that the new school at Hickox was being built for him. His father had generously contributed time, money, and material to help make the building possible. His father had advanced him his money to go to school, with the understanding that he was to be the principal of the new school. He had an uncle on the Hickox school board, and there seemed to be no doubt about it: he was to be the principal.

I was very tired and busy, and my time was short. I had written the Hickox trustees when I would be home and that I would be glad to see them at their convenience. I had not heard a word from them, only the gossip of this young man whose voice had not changed as yet. I don't think he had ever taught anywhere. Every day someone would come to see me with a new piece of news the young gentleman was spreading from the community bench on the post office porch. I stayed home. I said nothing. No trustees came. I had not answered Mr. Purcell's letter. Toward the end of the week, my beloved teacher and blessed counselor, Mrs. S. B. Lary, came to see me. She said, "Martha, I want to see you privately in your bedroom, with the door locked." So we went in, locked the door, and she said, "I suppose you've been hearing all the news about Hickox School." I told her I had heard a good bit, but I had never made one comment, and I had not been uptown since I came home. Lula had been doing the shopping and other errands. She said, "Well, don't you comment. That young man has not missed a day coming there to the post office and telling about the fine new school being built just for him to be principal." She wanted to know what I actually knew. I showed her Mr. Purcell's letter to me. She said, "Mr. Purcell will never hear from those trustees." She wanted to know had I heard from them. I told her no, but I was expecting them any day. She told me to let it go; the odds were against me, and I could not overcome the politics, kinship, and the arrogant young man who would be there to try to make my work fail. She said that I could easily get a full-term at a good salary and not have to overcome all the hazards that lay in my pathway now. She left me saying, "The least said is the easiest mended," and pray never let on the advice she had given me. I promised her faithfully that I would not. It has been more than fifty years, and I have never breathed a word of it to a living soul.

I stayed home all week. Late Saturday afternoon all three of the trustees came to see me, and of course they were full of politics, wondering where the county seat and the county high school would be. I told them they seemed to be further on the way to a high school than was any other community. I was ready to lay the foundation with a fully accredited eighth grade and had plans for the other grades to follow as needed. Then they told me they had let the sixth- and seventh-grade teacher go and had elected this young man to help me. They said they thought I might need some help controlling the older boys and girls. I told them, "No, I expect to treat them as young ladies and gentlemen to be, and I expect the same respect from them. I have never had any trouble controlling a school, and I do not expect any trouble there. Had I not thought myself capable of controlling your school, I would never have accepted the principalship, and I do not need any help along that line. I cannot work with that kind of setup."

Two of the trustees said they wanted and needed me badly. But the third one, the boy's uncle, said, "But you two men know full well that we had to hire him. There was no way around it." The Hickox School trustees offered to loan me the money for a whole year of college from January 1, through the summer quarter, to September 1, 1921, if I would stay with them. I told them I was not able to accept, as I had financial obligations I had to meet. So I quietly told them, "I will fade out of the picture. I think it would be best for all. I am in a financial bind, and I need a full term of schoolwork to meet my obligations. I will have to go where I can be assured of a five-month school term." I wished them luck with their new county and new principal. I told them how hard I had worked to develop a full-fledged accredited high school for them and that I appreciated their choosing me. Then I told them I had enjoyed the work and the time spent making the plans. That concluded our meeting. I have never seen them since. I understand that the young gentleman was soon running for county school superintendent of Brantley County and was elected. I do not know of his schoolwork. He was killed in an automobile accident very young in his life.

That night I wrote to my superintendent, telling him that I would accept Farm Life and to please notify the other two teachers to meet me at his office Thursday morning, September 2, for our supplies and instructions. I asked him to notify the trustees of Farm Life to meet us at Screven at noon the same day; to ask them to arrange a boarding place for us; and to inform the trustees that cleanup day at the school would be Friday. As yet, schools did not have janitors. You cleaned it up or went to work in a collection of summer dust and dirt. I always preferred going on ahead and getting everything clean and in order for the opening day of school. I felt as though a great burden had been lifted from me; I was happy over my decision, and I believe all concerned were relieved as well. No one's feelings were hurt, and no unkind words were said.

Lula had promised to make a visit to Hortense to see some friends and to attend the old-time camp meeting there on the fourth Sunday in August. Then we were to go on to Savannah to see our two older brothers for a week before we began our fall work, leaving Sunday night from Hortense and returning home on

Saturday afternoon. I was to accompany her on this trip, since neither of us had had any vacation for a year, and we were to be back to work again in a few days for another year.

I had received a letter from Mr. Puckett every day during the week, also a box of one dozen long-stemmed red roses. Mr. Puckett arrived as planned on Sunday evening. I had prepared a nice evening meal. We all three ate and enjoyed the meal together. Lula asked about each of his children and whether they had enjoyed their vacation. He told Lula that his sister, Daisy, was going to Spencer, North Carolina, to teach first grade, and he had secured Miss Anna Gentry, an elderly lady and practical nurse, to stay with the children while he was away at work. He felt they could get on quiet well. He still had the same cook and laundress that he had when she was there, and the little boys were getting on very well with the milking and other chores. He said the two small children seemed to like Miss Anna very much, and the two older girls were busy making plans for their fall clothes, classes, and music. After the meal my sister excused us and said she would do the dishes. We retired to the front porch, enjoyed the evening breeze, and talked of many things. I told him that I had let my school at Hickox go because they could offer me only a half-term; instead I would be at Farm Life. He seemed to like that part of the plan. He asked about another visit before we went to work, and I told him of our visit to Hortense. He said he would plan to see us at Hortense, that he had friends, Mr. Jim Harper and family, who were always begging him to go to the camp meeting at Hortense with them. He never had been, and that would be a good time to go. He would plan accordingly and would see me there the next Sunday. The train was blowing; he had to go.

The next week there was a big road and bridge meeting at Nahunta about the new county's getting the Little Satilla and the Big Satilla rivers bridged at Trudie. Wayne County was to build a road as far as Wayne County would now extend. This was to be Brantley's first try at road development. The ladies were to prepare a delicious noonday meal. There were a great number of northern settlers in Brantley County at that time, and their plan for an outdoor meal of that type was to make up a menu to feed the number that were supposed to be there. Each lady in the community would choose one item from the menu and furnish enough of that item to feed the number expected. I was given the job of preparing pumpkin pies. We had a large woodstove, and I could bake four large pies at a time. I made up my filling in a dishpan, and my piecrusts in Mother's bread tray. I baked pies all day long. The dinner was great. The crowd was large. The speaking was loud and long. The pledges were strong from both counties. Everyone seemed pleased with the meeting. After the dinner was served, I gathered my plates and went home.

While I was there resting on the front porch, I heard someone coming down the street whistling a little tune. When he got to the gate, he came in. It was Colonel James R. Thomas. He said he thought he would come up and visit awhile with us until train time. The Jesup crowd had come on the Bogey and would return the same way in the late afternoon. So I invited him in. He began to tell us how much he thought of our father and how he had enjoyed talking to him on various and diverse subjects. He remarked on what a great Bible scholar my father had been, on how well-versed he was in everyday law. Col. Thomas said he enjoyed Father's great knowledge of plant life and his understanding of human nature. He mentioned that Father had often spoken of his daughters and our thirst for knowledge and how he hoped he would live to see us succeed in our professions. What a great loss his passing was to all of us. Then he spoke to me about my new friend, Mr. Puckett. He said he was a mighty fine man, that he had some faults; but, he said, all men have some failings. I told him I supposed all human beings had failings more or less. Then he spoke of the six children and said they are all nice, obedient children. I told him that children were my stock and trade, that I worked with and loved children every day of my life. He stayed and visited until his train was soon to arrive and then he departed.

We left for Hortense on Friday night for a good visit with the George Baxter family. His wife was Lillian Lewis Baxter, one of my mother's favorite cousins. We enjoyed being with her two fine daughters, Pearl and Alma, and two sons, Henry and Ira. Sunday came, and we all went to the camp meeting. There we were met by Mr. Puckett, his two daughters, Gertrude and Angie, and two nieces up from Florida, Lois and Louise Puckett. Mr. Puckett's friend, Mr. Jim Harper, and his family were there, as were hundreds of other people. They had brought lunch, and Mrs. Baxter had fixed a lovely lunch; we all spread together at noontime. Lots of people were camped in the cottages. There was a lot of good preaching, singing, visiting, eating, and enjoying each other. We were persuaded to go with Mr. Puckett in his car on to Jesup, where we could get an earlier train to Savannah, Train No. 22, which came by about seven. So two of Mr. Puckett's load went in Mr. Harper's car, and Lula and I went in Mr. Puckett's car. The road was very bad, filled with deep ruts and bog holes, but we left early and made the fourteen miles before sundown. There we had supper and boarded the train. Mr. Puckett went on the same train on his way back to Charleston.

Mr. Puckett got off the train in Savannah and saw us to our brother Frank's home in a cab, as they were expecting us on the late, late train. Before Mr. Puckett left he told me he had to be in Savannah Wednesday for a meeting at the ACL roadway engineers office to see about some more contracts for further work and asked could I arrange to go to Tybee with him for an outing. So we set the time and place of meeting at the Tybee railroad depot. He was then gone to catch the late train to Charleston. Wednesday came bright and clear. My brother's wife and children and Lula decided they would also like to go to Tybee that day for a swim and shore picnic. So we all packed a nice lunch and bathing suits and took the trolley to the Tybee depot. The appointed time came, and there was no Mr. Puckett. The others went on the train to Tybee. I told them I would wait until the next train, that he must have been delayed at the ACL office. By and by he came, but alas, the last morning train had gone. They ran every thirty minutes until 11:30 A.M. and then did not run anymore until 2:30 P.M. So there we were, our picnic lunch and our folks at Tybee, and we were at Tybee depot in Savannah. Mr. Puckett quickly said we would catch the next trolley uptown and have lunch; we did. He was very sorry that he was late, but the business was about rather detailed construction of tracks to the big vegetable fields around Charleston. He showed me the contract that he had signed that morning and said that it would keep him, his foremen, and workmen exceedingly busy until far into the coming year. There was promise of work, plans already on the drawing boards being made ready for bidders.

We had a lovely seashore lunch, for which the restaurants of Savannah were world-famous. Then we went for a stroll in beautiful Forsyth Park. I have always loved its magnificent beauty. After a while we sat down to drink in its refreshing splendor, and there he proposed to me again. I told him I loved my work the same as he loved his, and I was preparing myself as fast as I could to go forward in the field of education and child development. I could not lay it aside easily. I enjoyed his company and enjoyed his letters, but I would have to have more time and more thoughts on the matter before I could make such an important decision. I had put a whole lifetime of thinking and planning into my teaching career.

We hurried back to Tybee depot and went on the first afternoon train. My folks were at the depot waiting for us. They had enjoyed walking on the beach and having their lunch, but they had not had their swim. We were all soon in our bathing suits and out for a nice dip in the ocean. Afterward we had refreshments on the pavilion. Then it was time to head back to Savannah.

Mr. Puckett felt that he had let me down by not being on time, and he insisted that he should take me that evening to the Isle of Hope, where there were always lovely seafood dinners, dining and dancing, and beautiful orchestra music. There was an open deck over the water, and at full moon it was extremely beautiful. We neither one danced, but we enjoyed the dinner, the music, and the cool open-air trolley ride out there and back. He had to take a late-night train back to Charleston and wanted to know when he could see me again. I told him we were to go to the home of our oldest brother, Frank, on the morrow. We would go to our home in Nahunta Saturday afternoon. Sunday we would go to see our mother in Camden County; then back home on Wednesday. We would leave for our schoolwork via Jesup on Thursday.

I did want Mr. Puckett to meet my brother, Frank, a locomotive engineer for the Seaboard Airline Railway. He had met my next-oldest brother, Bob, a fine interior coach painter for the Central of Georgia Railway. They seemed to like each other. So he told me he would be very pleased to meet Frank. He would come from Charleston early Saturday afternoon and join us on Train No. 83, as that was the train he had already planned to ride home. I suggested that we all meet at Jerry George's, a very nice ice cream parlor on Broughton St., not too far away from Union Train Station, where we would have to board. That was our plan as he left for Charleston that lovely night.

We went to Frank's home to visit with his good wife, Rintha, and son, F. M. Jr., and beautiful little daughter, Jessie Mae. When he came in off his run I told him I wanted him to meet this friend of mine, Mr. L. P. Puckett. I asked if he knew him. He said no, but he had heard of him and reports seemed good. You see, they all three—my two brothers, Frank and Bob, and Mr. Puckett—worked for different railroad companies, and there was not much communication between railroads in that day and time. So he told me he would do his best to arrange to be with me there on Saturday afternoon. He did, and we all had a nice social hour there together. Lula and I had a social visit with each of our brothers in Savannah and with their wives and children. It was the last long visit I ever had with them.

Our train was on time, and our brother Frank saw us off to Jesup (this train did not stop between Savannah and Jesup), where Mr. Puckett was to get off. He wanted to know when he could see me again; I told him I would have to let him know. We were home in a few minutes, as the train stopped only at Nahunta on the run from Jesup to Jacksonville, Florida.

Early Sunday morning we were up, with our grips packed with what clean clothes we could gather. Soon we were on the noonday train for our less-than-ten-mile ride across the Big Satilla River on the Old Brunswick and Western Railroad to Atkinson, where Mary Ellen was to meet us for the nine-mile ride on the dirt road down into Camden County. We visited until Tuesday afternoon, when we had to return home to get our clothes clean and ready to be packed again into our trunks and suitcases for a year's work. After long, hard hours of work, we were ready to call Edwin Roberson to take our baggage to the depot. We locked the door to our home and walked down to the depot to catch the Bogey. Edwin, who in years to come made a mighty fine schoolteacher, told us to hurry back. We told him we would be back in the late springtime. I was going to Screven to be the principal of Farm Life School. My sister was going to be the principal of Piney Grove School, out from Odum.

I had not thought that I my lengthy visit with my mother that summer would be the last I would have with her on this earth, but so it turned out to be. The eventful summer of 1920 had come to a close, and I was off for another year of hard work, Wednesday, September 1, 1920.

CHAPTER 18

I Marry, and My Life Is Changed

Lula and I left home to go to Jesup, where we spent the night at the Ingleside Hotel. Arising early the next morning, we went to Mr. Purcell's office. There we signed our contracts, received our supplies and book lists, and purchased crayons. Lula then departed for Piney Grove. My two teachers, Miss Nellie Sports, for grades three through five, and Miss Sallie Lou Howard, for grades one and two, joined me, and we were ready to depart. When we started out the door, Mr. Purcell said, "There go three of my finest teachers, and I am expecting a mighty fine school."

News was coming through about how despondent the people in the Farm Life school district were over the invasion of the boll weevil, but Mr. Purcell hoped we could cheer them up along the way. At that time, no one knew of the mighty force of this small insect, nor of the power it would exert over the economy of a people; it would change their entire way of life.

As I passed by the post office, I dropped a letter in the mail to Mr. Puckett, telling him I was on the way to my school for the term of 1920–21, and I would let him hear from me after my arrival as to my address and my situation in general. As for now, I was leaving on Train No. 185 for Screven with my two teachers. We were to get our school building in order on Friday and begin school on the following Monday.

We were met at Screven by Mr. Walton Long, the head trustee, and his big cotton-hauling truck. We sat in chairs in the bed of the truck just like we did in the two-mule cotton wagons. He was taking us to his home on the Nine Runs Road between Reedy Creek and Coleman Creek. On our way out we passed many still-green cotton fields in place of the snowy whiteness that was the usual scene this time of year. I asked Mr. Long the reason why, and he said the boll weevil had eaten all the cotton squares, so there were no bolls to pull the strength from the cotton stalks, causing them to turn brown, shed their green foliage, and show the snowy-white bolls. Where there had been one and one-half bales per acre last year, there would be one-half bale or less this time. Every farmer was facing financial ruin.

We drove through some seven miles of this desolation before we were at Mr. Long's lovely home and met his good wife, Mrs. Maude, and his younger daughter, Estelle. His older daughter, Della, was away at college. We were invited in to share a delicious country dinner, already on the table waiting for us. My, it was so good. Every mouthful cooked to perfection, field peas, ham hocks, hot corn bread, beef stew, sweet potatoes, rice and gravy, hot biscuits, fresh sweet butter, and new Georgia cane syrup. It was a meal fit for a king.

While we were yet at the table, we approached Mr. and Mrs. Long about boarding with them for the next school term. There were three of us, and they had only one spare room. I quickly told them that all three of us could occupy the same room and could eat the same type food they ate, that all three of us were raised in the country and knew the worth of good country cooking. We would do our best to be no trouble anywhere, to arise and eat at the same time of day they did, and eat our big meal or dinner when the day was done after we returned from school. I told Mrs. Long we would care for our own room and see to our own laundry. They agreed to keep us at a very reasonable price.

We had a nice room with a fireplace, two double beds, a wash stand, dresser, three chairs, and a good worktable—by my request. With our three trunks and three grips, we just about filled it up to capacity when our shoes and other small items were slipped under our beds. Miss Sports and I chose to sleep together, as we had roomed together before when teaching at O'Quinn in 1919–1920. Miss Howard seemed very happy that she had a big double bed all by herself. She said she liked to sit in bed and do her work, while I prefer to do mine at the table and go to sleep when I go to bed.

They brought in our trunks, and we told Mr. Long we wished to work at the schoolhouse on Friday, as I had previously written to him, and asked did he have some help for us rounded up? He said he was sure we would have enough help to do everything that needed to be done. I told him we wished to start early so as to have plenty of time to get everything in order. He promised to spread the word around for us among the neighbors and any other patrons who passed that way and to get the word over to Kayville. Kayville was the nearby county village from which news quickly spread over the countryside that Friday was cleanup day at the school and that school would open Monday, September 6, at eight o'clock.

We spent all afternoon getting our trunks in place, getting out the clothes we needed first, and hanging them in the closet. We also got our school material ready to be used. I had brought many scrubbing and polishing cloths from home. So the cleaning, dusting, and polishing of everything could go forward in an orderly way. We had a wonderful supper and a delightful visit with the family afterward. Soon we were off to bed, as we had a hard day on the morrow. We planned to arise early and to get the work done in the cool of the day, knowing full well it usually took all day long until the setting of the sun to get everything in order. We had asked Mrs. Long for a lunch to take with us. Mr. Long told us he would take us and our working tools over to school early in the morning, and he would get the pump in good working condition. Then he would have to return to the farm to see after his cotton harvesting and other farmwork. He would return later in the day to see if we had sufficient help to get the work done on time. I was so glad he said he would get the pump to work first, for an open well was one of my greatest fears on a school ground. I had one at Burnt Bay and at O'Quinn. It was a dread on my mind every day that I taught at those schools.

Friday morning came all too soon. We were up early and on our way early. I had borrowed buckets, scrubs, and mops from Mrs. Long, and Mr. Long brought us six new brooms, two for each room. We borrowed hoes, rakes, shovels, and axes for work on the grounds. Mr. Long also got new pump valves, as the leathers usually became so dry during the summer they would crack and not hold the pump's prime in the fall.

We had good help until mid morning. Then many of the ladies had to go home to prepare the noonday meal for their families. We worked on. We cleaned all the walls and ceilings, washed windows, scrubbed floors, dusted and polished the desks, and cleaned and decorated the blackboards with a happy welcome greeting. We posted a tentative daily schedule, got cloakrooms, lunch shelves, and coat and shoe racks in order. We stopped for a late lunch and rested some. By then we had some fresh afternoon help, and we began to tackle the dooryard and soon had it looking in good order. Many hands make light work, you know. The campus was fenced and ample for baseball playing and singing games, with quiet corners for those who wished to set up permanent games like Lady Come to See Me. All of this contributed to the attractiveness and control of the school. The building was only a few years old. The furniture was new, modern, and adequate. The teachers' desks, maps, charts, blackboards, globes, dictionary, and other equipment were of good selection.

After we had everything clean, polished, well arranged, I said, "I don't see but two things we need to make the rooms complete." And one of the dear ladies said, "Well, what is that? We shall do our best to get it." I said, "A beautiful bouquet of flowers on each teacher's desk, and every desk with a well-behaved child sitting in it." They all laughed and I said, "No children, no school; that is the reason we must take good care of them, or we would have no children to teach and therefore we would have no position. They are our 'stock and trade.'" They all laughed again and another lady said, "You must surely love children." My reply to her was, "I do, or I would not be a teacher trying to lead, guide, and direct their young lives."

We put all the schoolhouse tools in their correct places, locked the doors, gathered up the tools we had borrowed from Mr. and Mrs. Long, and took them down to the gate at the campus entrance. We were standing there, visiting with some of the ladies and gentlemen who had come to help us, when we saw Mr. Long coming to get us. He wanted to know did we get everything fixed okay. I replied that we had it in right good shape and could begin work Monday morning. He told us he was sorry he had not gotten back, but he was trying to get some fields open to change stock over on to more feed so they would begin to fatten for the winter meat supply. We fastened the gate, got in the truck, and soon arrived at our new home.

On my way out that morning, I had placed a letter in the mailbox to Mr. Puckett addressed to Jesup, so he would get it when he arrived home Saturday night from his work. I was telling him where I was located and giving him my mailing address and also my telephone number. It was party line, not very reliable; no privacy could be expected at any time, but it was for use in an emergency.

We had a good country supper, with an overflowing variety of foods. After a nice visit with the family, I talked to Mr. Long about grade eight. I told him I had come licensed and prepared to add it on if the student enrollment called for it. He said we would wait and see; many of the older boys and girls had gone away to Professors Little and Khul's school in Douglas to study business, typing, shorthand, banking, and other business subjects, and some had married. He did not believe we would have enough for a class. Not knowing they could get a teacher qualified to teach them, many parents had entered their children at distant boarding schools.

The other teachers and I soon excused ourselves and began to work on our tentative schedules for the school opening. I told Miss Sports and Miss Howard that I expected we would have to work on an early schedule until the cotton was gathered. There was no fast time then. You just went to work one hour earlier and, of course, got out an hour earlier in the afternoon. They both liked the idea, so I told them I would approach the patrons about it Monday morning. We all three set our schedules up accordingly. Miss Howard was to have five relief periods a day, while Miss Sports and I were to have three. A lesson every hour for every child was to be followed by a study period for every lesson, as no one could expect any studying to be done at home as long as those fields were white unto harvest with cotton. All the children picked from the time they got home from school until nightfall, then home for supper, and then to bed. They would arise early in the morning and walk to school. We made out our duty schedule for room cleaning, wood gathering, water getting, and all the other necessary tasks that make a school run smoothly.

I told them we would be loaded to the hilt with students and that we must have order and routine from the very beginning, or we would never be able to swing the job. It takes time and strength to correct and punish. I preferred order and obedience to chaos and misbehavior. I would expect each one of them to keep order in her room and be on the playgrounds with her children at relief time. In other words, they were on full duty for eight hours every day. The children were theirs from the time they arrived until they left. I would be loaded as heavily as either one of them. Every time I was called on to assist either of them, it took me away from my work and made them weaker in their control of the classroom. I expected every tub to sit on its own bottom, but they were never to think I was not there to assist and help them when needed. We worked and talked far into the midnight, but to sleep we had to go, for there was much to do and learn on the morrow. Tomorrow, Saturday, would be our most leisure-filled day of the whole term.

We visited with Mrs. Long off and on during the day and learned the first Saturday and Sunday was the preaching day at Old Ritch Baptist church, to which a lot of our patrons belonged. She, the Joe Tyre family, the Josh Lary family, and a few others scattered about, belonged to Effies Chapel Methodist Church. Quite a few patrons belonged to Big Creek Primitive Baptist Church, and their big meeting day was second Sunday in October, and everyone in the whole countryside went. A few went to Lake Chapel Progressive Primitive Baptist over near the Tyre Bridge, and on the third Sunday in September, everyone went to Jesup to the singing convention at the courthouse in Jesup. Ritch Community always had a winning choir. The circus would be coming to Jesup in October. Big, little, old, and young went to the circus. Everyone tried to go to the Wayne County Fair on "school day," when all the 4-H club boys and girls showed their exhibits, and many of the farmers and farmers' wives exhibited as well.

From the information I gathered that Saturday morning from Mrs. Long, it looked like we were to have a very busy and exciting time in our school and community that fall, and we were only eighty school days away from Christmas. We had already been given our instructions by our superintendent to plan to teach one Saturday, so as to get out of school Thursday, December 23, and not have to teach Christmas Eve day, and still get our four months of school in before Christmas Eve. We did not want to have children come to school on Christmas Eve. This Saturday of teaching was set down in December, so as not to interfere with the children helping gather the cotton on Saturdays during the cotton-harvesting season.

I also learned that everyone had Santa Claus at their own homes for their children on Christmas Eve night, and the Christmas program, put on by the church people, was usually at Old Ritch Church. But there had never been much of a Thanksgiving program, and the patrons thought that was a shame. I relayed all this information to my two teachers and told them that was where we could shine—by developing an appropriate Thanksgiving program for the whole school. We would invite all the countryside to come and enjoy it. We would plan to use their bountiful harvest as the decorations, use the first Thanksgiving as our theme, and use songs the whole community could help us sing. I thought we could develop it easily and have a beautiful program without too much time away from routine work. We talked, planned, and worked all day Saturday. We usually did not have many chances for such a day, as one Saturday out of each month we attended a teachers meeting in Jesup. We had to use one Saturday to complete report cards. Saturday was the only day we had to attend to our personal affairs and to clean our clothes, keeping them in good clean condition and ready for wearing every day in the week.

Sunday came bright and beautiful. We all dressed in our Sunday best and went in the big new cotton truck with the Long family to Old Ritch Church. We had a good sermon and fine singing. After church we met many of our patrons, and they told us they would see us Monday morning at school. Some of the young folks asked Mrs. Long could they have a sing at her home that Sunday afternoon; she readily agreed, telling them to come early, bring their songbooks, and have a good sing. She told them to get the word around to all the young people.

We came home to a good Sunday dinner of chicken and dumpling, fall vegetables, pound cake, and custard pie. We helped Mrs. Long do the dishes. By that time, the young people were coming in. Soon the living room was full, the organ was putting forth its melodious sounds, and the country voices added to the harmony of the music. Everyone seemed happy. Some were singing, others listening, and a very few were quietly talking. The afternoon was soon gone, and the happy people were telling Mr. and Mrs. Long good-bye and how they appreciated being invited. They also told us how happy they were to know us and hoped we would attend their Sunday afternoon sings often. We told them how much we had enjoyed their singing and that we hoped they would be coming back soon. Quickly, they were gone. The day was done. We all had a good Sunday dinner. After a family chat around the table as to who all we had seen and what we had heard, we were off to bed. Tomorrow was coming up fast, our work was to be long and hard, and we needed to be there on time and at our very finest.

Monday morning we three teachers were in our places. Lovely bouquets were on each of our desks, and the seats began to fill with bright-eyed children, all nicely dressed and attractive in every way. Many patrons were coming in. At eight o'clock I rang the bell, and we assembled our children in the auditorium that we had made by opening the folding doors between Miss Sports's and Miss Howard's rooms. The auditorium was soon filled. We had a nice opening, with Bible reading, a prayer, and the singing of "America." I asked the trustees to talk, and they made a few pleasant remarks and turned the meeting back to me. I then inquired about the length of the school day and mentioned the early schedule until the cotton was harvested. They liked the idea, so the time was set from 7 A.M. to 3 P.M. each day until late fall. I also inquired about the fuel for the heaters, and they told us to use off the ten acres belonging to the school. I told them the supply looked good for fatwood, but I would like some oak or gum to go along with it if anyone could bring us a load. Several spoke up and said they would bring a load the first rainy day that was not cotton-picking weather. Then I went into the teaching of grade eight. I told them that after we had registered the children, I would know if it was needed. We decided we would wait to go further into the matter after the registration was finished. Several of the ladies spoke up and said they thought all the eighth-grade prospects had gone away to boarding schools or had married. I next asked about getting books for all the children. Mr. Burley Thornton said he was going to Jesup early the next morning and would be happy to come by the schoolhouse to pick up the list and the money, get the books, and bring them back to us in the afternoon. We were all happy about that.

I now introduced our teachers and told the patrons what excellent teachers they had secured, that we would have a wonderful year together and do them a good job if they would see to it that we had the children every day. I then brought in my plea for perfect attendance every rainy day. I told them I always made special plans for taking care of the children every minute of those days and that the lessons could be learned on such days as well as on days when the sun was shining brightly. I told them that going to school was like reading a letter; the days you stayed home were like pages missing from your letter, and ofttimes a day you stayed home was the most important page.

I asked the patrons if any of them wished to say anything. We had now been in session some two hours, and I told them I would have to let the children be relieved. So they all said the dew had now dried, and they would have to get to their cotton-picking. They seemed despondent over the outlook for the year's cotton yield. They said they could not afford to lose one lock, for it now appeared they would have not one-half of a crop. They told us good-bye and asked us to come to see them when we and they had time. They hoped to get the cotton picked ahead of the October storms. We invited them to come to see us when they could.

All the patrons were gone. I thanked the children for their quiet behavior, gave them our schedule for the day, and told them when the bells were to be rung and the length of the relief periods. First recess would be for thirty minutes to get water, be relieved, and play a little if time enough. There would be only one bell, and they were to come in when it rang. I gave directions for their going out, coming, getting water, and other behavior. I then had my pupils—grades six and seven—return to my room for their drinking cups and a bite of refreshment if they desired. All were to pass out, in order, and quietly.

After recess, we began registration. I called for grade eight; not a soul came forward. I began to check last year's register for those who had finished the seventh grade and asked where they were. And as we had been told, some had gone away to boarding school after the seventh grade, some had married, and some had gone to work. None knew they could have come to Farm Life School for the eighth grade. So I passed on to grade seven. Some twenty-five fine, eager boys and girls registered. I began by assigning the spelling lesson for the morrow and made out lists of needed spelling books. Then on to grade six, following the same procedure, asking them to prepare the assignment for tomorrow's lesson. We went forward with English, mathematics, history, and geography. At noontime, the children washed their hands, ate lunch, and played games until they heard the first of two bells. On the first bell, they quit playing, relieved themselves, got drinks, and were ready to move to classes on second bell. The whole school moved by the same schedule except that there were extra relief periods for the primary grades. When we returned to the classrooms at one o'clock, we continued to assign lessons and make out a book list.

I assigned reading and health for grades six and seven. I still had civics, agriculture, and writing to get in somewhere somehow. I set first period one day a week for each of these subjects, and chapel two times a week. With that taken care of, I gave grade six two extra study periods per week, which they could surely use to an advantage while I had the other extra classes for grade seven. After a fifteen-minute afternoon relief—there was no playtime at this period—I asked for assembly again. We folded open the doors between Miss Sports's and Miss Howard's room. My children marched in; the sixth grade sat on long benches on one side of the room, and the seventh grade sat on the other. There was no mixing with students in the other grades. I gave instructions for those bringing their money to buy books the next morning. The collected money would be given to Mr. Thornton. Everyone had a completed book list. Then I told them that each day I wanted to know how many pounds of cotton they had picked after school. They were to keep a record for each grade, then to select a champion for each grade and the champion for the school. They were cautioned to remember to be at school at seven o'clock the next morning.

We then returned to our room. The children were prepared for home-going and cotton-picking. The bell rang at four o'clock, but it would ring at three on the morrow and until cotton-picking was completed. The children moved quietly and quickly on their way toward home. We soon had the school building locked and the gate closed and were on our way to our boarding place.

We had a little rest until suppertime, then a nice chat with the family. Afterward each teacher went to make out her own schedule of work. We were heavily loaded with forty-five to fifty students each. We did all the planning we could, then talked a spell about rainy-day attendance, and what games and physical exercises we could do indoors on those days. Each teacher was to take care of her own activities. We went to bed, as 7:00 A.M. would come mighty early, and we had to walk to school. There were no school buses as yet, and very few cars, and they were used only for church-going on Sunday and maybe a trip to town once a week. Gas cost money, and the farmers were not yet used to turning loose much of their hard-earned cash.

Tuesday morning school began right on time. Our lessons began to roll by, and assignments and study periods for the lessons were set in motion for the recitations for the morrow. We had only one caller: Mr. Thornton came by for the book list and money. We quickly had that ready for him, and he was on his way. He arrived back just as we were preparing to close for the day. I told the children we would have to wait until Wednesday morning to issue the books, and they were to be sure to come with extra-clean hands the next morning so as not to soil their brand-new books. We thanked Mr. Thornton very kindly for being so generous to us with his time and for getting the books to us so promptly. Everyone left happy and hurried home to get to their cotton-picking.

Wednesday morning came bright and fair, and the children were excited over having their new books and not having to share them with two or three other children. The work seemed to be going well for the other two teachers as well. We had set up our system of daily grading of all class work so monthly averages could be easily totaled at the end of each month. All absent pupils drew zeros in their daily grades, and they all decided then and there that they would not be absent unless it could not be helped. The fall was beautiful. Our attendance was almost perfect, which made the classroom work easy and pleasant for pupils, teachers, and parents.

There were practically no disciplinary problems, as each teacher looked well after her own students; they all seemed happy in the classroom at work as well as on the playground, and on the road home. It was a very happy school, although I was disappointed that I did not have a grade eight to develop so as to start Farm Life School on the way to being a model high school for rural boys and girls. At the end of that week, my weekly report to Mr. Purcell was one of the very best as to attendance, enrollment, parent interest, and student response.

I had heard from Mr. Puckett every day, and he said he would call me Saturday night when he got home to see if he could possibly drive out to see me Sunday afternoon. He called. I tried to tell him the way, of the poor condition of the roads, and of bridges he would have to cross. I told him I was three creeks away from Screven, and he would have to cross Satilla Creek four times. First he would have to cross Satilla Creek near Mr. Isham Bennett's home, near Screven, then at Nine Runs as well as at Reedy Creek and nearby Coleman Creek, all lovely waterways flowing into the Little Satilla River. They bounded beautiful fertile fields filled with lush crops. When he came, he brought his daughter Gertrude and his two youngest children, Virginia Mae and L. P. Jr. We all had a nice visit on the front porch. He and Mr. Long seemed to get right off with their conversation about farming here in Wayne County and back in the Carolinas, where Mr. Puckett was raised. Mrs. Long seemed to enjoy Gertrude and the younger children. He had a new car, a Buick, larger than the small Chevrolet he had when we made the trip from the camp meeting at Hortense the last of August. He asked me to ride with him. The children stayed with Mr. and Mrs. Long.

Before we had gone very far we had bogged up in a sand bed on the road to Old Ritch Church. Several of the boys of the community came along and helped us push the car out. He tried to pay them, but they would accept no pay. Then he tried to take them for a ride, but they would not accept that either. They advised him not to go any further on the road, as the farther you went, the sandier it got, and the car seemed to be too low to take the deep sand beds or deep ruts. We turned around as soon as we found a suitable place. Our ride was a short one. We laughed it off. It was almost time for him and the children to go.

While we were gone the children had been invited to the pecan trees and the cane patch, so they were all supplied with the refreshments of the countryside. Mr. and Mrs. Long told Mr. Puckett that we would all be in Jesup the next Sunday, the third Sunday, September 20, at the Wayne County singing convention and that he must be sure to come hear the Ritch choir sing. Mr. Puckett promised them he would do so but for them to be sure that I was in the crowd going. They said, "Surely, everyone goes." Next Mr. Long told him of the big meeting at Big Creek Primitive Baptist Church and said he must plan to come to that. He told Mr. Puckett he could see some mighty pretty cotton farms on the way up there. The meeting would begin at ten in the morning and would last till late afternoon. You didn't have to stay all day long if you did not care to—that would be October 10. Mr. Puckett promised he would try to arrange to come and enjoy the whole day at the old-time camp meeting. They were soon gone, as the way was difficult, travel was slow, and no one cared to travel over those roads at night. All the folks he had met seemed to think him a fine man. The next week of school went off nicely, but I had to take the teasing about bogging up in the sand.

Everyone was getting ready for the singing convention, planning what they were going to wear and what they were going to take for the noonday meal, bragging about which choir would get the highest rating in the county. Ritch always stood mighty high. The day came, all bright and fair. After breakfast, we packed the noonday meal securely in the large wooden cracker box that was kept for that purpose. We were well on our way by sunup. The singing began at ten sharp, and no one wanted to miss a single one of the choirs, as everyone wished to be his own judge of the winners. We arrived in due time. People were everywhere. There were a few cars and trucks, but mostly it was horses, buggies, mules, and wagons. The courthouse was filled to overflowing, and soon the music was resounding all the way down to the first floor and out on the streets, where people sat in chairs under the large oaks on the courthouse square.

Mr. Puckett had called me the night before. He had received my letter telling him that we were to arrive at the courthouse around ten Sunday morning. He told me that he would meet me there at the stated time and said for me not to get lost in the crowd before he got there. We were getting unloaded from the big new cotton truck and finding out about lunchtime when Mr. Puckett came up. He spoke to all he knew, and I introduced him to the others who had come with us. Mr. Puckett told them that he wanted to borrow me for a little while, to take me for a ride. Mrs. Long told us to be sure and be back in time for lunch, around noontime. We thanked her and soon drove away. We went down to Doctortown again, and there Mr. Puckett pressed his proposal with greater determination than ever before. He wanted to know why I could not give him an answer. He said that my letters to him daily for some four months now led him to believe that I did care for him. Why did I continue to hold out on him when he loved me so dearly and needed me so much to make his life complete? He asked for me to please just tell him why I was still undecided. He wanted to know, if I did not mind telling him. I told him I did not like to bother other people with my affairs. I always thought everyone had enough troubles of their own without shouldering my responsibilities. He pressed me harder still.

I told him I was the youngest of twelve children, and my father had passed away in October 1919. My mother was too feeble to live alone anymore and was with my sister Mary Ellen, who had two small children. Our mother was becoming feeble and required more time than my sister could provide. All our other brothers and sisters were married and had about all the expense they could carry taking care of their own large families. My sister Lula, whom Mr. Puckett knew, and I had taken care of our mother and father for many years, as Lula and I had a nice little home, and our mother and father had lived happily until the passing of our father. Now it seemed that Lula or I would have to quit teaching to care for our mother. The other one would have to teach on to provide the necessities of life for our mother and whichever of us was to take care of our mother. Lula and I had discussed this at length, and it seemed that I would be the one to continue to teach. Therefore, I was not in a position to think about or talk to anyone about marriage. I had tried to equip myself well to go forward with my educational work, and I would try to be happy with my lot. I could not leave my mother without care. I told Mr. Puckett that I hoped he would not feel hard toward me, nor think I had led him on. I had enjoyed knowing him and had always enjoyed every minute with him and found his company delightful. I was exceedingly sorrowful if I had caused him any disturbance in any way. I also told him that my mother owned a small farm with a good home on it. It was where all twelve children had been raised, and it had produced abundantly for us. Now it was not being tended and was unproductive, just lying there.

So there we sat, I had no more to say. Finally he asked me did I care if he talked to Lula about the matter. I told him that I did not mind if he did. Then he wanted to known if I would go with him to see her. My answer was yes, when it could be conveniently arranged for the three of us. We drove back to the singing convention in time for lunch. Mrs. Long and her folks had spread theirs in the back of the new cotton truck and on the ground nearby and were ready to eat when we arrived. Mr. and Mrs. Long both invited Mr. Puckett to have lunch with us, but he declined, saying he would have to return home to have Sunday dinner with his children, the only noonday meal he would have with them until the next Sunday. I did not know whether I would ever see him again. We had a nice lunch, and the singing was soon going again. All the folks were trying to decide which community had done the best job. They would still be discussing it until next September, when it came time to battle it out again with their voices.

The convention closed at three, and we were soon on our way. We were fortunate to be riding in the cotton truck and were back to Farm Life before sundown, while those with horses and buggies and mules and wagons traveled far into the night on their return trip. Everyone had a delightful time; they had seen old friends from all over the county, from Mt. Pleasant, Union, Hopewell, Midway, Bethlehem, Oglethorpe, Piney Grove, Liberty, Red Hill, Bethel, Ritch, Screven, Odum, Reddishville, Kelly, O'Quinn, Flint Branch, and many other places that had choirs. It was a happy joyous time for all concerned and gave us many good conversation pieces during the week to come.

Another Monday morning came. School was moving along nicely, attendance was almost perfect, the weather was fine. I did some visiting, not from necessity, but just for the joy of visiting my pupils in their homes and getting better acquainted with their parents. I had enjoyable visits to the Pat Dennison home, the widow Mikel home, the widow Clary home, and several others. My other two teachers did not care for visiting like I did, so I usually went alone.

My good trustee, Mr. Thornton, was always doing something needful for the schoolchildren, like the time he came to the schoolhouse early one damp and chilly morning. We had nice warm fires going in all the heaters, and the schoolrooms were quite comfortable. He had a large roll of brown paper under his arm and a tin cup full of soft bacon drippings. He set the cup on my desk and laid the roll of paper down; then he asked me how many children were there without shoes that fall morning. I told him I did not know. He asked me to please check. So I asked him to sit at my desk until I could go to the other rooms and see. He asked me to bring the barefoot ones back with me. So I did, and he asked for them to be seated on the bench nearby. He took the brown paper and the cup of grease and went over to the barefoot children. He greased the bottoms of their feet, had them to stand flat-footed on the paper, and had me to write the appropriate name by each set of footprints. He had a big old soft cloth with which he wiped all the grease off their feet before he let them put them on the floor. He had about one dozen children's footprints on the papers. Then he was soon off to town with his measurements and names. A little after noontime, he returned with socks and a soft, good-looking, well-made pair of shoes for every one of them. I called for all

[205]

the barefoot children to come back to my room, and he soon had them all fitted with socks and shoes. He told them to tell their mamas that Santa Claus had came early to school that fall so they would not have to miss any days of school that winter. He seemed to be the one-man social-services committee for the whole community. I never did hear of any collection for these funds, but I always thought the whole community had paid for the shoes. You see, this was long before there was any welfare department to see after the needy of a school or community. The little boys and girls were surely proud of their new Christmas shoes.

Mr. and Mrs. Burley Thornton's daughter, Rosa, was to be married at high noon at home to Mr. Amos Altman, and Mr. Burley came and invited all three of us teachers and our students to the wedding. It was a beautiful, crisp fall day, and I told him we would come. So we turned out a little before noonday to give us just enough time to walk the short distance from the schoolhouse to the home of Mr. and Mrs. Thornton. There we lined up our children, with tallest ones in the back row by the lawn fence, then the next tallest, and so on. We had about 150 students and had four long rows the full length of the front porch, where the wedding was to be. By the time we had them ready, the bride and groom were coming onto the front porch from the front hall. All the houseguests had preceded them and were in the front yard with us. Their "waiters," which meant their young lady and gentleman friends who were going to stand with them during the ceremony, had made a nice-appearing line on each side of doorway for their company during the ceremony. The minister stepped forward from the crowd and performed the wedding ceremony, which was very beautiful. The holy bonds of matrimony were sealed with a kiss, and they were declared man and wife. Congratulations were now in order. Mr. Burley had asked us to stay for the wedding feast, but I told him no, that it would take too long and would be too hard on Mrs. Thornton and the other girls to prepare a feast for 150 schoolchildren. Then he said we must not leave until all the children had a piece of Rosa's wedding cake. So as soon as the ceremony was over, the girls were there with large trays of sliced golden pound cake. Each of the children took a slice, and we were soon on our way back to the schoolhouse.

We had our lunch at school, somewhat late, had our relief period, and then were back to school for regular work. Only the work was not regular. It was the first wedding that most of them had ever seen, and they had quite a few questions to ask about it and how it was all carried out. They wanted to know about the license, the ceremony, the marriage certificate, and all the vows of matrimony that had been spoken. It gave them food for thought for many days and a delightful story for them to tell when they got home. When they were asked why they went, they answered that Mr. Burley had invited us, and Miss Mizell had thought it would be a good trip for us to make. We all enjoyed every minute of it. I had the children write thank you notes to Mr. and Mrs. Thornton, and they told me afterward how much they had enjoyed reading them and how glad they were that they had invited us. I thanked them graciously.

Mr. Puckett made his trip to Big Creek's big meeting as he had promised. He brought his two oldest daughters with him, Gertrude and Angie. I had asked Miss Sports and Miss Howard to go with us. We arose early and were ready to go when they arrived about nine o'clock. The day was crisp and cool. We enjoyed the ride over the countryside and enjoyed the old-time preaching and singing. Mr. Puckett met quite a few of his friends he knew from Baxley, when he had lived there in the early 1900s and was laying the rails for the Southern Railway. We had a very pleasant day indeed. Mrs. Long had brought lunch, so we and the friends they had invited, who had come unprepared, all enjoyed the lunch together. Here the crowd was so enormous that people ate in groups, and I expect there were some people there who had no group to go to for lunch.

The home-going time was set for rather early. Church usually lasted until near sundown, as there were three long sermons, singing, the serving of the bread and wine, and also the washing of feet. We set 3:00 P.M. as our leaving time, and were soon all back to Mr. Long's. Mr. Puckett and I set a date for us to go to Piney Grove to see Lula and talk with her. Lula and I were to be in Jesup for a teachers meeting, and he was to take us both back to Piney Grove from the meeting Saturday night and return for me on Sunday afternoon in time for me to get Train No. 21 back to Screven. The road was better to Piney Grove than to Farm Life. On the way to Piney Grove, there was only one creek to cross, Goose Creek, and the Altamaha Ridge was pebbly clay, which made a far better road. The trip by car to Farm Life was difficult and long, yet Mr. Puckett would try it every so often.

Soon circus time came. Mr. Puckett arranged to be at home to take his six children. I went in with the crowd in Mr. Long's new cotton truck for the night performance. All those who drove horses and mules, which was nearly all the people on the farms about, went in for the circus parade and the afternoon show. We did not have many at school that day. We met them coming home as we were going to the evening show. Mr. Puckett and I took the children to the early sideshows and then to the big tent where all the famous circus acts were performed. Everyone seemed to enjoy the excitement of the actors. I believe that was the last time a big circus ever came our way. The boll weevil swallowed up the delight of the coming of the big-top circus, the same as it did many other timely traditions of the cotton country. There was much talk in the weeks that followed about the different circus acts, the fat lady and the lion tamer, the beautifully spangled bareback riders, the trapeze actors, snake charmers, fire-eaters, and sword swallowers, and on and on about the circus folks.

I was told many times by many of my students, "Ma wants to know who the handsome gentleman was who was taking you through the circus that night, and who were those six lovely children who were with you." I told them to tell their mothers that he was my gentleman friend, Mr. Puckett of Jesup, Georgia, a railroad contractor, and the lovely children were his, and that he was a widower, his wife having died in the terrible flu epidemic of 1918–19. I also told them that he came to Mr. and Mrs. Long's sometimes to see me, when he was home on the weekends from his work at Charleston, South Carolina. That seemed to satisfy them, and their mothers also, for they told me that "Ma" said, "He surely was good looking, and the children were pretty too, and you had better try to hang on to him." I laughed and told them that was what I was trying to do just as well as I knew how. They did not tease me anymore.

As time passed, our patrons became more and more despondent, as the cotton acreage was picked clean as clean as could be, and the yield was not reaching half the usual amount. The county fair came and went. The exhibits were made, and most everyone attended, but the talk with neighbor after neighbor from one end of the county to the other was a lamentation of the great loss the little boll weevil was pouring out on them. They were at a loss as to what to do. We did not plan a community cavalcade to the fair as we had at O'Quinn, as there were getting to be more and more Ford cars, and trucks of different makes. Yet the majority were still buggies and wagons. All who could get a seat rode in the trucks and cars, which was a great letdown for the buggy and wagon folks. Quite a few prizes were won by the men, boys, ladies, and their daughters, but this could not overcome the great economic disaster facing each one of them.

On November 1, the Monday after the fair, I told the two other teachers that the time had come for us to work on our Thanksgiving program, planned for Thursday night, November 25, at the school. We would have to complete our program plans that night, and I expected them to include every child in the program and to get a special invitation to all the parents, asking them to come and to contribute to the decorations for the occasion. I considered it a patriotic duty to celebrate Thanksgiving Day. But it was also our bounden duty to our community to do our best to help them raise their morale; for I could see it sinking lower and lower each time they met and talked of the economic chaos around them. It was becoming an obsession with them, from the oldest to the youngest. The older children were used to getting their Christmas money by scraping the fields for stray locks, but they told me there would be no scraping this year, as "Pa" had said he had to have every lock, and even then there still would not be enough to make ends meet. So the whole family was suffering from the boll weevil invasion.

I told my teachers to be sure to take their roll books home with them so we would have an accurate list of all children and parents, and I would do the same. They were to take home any material they thought we could use. We had to have the plan perfected before we slept that night so the children could begin work on their lines and have them memorized before the end of the week. We would take only enough time from classes to tie the program together. Learning the lines of the songs and poems would be a part of the English work each day, as would be writing a special invitation to their parents, grandparents, uncles, aunts, and cousins. We taught our day through, looking over our children and surveying their ability as to the contribution they could make to a lovely community program. In arranging our evening of celebration, we had to consider time, space, and audience as well as the children. Although we were still working on our fast-time schedule, the sun would be sinking low by the time we walked home, and it would soon be suppertime. We would have to forego our happy visiting hour around the dining table at the close of our evening meal, and one of us usually helped Mrs. Long with the dishes so she could hurry and join us around the table. This day we had to excuse ourselves and get into our own room to begin on our Thanksgiving program. Here is what we decided.

A. Decorations

Decorate the stage and front of the auditorium with Farm Life "goodies," right off the farm: cane, potatoes, peas, corn, and cotton; hay fodder, peanuts, pumpkins, syrup, and lard; hams, bacon, and sausage; dried peppers and sage; canned tomatoes, berries, pears, jellies, jams, figs, and watermelon rinds; soup mixture and dried apples, peaches, pears, and beef; cotton, cottonseed, cottonseed meal, cottonseed hulls; homemade soap, big hominy, honey, and butter.

B. Costumes of children

Everyday school clothes with a Pilgrim collar and cuffs of stiff white wrapping paper to be pinned on over their regular clothes. (We decided we could not use the tall black hats on account of crowded space on stage.)

C. Program

1. Open with singing "America"; ask audience to stand and sing with us. Repeat Psalm 100 in unison by whole school and audience if they care to join us while yet standing.

2. Welcome by first-grader Randal Tootle.[1]

3. Primary group singing "Over the River and through the Woods to Grandmother's House We Go." (They then retire off the stage and go to sit beside their parents.)

4. The story of the first Thanksgiving told by a group of fourth- and fifth-graders. Fourth- and fifth-graders singing "Swing the Shining Sickle"; they then retire to their seats.

5. Recitation of the poem "Landing of the Pilgrims" by a sixth-grader. Essay on the national Thanksgiving.

6. Remarks about our bountiful blessings. Blessings that are here on display tonight by sixth- and seventh-graders.

7. Singing of Whittier's "Corn Song" by sixth and seventh grades. Announcements given by me, Miss Martha Mizell, principal of Farm Life School.

   a. Thanks to everyone for contributing to the bountiful harvest decorations; remind them to be sure to get theirs before going home.

   b. Thanks to everyone for furnishing the lanterns for lighting our stage and decorations; ask them to be sure to linger after the program to get their lanterns.

   c. Call for the wishes of the parents about whether to discontinue our early-morning taking-in and return to a time schedule of 8 A.M. to 4 P.M. Many had asked for us to return to that schedule, as days were getting so short. Everyone voted for the later taking in and dismissal. There would be no more cotton-picking for the children except on Saturdays now as it would be almost nightfall when they arrived home. So I announced come Monday morning we would begin the later schedule.

   d. Announce that we had been instructed to teach Saturday, December 4, to make up for Friday December 24, Christmas Eve Day, which would be a "no-school day."

e. Close the program with a prayer of thanksgiving after I invite everyone to stay, visit, and get their produce with which we had decorated
the stage.

The program was a big success. The decorations were bountiful and beautiful, and everyone seemed happy, thankful, and joyous. The crowd was well
behaved and enjoyed seeing one another as well as they did the children's program. Many of the people exchanged their contributions to the decorations with
their neighbors for something they did not have. All the gifts and lanterns were
taken home. For you see, we had to teach on the morrow. In that day and time we
did not have days off, only our Christmas vacation each year, from just before
Christmas until the first Monday in January, and we received no pay for that. Our
program had taken very little time and had helped lift the despondency of our
patrons. Only four weeks remained until Christmas Day, and there was yet so
much to do for myself and the school.

Mr. Puckett and I had continued our courtship. We had talked with Lula, and
he had promised her that our mother would never want as long as he lived. She
died two years to the very day after my marriage, and he provided for her funeral
expense. After her estate was settled I insisted that he be reimbursed for those
expenses, and he accepted. I know that was the way she would have wished it, for
she never was a person to wish to be a burden to anyone; she wanted to carry her
own load at all times. He gave me my ring in October, and we set our wedding
day for Wednesday, December 29, 1920, in my home at Nahunta at four o'clock
in the afternoon. So I was very busy getting myself ready for my wedding, for our
wedding trip to Miami afterward, and for my home duties when I became a house-
wife instead of a public school teacher.

I had to begin to plan my wardrobe. Most all ladies dresses were made by
dressmakers in that day and time. I got Mrs. M. L. Parker in Jesup to make me two
beautiful dresses, a black satin dress trimmed with small tucks and gold lace, and
a well-tailored light blue wool broadcloth dress finished with black military braid
and a colorful ribbon vest finishing in the front. Lula and I made a trip to Savannah to get my wedding invitations, my wedding suit of blue wool, hat, shoes,
blouses, bathrobe, and bedroom shoes. She and I made all my negligees, underclothes, and housedresses. I made four nice gingham, chambray, broadcloth, and
Indian Head linen dresses for my household duties. I also bought the material to
make a nice supply of sheets and pillowcases. Bridal showers were not yet in style
then to help out. I went to a good friend in Screven, Mrs. Lawson Morgan, and
sewed there the whole weekend.[2] I did a good bit of crocheting for pillowcases,

dresses, scarves, and centerpieces. In fact, I had quite a bit of my trousseau already on hand, all nicely laundered and folded away in my trunk.

Before the wedding, there were many items of business I had to attend to. First I had to be sure that all my financial obligations were taken care of while I was still a working woman. By counting every penny, I paid the last payment on my three-hundred-dollar note at the Merchants and Farmers Bank and received the note marked "paid in full." That concluded my outstanding personal obligations. Then I had to turn to my professional obligations. I had never broken a school contract in all my eight years of teaching. So I told Mr. Puckett that I could not give up my school without the consent of my superintendent and that I must see him the next time I got to Jesup. I think Mr. Puckett beat me to the draw, for when I told Mr. Purcell that I needed to see him privately on some personal business, he laughed and told me to come on in, and we would see what he could do for me. Then I told him I wished to be relieved of my contract at the end of the fourth month, as Mr. Puckett and I wished to be married in December. I told him I had no idea when I signed my contract that I would be asking to be relieved so soon.

We had a wonderful school so far. The patrons were among the best. Every student was above the average, and their behavior had been above reproach. In other words, I considered it some of the best and most pleasant teaching I had ever done. I would do my best to leave everything in order. I would grade and check all areas of study for every child and leave a full record of all their accomplishments. I would have their report cards filled out for half a year, as well as the permanent scholastic record of each child I had enrolled. I would bring them to Mr. Purcell on December 24, along with the attendance records, so that he could give them to whomever he hired to follow after me. We talked at length.

He said Mr. Puckett was a special friend of his, that he had rented Mr. Puckett's home on the corner of Brunswick and Pine streets and had lived there for several years while Mr. Puckett was building the Georgia and Florida railroad from Augusta to Moultrie. He said that he considered Mr. Puckett one of the finest men he had ever known, and he was so glad to know that we were to be married. He would not only relieve me of my contract, but he would add his and Mrs. Purcell's blessings. He hoped he and Mrs. Purcell could always count Mr. Puckett and me among their dearest friends throughout their lives.[3] I thanked him profusely for being so considerate of my wishes. I told him I believed he had given Mr. Puckett encouragement in being so ardent in pushing his suit to a successful conclusion so rapidly. Here he laughed out at length. He said, "You do not mind if I gave you a good recommendation, do you?" He said that when Mr. Puckett inquired of him about me he had told him if he had searched the world over he could not find a finer woman to bring to his home and to help him raise his children to be noble ladies and gentlemen; he prayed that Mr. Puckett would love me with all his heart all the days of our lives. Mr. Puckett's reply was, "You need never fear about that. If you would just relieve her, as she will not break her contract without your consent." I told Mr. Purcell how much I appreciated his advice and kindness through the years and that I would see him with my records at eight o'clock the morning of Christmas Eve. I said I would be much obliged if he would write a letter to Mr. Long and tell him of my request to be relieved of my contract. He promised me he would do it that very day.

Mr. Long had received the letter on Monday, and after supper that night, around the dining table at our usual chitchatting hour, the news of my upcoming marriage to Mr. Puckett was the topic of the hour. Here again I had to express my appreciation for all they had done for me. Mr. and Mrs. Long both told me how much they hated to see me go, but they thought Mr. Puckett was a fine gentleman and that his children seemed to be mighty fine and sweet, so they would have to add their blessings to our happiness. They, too, hoped to always number us among their dearest friends.

With my professional obligations attended to, I then had to turn to my duties concerning my marriage. So the next weekend, I went to my home in Nahunta. We had rented it completely furnished for forty dollars a month to a Mr. Waters, one of the incoming colonists of Mr. L. S. Robb from the north. I went to see them as soon as I arrived and asked them may I use my home for about five days to prepare for and have my wedding there. They very graciously said I could. I asked them their fee for the use of the house, and they said, "Oh, not much. Just enough to cover the expense of the wedding." I told them I would bear all expenses. Next I went to see three of my friends of the village: Mrs. Rosa Peek, Mrs. J. B. Lewis, and Mrs. S. B. Lary. I got them all three together and told them I was to marry, and I wished them to help me with the refreshments. I told them my wedding wardrobe was about ready, that the invitations had been ordered, and that I had come home to arrange for the wedding.

Mrs. Rosa spoke up at once. She said to just let them know who I was to entertain and how many; they would see to it all. I told her I expected most of my guests would be my friends, neighbors, and kinfolks of my childhood up on the banks of the Big Satilla, all the way from the Rattlesnake Bridge to the Ammons Ferry Bridge. They would drive horses and buggies, mules and wagons, and would bring their children. It was a long way, from ten to twenty-five miles to come to Nahunta, and they would be tired, cold, and hungry when they arrived.

Then Mrs. Rosa looked at the other two ladies and said, "Let's make it chicken salad, deviled eggs, saltines, hot coffee, wedding cake, and two pounds of coffee." They all agreed. They said that enough nice plates, forks, cups, and spoons could be easily gotten. With ours and theirs, we would not have to do many more askings among the neighbors, and I could buy the paper napkins. Mrs. Rosa said she would bake a huge pound cake in a giant pan, and ice and decorate it well. She was rated as one of the finest cake bakers anywhere around.

She would give me a list of material to bring from the grocery store in Jesup when I came home on December 24. This was for the chicken salad dressing, celery, olives, lettuce, thin saltines, and napkins. I would arrange for the eggs and chickens and some other items at the local grocery store. On Monday, the twenty-seventh, I was to get the chicken and eggs; and dress, cook, bone, and mince the meats. They would come the morning of the twenty-ninth to prepare, mix, and serve the plates; they would be through before noontime. They would then go home, dress, and be back in time to serve for me after the wedding. Mrs. Rosa would also bring the wedding cake and fix the bride's table. Who could have asked for greater love than this? I knew my worries were over in the arrangement of my wedding reception, for these were three dependable women. So I hurried to our local general store, where Hon. J..B. Strickland was the general manager. I told him I wanted twelve fat hens, six dozen fresh eggs, two pounds of Maxwell House coffee, five pounds of sugar, and cream. All were to be picked up Monday morning. While I was in there he told me he wanted to buy our northeast corner lot for the Masons, who hoped to erect a lodge hall on it. So we traded on that as to price, and I told him that as soon as my sister Lula and I could get together, we would make the deed, and he could pay us. I would get half the price of the lot, and that would help me meet the expenses of my reception.

I hastened to complete my day's work. I had to see my dear young friend, Mrs. Naomi Brown (Mrs. Ralph Brown), and ask her to furnish the wedding music, which she graciously did. The minister of the First Methodist church of Jesup, the Reverend Mr. Arnold, had just arrived at his new appointment. Neither of us knew him, so we chose a minister from Jesup, the Reverend Mr. Bush, minister of First Baptist church, whom both of us knew. I had raced and chased all day, but now all was well. I was satisfied, and I could return to my schoolwork and know that all would be well with me on my wedding day. I left Nahunta Saturday afternoon to ride to Jesup, where I would change to Train No. 57 for Screven. That was my last time to make that run as Martha Mizell.

My plans were now complete, and I had only four more weeks to teach. I still had my wedding invitations to mail out as soon as they arrived from the engravers.

When we were compiling our list of those we wished to invite, Mr. Puckett had very few. But before we had come down to the addressing and mailing, his list of brothers, sister, father (his mother had passed away), uncles, aunts, and favorite cousins was quite lengthy. So my supply of invitations was soon exhausted, and most of my close kin were invited by special letter, which they appreciated very much. Most of them came, while Mr. Puckett's people in far away North and South Carolina were unable to attend. I was always glad they had been invited, as they each and every one became very near and dear to me as we visited them in the following years. They never failed to tell me how much they appreciated that invitation, even if they did not get to come to my wedding. They felt like they knew me from that day forth, and I at once became a part of their great family. I was so graciously accepted by the whole generation of Carolina kinfolks.

All necessary plans had been brought to conclusion now except for one thing. What was I going to give the Puckett children for Christmas? My obligations had been heavy, and my money was getting to be less and less. My invitations were yet to be mailed, and I had to pay my way to my home once more. I wanted the gift to be nice. I wanted them to enjoy it. Then it came to me out of the clear blue sky. Mrs. Long cooked the best fruitcake I had ever tasted, and I could get some sprays of the most beautiful holly I had ever seen out of Coleman Creek Swamp with which to decorate it. The next time Mr. Puckett came out to see me I would send it to them all beribboned and with a card saying, "Do not open until Christmas." Mrs. Long and I did this the very next Saturday.

I got a large green box—we had baked the cake in an extra-large pan—and placed the cake in it on a bed of soft tissue paper. I tied the box with a big bow of red ribbon, tied on sprays of fresh green holly loaded with red berries, and placed my card on it. So when Mr. Puckett came out to see me the last time before my leaving, I gave it to him to take to the children from me for their Christmas. They would smell it, all their friends were invited to come and smell, but no one peeked. Everyone wanted to know where they got it, and they always replied, "'Our Mother Martha' sent it to us for our Christmas." So that was how I got my name in the family. From that time forth I was Mother Martha to them, and for lo these fifty-two years I am still their Mother Martha, and I love them every one so dearly. I never have missed baking and sending fruitcakes to them, wherever they might be, since they have been away from home. So in place of the one fruitcake I baked at Christmastime, it has turned out to be many, many fruitcakes. After the grands and great-grands came along, it multiplied still more.

During the time I lived with Mr. and Mrs. Long, I had not missed the opportunity to learn of the workings of that great plantation and its happy, businesslike management. It had come into being through the efforts of one man, Mr. Walton Long. He had worked as a day laborer and bought the land when Wayne County land was selling for twenty-five to fifty cents per acre, and some swampland for as low as ten cents per acre. He had cleared every foot of it with his own hands and strong back, a club ax, a crosscut saw, and a grubbing hoe. He worked all day for his employer until nightfall; then he would clear his land until midnight. He did this until he had enough cleared to make a one-horse farm. Then he had to work out a horse and a few plow tools, such as turn plow, opening plow sweeps, and scooters. He next had to build a log cabin, barns, and other outbuildings. He split rails to fence his fields, as we had open range then and for many years to come. He married a Miss Harris. She did not live long and left him with three children, two girls, Viola and Della, and a crippled son (from polio I think), Stog. Sometime later he married Miss Maude Moody. Three of their children were born there, one daughter, Estelle, and two sons. One son died with typhoid fever. The other baby was born when I was there.

His plantation had grown from one small log cabin and small amount of cleared acreage into the largest and most scientifically controlled plantation of any in this section of the state, with fifteen one-mule tenants and Mr. Long with a large acreage for himself and some hired hands. After he had cleared more land than he could work well himself, he asked one of his friends to come and work a portion in partnership with him. This was his plan: He would furnish a house, barn, mule, tools, fields, fence, fuel, and water well or pump. The man would furnish feed for the mule after the first year, and he was to grow a supply crop of corn, potatoes, peanuts, peas, beans, sugar cane, meat, milk, and honey. Mr. Long would provide a sow, a cow, and bees. He, the tenant, was to fertilize the supply crop and the summer and winter gardens of all varieties of vegetables and to have all varieties of fruits, nuts, grapes, and figs as soon these could be established at his homesite. The tenant was to feed his mule, cow, pigs, chickens, and other animals, and to have the returns of his stock. Mr. Long was to get all the heifer yearlings. The partner was to get half of the steers when they were butchered, and he was to grow and harvest thirty acres of long-staple Sea Island cotton; Mr. Long would furnish the land, seed, tools, mule, and half the fertilizer. The man was to pay half the cost of the fertilizer and grow and harvest the crop in due season. They were to share the total income on a fifty-fifty basis. To save the cost of fencing, the cotton was to be grown in the cotton field right beside Mr. Long's large acreage, and planted and worked according to the best methods of that day and time and harvested accordingly. All cotton was in one great field, five hundred acres. The fields were quite a showpiece when they were in full bloom or ready to harvest.

Mr. Long used to laugh and tell about when he used to have to work so hard to split the rails to fence his fields. He soon learned that the larger the acreage to be fenced, the less rails it took per acre to fence. His neighbors would tease him and tell him, he must be trying to get it so large that one rail would fence an acre. The homesites for the tenants were built here and there over his large holdings, the finest of soil and timber and abundant forest and water supply. A pretty site would be selected, and there the tenant would build a nice, neat log cabin, with one good chimney, a front porch, a back shed to be used for cooking and dining, and a second back shed area as an extra bedroom. When more room was needed, he would add another cabin for the kitchen and dining room, and the space once used for cooking and dining would be made into a bedroom. A walkway connected the kitchen and big house. Outbuildings consisted of a log smokehouse and a log chicken house with a shed for the chicks. The varmints from the creek swamps were so abundant and fierce that they could easily overturn small coops, so the younger chickens were cooped within the larger chicken coop. A large, strong log corncrib had a good loft to hold forage for the milk cow for winter feeding. Each side of the crib had a shed, one side for a milk cow, the other side for the cow's calf. The mule barn was a large stable with a loft for forage for the mule. A shed to one side was for the wagon and harness. A shed on the other side held bins for sweet potatoes, pumpkins, peas, beans, onions, Irish potatoes, and other supply crops.

Of course there was a strong hog pen for the fine sow and her brood of pigs to keep the varmints from eating them, every one. Every domestic animal had to be made secure at night. Sometimes the alligators would get them in the daytime if they grazed too near the creek swamps. All these timbers were cut from the strip of land that was to be cleared the next winter as well as the trees to make the ever needful rails to fence the new ground.

All the buildings were made from the slender pine saplings of Mr. Long's higher ground and were covered with pure heart-cypress shingles from his big trees in the creek swamp. The long, thin cleats were made from the same heart cypress. The limbs would be cut for firewood, and the pine needles would be raked and hauled to make bedding for the animals and to help supply the enormous amount of barnyard fertilizer ever needed to keep the land fertile for the supply crops. No money came forth from these crops, as they were consumed by man and beast right there on farm, so it was necessary to grow them without money being involved. They saved their homegrown fertilizer, grew the crops, consumed them for their own benefit, and owed no man for what they consumed.

Mr. and Mrs. Long's gift to a bride and groom who came to them to live would be twelve hens and a rooster to the bride and a bred gilt to the man. The milk cow would be loaned so the family would always have a milk supply, for their children, and milk, butter, cream, clabber, and buttermilk for the family. They usually would become attached to their milk cow. Mr. Long would always go on a note for them to buy a Home Comfort stove and a Singer sewing machine. The note was to be paid when the cotton was sold. Mr. Long said it was as essential for a man's wife to have a good stove and a good sewing machine as it was for a man to have a good mule, plows, hoes, and axes.

As years rolled by, more and more families came to live on Mr. Long's farm. They traded seeds and improved their supply crops by careful seed-selection and better fertilization and cultivation. They swapped messes of all kinds of vegetables, fruits, and fresh meats and thereby became very good neighbors in their way of life. It has often been said that a man never left Mr. Long unless he had saved enough to try to buy land and develop a farm of his own. Not many did that, as they felt that they had it better with Mr. Long than if they were off alone trying to make it on their own. There was always someone waiting, hoping against hope, that he could get established in this great plantation system. The new man would usually be ready before another unit could be added to the plantation. When I was there in 1920 there were fifteen complete units of homes, barns, and supply crops, and a cotton field of five hundred acres. Fifteen thirty-acre sections plus fifty acres that Mr. Long tended the best, fertilized the best, and planted with the best seed offered on the market. It was test acreage planted to see if the fifteen other units should follow the procedures established there. On account of the boll weevil, I don't expect any more units were ever added.

Mr. Long had a few rules he asked each of his men to follow. First, he was to take care of the tools, vehicles, and animals placed in his care. Second, he was to keep his new home in an attractive, clean manner and to keep it in good repair. Third, he was to practice seed selection on all his crops. Fourth, he was to provide a good table. Fifth, he was to keep plenty of wood to keep his family warm and happy. Of course, that included plenty of well-prepared wood for the Home Comfort stove. He should always plan for his wife to spend at least one week a year visiting her people and for one week's attendance at the church of his choice each year (usually the protracted meeting). It was necessary for him to be at home between Christmas and New Year, as this was the season when all plans were made for the crops for the coming year, and he needed to know if any changes were to be made in seeds, fertilizers, cultivation, and harvesting plans. He also needed to know if the supply crops were adequate for their needs—and if not, why not—and where changes could be made to make sure there would be enough. Mr. Long told me he always felt this to be the most valuable time of the whole year. It was important that everyone know what was expected, and whether they were pleased with their returns. He always advised them to try to put some of their profits aside in savings to have something to help them out should sickness, accident, or hard luck hit them.

There were two great merry-making times on the plantations when they all came together to rejoice, Independence Day (the Fourth of July) and New Year's Eve. On the Fourth of July, after all crops were laid by, they would have an all-day picnic on the front lawn of Mr. Long's home; the dinner, consisting of goodies prepared by all the ladies of the plantation, was spread at noontime. Then later in the afternoon came famous watermelon-cutting, where every man brought from his own patch his very finest melon, sliced, and served it.

Everyone could have the seeds from their portion if they so desired. Many of the seeds were gathered for next year's melon crops. Games were played by old and young until late in the afternoon. The ladies did much talking while the men wagered the yield per acre of their cotton acreage. The setting of the sun would see them going home with their empty dinner baskets and a great quantity of melon rinds to be made into pickles and preserves by the ladies for winter use by their families. Everyone would tell Mr. and Mrs. Long what a wonderful, happy day they had had and how they hoped they could all be together the next Fourth of July. The ladies hoped they would have time to try out all the recipes they had collected before next July. Of course, the men had enjoyed the horseshoe pitching, the high jumps, and the many other games they had entered into. The children had played ball, marbles, and singing games and had sung the latest love songs. After a day of enjoyment, the people would load their wagons, and everyone would wind their way home, weary from a happy, well-earned holiday. And on the morrow they would be ready for canning, sewing, fall garden planting, or getting ready for that weeklong visit to Grandmother's house or for the week's "protracted meeting," or any other summer activity until cotton-picking time.

The other great holiday for all the farm was New Year's Eve, when great bonfires were lighted to giant piles of the huge Sea Island cotton stalks. After all the cotton was picked and the heavy winter frost and freezes came, the larger children would take the strong hickory cudgels and break off rows of cotton plants so that just the giant main stalk was left standing. Then the father would take his turn plow and rip those stubs of stalks from the earth. The larger children would follow their father, pulling the stalks and roots, putting four rows into one pile row, making the piles as high as they could. The piles would dry there in the cold, crisp air until New Year's Eve, when all the families on the farm and neighbors from far and near would come at dusk. The long fat-splinter torches would be lying at the end of each heap row, ready to be lighted. Each farmer would provide the torches and select the torchbearers for each row from among his children or from his neighbors' children. It was quite an honor to be selected as a torchbearer, and there was always a handsome prize for the one who made the run and finished first, having lighted every pile well so they would all burn evenly. No little children were allowed; they sat on the long porch of Mr. Long's home with the ladies and watched the bonfires from there.

It was a beautiful and exciting sight, all those great piles of flaring stalks up and down the rows—over five hundred of them. The older men followed after and made a tour of every pile on every heap row, raking the ends of the stalks into the middle of the hot, red coals, where they would burn to clear, clean ashes. The young folks would go back up to the large space in the lawn in front of Mr. Long's home where a large bonfire had been built of fat stump-wood so there were no sparks to fly. There they played singing games and other active games. By and by Mrs. Long and the other ladies would serve peanut brittle and pecan candy made from good Georgia cane syrup. When the men arrived from tending the stalk piles until the last nub was burned, they would find the cold cane juice that had been ground early in the evening—so cold it would hurt your teeth. Everyone would drink until they could drink no more, knowing full well there was no more until next cane-grinding time, one year hence, as all the cane had been ground. The sweep would be taken off the cane mill and stored under the house, and a small shelter would be placed over the mill until next fall.

My children had begged me so hard to return from my Christmas vacation in time for their New Year's Eve bonfire; I kept telling them I could not promise for sure, but I knew they would have a lovely time. They would always tell me that they wanted me to be there to enjoy it with them. The boys could hardly wait until they became old enough to be chosen to carry the torch for their father's acreage.

Everyone laughed and talked. They had a lot of jokes to tell about the dry peas and hog jowl dinner they were going to have on the morrow for New Year's to give them luck and health for all the next year, with the meal's added delicacies of crackling corn bread, cabbage coleslaw, sweet potato pie, and sweet milk or buttermilk. It was early to bed on New Year's night and up before sun on January 2, as that was when the plows and teams would begin to roll for 1921 crop. Of course, the men had all gone out New Year's morning, each with his mule and wagon, stone crock, and clean shovel to gather the clean cotton-stalk ashes; for this was to make their supply of lye hominy for good winter eating with collards, turnips, rutabagas, and sweet potatoes. What could be better than a large bowl of lye hominy fried in sausage or ham drippings? This job was never delayed, for fear of a winter rain on them; nor ever entrusted to the children, for fear they would dip beyond the clean ashes and get sand. Not a spoonful was to be wasted, as all the ashes not needed for the hominy would be used to make the year's supply of soap from the wasted fat at hog-killing and beef-butchering time.

Our talks were enjoyable to the very last night of my stay in this wonderful, hospitable home. I learned of all the small tasks that were performed to make the guest who entered there feel welcome and happy. Mrs. Long told me of many little acts she performed every day to make Mr. Long at ease, so he always knew that everything would be in order anytime he brought any of his many gentlemen callers to the home. She always put their bedroom in order as soon as they arose, for Mr. Long kept his desk and all his business papers in that room. It was always kept warm in winter and cool in the summer. She always set the table nicely for dinner as soon as breakfast was completed. She never failed to see that a fresh towel, clean comb, washbasin, and a full bucket of water were on the wash shelf on the porch. Then if anyone came, it would all be ready—and there was usually someone there for the noonday meal every day. She prepared her food to perfection; no matter what the menu, it was always a delicious meal. She served them all with the "golden sauce of hospitality." I never knew a person who could do better than she.

On my last night with the Longs, I set myself to pack my trunk, excusing myself early from the family hour of conversation around the dining table. I asked Miss Sports and Miss Howard to go with me, as I had promised them all of my teaching materials, and I wished to divide them as they so desired. I had acquired a large collection over many years: *Normal Instructors and Primary Plans, Progressive Teachers,* many art supplies, all my program books for "special days," and other teaching devices. I divided the teaching aids between the two. Then I began to pack my clothes, the year's supply I had brought with me in September plus my new fall wardrobe and my wedding outfit. I packed layer after layer until my trunk was solid up to the tray. On one side of the tray, I put my precious wedding hat stuffed with plenty of tissue paper. As I was pondering what to put in the other compartment, Mrs. Long came in with a delicious fruitcake baked in a large pan and decorated with sprays of beautiful red-berried and waxy-leafed holly from Coleman Creek. She said she wanted me to take it home to serve to my hometown friends as they came and went during the few days before my wedding. My! It smelled so good and was so pretty. She had it in a strong box, well packed with

tissue paper, that just fit the other side of the tray. I told her she must have measured it. She said she had not, but Miss Sports had measured it for her, and she
baked and packed the cake accordingly. My trunk was now ready.

When we returned from school the next afternoon, I would need to hurry to
catch Train No. 180 from Screven to Jesup. I had left my grip almost empty so
that I could put in my overnight clothes, a few pieces of soiled laundry, and some
toilet articles and still have room to carry my teaching supplies and the report
cards that I had to finish for the first half of the term to turn over to my superintendent. He would then turn them over to whomever he secured to follow after me.

That day, Mr. Puckett had paid me his last visit at the Long home. Around
the dining table with the family after I had told Mr. Puckett good-bye, I thanked
them for how nice they had been to me during my stay. I conveyed Mr. Puckett's
thanks to them for the kindness they had shown him during his many visits in
their home and said he had apologized for any trouble he may have caused them.
They quickly said it had been no trouble at all. They were always glad to have
him and had enjoyed his company while he was waiting for me to come from
school. I had asked him to never come to the schoolhouse for me; I was there to
work not to court. This day was the only time I had ever asked to use the living
room. Mr. Puckett and I usually went for a ride during the short time he would
have with me. This day it was pouring rain, and I knew he could not stay long, as
the roads were so bad, and night was close by, but there were some final plans we
needed to talk over. I asked Mrs. Long to invite the two other teachers and their
beaus down to the dining room with her, which she graciously did. I think then
was when they measured the compartment of my trunk tray to get a box to fit the
space and the cake.

Mr. Puckett told me he had to return to Charleston that night with his pay-
roll. He had to get his books in order to pay off his hundreds of railroad workers
early Thursday morning, and had to give his men and foreman instructions about
what to do until he returned early in the New Year after his marriage to me and
our wedding trip. I had a date with Mr. Purcell in Jesup early Friday morning,
and I told Mr. Puckett that I could see him after that if I had the time, as I would
be trying to make it home on the Train No. 85 around noontime. He was soon on
his way back to Jesup through the mud and slush on a cold and rainy December
evening but not before I gave him the beautifully decorated fruitcake for his children's Christmas present from me. He called me late in the evening, saying he had
just arrived home and would soon be leaving for Charleston.

Mrs. Long kept a gracious home and was always pleasant and hospitable to
everyone who entered her door. She was always ready to receive them, feed them

well, and sleep them comfortably if they were overnight guests. I loved her with all my heart, and I let her know it before I left her home and for years afterward. I told Mr. Long good-bye, and I begged of him not to lose faith in me because I had not fulfilled my contract. I let him know how much I had enjoyed his talks about his great plantation and his wonderful rules of conservation he had set up as guides for his people to follow, so as to make everything count, even to the smallest item. Nothing was wasted. He believed that "willful waste made woeful want."

Below are some of his rules for the plantation, his forest, and creek lands.

1. No tree would be cut unless it was needed for a special purpose. The whole tree must be used, even its foliage and needles. The body of the tree was to be used for the purpose it was cut, such as for rails, shingles, pales, rafters, sills, or stove wood. The limbs would be prepared for firewood, and the tiny limbs and twigs of hardwood would be cut up for kindling, for small stove fires, or hearth fires. The straw would be raked and hauled for bedding for the animals, to keep them warm, and to catch their urine. It would be stored then used for fertilizer for the supply crops. His forest-lands were to be kept as clean and beautiful as a park.

2. Sugar cane could be cut for chewing as soon as it was sweet enough to smell, provided the top was brought up to the barn to give to the milk cow to help her produce good sweet milk, butter, and cream.

3. Peanuts could be pulled as soon as they were full enough to be edible and tasty, provided the vines were put on top of the shelter to dry for winter forage for the milk cow.

4. All shucks from the corn were always to be packed in sacks and dried for the winter feeding of cattle.

5. All corncobs would be burned for ashes and used on the trash heap to help make compost.

6. All dry pea hulls were to be stored for winter forage for cows. It was as sinful not to take care of your animals as it was to waste your forest and crops.

7. Live within your means, and be happy with what you produce. He had grown cotton for five cents per pound, and now it was $1.25 per pound, and he had lived well through it all, for he believed that providing for your living was the first thing.

We sometimes talked about his rules until late in the night. His wisdom was tried and true, and all his men respected him for it. All the ladies admired Mrs. Long in her role as the helpmate in such a great enterprise.

School closed at its regular time on Thursday, December 23. It was to open again on Monday, January 3, 1921, but I would not be there. Quite a few of the children were very sad, knowing I would not return.

Once we were back at Mr. Long's, Mrs. Long had us each drink a glass of milk and eat a generous slice of her Christmas fruitcake. She wanted to serve us supper, but there was no time. Jesse, the handyman, had all our suitcases and my trunk already loaded in the cotton truck. We said good-bye and were soon in the truck and on our way.

The train was coming down the track when we got to Screven. We boarded and were in Jesup in a few minutes. Miss Howard went to her home on South First Street. Miss Sports had friends who met her, and she went with them to her home out Goose Creek way. Said she would see me Friday morning before I left for my home. I bought my ticket to Nahunta and checked my trunk for the next day, as I knew I would be so pushed for time Friday. I took my grip and walked across the street to Mr. Harry Surrency's store.

Mrs. Peek had told me I could get everything I needed there to make my wedding reception complete, the little extras that the Nahunta general store did not carry, such as olives, lettuce, Durkee dressing, celery, thin saltines, nice napkins, and doilies. I showed Mr. Surrency my suitcase and told him to make the packages to fit it, as I wanted to put them in there to take on the train. I asked him to get a cab to take my bundles, my grip, and me to the Wayne Hotel. I would spend the night and complete my school records. I would be right across the street from the courthouse, where I would deliver the records to Mr. Purcell early the next morning. Mr. Surrency said, "Oh! No cab"; he would take my groceries and suitcase in his delivery wagon, and I could walk around. I paid him and was soon on my way over to the hotel, little realizing that he would be the first person I would ever address myself to as Mrs. L. P. Puckett. As it turned out, Mr. Surrency was the grocery man who supplied Mr. Puckett's family, and when I called him for my first order of groceries, I identified myself with my name from my marriage.

I began work after telling the hotel lady that I had a lot of record work to do and did not care for supper, but to please awaken me in time for breakfast, as I had an appointment and must be on time. I worked until the wee small hours of the morning. I had everything ready, in perfect order, and stacked on my dresser. I packed the groceries in my grip with just enough space left for my toilet articles and my nightclothes. I thought I was burning my last midnight oil grading and recording children's report cards, but this was not so. If you read the story to completion, you will find out.

I lay down to sleep, and it seemed like just a few minutes until the maid was saying, "Last call to breakfast." I got up, dressed, packed my grip, and ate a hurried breakfast. I paid my bill and asked if I could leave my grip at the clerk's desk while I went across to the courthouse to turn in some school records. They very kindly assured me that I could leave it. I told them I would not be gone but a few hours.

I walked over to the courthouse, turned in all my records, and thanked Mr. Purcell for all his kindness throughout the years. I sent my love and best regards to Mrs. Purcell and their daughter Evelyn, and told Mr. Purcell good-bye. When I came out of he courthouse I saw I had some time before my train, so I walked across the street and one block down to Mr. Puckett's home, so soon to be mine also. He was there, having gotten home after riding all night from Charleston. All the children were there and all in a buzz about their Christmas tree and presents. I went in and let Mr. Puckett know that I had made my final teaching report and must be on my way, as my train would soon be in. He, the children, and I got in the car, stopped at the hotel to pick up my grip, and drove up as the train was pulling in. My good friend Miss Sports was there to see me off. Mr. Puckett said he would see me on Sunday, December 26; he must spend Christmas day with his children. He reached over and kissed me and was gone. I got on the train and waved good-bye to all of them. It was only a short ride to home.

When I reached Nahunta I went uptown to find my pleasant drayman. I saw his little gray mare hitched to the front porch of the general merchandise store and saw him sitting on the whittling bench. He was so glad to see me, as he knew he now had some business. I told him I wanted him to get my trunk and suitcase from the depot and to take them to my home. I asked him to wait a minute. I stepped inside and asked Mr. Strickland if he had the twelve fat hens for me for Monday morning. He said he surely did, at fifty cents each, nice fat Plymouth Rock hens. He also had the eggs, sugar, and bean coffee all ready to give me. I told him I would be in for them early Monday morning, and would he help me wring their necks. He said he would get the drayman, Edwin, to help. I stepped back to where Edwin was waiting and told him I would also want him early Monday morning to help me get some chickens to my home. He could just bring his wheelbarrow for that. I would need him to get my trunk and suitcase to the depot on Sunday, January 2, to be taken to my new home at Jesup by my sister Lula as she returned to her school at Piney Grove. I gave him a dollar for all three jobs, twenty-five cents twice for my trunk, tens cents twice for my suitcase, and thirty cents for helping wring the hens' necks. He seemed so happy. He said, "I can now get an extra present for my father, for my aunt Sallie (his mother had been dead for years), and for my two younger brothers." I thought how kind and considerate, not a penny to be spent on himself.

He soon had my trunk and suitcase at my home. Although it was heavy, we got it out of the tail of the wagon and onto the porch, where I could, with his help, push it into the room I was to occupy with Lula until after my wedding. He helped me untie the rope around my trunk. I unlocked it and took out the fruitcake. It had shipped perfectly. Everything else seemed okay. We took the cake to the dining room and asked Mrs. Waters, the landlady, for a large cake plate and a sharp knife. She brought the knife but did not have a large cake plate, so we took the lid off the box, turned the box upside down, and put the cake on top. I cut it and gave Mrs. Waters a slice. She said, "Yum, yum! So delicious" and further added that one of her lifelong dreams had been realized—to actually eat a slice of real southern fruitcake. I sliced a piece for Edwin and cut pieces for his father, his aunt, his brothers, and his sister Eppie. Mrs. Waters gave me a napkin and small box for Edwin's slices. I fastened a spray of holly on top of the box and gave it to him. He was soon on his way, with me admonishing him to come early Monday morning to help me with the chickens. He said okay, brought in my suitcase, and was gone. I told Mrs. Waters to be sure to serve her family a slice of the cake for supper and that I would not care for supper. I was so tired that I would retire. I was looking forward to the arrival of Lula. She had had some official business to attend to and would not get home until Christmas morning. So to bed I went, promising myself to unpack on the morrow.

Christmas Day came and went. Many friends called. I gave them all a nice slice of fruitcake. It was fast disappearing. I unpacked my trunk; everything had kept perfectly. I had worried about my hat, but it was okay. I took out my wedding clothes, boxes and all, and left space for some of my things—like quilts, pillow, and spread—to be put in my trunk. Lula and I had a lovely visit and were off to bed early after having visited with many of our friends on Christmas afternoon. All had been served a slice of fruitcake and a cup of hot coffee if they chose.

Mr. Puckett came Sunday afternoon, bringing me a large wooden box of long pods of dried raisins, a mixed box of citrus fruits (grapefruit, orange, tangerine, kumquat, and lemon), and a beautiful toilet collection. He said it was all ready for me on Christmas Eve day, but he had not wanted me to have so many boxes while getting off the train. He just waited until he could bring them. Mr. Puckett said they had had a lovely, although lonely, Christmas. Sunday morning, before he came to see me, they had all gone to church. He was to return to Jesup that night.

He wanted to come back again Monday, but I told him no, I would be busy getting everything ready for our Wednesday departure. I did not tell him of those fat hens I had to butcher Monday morning for the chicken salad. He said, Tuesday then, and I agreed to that.

He came on the Bogey, bringing a beautiful leather luggage set, a large tan suitcase and a large overnight bag to match. They contained his extra shirts, collars, ties, nightclothes, and toilet articles. He asked me to pack my clothes in them also. I told him I had planned to use the regular suitcase I had used to go to my schools. He then asked me to please use his; he had bought them as our wedding present to each other. So I agreed. Lula had given me a beautiful overnight bag as her wedding gift to me. We had a nice set of luggage with ample room. He had also brought the flowers and ribbons for my wedding bouquet (there was no corner florist in those days). My good friend Mrs. Peek made it for me, a beautiful arrangement of white carnations and white ribbon, not fancy, just elegant. It went well with my tailored blue wool suit and hat. We had a pleasant day. All my friends were coming and going and enjoying the luscious fruits, the same as they had the delicious fruitcake. Mr. Puckett left, to return on the morrow to claim me as his bride.

All the while those fat hens had been boiling tender on the woodstove. As soon as Mr. Puckett left, I boned and minced them, ready for Mrs. Peek, Mrs. Lewis, and Mrs. Lary, who were to arrive early the next morning to prepare the salad plates and the bride's table. I had nothing to do with the preparation of the food on the morrow, but on this day there was much for me to do. Our latticed back porch had a wide shelf the length of the porch. On it I put platter after platter of boned and minced chicken and bowls of the hard-boiled eggs I had peeled. I laid out the boxes of celery and lettuce and set the box of Durkee salad dressing, saltines, olives, and napkins nearby. I used some empty two-quart fruit jars for standards every so often and covered everything from one end to the other with some of our clean old sheets tucked well on each side and at the ends. I had all our plates, cups, and forks clean and ready nearby, as well as Mother's large brown bowls for mixing salad on the back-porch table. My part of the preparation of my wedding reception for my wedding day was finished. I would not be on the scene tomorrow.

I slept well, arose early, and took my time preparing my morning toilet. The Bogey arrived at 10 o'clock; quite a few of my kinfolks came on it, but I did not appear. Around noontime, Train No. 85 came, bringing Mr. Puckett and his daughters Gertrude and Angie. His two oldest boys, Osborne and Harry, did not care to come, and he could not run the risk of bringing the two smaller children,

Virginia Mae and L. P. Jr., for fear they would cry to continue the trip with him and not want to return to their home without him. The four children who did not attend were being cared for by their uncle and aunt, Mr. and Mrs. B. F. Puckett. Mr. Puckett and his daughters had to entertain themselves as best they could with Lula's help. My sister Bessie helped me with my toilet, especially my hair, and with my last-minute packing, picking up and cleaning up my bedroom. After I had dressed, I locked my grips, readied my handbag, laid out my hat, and sat down to await the appointed hour which was drawing nigh.

Friends, neighbors, and kinfolks kept arriving. I could hear the buggies and wagons coming, folks talking and laughing, asking, where was the bride? I had told my sisters Lula and Ellie (Mrs. B. C. Lang) beforehand, that there would be no visits to me. My door was open to no one that day until I came out to meet Mr. Puckett and the minister to be married. Mrs. Brown rendered a beautiful selection of nuptial music. When the strains of the traditional wedding march, "Lohengrin," were heard, Mr. Puckett came forth to meet me. He being a widower, it was thought in those days not to be in good taste to make a big show at the wedding ceremony. We advanced to the far corner of the room where an altar had been prepared. At 4:00 P.M., Wednesday, December 29, 1920, we were joined in the holy bonds of matrimony by the Reverend Mr. Bush, minister of the First Baptist Church of Jesup, Georgia.

Congratulations were in order. We were seated at the beautiful bride's table, and my three friends were soon serving the most beautiful and elaborate salad plate I had ever seen, along with steaming cups of coffee. Cream and sugar were on the bride's table. When the reception was over, kinfolks and friends gave their congratulations and departed for their homes over deeply rutted roads. They had brought gifts of smoked sausage, hickory smoked hams, and bacon; canned peaches and huckleberries; jams; mayhaw, grape, and blackberry jelly; homemade quilts and crocheted-edge pillowcases. I appreciated all of it very much. As the December sun set, Mr. Puckett and I were on our way to the depot, destined for Jacksonville, Florida. I threw my beautiful bouquet from the train door as the train moved quickly away from the station; I never saw who caught it, the train moved away so quickly.

We spent the night in the Seminole Hotel in Jacksonville and were up and away early Thursday to catch the train to Miami over the famous East Coast Railway. We were there by nightfall and were quickly to our hotel, the St. Francis. We arose early Friday morning and went to call on my beloved cousin Mrs. J. H. Paterson (Molly Brown Paterson). She took us sightseeing and then said we must have lunch with her, her three children, and her Negro maid (who was from Georgia also). We had a wonderful lunch; then the children, Mr. Patterson, and Cousin Molly took us to the Indian villages, Flamingo Park, and many other places of interest. They dropped us off at our hotel at the close of day. It was such a pleasant afternoon. It was early to bed, as we were to arise at dawn on Saturday to catch the train home.

It was midnight by the time we arrived in Jesup, and we were met by all six children with the Buick. We were soon home, and everyone was off to bed, as tomorrow was the first Sunday in January, and we were all to be in church on time. The cook would have a good noonday meal for us upon our return from church. All went well. Lula came in from Nahunta and brought my trunk on her ticket. She had lunch with us. Soon after lunch, Mr. Puckett, all the children, and I took Lula to her school at Piney Grove, where she boarded with Uncle Sol Pye. The day was about done by the time we arrived back home. The two beautiful Jersey cows had to be milked; this task was performed by the two older boys. Mr. Puckett and I went to the barn with them while the two older girls set supper, and we were soon from the barn with two large pails of steaming milk. (I did not at this time let it be known that I knew how to milk cows.) We strained the milk and put it in pitchers, pans, and bowls, then put away in the ice refrigerator to cool for drinking and set for cream to make butter and buttermilk for the family.

When supper was over, the table was cleared, and the dishes were stacked in the sink to await the cook's arrival the next morning. She never stayed for the evening meal and never arrived in time for breakfast; she prepared only the noonday meal and cleaned up. Mr. Puckett packed his well-used traveling bag, as he was to leave on Train No. 22 to return to his construction work at Charleston by Monday morning. I asked what he wanted me to do while he was gone. He said to do whatever I wished to do, to be sweet, and to meet him Saturday night when he arrived home on Train No. 57. There I was, in my new home, not knowing what to do or where to turn. I had a house full of children and did not know how they would react to me, nor know what I should do or say. I went to bed in my room alone. All the children retired to their rooms. Osborne and Harry slept together. Gertrude, the oldest girl, cared for the youngest child, L. P. Jr.; Angie, the next-oldest, cared for her younger sister, Virginia Mae. I never closed my eyes. I just lay there. By and by the night passed. I began to hear movements in the household. I knew not where or how to turn, so I just lay there.

I heard a gentle knock on my door. I said, "Come in." It was L. P. Jr., dressed so pretty in a Buster Brown playsuit, with a red tie, red belt, and red socks. I held out my arms to him, and he came, laid his head on his father's pillow, and said to me, "Did you know my daddy was married?" I said, "Who told you?" He said,

"Gertrude, and she said we don't have to mind anyone but you." I asked him, "Where is everyone?" He said, "Osborne and Harry are milking, Gertrude is preparing breakfast, and Angie is dressing Virginia Mae." About that time we heard a cry from down the hall. He said, "That is Virginia Mae now. Angie is trying to comb her hair, and it is so curly it hurts her." So I thought to myself that I had better come forth and see what I could do to help the family along.

It seemed everyone except me was busy. So I hastily arose, dressed, and went to the kitchen. I asked Gertrude, "What may I do?" She said, "Well this is a school morning, and the boys have not returned from the barn. I have breakfast ready. We don't have a minute to lose and still get to school on time. If you can go hurry them along I will surely be much obliged." So I hurried off to the barn, Kabo corset, nice shoes, and all. I arrived in the midst of a corncob war, Harry upstairs and Osborne on the ground. When they saw me, Osborne quickly grabbed his bucket and went to milking. Harry came down the stairs and got his bucket off the shelf. I asked him for it, stooped over as best I could, and soon had a pail full of good rich milk. We set buckets on the shelf, put the cows out in the lane, and turned them toward the woods for a short ways. There was free range then, but we didn't want them to stray uptown. We gave the calves plenty of hay and water, fastened the barn gates well, and took our buckets of milk and hurried to the house. I strained the milk, put it away in containers to cool, and told the boys to hurry and dress for school. Soon they were dressed and returned to the dining room. We all gathered around the table. I graced the table, and we sat down to our first meal together without their father, just as we did thousands of time thereafter.

Before Gertrude left, she gave me the keys to the car, although I could not drive, her father's checkbook, the Smith and Wesson pistol, and the combination to the family safe. She told me that Mr. Frank Scott would come by to pick up the laundry and take it to Pepper Hill to the colored washwoman; I could order groceries by telephone from Mr. Surrency, and he would deliver twice daily. The children were supposed to come home by 3 P.M. And off she hurried to school. I was left with two small children: L. P. Jr., aged three, and Virginia Mae, aged five. I thought how magnanimous Gertrude had been to me, how much she had helped me along the way, and how I could never do enough for her in my whole life for the kindness she had shown me that morning. I turned back into the house and went to work doing whatever my hands found to do. From that day to this, some fifty-two years later, I have never found time for an idle moment. I cleared the dishes away, checked over the food supply, planned a well-balanced meal to be ready when the children returned from school, and made my first order from the grocer. Mr. Surrency answered the telephone, and I spoke my name, Mrs. L. P. Puckett, for the first time. Then it dawned on me what Mr. Puckett had done; he had given me his own name. I leaned over on the telephone (an old-fashioned wall type) and took a vow that as long as I drew a breath of life I would bring honor and goodwill on that name that had been entrusted to my keeping; so help me God. I can truthfully say that through those fifty-two years, I have kept that vow.

CHAPTER 19

My Teaching Career, 1921–1932

This covers quite an active period in my life, yet teaching touched me throughout all these years. I never did let my teaching licenses lapse. I thought too much of them to ever give them up. I could keep them in force by reading three professional books on teaching and taking a state teacher's test to have them renewed every three years. I often supplied for different teachers from a day to a month or more. You see, I had a ready-made family, with four children in school and two nearly ready to be enrolled, so my interest in education stayed at a high level.

It was not long before we had children of college age. Gertrude entered Georgia State College for Women at Milledgeville in September 1923, and was graduated with a B.S. degree in home economics in June 1927. She made a wonderful career in that field, until her retirement from the educational system in Hawaii in 1969. Our second-oldest daughter, Angie, entered the State Normal School at Athens in 1926, but the Depression arrived full blast in 1929, and she never did get to finish. She worked in the WPA days as a county supervisor and from there went to Red Cross work for many years, some school-teaching along the way. Our oldest son, Osborne, entered Georgia Tech in the fall of 1927 in a civil engineering curriculum. The depressed economy caught him also, and he had to come home. He got work in July 1928 with the state highway department, beginning as an axman on State Highway 38 (now U.S. Route 84) cutting right of way in the Altamaha Swamp. He was promoted to rodman, and soon he was using the theodolite. He continued with the state until he joined Bowe Construction Company, a private highway contractor in Augusta. He then went to work for the Clausen Highway Construction Company, also in Augusta, until his retirement in 1971. He made a very enviable record all through those years.

I kept my interest up by doing church work in the Jesup First Methodist Church, and I joined the Eastern Star, where I served for ten years as secretary. It was very rewarding work. I also was one of the directors of the Georgia parent-teacher movement. I was chairman of the citizenship division for the whole state. I served under Mrs. Bruce Carr Jones of Macon, Mrs. Fred Wessels of Savannah, Mrs. Charles D. Center of Macon, Mrs. Gordy of Columbus, and Mrs. Ginter of Atlanta. I organized the Parent Teacher Association (PTA) at Jesup, Odum, Piney Grove, Empire, and Screven. I also organized the Eleventh Congressional District (now part of the Eighth) into one large district working group. I often attended regional meetings at Brunswick and Waycross, and state meetings at Savannah, Macon, and Atlanta. I served until the Depression wiped out our way of life, when for financial reasons I was not able to attend the board of directors meetings. I quietly withdrew from the board. I had served three terms as president of the Jesup High School PTA. I had also formed the Wayne County PTA council and served as its president for three terms, and I had attended the PTA training councils at the University of Georgia for several summers.

Our family life had continued on. Mr. Puckett traveled hither and yon with his work, all the way from Richmond, Virginia, to Miami, Florida, over into West Florida and Alabama, and all up and down through the Carolinas and Georgia. I stayed at home taking care of the children and seeing after their education and health and the business of them getting grown into fine ladies and gentlemen. Along the way, on December 31, 1921, we had a beautiful daughter born to us, Lawrenna Mizell Puckett, weighing ten pounds, five ounces. She is now Mrs. Howard W. Powell Sr. of Jesup.

Mr. Puckett bought some land three and a half miles west of Jesup. It is now traversed by U.S. Route 84, but it was right in the woods when he bought it and thereon built our beautiful country home, The Pines, a large ten-room, two-story home with eight fireplaces and two flues for a wood-burning heater and a cook-stove. We moved there on December 24, 1925, with our six older children, our little daughter, and our brand-new son, Hoyle Brooks Puckett, born October 15, 1925, weighing twelve and a half pounds. Mr. Puckett developed a large farm, garden, orchard, and pastures from the tract of 490 acres he had bought from Mrs. G. B. Whaley. We furnished it well and framed it with a beautiful lawn and flowers, preserving the native beauty of the pines for which it was named. Here we enjoyed ourselves, took care of our aged and orphaned kin, and entertained our friends. The children drove back to Jesup to school through the then mud and water. Mr. Puckett was prospering with his railroad work and the sale of the railway-tie spacer he had invented and for which he had the patent rights.

Railroad building was among the first industries to feel the effects of a weakening economy, and Mr. Puckett moved his construction outfit to Jesup in the fall of 1927. He parked his ten sleeping cars and three tool cars on a spur track, and there they sat until they rotted down. Years afterward he sold the running gears for thirty-five dollars per car. So there we were with a family of ten of our own and two orphans of Mr. Puckett's brother Ben; his elderly uncle Madison Goodyear, his mother's oldest brother; his first wife's baby brother, Horace Jones of Mullins, South Carolina; and "comers" and "goers" and "stayers" from every direction. Many were the times that the number who depended on us for their board and keep and lodging would be more than twenty-five. With no money coming in, it did not take long for a large bank account to fade into oblivion, and money was not at our command anymore. If we had not had the very finest garden, orchard, dairy, farm and forest products, I don't know how we would have ever gotten through those lean years. During those terrible years, there was never a meal that our table did not groan, laden with the finest of foods. Our fireplaces were cheerful with the glowing warmth of oak and gum logs and lightwood knots from our own forest. Our beds were made up with sheets and pillowcases of snowy whiteness and soft, warm handmade quilts, feather pillows, featherbeds, and soft pure-white lint cotton mattresses. All of this took long hard hours of work, many happy hours spent around our festive board by hungry kinfolks and friends, but never a penny for clothes and shoes or gas for the numerous cars we owned.

As we got further into the depressing 1930s, we had more children ready for college. The next two boys, Harry and L. P., were each granted football scholarships: Harry, to the Agricultural and Mechanical College at Madison; L. P. Jr., to Armstrong College in Savannah. Virginia Mae, with a 4-H club scholarship, went to Abraham Baldwin College at Tifton. We had to pay for board, books, clothes, and traveling expenses to and from. I canned foods for board and keep, but I could not manage the clothes and traveling expenses. They all had so far managed to graduate from high school, where the cost of the diploma and the hire of the graduation clothes could scarcely be met. Somehow we got by. I was home working every day, cooking, milking, washing, ironing, scrubbing, packing, preparing, canning, and churning as we waded through the Great Depression.

On the morning of the first Saturday in September 1932, a mule-drawn wagon bearing Mr. Aaron Nichols pulled up to our gate. Mr. Nichols, a good friend and a member of the school board of the Empire community school district, asked me to become a member of their school faculty, teaching grades six and seven, beginning the first Monday in September and continuing until the next April and year after year if I proved my ability as a good teacher for the place. I told him how badly I needed the job to get funds for our older children's education as well as funds for the care of those left at home. I had more than I could do day by day, from early morning until far into the night; Mr. Nichols said I would just have to learn how to let some of the tasks go undone to be able to do the grading. He kept telling me how much they wished me to accept the work. So I finally told him I would accept the offer.

Monday morning, September 5, 1932, came bright and fair. I arose early and milked the cows, prepared lunch for all our children in school, prepared enough lunch for all those left at home, and told them they would have to make do on that until I returned in the afternoon. I fixed myself a small lunch. We had cars, but gas was hard to come by. Our children had to drive a car to school, as there were no school buses at Jesup. They went one way to school, and I went the other way, five miles west to Empire School. I got the few supplies I needed for the school day, locked the front door, got into the car, and drove to Empire to start my teaching career all over again. As soon as I had the car started, the tears began to flow. I cried until I could scarcely see my way down the road. I tried to overcome my anguish, but nay, not so, and finally I cried aloud, "O Lord, why did I have to leave my beautiful home and my husband and my children and enter the teaching field again? I thought I had fought this battle to completion in 1920 before I gave up my school at Farm Life to marry my husband, Mr. L. P. Puckett, and assume the charge of caring for, loving, and guiding his six children orphaned by the terrible flu epidemic. Why, oh, why, must this be? Have I not done my part well? Why is it necessary that I now return to try to make a living for my family of eight children, two of my own and Mr. Puckett's six added on to the numbers? So now we are ten." I prayed again aloud, "Oh! Why! Will you tell me why?" Alas! The answer came back aloud to me, "I have need of thee." By now I was to Satilla Creek. I pulled my car to one side, got out, went down to the water's edge, praying all the while. I took my handkerchief from my handbag and dipped it into the cool running water and washed my face again and again until I felt all tears were gone away. I stood there on the banks of that beautiful slowly moving creek, and I prayed one of the most fervent prayers I ever prayed in my life. "O God, if thee hast need of me, help me to do thy work joyously and happily and let me be so ardent in my work that I shall always be counted as one of the best and most faithful of thy workers and further dry the tears away from my eyes and place joy and happiness in my soul, so truly and deeply that it might shine forth to all those with whom I must come in contact; students, parents, teachers, principals, superintendent, all of our citizens who have to pay taxes to support the schools, and other human beings that I may have to come in contact with from day to day. And, O Lord! Let me not forget those of my own home, whom I left behind this morning: my husband, my children, my guests, my neighbors." I once more wiped my face,

[235]

walked back to my car with a song on my lips and music in my soul, and I arrived at school in due time and met everyone with a cheery smile and a happy greeting. I had a lilt in my walk and a firm grip in my handshake and thanksgiving in my heart for Mr. Nichols and his school trustees, who decided they would like to have me on their school faculty.

At the opening that morning Mr. Nichols gave me such a beautiful introduction. He said that when they planned the school consolidation of Flint Branch, Liberty, Bethel, and Empire I was one of the teachers they had set their hearts on to teach and direct it, but I had married before they got the consolidation perfected and the building constructed. How happy they were that they were able to secure my services for their school and community. I was given a roaring standing ovation by all the community present. I served on their faculty for eleven years during my teaching career, and many are the letters that I get until this good day from former pupils I taught there, telling me of the knowledge, hope, joy, love, and happiness I brought into their young lives.

CHAPTER 20

Empire School Years

I entered the Empire community school faculty as the sixth- and seventh-grade teacher under the direction of Mr. Helms as principal. He also taught eighth and ninth grades. The other teachers were Mrs. Augusta Durrence, the first-grade teacher; Miss Sadie Smith, the second- and third-grade teacher; and Miss Doris Nichols, the fourth- and fifth-grade teacher, who also taught home economics. We had a very nice setup for the school as far as the girls were concerned, but for the boys, there was only an academic program, no vocational work at all. I soon set myself to see if something could be done about this.

Mr. Helms's wife became seriously ill, and he had no money to hire anyone to stay with her. She grew steadily worse, so he gave up his schoolwork to be with her. She lingered on into spring, when death claimed her. He was so spent by the time she passed on, having nursed her day and night, that he was never able to return to his school duties, which we all regretted very much. The trustees met and asked Mrs. Durrence to take on the duties of principal. She would continue to teach first grade. The county board of education sent Mrs. Lucille Dowling to take over grades eight and nine.

Our schoolwork went on very well. We had a nice school-closing, and a graduation ceremony for the ninth-grade pupils, who were going to the high school in Jesup or Screven, whichever they preferred. I also had a promotion exercise for my seventh grade and gave them certificates permitting them to enter the eighth grade at Empire the next year. This program was held in the evening, with a good speaker from Jesup. A public program was held for all the children from grades one through nine. This included a picnic dinner for all the pupils and their parents. It was an enjoyable year of work. I had to do two extra classes a day for Miss Nichols so she would have time to teach home economics. I did an arithmetic class for her and a fourth-grade reading class also. This arrangement went off well.

The school had a teacherage, where the teachers could live together and save the price of board. They could bring food from their own homes, and the country children would often bring them nice foods from their mothers' gardens, pantries, and food supply at butchering time. The school board furnished them with wood for heating and cooking. Their water came from the school pump, and their lights were kerosene lamps. So, their expenses were few. I understand they had a pleasant time all living there together. I never lived there, as I was only five miles away and had to be home every night. At this time, Empire was the only rural school that had a seven-month term, late in September to early April. The other rural schools of the county had five or five and one-half months of school. Empire had Roger Barrett money, a grant from a private fund, to assist with the two extra months of time.

The 1933–34 term began in due time, with several changes in the faculty. Mr. L. L. Purcell, a fine young man of Wayne County, was chosen as principal, and Miss Dugger, from Effingham County, was to teach grades six and seven, and I was to teach grades four and five, as Miss Nichols had returned to college to complete her education. Miss Sadie Smith continued to teach grades two and three, and Mrs. Durrence was to teach grade one. Our work went along well, with everyone enjoying the new principal. There was no one to teach home economics, and this work was dropped, which I regretted very much, as well as did many others. Now both girls and boys had only a narrow academic program with no vocational work at all. I kept my eyes and ears open for a department for the boys and girls. I attended all the educational meetings of the district and state, and I always attended the vocational meetings to find out how those departments were developed and maintained. I set apart time each week in my fourth and fifth grades for some work with the hands, like sewing, carving, or drawing. The children really loved that work, and I held them responsible for their work and their tools. They were to report the amount of work they had done each month so I could grade them on their accomplishments.

The faltering economy during Governor Richard B. Russell Jr.'s term (1931–33) drastically reduced state revenues, preventing the state from paying teacher salary supplements, so the teachers were given vouchers which would be paid when the state had the money. Large and wealthy districts continued to pay their teachers, using local resources. Rural districts had no such resources. Except for the kindness of a wealthy merchant, the owner of Nathan's Department Store, who bought our vouchers at face value and held them until the state redeemed them, I and many other teachers would not have been able to survive.

Our pay was coming in very poorly. Governor Eugene Talmadge tried to pay us the deficit that had occurred during Dick Russell's administration, but it was sent to the county school superintendents, and they took it. They pulled the "grandfather clause" on us: bills from past fiscal years not paid for lack of funds could not be paid from the current year's fund. If we were not paid by December 31, come January 1, they owed us nothing. So there were months and months with no pay. It went down the drain, but we built hope on hope attending Georgia educational meetings, trying to get legislation passed so we would have some assurance of pay. Governor Talmadge ran for a second term and promised to pay the teachers. This he did in 1936, before his second term ended in 1937.

Times grew worse. The Red Cross came in with cloth, and we set up sewing days at school for ladies to bring their lunch and sewing machines. We got clothes enough made to cover the nakedness of our children. I had many girls in fourth and fifth grades whose clothes were worn so thin over their stomachs that you could see their naked skin. The little boys were so bare that 100 percent of them were bare on their buttocks. So the need was great. We saw that the clothes were made to fit the children who needed them. The old worn clothes were neatly rolled and tied in a bundles to be taken home with a note saying that the new clothes were a gift from the Red Cross and were made by the good women of Empire. After the old clothes were laundered, they were used as patches to make other worn garments wearable. We made dresses and underclothes for the girls, and shirts, trousers, underclothes, and jackets for the boys.

Many were the mothers who came to sew. Some would bring thimbles and needles and work buttonholes while the others sewed on the machines. The teachers continued with our classes day by day. We took our children in when the ladies called for our age group to be measured and again when they were called back in to be fitted. We never had a family refuse one of the well-made garments, and many were the words of praise that came to the teachers.

The small scraps of cloth that were left were made into beautiful quilt tops and linings. The community furnished the padding. The lining, padding, and tops were quilted by the mothers and wives of the Empire school district and given to the most needy families in the community. The quilts were made at the schoolhouse. The women used the room that had been used for home economics and library work. It was secure, well lighted, and equipped with several large tables and plenty of shelving. There was no problem with leaving their work and tools in the building overnight or weekend. The ladies rode the school bus to and from the schoolhouse with the children. Empire was the one school in the county that had buses. They were homemade ones built on as truck chassis and were owned by Mr. Ed Lastinger. The county paid him a fixed amount to transport the children from their homes to the school and back. Mr. Lastinger did a good job, and his operation was copied for other areas of the county as schools were consolidated and more and more students were transported to more distant campuses.

The Depression seemed to get deeper, but we tried all the harder to bring joy, pleasure, help, and hope to the children we were teaching. The orphans' home out from Baxley would come, sing for us, and put on playlets if we could get them a collection of foods. They would allow us ten cents (the price of admission) per dozen eggs; quart of canned peaches, huckleberries, pears, or blackberries; large bunch of greens; or pound of cured meat. A smaller amount would be allowed per pound of cornmeal, home-ground hominy, lard, syrup, honey, homemade soap, sweet potatoes, dried peas, or dried beans. A larger amount was allowed for a coop of chickens in good condition. The orphans entertained us several evenings, and a large crowd would come in wagons, as no one had money to buy gas for their cars. The orphans would always leave with bountiful boxes of food and, usually, a date for a return visit. Their performances were well worth the small fee they charged. They were never charged for the use of the building. The school trustees donated that to help the orphanage.

Word gets around, and it was not long until a small camper-type trailer and an old car appeared with a showman, his wife, his daughter, and two fellow showmen. They wanted to camp for the winter and put on shows each weekend of magic, slight-of-hand, and laughable skits. Our principal referred them to our trustees, as they had full control of the grounds and building. The visitors had their conference with the trustees and promised them that their show would be clean, educational, and enjoyable to both old and young. All that they asked for was a clean place in the far corner of the campus to park their car and trailer and enough waste wood and limbs to make a campfire every evening to cook their food and warm themselves. They would request small amounts of foodstuffs as entrance fees to their shows to keep themselves from starving. They also told the trustees they wished to use each day to practice their new acts and did not care to have the children visiting their establishment.

They wanted to get water from our pump and use our toilet facilities to relieve themselves. They wanted to dry their laundered clothes on lines they would set up from tree to tree. All arrangements were made, and we had delightful shows where we could go and refresh ourselves from our week of hard work. They would sometimes talk from the stage, asking how to cook so and so, on and on. The replies would be so humorous that the whole house would come down in roars of laughter. Then the master of ceremonies would tell the crowd that they did honestly wish to know how to prepare a particular product for human consumption, and would someone tarry long enough after the show to tell them the exact procedure in making it edible.

Last, but not least, they wished to place their daughter in our school, as we had been recommended to them as a good school. They said they would send her to school regularly with a lunch (we did not have a lunchroom yet). She would do her training each day after school, as she was a part of the troupe. The little daughter was in grade four, and I was her fortunate teacher. She was a delightful pupil. She had been to so many places, met so many people, and helped with the show programs ever since she could remember. She never divulged any of their magic tricks. She always told the children that was a part of their "stock in trade" and the way they made their living. She was lovable and well liked by all the children. For some three winters, they camped with us. Then one spring day, they drove away and never returned. We all missed them. They had brought us joy and laughter when we needed it most, and we had given them food, water, sunshine, fuel for warmth, and a place to camp.

The Depression deepened. The legislature did not pass the education budget during Governor Talmadge's first term, and we received no pay. The governor ran for a second term and again promised to pay the back salaries of all teachers. This time he trusted no one to dispense the money but had each county board of education send him a list of the amount owed to each teacher in their county. That was the way the money came, to each individual teacher. The first payment of back pay was received in 1936, before E. D. Rivers became governor.

I continued to attend the vocational meetings when I went to our educational meetings, and at one vocational meeting, I met Dr. Thomas Quigley, an extension worker from the Georgia Institute of Technology. He was anxious to find boys who were mechanically or vocationally inclined while they were still in the lower grades so engineering and the related subjects of mathematics, chemistry, and physics would not seem foreign to them when they enrolled in college level engineering courses at Georgia Tech. About this time WPA officials turned their minds from unemployed ditchdiggers to other unemployed persons of our nation. Many teachers fell into this class.

Dr. Quigley sent Mr. Norman C. Smith, a graduate of Georgia Tech, to establish a shop course for school-aged boys. Mr. Smith arrived at our home about noontime on Sunday. We were having Sunday dinner, and we quickly cleared a place for him to sit and invited him to dine with us after he had relieved and washed himself. I think he had walked most of the way from Atlanta. He was very tired and hungry, and his spirits were low. He was soon busy devouring a good meal. Monday we launched the program for a shop at Empire School. Mr. Smith went down to the WPA office and signed on as a shop teacher for Empire at thirteen dollars per week. I agreed to provide him a room, board, fuel for warming, water for washing, and electricity for lights for four dollars per week. I had no maid service, so he would have to keep his own room. I would furnish him clean towels, sheets, and pillowcases each week. It had been years since I had seen that much money per week. And it still left him $9 per week to use as he chose. He picked up an old Ford car and soon had it rolling. I rode to school and back with him, saving me the price of gasoline to drive my own car.

The schoolboys were to attend classes in the shop during the school day, and farmers could make use of it during late afternoon and evenings. The farmers would use the shop to mend and repair their tools and equipment. We had far more patrons than were necessary for the establishment of the shop course, but we did need a shop. There seemed no way except to build one. So the trustees gave a portion of the campus for that purpose. One trustee gave the heart-cypress tree from which to rive the shingles; a second gave the long, slim saplings to build the walls; a third gave the yoke of oxen to pull the poles to the shop site; and a fourth trustee gave the smaller saplings for joists, rafters, and laths on which to nail the shingles.

The cuts from the large cypress tree given by Mr. Nichols were hauled from the creek swamp in a cart by a yoke of oxen to the shop site, where they were split into billets, then cut into well-shaped shingles with a drawing knife. The longer saplings were also pulled to the shop site, where they were debarked with drawing knives, notched, and made ready to be raised into the shop building. Joists were put at the proper height to tie the sides of the building together. Cupboards were put on each side of the wide entrance door to hold the needed tools, such as hammers, drawing knives, augers, bits, adzes, planes, crosscut saws, handsaws, and awls. There was a lathe, a stand for the anvil, space for blacksmith tools (flat tongs, round tongs, hammers, chisel, and punches) and for the forge and bellows, with a flue to remove the smoke. Most of these tools were gathered from some deserted shop and restored to their usefulness.

The day that Mr. Smith had his "shop raising," quite a few dignitaries from different work programs came to watch. They saw the shop raised from the ground upward by friends and neighbors of the school; the roof, rafters, and laths were built on top in place; and the roof was well shingled before nightfall. The ladies of the community provided an abundant noonday meal for pupils, friends, and visitors. That day will always be remembered as a red-letter day in the life of the Empire school district, and Mr. Smith's contribution to that school will be long remembered.

The work went forward day by day. Mr. Smith set up a class period for each section of boys from grades one thorough nine. That made six classes per day, one hour for each age group. They enjoyed every minute of it. They made new things and repaired articles the farmers brought over. Mr. Smith became a great asset to the community, a friend of all the young men, and a great help to the principal, helping with any community entertainment (inside or outside). He was highly trained in conducting public affairs and was willing and eager to help wherever he could. He was happy in his work and the good he was doing for the community.

Our own daughter, Virginia Mae Puckett, was hired to set up and teach a course in home economics through the WPA at thirteen dollars per week. Miss Sara Peavy was paid the same amount for teaching public school music and remedial reading for grades four and five. Our teaching was greatly enhanced by these additions to our faculty. We began to develop our own entertainment and did not have to depend on the orphan's home and the passing show troop.

This plan continued until Mr. Roosevelt got industry on the move, and it began to call for such types of men as our Mr. Smith. Mr. Smith went to South America to establish Lomus Gins in the great cotton section of Brazil. After a few years, he returned to Augusta and became a teacher in Richmond Academy. He married and was doing mighty well the last I heard.

Time rolled merrily on. Teachers began to be considered human beings and worthy of their hire. Teachers improved their training by enrolling in college and by taking extension courses and correspondence courses. Mr. L. L. Purcell went away to college for further training. He did a good job at Empire during a difficult time. He had a well-organized school and rendered many community activities, such as planning entertainment for Halloween, Thanksgiving, Christmas, Valentine's Day, Easter, and school-closing. He had good chapel programs twice weekly. They were always a delight for all the pupils and teachers, as well as for the many patrons of the school. We all hated to see him go after three fine years under his strong management.

The year of 1935–36 was wonderful for all of us. Mr. Blackwell of Atlanta was the new principal and taught grades eight and nine; Mrs. Lois Nichols Kicklighter taught grades six and seven; I taught grades four and five; a new teacher taught grades two and three; and Miss Ruby Ashmore taught the first grade. Mr. Blackwell was a 1904 graduate of Mercer University. His was in the class of the famous

Reverend Wilder, the minister of Calvary Baptist Church in Savannah for more than sixty years. Mr. Blackwell lived at our home, and we found him to be a very compatible member of the family and a delight to have around. His year at Empire was a fine one, but Mr. Blackwell did not care to return, and a new principal was sought for 1937–38.

Our 1937–38 school term began in September, with Mr. Harold O'Quinn as principal and teaching grades eight and nine; Mrs. Albritton taught grades six and seven; I taught grades four and five; Miss Evelyn Brannon taught grades two and three; and Miss Ashmore taught first grade. No one lived at the teacherage and had not since the going of Mrs. Spivey and Miss Smith. Mrs. Kicklighter, Mrs. Albritton, and I lived at our homes; Mr. O'Quinn lived at Mrs. Isham Bennett's; Mrs. Ashmore lived at the home of her uncle, Mr. Peal. The term did not move off well and seemed never to get to running smoothly. At the close of the term, there was quite a shake-up in the school. I went away to Gardi to be the principal, and most of the other teachers changed to other schools. I lost track of Empire after six successful and enjoyable years of teaching children of the community.

CHAPTER 21

Lunch at Gardi

I went to Gardi School in September 1938. I was to be the principal and teach grades four through seven. My assisting teacher, Mrs. Mark Henderson, was to teach grades one through three. I had returned to Georgia Southern College at Statesboro for a quarter of summer work. I took courses I felt I needed to make my work more appealing to the children and patrons of the community. Most of my students were the children of pulpwood, timber, and turpentine workers. Their parents' incomes were low, but pupils were good-hearted, kind, and very appreciative of anything that you did for them. They all applied themselves well to their studies, and they liked to put on programs. We had an interesting and happy time together. Mrs. Henderson was an excellent primary teacher, and I did my best with the elementary work. We put in eight hard hours every day in the basic subjects.

We had a strong 4-H club with Mr. J. H. Chaffin, the county agent, and Miss Bobby Hicks, the home economist. Every boy and girl from age ten through grade seven belonged to the club. They were happy with their club work and carried on their projects well. We had interesting chapel programs for special days. We were always quite busy. Except for the Christmas and school-closing programs, when all grades would be participants, one grade would put on the program for a special day, and another, for the next special day. We always had a nice promotion program for grade seven before they went to Jesup to Wayne County High School and entered eighth grade. I always took them to Jesup to look over the high school in their seventh year so they would have some idea of what they could expect when they became students there. I tried to prepare them well, and most of them could go forward in their work without any difficulty. The Jesup superintendent always bragged on the Gardi children, saying they came well prepared, knowing how to study, behave, and enjoy themselves.

At this time, through our great president Franklin Delano Roosevelt, the school lunchroom program came our way. First we received only vegetables, shelled pecans, canned milk, and fresh and dried fruits, such as apples, oranges, pears, and raisins. As soon as we could provide facilities, we received foods of almost every type. We were also provided with a cook from the WPA rolls. We soon converted a garage, loaned to us by Mrs. Mary Murphy, where we could set up a stove, sink, worktables, and eating tables and benches and began serving the most delicious lunches. We had to provide lard, syrup, sugar, salt, fresh vegetables, fresh meat, fresh fish, and fresh milk. A small fee of five cents per meal was charged. This provided all the funds we needed, as we paid no rent, and the wood for the lunchroom was furnished by the patrons, the same as the wood for our large wood-fired heaters in the school building. Mr. Bill Flowers owned the forest surrounding the lunchroom and the schoolhouse. He was delighted to have us pick up fallen limbs. This greatly added to our supply of fuel for the lunchroom and the school. We were never without an abundance of fuel for the cold winters we had during those four years. I well remember when the temperature dropped to three degrees Fahrenheit and my car froze up. Although I had antifreeze in my radiator, it froze, and my engine burst. The engine was ruined, but I escaped unhurt.

Our average attendance was excellent; in fact, almost perfect. The school building was the old-fashioned design, sixty-five feet by forty feet, with a door on one side for entrance into the elementary room, and the original entrance into the primary room. We were soon to need a third room, so we had the primary room divided with a wall across its middle and installed a flue in the new room for a heater. We made a door opening from the middle grades into the primary grades but soon discovered that this disturbed the workings of both rooms. We had a door cut from the middle room to the back lawn of the school, with a good set of steps to serve that door. We also had a door installed for the upper grades to the back lawn, with another set strong of steps. Locks were put on each door. Now each room had an outside entrance, away from the main highway as existed heretofore. There was also a door between each of the three rooms. All rooms were well lighted and heated.

When McKinnon School was closed for lack of students (only five students were enrolled), the students were transferred to Jesup elementary, transported there on the same bus as the upper-grade students. The teacher, Mrs. Vaughan, and the school's equipment were transferred to Gardi. The equipment was welcomed. It consisted of a globe, maps, charts, many good books, several lengths of blackboard, and good extra chairs, which could be offered to visitors who might come to see us. Our average attendance was now ample to warrant three teachers, and with the added equipment, we were better equipped than ever before to do good work. The schoolwork and play periods were joyful. We had a happy, well-organized school, and the learning was going forward in an excellent manner. You could see happiness gushing forth from the children; there was never any disturbance among them. Their health was improving day by day from the good lunches served by the lunch program and because of the wonderful health program set up by Dr. Rice, the Wayne County health physician, and his good county nurse, Miss Nan Smith (now Mrs. Robert Harris).

When Mrs. Henderson retired because of ill health, Mrs. Joe Wilkins joined our staff; she was one of Wayne County's best primary teachers. She joined the Jesup teaching staff in 1942 and served well there until her retirement from the Wayne County system in 1968.

Our school was known far and wide for our successful lunch program; we served delicious lunches to every child and had no deficits in our accounts. Gardi was also known for its excellence in learning and for the extracurricular activities in which students and patrons alike participated. We had one of the oldest school plants in the county and one of the best educational programs.

We had established a high school bus run from Gardi School to the Wayne County High School, some seven miles away. All the children were gathered at Gardi; the high school students boarded the bus, and the other children entered their respective Gardi School classrooms. In the afternoon, we held school in session until the bus arrived from the high school. Then the bus children went from their classrooms to the bus with all their books, shoes, and wraps in order. This gave us some thirty minutes extra per day. This extra time was used in our lunch period and a little added to our morning and afternoon play periods. So we were never burdened with extra time and the children getting out of hand and out of place before the school bus arrived.

We never charged up lunchtime to play period. It was just part of our day's work. We ate in three shifts: primary grades at 11:30 A.M., middle grades at noon, and upper elementary grades at 12:30 P.M. This gave the cook time to prepare the meal, to clean up, and to leave everything in order during her eight-hour workday, the same as ours. Our three play periods were at 10:30 A.M., at the close of lunch period for each grade, and at 2:30 P.M., when all grades had relief and playtime before the last lessons and home-going preparation. Each day ended perfectly, just as it had begun.

I carried all the teachers with me from Jesup. There were Mrs. Henderson and Mrs. Vaughan and, later, Mrs. Wilkins, also the two Negro teachers for the

Negro school. This was in the forties, before integration. For four years Ellen Cogdell and Henrietta Henry met me at the post office each school day morning. I carried them to their school and brought them back each afternoon. They appreciated it, and I enjoyed doing it for them. They were both good teachers and did a good job for their community. I was glad I could be of a little help along their way.

I don't think I ever had a better set of trustees than the three men I had at Gardi. They were Bill Flowers, A. J. Hopkins, and Kel Yeomans, all princes among men. They usually sensed our needs before we ever voiced them.

During this same period of time, I was president of the Jesup PTA (my youngest daughter and son were still in high school). Mr. W. G. Nunn was the superintendent of the Jesup school system (Wayne County High School) when he heard about the wonderful lunch program at the Gardi elementary school. He asked me why we could not have one at Jesup. I told him he could if he wanted it badly enough. He asked me to help him. I asked him how quickly he wanted it done. He answered, "Right now!" I asked him to let me have Mrs. Ina Carter and Mrs. A. G. Williams, and for Mrs. E. T. Youngblood to assist us. I wanted all of them to meet me the next afternoon when I came from Gardi School. I thought we could get the ball rolling.

When I went to Jesup School the next afternoon, he had those three ladies waiting for me. We went into a conference, and we were soon down to the facts of the matter. Mr. Nunn wanted an electric kitchen, which meant a new range, a new refrigerator, an electric water heater, and electric aids such as a heavy-duty mixer; we would need tables and benches, a lot of closed storage space for dry staples, shelves for canned fruit and vegetables. A full complement of cooking tools would be needed, pots and pans, bowls, spoons, and knives. The children would bring their own eating utensils. We estimated that one thousand dollars would be the minimum amount required. Mrs. Carter suggested that we sponsor an old-time box supper Friday night in the gymnasium. We had three days in which to make preparations. She would procure Mr. Glover from Odum to be the auctioneer to sell them. Mrs. Youngblood, with Mr. Youngblood's help, was to get the word across to the grown men and women to come out and participate by bringing beau boxes of delicious food for a festive supper. The men were to bring money with which to buy the boxes. Mrs. Williams was given the job of arousing the interest among the older boys and girls of high school age and to enlist their active participation. Everyone was to tell everyone else.

Friday evening came all too quickly. The gym at the then high school (now the junior high) was filled to overflowing with beautiful ladies, young and old, their gentlemen escorts, and their attractive box suppers. Mr. Glover, Mrs. Carter, Mrs. Williams, and Mrs. Youngblood were present. The bidding began fast and furious, and before nine-thirty we had more than $750.00 in our hands. Everyone was having such a glorious time.

At that time there were no electrical equipment suppliers in Jesup. Mr. Nunn set Saturday aside to go to Waycross to Bradshaw's to buy the needed equipment. Harry Burns, our only electrician, was secured to install the equipment upon its arrival from Waycross Saturday afternoon and promised to work into the night if need be to get the equipment installed. Norris Cabinet Shop was alerted to make tables, benches, and cupboards. Mrs. Roy Breen agreed to be present to supervise the preparation of lunch to be sure it was done correctly. A system of serving the meals was established. The cooks were granted from the WPA rolls, and food was sent to the local lunchroom warehouse, located on the courthouse grounds near the county jail.

Monday morning came and Mrs. Breen was there with all her dignity, charm, and firm businesslike ways to supervise the first day of operation of the Wayne County High School lunchroom. When I returned from Gardi School Monday afternoon, one week to the day from when Mr. Nunn had asked me to get it done, the Jesup School lunchroom program had begun with a perfect day. Although that happened some thirty-four years ago, there has never been a skip in the serving of lunches to Jesup school children from that day to this. I thank all those who helped with this much-needed project. I think back about how quickly and efficiently it was accomplished and about what great good has issued forth from this one project.

I was at Gardi when the terrible blow came to Pearl Harbor December 7, 1941. I had charge of registering all male citizens of the Gardi military district between eighteen and sixty-five years of age. This was done at Gardi School. I began work at 6 A.M. and worked until 9 P.M.; it was one of the longest days I ever worked without any rest. At the Jesup high school, I wrote 375 sugar ration books for the Jesup public schools and for patrons in the whole county. We had no school on either of those days and worked all day long, swearing we would never take any pay for our labors. We were drilled in protecting our children from mustard gas attacks. For many months I kept large zinc tubs filled with one-pound boxes of tea under tables in my schoolroom, ready to make a hot tea bath for those who might become saturated with the gas. We were ready to crawl under the tables should we have a moment's notice of an attack. We were only thirty miles from Brunswick, where German submarines were captured and destroyed during the early part of World War II.

The four years I spent at Gardi were some of my happiest and most rewarding; yet I let myself be persuaded to return to Empire as principal in 1942. It was a much larger school and nearer my home. I hoped it would turn out to be a greater field of work. I received no increase in salary, although I would have four teachers to supervise, twice as many as I had at Gardi.

CHAPTER 22

Empire Community School in World War II

When I returned to Empire School from Gardi School, I found that the two high school grades, eight and nine, had been dropped somewhere along the way during the four years I was gone. I never have known why or when or by whom. I was to have only grades one through seven. During these years at Empire I had the following teachers: Miss T. C. Withrow (grade one), Mrs. L. B. Spivey (who had been Mrs. Augusta Durrence), Mrs. Johnny Crawford, Mrs. Lucille O'Quinn, Mrs. Ruby Nichols, and Mrs. Page Nichols. I began with four teachers and climbed to five before I left. I thought surely I would have made a raise by then, but the word came to me that you had to maintain high enrollment and five teachers for one year before you received any reimbursement.

I tried my best to teach in every way that I could to help the school, community, nation, and every single human being with whom I came in contact. The war was in full swing. Our boys were being called every day. Foods were rationed along with gasoline and tires. New automobiles did not exist. I had to ride the school bus, as I was permitted no gas or tires. Therefore, I had to go the full route, which took some three hours over bumps, mud holes, and deep creeks. The winters were cold and wet. The bus was unheated. I was the first one to get on, five miles away from the schoolhouse, but I had to ride some twenty miles over the route to get there. I would take good wool blankets and soft warm quilts in which to wrap up. I always shared them with our small, thinly clad children who had to get up so early each morning.

We ran on fast time (one hour ahead of standard time). The Brunswick shipyard did the same. Every able-bodied man and many of the women worked there. Their children were all up, dressed, fed, and ready to go. Their parents preferred them on the bus going to school rather than at home alone and unsupervised. Also, the children would get home early enough in the afternoon to bring the cattle from the pasture, feed the pigs and chickens, milk the cow, bring in wood, and gather vegetables for the family's evening dinner. We gladly agreed to this time schedule. I liked it too, as I was alone at home and had to secure the stock for the night, gather wood, eggs, and vegetables, and do the milking in daylight hours. Being on fast time permitted me to get into the house and bar the doors before nightfall.

Our four sons were in the war effort. Osborne was a chief petty officer in the Seabees in the South Pacific; Harry was a heavy-equipment operator at Camp Lejeune; L. P. Jr. was in a railroad battalion moving much-needed supplies to the Allied forces; and Hoyle was an aviation cadet in the Army Air Force and stationed at San Antonio, Texas. Our daughters were also involved. Gertrude worked with General Cable in New Jersey; Angie, with the Red Cross; and Virginia Mae, with the USO. Lawrenna was a secretary in the quartermaster warehouse at Camp Stewart (now Fort Stewart) near Hinesville, Georgia. I was at home by myself, but I never told anyone.

Mr. Puckett was past the age to be called into service in the military or for work, but he was asked and begged to give his time and knowledge to railroad work where it was sorely needed. He took up fifty miles of track near Florala, Alabama, and built the tracks needed for the Brunswick shipyard. He built sidetracks and spurs all along the existing railroad lines to facilitate movement of materials and men. He went to work on the Pennsylvania line from Washington to New York to upgrade their track and enable them to run their trains faster. His last job took him to St. George, South Carolina, to build twelve miles of track from Pregnal, through the pinewoods, to a bauxite mine site that was supposed to become a twelve-billion-dollar enterprise. Just as the work was finished and the heavy equipment put in place, the war ended, the work was halted, and the equipment was put to sleep. If the mine was ever developed, I have never heard of it.

Empire had developed its old teacherage into an excellent lunchroom, with a good kitchen and equipment, a Home Comfort Stove, a safe, and a cupboard. There was a storeroom and a large well-lighted and well-heated dining room. Although the food was rationed, every child had a bountiful noonday meal every day. We had a large abundant community from which to draw our fresh foods, meats, vegetables, chickens, eggs, and milk, so our diet was among the very best. Lunch was not free. I accepted whatever they had to offer: wood, eggs, chickens, vegetables, syrup, sweet potatoes, fresh meal, hominy grits, honey, or what have you (I did not have the good fish that we had enjoyed at least once a week at Gardi). Very few failed to keep their lunch bills paid up, and some were ahead most of the time.

At first the WPA paid all the labor, but as time moved on, our WPA workers were placed in private industry, and there were no WPA workers available to take their places. We had to assume the cost of the workers. We began charging five cents a meal, and we never did have to go above ten cents. Many were the citizens of our community who came to eat with us from time to time. We always charged them twenty-five cents. The fame of our lunchroom spread near and far. Mr. Nunn did his best to hire me as supervisor of the Wayne County High School lunchroom. Although it was at a much higher salary than I was getting as principal of Empire, I refused. I told him I was a teacher not a cook. Many were the birthday parties that mothers put on for their children after noontime of a day (such parties were to never interfere with serving of lunch). We used the facilities to put on the banquet for our graduation class at close of school. We used it for our Thanksgiving, Christmas, and Easter celebrations. The lunchroom was a great asset to school.

The war was pressing harder every day. At one time it looked as if the enemy would invade our section of the nation. Our community was alerted to be moved out at once. Everyone was told what to have ready. I was to assemble the children by families and have them prepared to go at a moment's notice should their parents come by for them. I had the children listed by families, and to see that no child was left behind, each family was to leave my room with this list closely checked. We sold savings stamps every day. Mrs. Spivey agreed to do this job for me. The two "children of the day" from my room collected the money for the stamps each morning as they collected the lunch money and produce to take to the lunchroom. They also delivered the stamps back to the children according to how many they had purchased. The same children met the postman each day and bought more stamps as needed. We always had a sufficient supply on hand. The American Legion gave us ten dollars at the beginning of the school year to purchase the initial supply. I always paid this back at the end of the school year and got it again in September. Whenever a child had bought $18.75 worth of stamps, we gave the child a $25.00 savings bond from the stage at the next chapel program. Usually some member of the family would be there to see this.

The people of our community heartily endorsed this work, but they felt they should do more. They asked me to try to get this message across to our grown people, that it was necessary to help the government as well as to lay something aside for themselves in savings bonds. So we got our heads together and asked how many ladies would bake a beautiful cake in honor or memory of their sons in the service. The cakes were to be auctioned off to the highest bidder in savings bonds. This went over big. There was not an Empire boy in the service who did not have a cake offered in his honor. The bond sales would go into the thousands of dollars at each sale. Of course, they got the cake. This was really having your cake and eating it also! The chairman of our bond sales, C. W. O'Quinn, and his helper, Chris Harris, highly endorsed the plan. Sometimes we would have a short program by the school children. Other times we would have a show of war materials and personnel from Camp Stewart; the commander would see that we had a good show when we called upon him.

Our bond-sale evenings became larger and larger. With people coming from far and near, our sales became greater and greater, running into many thousands of dollars at each event. One of my most treasured keepsakes is the award from President Harry S. Truman that was given to me by Mr. O'Quinn for my bond work. Empire community had sold more bonds than any other community of its size in the nation. Everyone in the school district swelled with pride and patriotism. Many of the boys' cakes carried the boys' names in decoration, as well as the branch of service to which they belonged. We encouraged the children to collect waste iron at home and at school. We got trucks to come from Camp Stewart to take it to the loading station. We had everything, old stoves, cane-mill rollers, broken plows, axles, tires, and hubs. All in all, we had thirty-seven big dump truck loads, which provided a good return to those collecting as well as the needed iron for the nation to use in vital war work. When the call came for copper, we planned a chapel program, featuring a penny march. Each grade passed across the stage to the collector of the copper, who dispensed other money in exchange for the copper. We had many large cookie jars full of pennies that were counted, transferred to strong money sacks, sewn up, and given to the postman on his next daily run.

While our activities for the war effort were being carried on, we went on with our academic work. We looked forward to seventh-grade graduation. We also tried to keep our American way of life to the forefront by remembering our festive days such as Halloween, Thanksgiving, and Christmas. At Halloween, our good PTA would try to make enough money to support the extracurricular activities for the whole year. We would have bingo, cakewalks, candy drawings, a country store, wiener roasts, marshmallow roasts, the witch's tent of fortunes, the house of horrors, guessing the number of beans in the jar, hot dogs, hamburgers, and fortune cakes. All in all we made money at every turn, and everyone had a wonderful time, especially with the crowning of the king and queen, who were elected at one cent per vote. We also had prizes for the best costumes. There never was a time better than the Halloween carnival at Empire, with its great array of home-baked cakes, pies, fudge, divinity candy, and boiled and parched peanuts.

At midnight, when black cats are let loose and the old witch rides away on her broom, it was hurry to home and to bed before we got caught up in all the mystic charms of the season.

Thanksgiving followed quickly, with our traditional feast, music, historical pageant, songs, and display of bountiful foods. It was a day long-remembered by everyone from year to year. The Monday morning after Thanksgiving we began our month-long preparation for Christmas. No room-to-room visiting was permitted for teachers or pupils during this work period, when each teacher was to tell Christmas Bible stories to her children and also practice singing the Christmas songs they were preparing for the Christmas program.

Christmas week each teacher held an open house in her room for the other teachers and their pupils. They came at a stated time to view the beauty of the room and hear a favorite Bible story or song as they enjoyed light refreshments (homemade fruit punch and Christmas cookies provided by the mothers of that grade). I can tell you that the Christmas spirit really ran high by the time all these visits were completed. No child ever felt slighted or left out, and no room was ever left bare and barren because of a teacher who did not want to go the "second mile." Just think of all the wonderful Christmas ideas we shared: various decorations, different types of Christmas cookies, wonderful homemade punch made from blackberries, huckleberries, spiced peach or pear juice, and the many other combinations. Thirty years later, I am yet using some of these ideas. I always made a sugar plum tree for every room, using bare hog haw branches covered with brilliant colored gum drops. I well remember one time during the war years when it looked as if I would not be able to secure the beautiful candy gumdrops. But my daughter Lawrenna was able to find them at the PX at Camp Stewart.

Right after Thanksgiving we would begin making beautiful cedar wreaths decked with the holly sprays and berries from the Satilla Creek. We made garlands of cedar roping, with beautiful senna-berry sprays woven intermittently along their length. We placed bunches of mistletoe over every door in the school and lunchroom. In the far corner of the stage, we would have a giant, beautifully decorated holly tree, and in each classroom, a small cedar tree, on which the children placed their personal gifts to each other. Santa would arrive with his enormous sack filled with bundles of fruits, nuts, candies, and raisins for every child.

Each year the decorations became more beautiful. People would come from far and wide to view them. Some of the children became very proficient in making garlands, wreaths, and swags. So the job of decorating the halls, auditorium, and individual rooms was a joyous occasion instead of task of tedious drudgery. No material had to be brought. As foundations, we used wire coat hangers or hay-baling wire from our barns. The handmade candle boards and candles for the windowsills could be used year after year, as we never lighted them on account of the fire hazards. I had bought the candles years before and packed them away carefully after Christmas so as no breakage or melting would occur. It was a set rule that all this work be done in time for the children and parents to enjoy decorations.

Of course we could never forget the wonderful yearly program telling the blessed Christmas story in song and story as related to us from the Bible. The auditorium would always be at its peak of beauty, with candles and wreaths in every window, visible from inside and out-of-doors. The doors and windows of the lunchroom would be decorated as well, and we always had a lovely little tree there for the lunchroom workers.

Every mother was remembered by a gift from her child, made at school, wrapped beautifully, and decorated with holly, senna berry, mistletoe, or smilax from our forest. These gifts were placed on the Christmas tree in the child's room. Some mothers with quite a few children had a rushing time going from room to room to get theirs at the gift-giving time in each child's room. Our large beautifully decorated tree on the stage was used only for its beautiful effect; it was always passed on to the local church that was to have the Christmas Eve party for the community. We left it intact and watered it well. The people from the church would get the keys to the school from the trustees and move the tree to their church in due time for their Christmas program. All we asked was for them to sweep up the fallen trash. The tree served two roles, and only one beautiful tree had to be cut from the forest. The church was always glad to get it, for it would have been quite a task for them to select the perfect Christmas tree from a forest full of them.

On the day of the Christmas program school was always called to order at the usual time. We called the rolls and collected lunch money and stamp money. Any gifts that were to go to other rooms were taken by the "children of the day." All the other children would make sure their gifts were well tagged before they put them on the tree as their turn came. Everyone would then move to the auditorium. The youngest children always appeared first, presenting to us what they had learned about Christmas. We had lovely songs, stories, delightful readings, and nice little playlets. As we proceeded up the grades, those who had just performed would be quietly taken by their teachers for personal relief and then brought back to their regular places in the auditorium, in time to see the next class perform. It usually took us some two hours to finish the program and the announcements for the New Year school dates.

And by this time the ladies at the lunchroom would be ready for the first grade and their parents. We would let them move out to get cleaned up and ready for lunch. All the room doors had been locked when we went to the chapel so that the decorations and gifts would not be disturbed when the first-grade teacher, pupils, and patrons moved about. All the other grades returned to their rooms, and Santa Claus began his tour, visiting second and third grades, then fourth and fifth grades, and then six and seventh grades. We each began the Christmas parties in our own rooms. Should we have any spare time before Santa Claus arrived in our room, the teachers were well prepared with Christmas stories of yesteryear or good Christmas games. We kept lunch moving as fast as we could so the lunchroom workers could get through on time to ride the bus home and have their Christmas party around their own tree. Everything went along on schedule. We had our parties, cleaned up, and were especially careful to take down the decorations. They would have become dry and brittle fire hazards if we had left them up. Instead they were taken back to the homes of the people who had furnished them.

By three o'clock our wonderful Christmas party would be over. Everything would be left in perfect order for our return on the first Monday of January. We would continue our work until the last of May. (All schools now had free textbooks and nine full months of schooltime, a far cry from the two-and-a-half-month term when I began in 1913.) Our 4-H club work had gained momentum as the years went by under the able leadership of Mr. Chaffin, who came to our county in 1925. He was always a welcome, charming, and informative visitor.[1] In the early 1930s, I had gone before the county board of education and asked for permission to have one hour per month for the 4-H club meetings during the school day. With the long distances the children had to travel on buses, we could not expect them to stay after school for a club meeting. They would have no way to get home. They agreed. This gave the county agents all the day to schedule the frequent meetings. Therefore, they were able to reach many more children and to plan their work much more efficiently. Of all the civic work I ever did, I have always considered this the greatest. The ruling still stands to this day in our county and has been a great boon to our extension agents and helped to get their 4-H club work done. "To make the best better" has meant too much to my life for me to ever leave any stone unturned for 4-H.

Our lady agents were not so long in tenure as Mr. Chaffin. Miss Hicks went into USO work; Mrs. Ryals died of a heart attack; Miss Ferguson, Miss Dyer, and Miss Bridges did not stay long. Miss Purdom and Miss Kirkland soon married. Mrs. Edwards and Mrs. Price retired. Miss Daniels moved on and on down the line. Mr. Hutcheson stayed from 1949 to the late sixties, when he moved on. Now Mrs. Avery and Mr. Deal are our agents. Empire had a strong 4-H club and often had county and district winners. When Mrs. Ryals was with us, we had a beef-canning demonstration at the school. I furnished the beef. It was done perfectly for me, and many farmers used the plan to save their beef after that demonstration. Freezers were not on the market yet, so canning was our only way to save foods for future use beyond the old-time drying methods.

Public speaking was a favorite project. We developed many worthwhile topics, and the children got involved in public issues. Our annual 4-H club tryouts were known far and wide and attracted state and national attention for the number of pupils enrolled in the work and the number of projects carried to completion. Our judges usually found it rather difficult to pick the winners to go to the county meet. Tryout day was always a great day at school, and the auditorium would be filled with interested parents, friends, and visitors. I gave fifty-four years of my life to 4-H work and was made a master 4-H club member in 1967 at Rock Eagle, a 4-H club park for leadership training in Eatonton, Georgia. It was my last public appearance for 4-H.[2]

Because there was no longer an eighth or ninth grade, we had two extra rooms. I had one fitted up as a workroom, with art supplies for posters, maps, bulletins, charts, and what have you to make the children's schoolwork more attractive. It also allowed them to learn color, form, balance, tints, shades, harmony, and contrast. Every teacher used the room for one period a day to do whatever could not be easily done at a regulation desk. All the tools and materials were always right there where you needed them. One set of tools sufficed for the whole school, and everyone was supplied. This art department added a great deal to the beauty and efficiency of our work, and many artistic pupils developed their talents because of this added facility.

The other vacant room was fitted up as a library. We had good lights, a good heater, and plenty of tables, chairs, and shelves. We used books from Wayne County Public Library. I went to the library for the books, and after I returned them at the stated time, I would be permitted to get another supply. This brought joy and knowledge to our community and showed the children what could be done through cooperation; the same way our art studio showed them how many children could be served adequately by one set of scissors or brushes. By sharing equipment, more funds were available for supplies such as paper, colors, and staples that needed to be replenished from month to month.

After Mrs. Page Nichols joined the faculty with her wonderful musical talent, we added public school music to our broadening program. We had a long, cold, wet winter, and day after day the children could not go outside to play. She would play for them while they engaged in singing games indoors. This made us think of adding an outdoor musical May Day to our music and health work. We also expanded our art program. During their music periods, each grade would practice for its chapel program, which came two periods every fourth week, and for the May Day festival. We had one of the most beautiful, fanciful, musical, and orderly May Day programs I ever saw—and I have seen many. We never took time out from our regular schoolwork to tie the program together but one time, when we would all practice together. After that came the presentation.

Oh! It was so beautiful. The grass was so green, and all the trees so lovely in their new, soft leaves. The sky was without a "cobweb," the early rain having washed all the dust from the elements. The piano was on an open truck. A special choir was nearby to reinforce the songs and dance of the different countries, polkas, waltzes, clog minuet, and many others, all in costume. Mrs. Ruby Nichols was the finest jester I had ever beheld, placing everyone in the right position after they had performed before the throne of the queen and king of May Day and their court of beautiful lords- and ladies-in-waiting. How stately they were as they walked to the throne and enhanced the royal pair. Our queen, Lady Scott, had a crown made of sweetheart roses by my daughter, a florist in Athens. Mrs. Kenneth Parks made her beautiful coronation dress. The king, Eugene Driggers, had his golden crown, kingly robe, and scepter. The music included the games they had practiced through the winter. Now it was beautiful springtime, and all the world was so happy and gay. It was a spontaneous performance and perfect performance.

We had chairs for the elderly, a throne for king and queen, and chairs for the royal court. The piano and choir were on the truck. All the others stood on the sidelines of the playground. The children had lined up in the front hall at the designated spot and moved outdoors as their special piece of music was played. They performed before the king and queen and then retired to their places to stand until all the others had performed. Then the king, queen, and court led the procession back into the building, and the teachers took their pupils to their rooms and rested until the bus arrived for home-going. The older boys and I got the piano and chairs back into the auditorium, and the tables back to the lunchroom. Everyone was saying how beautiful the program was and how little trouble and time it had taken to prepare and present.

The last month of school was used to get all academic work finished and to prepare the seventh-grade pupils for their graduation. They had their final test, a farewell supper for their parents and school officials, and a graduates party afterward. On the last night, they said their farewell to Empire School, speaking their pieces from the stage. After listening to the farewell address by their chosen speaker, they received their seventh-grade certificates and sang their farewell song. Another term of Empire School had come to an end. Now this seventh-grade class belonged to Wayne County High School. Thus, four years of hard work for me came to an end. I attended the summer quarter at the University of Georgia and took a special course in exploratory work for eighth grade, so as to be more able to assist the students when they selected their desired courses for high school. I enjoyed the course of study very much. This was the year that grade twelve was added to the high school course, and grade eight was the turning point between the set course of study through grade seven and the selected course of study from grades nine through twelve.

I went to the Odum School in the fall of 1946 to develop the eighth grade as a field of exploration for the boys and girls as they selected their courses of study for grades eight through twelve.

CHAPTER 23

An Unhappy Ending

I went into the Odum school system in the fall of 1946 as a teacher of grade eight. Mr. Aubrey Hires was the principal, and Mr. S. C. Harper was the school superintendent. I had fifty-four students. Grade eight at Odum was so new that there were no books and no curriculum for it. I was turned loose to set up my own course of study and schedule and went to work using the knowledge I had gained in my recent course of study.

I chose the following subjects set forth in the following manner:

First period

Roll call. Lunch listing, etc. Spelling every day, except on chapel days. All words to be copied from spelling book and used in many and diverse ways, this book to be made in art period, to use every phase of art as to color, balance, and form. Always showing grade, subject, pupil's name, date, period covered. At end of week we would have the test on all words studied.

Second period

English to include grammar, literature, and every needed form of communication for a full complete life, social, business, and family correspondence. This proved delightful to this age group. It opened a whole new world of learning. We made it real by mailing our letters and requesting a reply, if at all possible. This course also included dramatics, stage appearance, and club meetings—minute-taking, parliamentary procedure, agendas, motions, and programs. Great work was done in this section. In fact, we became so efficient in conducting our actual 4-H club meetings that we were asked by our county agent, Mr. Chaffin, to become a demonstration team for the county and to go from school to school to show other boys and girls how easy it was to conduct a well-organized club meeting. Our principal and school superintendent granted this request. Our club also received state recognition for this work. Recess and relief period of fifteen minutes

Third period

A double course: civics, two periods a week, and Georgia history, three periods a week. Here we tried to learn of our past and venture into the future of the workings of our local, state, and national government, as well as of our tax structure from sales tax on up. It proved to be a very exciting course. A lot of deep thinking was brought forward.

Fourth period

The students covered health, home economics, and athletics. Our lunch period came during the fourth period. The girls had a class using a text called *Girls Will Be Women.* It was a wonderful text, opening the great, noble avenue of womanhood to them and setting forth woman's role in our national way of life. The boys also had a text, *Boys Will Be Men,* in good, well-worded language that gave boys an insight into manhood. While the girls would be having their lesson, the boys would be with the basketball coach practicing for basketball. (Odum was a basketball town, there was no football.) The next day, at the same time, the girls would practice basketball with the coach, and I would have the boys for their class. On the fifth day, the girls would have their home economics lesson, and the boys would have a lesson in forestry. Wayne County forests have always been important to the economy of the county.

Of course, we got very deep into ecology: the forests' effects, watersheds, wildlife, weather, erosion, and windbreaks. It was a popular and excellent course. We used books on forestry and ecology written by Mr. Elliott. They had been stacked in the book room for years and never used. We came back from lunch each day knowing that "what we eat makes us what we are." Lunchtime was the most enjoyable period of the day. Our class ate together at one table, and we became known as the "happy group" and the "hungry group" because we always ate all the food that was served to us and never left even a drop of milk.

Fifth period

We were all back together again for mathematics. Everyone was eager to go forward. We had a wonderful text, *Making Sure of Arithmetic.* We had a review of all the vital parts of arithmetic, enumeration, addition, subtraction, multiplication, division, common fractions, decimal fractions, interest, measurements, equivalent tables, geometric figures, and rules for working same, money values (present value and future value), accounts, receipts, bank deposits, checks, notes, stocks, and bonds. It was a strong course, greatly enjoyed by both boys and girls. I always felt that after they had finished this class they were ready for higher mathematics. Otherwise, they had enough to carry on a well-balanced life. We always tried to do all this work within the hour of class time.

Sixth period

This was our blessed reading period, where we really enjoyed ourselves. We read many sets of books that opened many areas of thinking for us. One we especially liked was a biographical book of the great scientists of all time. It gave us a great insight into the scientific world with which we came into contact every day. We learned how scientific discoveries were made. We also had a series of Georgia literature. This added greatly to our study of Georgia history and government. We had another series of hero tales, which included heroines as well. It came at just the right age for them when they were so strong for hero worship. We had a series about faraway places, the people who lived there, and their way of living. I must say the children were happy during this period, and their test scores were always high.

They were many in number, but their behavior was above reproach, and their ability to learn and enjoy themselves showed at every turn. As a class, we never bothered anyone. We were in the high school buildings where classes were changed every hour. I had my students all day long, and what a joy they were to themselves, to me, to the principal, and to their parents. We were permitted every year to have one whole-day outing. We always prepared well for this day, knowing how much it would cost, how much time it would take to get there and back, and what good we could expect from the trip. Our trips included the Okefenokee Swamp, Crooked River State Park, and other nearby places of interest. These field trips always proved to be pleasurable and great sources of new knowledge.

When it was our time to give the chapel program, we always tried to portray some portion of our work and include every child in the class. We also tried to have every parent attend. We always enjoyed this portion of our work, and it seemed that the whole student body did also. I often heard people say that it was the first time they had seen so-and-so on the stage. They did not know "he had that kind of stuff in him." I am astonished by the very idea that a child could go through seven years of his schooling and never have a chance to show his stage ability.

Grade eight at Odum used to be a nightmare and was dreaded by all who entered its portals. It was now was a joyous experience for a teacher to look forward to. I delighted in them. Their advancement into grade nine, the first year of high school, was done in an orderly way, They seemed to know why there were the prescribed courses and moved forward with their work. In years gone by, many eighth-grade pupils habitually dropped out of school. My students came from old-line families of that part of Wayne County: Harris, Tyre, Hires, Griffis, Aspinwall, Moody, Odum, Ogden, Poppell, Stephens, Surrency, Tillman, Beasley, Collins, Overstreet, Davis, Jones, Sutton, Reddish, Copeland, Daniels, Thompson, Harvey, and King. Year after year my enrollment was heavy, yet my load did not seem to be so enormous, as each child came to me with full confidence that a wonderful year lay in front of him or her. Their attendance was practically perfect, which made our work easier. I was very happily situated.

In 1948 our principal was elected county school superintendent, replacing S. C. Harper, who, with twelve years to his credit, did not offer for reelection. He went into private business as the owner and manager of the Camilla Courts Motel in Jesup. Mr. Collins, of North Georgia, was selected as the new principal of Odum High School. He came highly recommended and was kind and good and considerate to every student, patron, and teacher. But he had been in a serious automobile accident, and he could not concentrate sufficiently on his duties to get the work done from day to day, so he was not rehired for the next school year. Next, Mr. Hallman was employed as the principal. He was young and inexperienced. His mistakes mounted month by month. The average attendance dropped in the high school to the point where he was to lose a portion of his faculty. To stand that off, he took grade eight and divided it among his high school teachers, and I was placed in an old dilapidated room in the grammar school with a section of grade four, thirty-two boys and eight girls. I begged him not to do it, telling him I was not prepared for teaching that grade level.

I had not taught the fourth grade for some twenty years, and within that time, every book in the curriculum had been changed, and the methods had changed to fit the newer course of study. All my begging was to no avail. He asked me, did I not believe that he had the authority to place me wherever he wished to. I told him I knew all that, but I did not want to go to those children so ill-prepared. But he made the change. Without a moment's notice I went from grade eight to grade four. Other teachers were handled in the same ruthless manner. Had I not been paying off a heavy mortgage on my home, paying for a car by the month, and helping out my youngest son, who was in college and had a young wife and baby, I never would have attempted such a drastic change. I did the best I could from every angle I knew to get help and create interest. From that class have come two fine ministers, one fine lawyer, many fine businessmen, and several distinguished ladies; so maybe their time with me was not a total loss.

Mr. Hallman accumulated his mistakes faster than he could get rid of them. He let me go in the middle of the summer of 1950 without letting the trustees know anything about it. He just wrote me a letter telling me I need not appear September 1, as I would not be needed. I had never received such treatment before or since. So I was left without work. I managed to get a veterans evening class at Screven. Then in a few months I was offered the opportunity to teach eighth-grade mathematics at Blackshear High School. I made a lot of friends from among the teachers, patrons, and students during my four years at Odum, and I feel that I did a fine piece of work there until I was completely upset and misplaced by Mr. Hallman. In fact, it was one of the best pieces of work I ever did.

During my tenure at Odum and as advisor to the Odum 4-H Club, Rock Eagle 4-H Club came into being. The Odum 4-H Club was a substantial contributor to Rock Eagle and holds a certificate naming Odum one of the charter contributors. My 4-H group did many other worthwhile projects. We sponsored a substantial gift-giving to a family whose home had been destroyed, and we contributed to a dinner that was held to raise funds to rebuild a farmer's tobacco barn that had been gutted by fire. We held a shower for an Odum girl, Miss Sadie Sports, who had gone into the mission fields, and we grew flowers and contributed them to the aged of the community at Christmastime. These are only a few of our many projects.

I always consider Odum one of my best-loved jobs, excluding the part of term 1949–50 under Mr. Hallman.

CHAPTER 24

My Short Stays

Early in the summer of 1950 I began a veterans class that met at the Screven High School building from five until eleven five evenings a week. I had some thirty students, all fine gentleman. They attended faithfully and applied themselves well. The class continued until late spring, when many of them had to discontinue their studies to make their various crops.

I began the class at Blackshear High School for grade-eight mathematics the first Monday in January 1951. I drove from home every day some thirty miles. Here grade eight was done in the old high school manner where a different teacher taught each subject. I had the same text as I had used at Odum High School. I liked teaching there, but I tired easily doing mathematics all day long. We worked on a short time schedule. We had six one-hour periods per day and only twenty minutes off. We could go to the restroom or to lunch, whichever we chose. I always had to go to the restroom, so I had no choice. My grading load was heavy, as my classes were enormous. My heaviest class was sixty-four, my smallest was forty-eight, and the others were somewhere in between. I managed somehow to get their papers graded every day. I sure taught a lot of arithmetic and had some brilliant students, among them, Alridge, Strickland, Allen, Brantley, Dubberley, Harris, Turner, Foremart, James, Dixon, Purdom, Walker, Odum, Colley, Batten, Kirkland, Riggins, Powers, Pittman, Kicklighter, Thornton, and Conner.

I arrived in middle of term and was never allotted any extracurricular activities. My class load was so heavy that I do not think I would have had time to do anything else but keep my papers graded and in order. Mr. Scheglal was the principal of the school. Mrs. Kicklighter was an eighth-grade teacher next door to me. I enjoyed knowing her very much. I participated with extra activities, like selling basketball tickets or seeing after concession stands, only when directed to do so by Mr. Scheglal. I did not ask to return. The work was too far away from home, and the load was too heavy.

CHAPTER 25

Gardi School Once Again

I returned to Gardi School in 1951. The school had only two teachers, as many more students were riding the high school buses to Jesup. We used the third room for a lunchroom; this was quite an improvement over the small garage more than a block away. My daughter, Lawrenna Mizell Puckett Powell, and I made up the faculty. She had grades one, two, and three; I had grades four, five, six, and seven. We had a nice school of forty children from the following families: Harper, Bennett, Hall, Riddle, Fultz, and Yeomans. Our work was light. The children were smart and well behaved. They were so appreciative of anything you did for them. It was a joy to work with them. The school was doomed, as the county board of education would not make any repairs to the building—it was one of the oldest in the county—nor would they put out anything for equipment or supplies. They were just waiting for it to take its last breath.

Two big, new sixty-seat buses were coming by Gardi every day, going to Jesup. I saw the handwriting on the wall. We just quietly finished out our school, checked all equipment, locked the doors the last day of school, and turned the keys over to the trustees. We did not say that we saw the end of their school. We thought it best for the county board of education to tell them. We told them how much we had enjoyed teaching the children and how smart and nice they were. They had done their schoolwork well, had excelled in all the 4-H club activities, and had participated in many extracurricular activities in forestry, as the forest was the very lifeline of the community, and provided for fishing, bees, and honey production. All the children were well versed in these great natural resources. They had great joy and respect for their way of life.

I felt as if I had turned my back on a dear friend when I locked that schoolhouse door for the last time, knowing full-well its portals would never open again to my dear pupils of the great forest and Altamaha fishing area.

CHAPTER 26

Back to Empire

I returned to Empire for the 1952–53 term to do departmental work in seventh and eighth grades, with Mr. Charles Withrow as principal. I had a heavy load, as the school had picked up grade eight again. I was to teach English, spelling, reading, and social studies in grades seven and eight. Mr. Withrow taught arithmetic, science, and health. My paper grading was heavy, the classes were large, and the subjects I taught were time-consuming. I enjoyed every minute of it. We did a lot of 4-H club work with Mr. Hutcheson and Miss Nell Daniels. Many of our pupils won district honors for their 4-H work.

The school had been repaired since I had last taught there. It had a new roof and new hardwood floors. The back porch to the main building was enclosed and made into an efficient all-electric kitchen. The ninth-grade room was now a nice dining room. Many new teaching devices had been added in the past several years. An electric deep well pump and a pressurized water system had been installed, and flush toilets replaced the pit toilets. Heating fuel had been changed from wood to coal, and electric lights had been added. The building was in good repair.

Community spirit was as high as always, and the school still held its own as a community center. News came to us that the county board of education might need the building for the overflow of several grades in the Jesup district, so Empire would not be a community school anymore, with its youth getting all their early training there. The faculty worked all the harder, determined to make it the best term ever taught there. We carried our academic and extracurricular activities forward in a glorious way. One of our pupils in grade eight, Terrence Nichols, won the county spelling bee prize. He continued his academic work and in high school was granted a Rayonier scholarship.

Our 4-H club won state recognition for its local meetings, community demonstrations, and preparation for the county meet, where we had many clubs scheduled for district tryouts. These meetings all had strong community support. We had a strong PTA, as always. The Halloween carnival, our annual fund-raising campaign, was the best ever. Thanksgiving had its traditional dinner for pupils, teachers, and families, and the usual lovely programs. It was well attended and enjoyed. Then came the glorious Christmas season with a beautifully decorated school building. As in the past, the doors and windows carried lovely door swags or window wreaths and candles, and the halls were festooned halls with garlands. We had the beautiful holly tree on the auditorium stage. Of course, every room had its own decorations and small tree, ready for each grade's Christmas celebration and visit from St. Nicholas. We still enjoyed our Christmas dinner in the lunchroom for all children and visiting parents. What a feast it was. As always, the lunchroom workers outdid themselves. The day was one of joy, never to be forgotten.

In the dark days of World War II, many of our boys were languishing in the Japanese camps after the fall of Corregidor in 1942. Lewis Withrow, who had been a pupil of mine at Empire, was in that group. In the wee hours of Christmas morning, he broke into song, "Hark! The Herald Angels Sing," and sang it all the way through. Then he sang "It Came upon a Midnight Clear," "Away in a Manger," "O Little Town of Bethlehem," "We Three Kings of Orient Are," "Silent Night," "Joy to the World," and on and on, singing every verse to every song. His comrades asked him how in the world he could do it. He quickly told them about his teacher at Empire School, a Mrs. Martha Mizell Puckett, of Wayne County, Georgia, U.S.A., and about how they had Christmas in every phase of their work beginning the first Monday of December. They learned these songs line by line in their English work so they could devote all their talent to the music when it came to their music period. He told me that after that faraway Christmas morning, his fellow prisoners seemed to take on new hope. Their long imprisonment was ended by Woodrow Anderson, from Piney Grove School, Wayne County, Georgia, leading the squad that freed them. I received word to the same effect from George Dart in Germany. So when you cast your bread upon the waters you never know how far your influence will travel. I have often thought, what if I had spent my time teaching worthless things instead of things of value? They may have had as great effect for wrong as these things did for values of true worth. Christmas at Empire was so happy and beautiful that it could last the children all their lives.[1]

New Year's Day came fair and cold. The news was definite now; the Wayne County board of education was to commandeer the Empire School building for their overflow of second- and third-grade students and would let the Jesup system absorb the other grades in their respective classes. Hearing that we made an extra effort to do all the good things we could in our remaining time.

I planned a historical tour for my eighth-grade social studies class in Georgia history. We left for the coast early one morning as soon as the buses had arrived. We toured St. Simons Island, taking note of Fort Frederica, Christ Church, Bloody Marsh, the great cotton plantations, and the lighthouse, among other sites. On to Butler's Plantation, Fort George, Midway Cemetery and Church, and Sunbury. By then the sun was sinking low. We did not get to Tybee and Savannah. We had to leave them for another day, which unfortunately never came during that school term. There was a scenic trip to the Okefenokee Swamp, which proved a laboratory of wonders for their young minds to ponder for years to come.

For our Valentine's Day there was the usual lovely lacy valentines, and valentine cookies for lunch, and a lovely Valentine's Day chapel program for all to enjoy. Easter brought its own celebration, including egg hunts. And I always had a display of Easter pictures for Holy Week, depicting the trial, death, burial, resurrection, and ascension, all the way from Palm Sunday until forty days after Easter. We carried the Bible verses for each picture. Many grown people came to see and hear this program year after year, and we always served refreshments from our room to all who came. We had a time schedule for each grade to come to our room for the beautiful Easter story. This was attended and loved almost as much as our Christmas celebration. Of course, 4-H club tryout day always brought a turnout that filled the auditorium. Throughout the years I followed the 4-H motto and tried to "make the best, better."

Spring arrived, and there was the all-day picnic for pupils, parents, and teachers at Dales Old Mill, a historical spot near Screven. The site was where, some seventy-five to one hundred years ago, Anne Nichols, the author of *Abie's Irish Rose,* was born. Annie's mother was Fannie Hopps, a local girl. Her father, a Nichols of Philadelphia, was the lawyer for the firm of Dales Mill. In the course of time, her father returned to Philadelphia and died. His beautiful southern wife had no support for herself and their young daughter. She did fine laundry for wealthy Philadelphia families. Annie grew up among the Jews and Catholics of the city of "brotherly love." Hence the background for *Abie's Irish Rose* was gained firsthand. When she lived at Dales Mill she often played with Miss Beat Bennett, the youngest child of Uncle Enoch Bennett, a nearby neighbor. Miss Beat still lives in Jesup, nearing ninety years of age, and she can tell you joyfully of those long-ago days. Mrs. Myrtice Westberry Clary and her sister, Madlyn, were close cousins to Annie Nichols, as their grandmother Morgan was a sister to Annie's father. She married a Mr. Morgan. They settled in Jesup, where she lived out her life. I remember her well.

In Dales Mill were long avenues of great live oaks, some ten feet in diameter and more than one hundred feet spread, still standing in all their grandeur and majesty, while the foundation markings of the great houses of the mill owners and operators could be traced on the ground. Also visible were the outlines of the cabins of the hundreds of workers in the virgin pine forest. Many tram lines brought trees from the distant forest to this giant lumber mill to be sawed and prepared for shipment to foreign markets all over the world. So the outing gave us a wonderful lesson in local history as well as a joy-filled day for swinging in the grapevine swing, playing in the shade of the mighty oaks, or just resting and dreaming of other little children who had once played so gaily on these selfsame sands. Everyone had their pictures made in the many lovely spots. It was a day of complete satisfaction to all and would be long remembered. The food had never tasted so good, lemonade had never been so refreshing, and breezes had never blown so softly. Many were the beautiful stories written about our day at Dales Old Mill. Even the first-grade students could frame lovely sentences about the day we all went picnicking. Several lovely chapel programs came from this trip. They highlighted the different kinds of games we played, the food, the resting, the beauty, the history, and the long, lovely unhurried time of this wonderful spring outing.

In our last six weeks of school, we concentrated on finishing all our work in due form and preparing for our eighth-grade closing exercises. Tradition called for a banquet in the lunchroom in their honor, with their parents as their guests. It was to be prepared and served by the pupils of grades six and seven and their parents. Then would come the farewell party in the auditorium, with the sixth and seventh grades doing all the decorating and game planning to be enjoyed by all until late evening. On the final day of school, everyone got their report cards, and the eighth grade decorated the auditorium and stage for their farewell. After receiving their certificates from grammar school for admittance to Wayne County High School, they listened to an eloquent speaker tell them of the firm foundation they had set for their educational career, of the marvelous work they had done in these eight years, and of the wonderful task now before them. The program over, at long last, congratulations were in order for each student, the speaker of the occasion, and all concerned. Another year at Empire School had closed with pride and joy and sorrow. In our hearts we knew this was the last of Empire's many years of valuable contribution to the community. It was to be swallowed up in the county system. Some people call this progress. I call it community destruction.

This was now two school systems I had seen go in two years. It was hard to work, knowing the end was so near. Odum, O'Quinn, Red Hill, Screven, Piney Grove, and all the other small community schools have gone the same way. I was not there with them when the breath of life was taken from them, as I had been at Gardi and Empire.[2]

National 4-H Alumni Award

In the fall of 1953 I went to Patterson School, Pierce County, Georgia, to teach the sixth grade for Mr. Ray James, the principal. Mr. Tom Strickland was the county school superintendent. Mr. Lecky was the county agent, and Miss Donovan was the home agent. There, I was connected with many lovely teachers in the various grades and departments.

Mrs. Crawford	Mrs. Florice Strickland Dean
Miss Virginia Lee Martin	Mrs. Charlotte Davis Roberson
Mrs. Effie Mae Tyre Womack	Mr. George Roberson
Misses Lightsey (two of them)	Mrs. Peggy King
Miss Bertha Walker	Mrs. Kitty Smith
Miss Marjorie Hyers	Mr. Oswell Smith
Miss Beverly Hyers	Mr. Marvin Anderson
Mrs. Izora Lloyd Thomas	Mr. Bud Still
Mrs. Inez Mikell Thomas	Mr. Casey King (coach)
Mrs. Sis Thomas (supply)	Mrs. J. E. Strickland Jr.
Mrs. Lena Dixon	Mr. Truman Riggins
Mrs. Gladys Wasdin	Mr. Shon Aspinwall
Mrs. Joe Beth Ellers	Mr. Billy Strickland
Mrs. Clara Echols	Mrs. Dubberley

I may have left some out. The teachers were well trained, the school was well organized, and the students were well behaved. The people believed in their children's teachers, superintendent, school, and community. The PTA was strong and had wonderful, lively, and enjoyable programs in parent education. The strong Farm Bureau, Grandmother's Club, Lions Club, Future Farmers of

America, Future Homemakers of America, 4-H clubs, Masonic Order, and Eastern Star all put forth great efforts of support for the school.

The school was well organized in every way and participated in all county, district, state, and national events, winning their portion wherever they entered. While I was there, Jim Thomas (Mr. Son Thomas's son) was elected president of the National Future Farmers of America. All of Patterson was so proud. They had a large billboard made and placed at the entrance of every highway into town, saying, "This is Patterson, Pierce County, Georgia, the home of Jim Thomas, president of the Future Farmers of America." At the base of these signs were planted beautiful flowers, shrubs, and a small section of well-kept lawn. Mr. and Mrs. Aaron Thomas's oldest son won the National Award in Recreation sponsored by the local 4-H club. Many were the district honors won in public speaking, debating, singing, instruments, music, including band, piano, and string ensembles. Many essays, scrapbooks, and other submissions brought home prizes and trophies as well.

The school and grounds were kept in perfect condition. Many of the maintenance duties fell on our shoulders. The work was divided equally among us. My duty for the five years I worked in this wonderful system was to see that the boys' and the girls' toilets on the curbside of the building were shipshape at all times. I was to inspect them as often as it took to keep them this way. My principal told me that I saved the school quite a sum of money by reducing the amount of toilet paper used and by preventing the destruction of toilet fixtures. No one knew when I was going to be there for inspection—I went at my own discretion—so it could no longer be used as a hangout. We were all requested to keep the bulletin boards, blackboards, and bookcases in our own rooms in a nice, orderly, and attractive way at all times. We were also asked to maintain the bulletin boards in the front hall at stated times during the year.

The teachers were responsible for their individual groups of children from the time they arrived until home-going. We had to see them get on the buses each afternoon with their correct books, shoes, and coats. It was a set rule that if you let a child leave without his books, shoes, or coat, you had to drive to the child's home and take the needed article to him. Very few teachers ever had to do that. A bell would ring loud and long at ten minutes until closing time. You would stop your work and get your children ready to go and have them to pass out of the building in order to get on the several buses while you stood there to see this was done orderly. They were in our care at lunchtime to see that they were exhibiting correct eating habits and nice manners. We had an enjoyable time during lunch. The food was always excellent. There were very few free lunches.

At the beginning of the school year, we were assigned the dates when we were expected to put on a chapel program. The programs were always excellent. We were assigned seats and the order in which we were to move in and out of the auditorium. We were responsible for our children's behavior going and coming and while there. The auditorium was in use every minute of the day, and you scheduled it as your needs called for it. We would watch movies there that we used in our classes. We also used it for all our club meetings, to practice for our chapel programs, and for PTA meetings. A strict schedule was kept for its use. It was an almost unforgivable error to muddle your time and appear in the auditorium on some other teacher's time.

Mrs. Echols, an efficient and highly trained musician, was always eager to help us produce music for any program we were planning, for special occasions or when we would sing just for the pleasure of singing. Her music period was a joy to all.

Our library schedule was run on the same strict plan we had for the auditorium. We went and came with the students and saw to their behavior while they were in the library. It was almost the same for physical exercise. Those who wished to practice basketball or football went with the coaches for these sports. The students who did not care for these competitive games remained with us to play singing games or to take part in other activities. We all went out together in an orderly way, and returned together, always quitting with time enough left to be excused and get back to our rooms in an allotted time. My play period came at the close of the day, so all going-home arrangements had to be made before we went out to play. Whatever the children were taking home with them was neatly stacked on top of their desks. We had to return to our room from play in time to be ready to move out when the home-going bell sounded. It was a severe offense for a pupil not to return from play, not to leave the building in the correct order, and not to leave with the correct bundle. If the weather was too bad for outdoor exercise, we had to be prepared for indoor exercise. Basketball was never hindered by the weather, but football and singing games were. I always had a supply of quiet games ready for rainy days. The children liked these and used many of them for their indoor party games at home.

In September we were given strict instructions to have our course of study covered by the last of May. We were to encourage the children to use charts, booklets, and maps in their work and to hand their work in on time. My course of study for grade six included spelling, reading, English grammar and composition, arithmetic, health, social studies, art, music, physical education, and library work.

Behavior control and discipline in our rooms were in the hands of the teachers. The principal would assist when and if he was needed, but we had to go with the child to his office, state the offense, and ask for the severity of the punishment, and tell how many times the child had been corrected for the same offense. We had to ask for help if we had to leave our rooms for this correction, as we were never permitted to leave our students alone for any length of time for any reason. I surely appreciated this help from the principal's office concerning punishment. I never liked to do it, as I had to do more than my share when I was the principal of small rural schools. Not only did I have to do my own punishment, but I had to do a good bit of the other teachers' heavier correction as well. After going into the Patterson system, I never did punish again.

We were on a six-week schedule. At the middle of the period I always gave out a worksheet that showed how much we would cover during this six weeks and within these limits would come our six-week test. I wanted my pupils to know the answers to every section of it.

I tried to always have a section of each student's art ready to be checked over at the end of each six-week period. I had them work with tempera paints, pencils, and finger paint on paper, and used various other techniques, woodwork, cutwork, papier-mâché, and appliqué. I always tried to make an exhibit of the art and invited the other grades to view it.

The art was usually connected to one of our regular academic subjects. I used the sixth-grade reader *Run Away Home* for our papier-mâché work. Each student chose one of the characters of the story to make, dress, and color. Just before Christmas we had an exhibit and performance, as the story in the reader ended at Christmastime. Although our class was large, we usually had more characters to make than there were students, so the ones who finished first would make the extra characters. Each student would tell his character's portion of the story. We arranged the class in a circle all the way around the room. Our invited visitors never sat; they stood and walked around the circle. Then we sang Christmas songs and served refreshments. We did this all day long, with each visiting group coming in at a scheduled time. When the day was done, the students took their character home to play with or to give to some other child for Christmas. Ofttimes they made more characters to go with the first one they had made. Thus ended one art project.

The children seemed happy in their work. They did their best at everything. We made artistic folders for each subject every six-weeks. All the work they handed in was graded and recorded in the grade book. At the end of each period, they put their work in their folders to take home to be signed by their parents and returned to me to be filed away as proof of what they had accomplished in that period. Then, we would start all over again for the next six weeks. With this system there was never any doubt about what grades they had received, for the proof was always right there in the folders. In each folder was the child's worksheet, showing what he had been assigned to do for that six-week period.

I was asked to take charge of 4-H club work in the school. I was to be assisted by Mrs. Gladys Wasdin, another sixth-grade teacher, Mrs. Izora Thomas, and Mrs. Joe Beth Ellers. We worked as one large unit. We presented programs and taught parliamentary procedure by *Robert's Rules of Order*. Our group became so proficient we were especially invited to carry out a full meeting before the school's PTA. Mr. Foster O'Quinn, one of the county board of education members, invited us to put on a similar demonstration before that august body. Somehow the time was never arranged for us to appear. At every meeting, we had a practice session to get our members familiar with the projects they planned to try out in the school club when it was ready for county meet.

The meetings were interesting, and we usually had visitors come to enjoy the meetings with us. We often had distinguished visitors on our programs. Some were foreign exchange students. Once, we had a German boy. Another was attending the school in Jesup and visited with us one whole day. An Irish student, Miss Ingram, from Ware County, appeared at "big chapel" one day and told us about the Emerald Isle. Our county agent and home agent would come and spend the day holding meetings with different sections of the club. We had our first annual 4-H club rally for Pierce County. The PTA, Lions, Masons, Grandmother's Club, Farm Bureau, and Farm Bureau Auxiliary contributed money to pay the expenses for our district winners. We always had a wonderful showing at district meets, a smaller showing for the state meet. We made it to the national meet only a few times.

In 1956 I was awarded the National 4-H Alumni Award by the Olin Mathieson Chemical Corporation. The Honorable J. P. Shedd, who had served for many years as the Wayne County agent, presented it to me at the close of a countywide 4-H rally in January 1957. In 1912 I had been one of his first club members. I was very proud of the award.

In 1954 our beloved principal, Mr. James, was transferred to Folkston to be the head of the Charlton County school system, and Mr. James Oliff and his lovely wife, Mae, came to us as school principal and librarian, respectively. They were highly trained and devoted school people. He brought strong rules and regulations to carry on a sound school system. He was hardworking and happy and expected us to be the same. We all thrived under his control. With my five years' work in the system, I never heard or knew of a major discipline problem. The perfect care and loving guidance of each and every child prevented such disturbances. Problems were caught before they became catastrophes.

Our PTA's major moneymaking project was the Halloween carnival. I was always asked to work on the bingo committee, securing prizes and then helping call the games the night of the carnival. I had good luck getting prizes of every worthwhile and unique value, which made the bingo tables ring with players until well in the midnight. We had a king and queen of the carnival. Each class could enter a couple if the class chose to pay the entrance fee, which was usually fifteen dollars. The pupils were permitted to work for one month before the carnival, securing votes for their candidates at one cent per vote. Whoever had charge of this work collected the money and posted the votes in the front hall every day. The school usually raised two thousand dollars on this project. Voting closed at noontime the day before the carnival, so at the beginning of carnival time, the king and queen could be dressed in their royal attire and crowned to rule over the festival, which was always so colorful and gay.

In our room the children picked up pecans on shares and sold their portion, usually about one-half of the nuts they had gathered. They made and sold popcorn balls, pecan fudge, candy pecan, divinity candy, parched peanuts, boiled peanuts, and cellophane bags of peeled chewing sugar cane. I made several lovely cakes and sold them at ten cents for a generous slice on a napkin at each recess time. A large cake would bring between four and five dollars. One mother made us a dozen fancy aprons that we sold for seventy-five cents each. Right there we had nine dollars. One lady tatted edges to lovely white and pastel handkerchiefs. We sold those for one dollar each. My daughter was in the florist and greenhouse business then, and she gave me several trays of greenhouse plants for baskets, planters, and dish gardens. Those went well. There never was a day we did not have a nice showing of money for our votes when the chairman came to collect. It was a rule you had to work for your money (not beg your parents for it).

We had one boy who liked to cook, and he would bring a large dishpan full of fresh, hot doughnuts. He never had enough. Several of the girls brought lovely iced cupcakes. We came up second in the contest. The senior class beat us. The senior boys donated money they had earned catching several thousand fryers to load on the large poultry trucks at the poultry-growing houses nearby. This amounted to big money, but we did not mind; we had lots of fun and excitement earning our money, and we sure put the senior class to working day and night. Everyone was happy about the large amount of money that was raised before the carnival even started.

The night of the carnival we had a country store, and at five o'clock we had a harvest supper. All the foods for the supper were donated, and it always raised a goodly sum. We also had the ever-present bingo table, candy drawings, and guessing the beans in the jar. Mrs. Smith and her home economics class would bake a fruitcake in a large "suit box," using donated ingredients. They decorated it beautifully with fresh holly from the creek and red ribbons and then sold chances on it. Mrs. Echols and the mothers always made and donated a large cathedral pound or wedding cake and sold chances; at twenty-five cents each, this would run into big money. We always had turkeys to raffle off, cakewalks, and Sunday dinner cakes to sell outright. There were hot dogs, hamburgers, hams, peanuts, games, and square dances. We drew crowds from miles and miles away. Some would come for the supper and stay for all the other festivities.

It was a well-planned and well-executed event. Everyone came at the setting of the sun, and we always tried to be through by midnight, when the costumes were judged and prizes were awarded. It was always a hilarious enjoyable affair for the youngest to the oldest of the community, and it made a good conversation piece for many weeks to come.

The carnival provided the school with a generous amount of money for every department—band, library, recreation, science, social studies, music, and art— and money for many other purposes throughout the year. We had a wonderful time planning it, and when it was over, we were ready to plan for next year. I helped for five full years. It seemed that each year it became more colorful, hilarious, and profitable.

Not too long after the carnival, we began planning our Christmas season. The work—who was to do what—was set up at the beginning of the school term. The first Monday in December the teachers and pupils were busy decorating their own rooms and the section of the public halls, windows, entrances, library, lunchroom, and auditorium that had been assigned to them in September. All materials and tools had to be cleared away on Friday of our last week before Christmas so the principal could inspect our work. The next week we enjoyed the decorations and the Holy Christmas atmosphere.

Visible from one end of the school grounds and buildings to the other, the beautiful live Christmas tree on the front lawn carried its five-pointed star at its top and was well lighted each night, and the front roof always supported Santa and his eight reindeer. The glee club always had a formal program of Christmas music, and everyone came.

On the last day before Christmas every class in school sang the wonderful Christmas songs we had been learning all fall and winter. This lasted until everyone was through with lunch. Each section went to lunch at the usual time, then back to program. After all had been to lunch, we returned to our own rooms and had our own Christmas parties, presents, and stories. The wreaths on the front windows, the garlands on the columns, and the gaily jingling swags on the front doors silently declared, "peace on Earth, good will to men" through the twelfth night. No one could ever have any doubt that Patterson School and community knew how to enjoy the wonderful Christmas story and helped bring "joy to the world." It was such a happy time, one never to be forgotten.

Valentine's Day was celebrated by the lower grades in the usual way, but the upper grades celebrated in a gay and beautiful way by selecting the "sweetheart" of the school. It was quite an honor to win, as the selection was made from a bevy of beautiful, talented young ladies. People came from miles around to gaze on all this loveliness, charm, talent, grace, and beauty. The event ended with a dance for the older students and young folks of the community.

Then came the spring holidays, when the community tobacco plants were "ready to set." Tobacco was now the great cash crop of the county, ever since the boll weevil had destroyed the community's record for being the most productive Sea Island cotton–producing community in the world. At the time, Blackshear was the leading Sea Island cotton market in the world. The Brantley Company had promoted both the cotton and tobacco crops and still supports the magnificent cash crops of the community.

We celebrated Easter and its accompanying religious holidays. There were various spring outings for all the grades, suitable for each grade. The upper grades were usually busy with the tryouts for their inter-district events in essays, debates, drama, music, business subjects, 4-H club, home economics, Future Homemakers, and Future Farmers. The whole school rejoiced when they excelled, which was quite often.

The last six weeks of school always meant hard work in the academic subjects so all grades might finish their work efficiently. The graduates were always busy preparing for their annual banquet, prom, class picnic, and graduation exercise. The public supported these events, and the boys and girls never disappointed them in their appearance and ability. Many of the graduates went on to schools of higher learning, many returned to the farms, and others went straight to their chosen professions, sometimes railroad work, carpentry, or highway work.

The year 1957 stands out as a special one for Patterson School and me, as so many important events happened that year. First came the public program given in my honor when I received the National 4-H Alumni Award. Next came the Pierce County centennial celebration.

Mrs. Smith, head of the home economics department, had for years wanted a bathroom for her department. She had saved her share of the carnival money for two years for this project, but she just could not wait on it for another year and then maybe never get it. So she came to me one day and asked me to help her with a plan that would bring her some quick substantial money but not take too much time away from academic work. It would portray the contrasts and likenesses of the events of 1857 and 1957. She wished to show off the articles of clothing each of her four classes was finishing and to compare them with clothes of the preceding one hundred years. She had made a collection of clothes worn in bygone days by the people of Pierce County. She asked for my help, as she knew I always arranged my public programs myself and based them on my grades' courses of study and included the local community in the productions.

I asked her how long she wanted the program to be and how much money she wanted to make. She said she wished a whole evening of entertainment and wanted to clear five hundred dollars, more if possible. She wanted to involve the whole school in the production and to draw the attendance of our community and our neighboring communities, Blackshear and Waycross. I asked her to give me the weekend to think about it and to plan it out.

I had to work like a Trojan to get it worked up and ready to deliver to her on Monday morning. I allowed one month for advertising and production and would involve every group in school and in the community in the effort to produce the needed amount. First off, I thought of all the things that would portray the one hundred years of Pierce County's life that could be produced and sold. I listed them and thought how they could be arranged by tables in the entrance hall for display and sale to all those who came.

Table 1—Sunday dinner cakes

Table 2—gallberry brush brooms

Table 3—sedge-grass hearth brooms

Table 4—palmetto house brooms

Table 5—corn-shuck scrubs

Table 6—dip gourds

Table 7—slat bonnets

Table 8—corn-shuck hats

Table 9—homemade quilts

Table 10—hoe and ax handles

Table 11—a lot of miscellaneous goods, such as knitted, crocheted, and tatted articles.

The entertainment would cost fifty cents for adults, twenty-five cents for children (not many would be there, as we intended to involve all the pupils in the production). First, we had to select a narrator of great ability who was interested in local history and events and who could ad lib freely. Second, we had to make a time schedule to hold all the major events of the one-hundred-year period. Third, we had to place the events within the bounds of the allotted time and ask one teacher to be responsible for each era of time. Fourth, we had to make a time and space schedule for the back hall and rooms on each side of it. The players of the pageant would wait there, and the "behavior committee" would see that each finished group came inside and had a seat or standing room in the auditorium so quietness would be maintained throughout the whole performance.

I made four copies of the list of eras, one for me for getting the right group on stage at the right time with the right props; one for Mrs. Echols, so she would be able to keep up with the musical score; one for the narrator (who was Mr. R. D. Thomas Sr.); and the fourth for the stage manager.

Era 1 (1857)—The opening of Pierce County, glee club singing "Dixie" and other southern songs in all their beauty, charm, and skill. Scene: antebellum home, telling of Uncle Remus stories (I and a large group of children).

Era 2 (1857–60)—Settlement, brush-arbor churches, log-cabin homes, quilting, house-raising, square dancing, stick and clay chimneys, rail splitting.

Era 3 (1860–65)—War between the States, singing of camp songs, returned confederate veterans.

Era 4 (1865–80)—Reconstruction.

Era 5 (1890–99)—Gay Nineties, singing, dancing, walking, etc.

Era 6 (1898)—Spanish-American War songs, uniforms, Spain, Cuba, Dewey in Manila.

Era 7 (1900–1915)—When cotton was king, picking, weighing, selling, prosperity.

Era 8 (1916–World War I)—uniforms, singing of songs, number called, number returned, famous saying, "Lafayette, we are here."

Era 9 (1920–21)—Arrival of boll weevil, coming of tobacco crop.

Era 10 (1929–33)—Hoover days.

Era 11 (1933)—New Deal, FDR, WPA, CCC.

Era 12 (1941–44)—Pearl Harbor, World War II, Patton, Eisenhower, MacArthur.

Era 13 (1945)—Death of FDR, end of World War II, Harry S. Truman.

Era 14 (1952)—"We want Ike."

Era 15 (1957)—One hundred years of growth and the exhibit by the present-day sewing class of Mrs. Kitty Smith.

The pageant developed well. I had arrived at school before seven that Monday morning, and I had it all on the blackboard before it was time for school to open. I put all the eras on the board and indicated the type of history we desired to portray. I sent for Mrs. Smith and asked her if it was what she desired. She said it suited her exactly. I asked her to ask the teachers to come by to select their era, as I wanted to use my blackboard before the day's end. Long before the day ended every era had been taken. Each teacher was to develop her era at her own discretion. We would practice it one time to tie the presentations together and determine what the narrator had to say to introduce each era.

Everyone seemed carried away with the idea, and the news spread like wildfire that Patterson School was developing a wonderful centennial celebration. Tickets sold at a rapid rate, and we feared we would not have enough standing room. We assembled all the extra chairs at our command to be used as needed. The numerous tables of centennial souvenirs filled to capacity rapidly; enough cakes were promised to fill the Sunday dinner cake table thrice and over. Each of us could see in our mind's eye the bathroom for Mrs. Kitty's department fast taking shape. This made us more determined to put on a perfect performance.

Our narrator, Mr. Thomas, was beyond comparison in his knowledge about each era, and could ad lib aplenty on each subject. The antebellum scene by the glee club was performed to perfection. For the settlement era, Mrs. Florice Strickland Dean showed brush-arbor churches such as the one that existed where Shiloh Primitive Baptist Church now stands, with the same pastor, Rev. Reuben Crawford, for more than fifty-three years. In those churches were sung the great old songs, "Amazing Grace," "Mixture of Joy and Sorrow," "Jesus, Lover of My Soul," and others so beautifully rendered in clear a cappella voices after being lined out to them stanza by stanza by their minister.

The presentation of the house-raising, rail splitting, new-ground clearing, all-day quilting, and "shaking the cat," a choosing game to see who would be the next to be married, climaxed with a hilarious and enjoyable "eight hands around" square dance called by a descendant of the original callers. This brought the house down, and many kept time to the toe-tapping music of the banjo and the fiddle.

Then the students displayed the costumes of times gone by. Some of the clothing was the equivalent of that worn by their great-grandparents to the big meeting at Patterson some seventy-five years before. The children told which of their ancestors had worn the clothing.

An authentic five-hundred-pound bale of the long silky fibers of Sea Island cotton was used for the era when cotton was king. The happy producers told the cotton buyers of Blackshear how they planned to spend the good price of one dollar per pound they were receiving. The happy pickers carried crocus bag picking sacks with bed ticking straps and sang field songs while gathering the precious snowy-fleeced staple. You would surely have believed with me that Mrs. Thomas and her field of pickers had been right there in the past and seen the joy in the faces of those long-ago pickers as weighing-in time came. You could hear their mournful happy songs as they wound their way homeward at close of day.

Then came World War I, "making the world safe for democracy." Hearing the casualty lists from Chateau-Thierry, Belleau Wood, and Argonne Forest read loud and clear by our narrator; seeing the original uniforms with their yards and yards of legging straps; and hearing the boys and girls sing their songs of the day, you would have felt you were "over there" with them.

For the Roaring Twenties, Effie May Tyre Womack and Virginia Lee Martin and their group sang "Five Foot Two" and danced the Charleston, the Big Apple, and the Black Bottom.

Another presentation depicted the first tobacco sales day at Blackshear, with the participants wearing the exact costumes that would have been worn on that day. You could hear the auctioneers shout. Then came the terrible 1930s and the Depression. If you had been there, you would have heard R. D. Thomas Sr. delivering one of FDR's great fireside chats, telling us that fear is the greatest of all destroyers. You would have seen the WPA workers and the CCC enrollees happily going about their reforestation projects and other public works.

Then came Pearl Harbor. Mr. Thomas read the list of servicemen called from Pierce County. There was a savings bond auction and a reading of the amount sold year by year. As time passed, Pierce County changed with the introduction of new technology.

The grand finale was Mrs. Smith's sewing classes, more than sixty students modeling the beautiful dresses they had made in their home economics class. After more than two and a half hours of fast-moving pageantry, the curtain came down on a happy, well-pleased audience. Miss Kitty would have her bathroom, as all the souvenir tables had long since been sold empty.

All those who had helped develop the show were so happy with its success. The presentations had gone smoothly; everyone had moved on stage with the greatest of ease at the correct moment. I was proud of the part I had played in making the pageant possible and in bringing great joy to the whole countryside and neighboring communities. We were invited to put it on at other communities, but we declined the invitations, as the transportation of our cast and props would have been too great a task and too time consuming.

In the spring of 1957 I was chosen Pierce County Teacher of the Year and was presented to the annual meeting of the Chamber of Commerce of Georgia by the Pierce County Chamber of Commerce. It was quite an honor for me, and I enjoyed the festivities of the occasion from early morning until late midnight.

This is the same year the Brantley Company celebrated their hundred years of continuous business by having an all-day celebration and giving away ten thousand dollars in cold cash to their past customers and serving a free old-fashioned Georgia barbecue with all the trimmings to all who came at noontime. It took them all day long to give this money away. Many gifts were one thousand dollars—to their oldest living customer, for the oldest receipt presented, or for the largest family doing business with them. Authentic receipts had to be presented on each call. It was an exciting event, and many happy souls left the show area that day.

I stayed all day. The Pierce County Board of Education granted a full holiday to all schools, providing that all teachers and pupils attended. It was a perfect field trip. I concluded my teaching in the sixth grade of the Patterson School system in the spring of 1958. I can truthfully say it was one of the happiest and most pleasant school experiences I ever had in all my fifty years of teaching.

The principals I had were efficient, competent, and delightful to work with. The children were intelligent, kind, loving, and efficient in their working ways. The teachers were friendly, helpful, and charming in every way. I think I knew them every one during my stay in the system. The people of the community were pleasant to be among at all times. My five years there were a joy.

All Things Hold Fast

I joined the faculty of Jesup Junior High School in September 1958. My principal was Mr. Bill Fordham.

I was given a class of forty-eight "repeaters." Quite a few of them were over-age and oversized for their grade. I could see no reason for several of them to be in that class, and I told Mr. Fordham so. He would never agree to move any to another class, saying there was a definite reason for each child's being there. I did the best I could for them and soon had the whole group working together, enjoying their work, and enjoying the work of the other students in their class. I kept them busy, and this they seemed to like. We maintained an average of forty-eight pupils during the year. We had a well-knit class and were doing excellent work.

We were scheduled to put on a chapel program for October 23. Not a one of them had ever been on the stage before to perform any kind of number. I told them we would all go on together and do the very best we could. So we arranged a "know-your-Georgia" program. Each one of us asked the audience a question. If they could not answer it right away, we answered it ourselves. We got along well with our program, and our master of ceremonies got on just fine.

At the time of our program Mr. Fordham was selling a great quantity of candy to get us a new movie machine. We hurried and sold ours and made Mr. Fordham a real money tree. In the limbs of the tree, we put all the money we had collected. We hung the dimes, quarters, pennies, and dollar bills on it. It was right pretty, shining so brightly. One of the girls (Sue Nell Parks) called Mr. Fordham up and presented it to him.

We sang several songs. One of the boys announced and led the songs. I thought we did well. We sang a cappella, as we had no musical instrument in our room, and we just pitched the songs and sang them the best we could. I told an

Uncle Remus story at the end of the program. One of the children called on Mr. Fordham for the daily announcements. Another had led the saying of the Twenty-third Psalm in unison. Everyone had done a part on the program and one extra part to make the program complete. We got through right on time. The performers were well received by the audience, and I was proud of them.

I arranged my class in five columns by days of the week, from left to right. On the first day of the week, the first child in Monday's column would do all the extra outside and inside duties of the day; when Tuesday came, we would cross over to Tuesday's column and begin with the first child there, and so on. Each week, the duty would move back one row. These duties included leading our line in and out of the classroom, adjusting and closing our windows, helping me carry my necessary teaching bundles, adjusting the TV set, giving out art supplies, and checking our worktables to see that everything was put away in order. Someone from our class would carry our lunch money and list to the lunchroom and collect the daily report from each teacher for Mr. Fordham each morning. Our work rolled merrily along.

We were asked to do the Christmas decorations for the front hall, which consisted of a good-sized bulletin board, the traditional tree, the door to Mr. Fordham's office, the small table that always sat near the front door, and the two large front doors. I had one student, Glynn Clark, who was quite artistic. He drew off the song "Holy Night" in red ink on a sheet of large paper. It had the music as well as the words. We put that up securely on the bulletin board. He brought me beautiful fresh holly, all full of red berries, from the Altamaha River swamp, and we wreathed it around the bulletin board. Oh! It was so artistic.

The next day I used another pupil to help me set up and decorate the small Christmas tree beside the bulletin board. We used colored lights on a fresh Arizona cypress tree that my daughter had grown. It was quite attractive and so very aromatic; its fragrance filled the hall. We fixed and decorated a lovely package for Mr. Fordham's office door. On it was a note that said, "Do not open until Christmas." On the table by the hall door we fixed a graceful arrangement of waxy smilax and brilliant red pyracantha berries in a large oval container. We called Mr. Fordham to come look at what we had done. I asked him, could we have all our class come over and see the decorations, as they all had helped make them and would not get to see them displayed unless we let them come, since they never used this hall. He gladly granted my request and furthermore told me the decorations were the most beautiful he had seen in the ten years he had been there and how much he appreciated what we had done. We yet had to add the beautiful swags of greenery, berries, ribbons, and Christmas bells that would announce callers who came and went during the holiday season. I hold in my hand now the note of appreciation he wrote to me and my class. It reads as follows: "Mrs. Puckett, I think the bulletin board and hall decorations are excellent. Thank you very much. —Bill Fordham."

We had our Christmas party in our own room, with a tree, presents, a party, and decorations, a lovely affair. The children enjoyed every minute of it. We had our usual lovely Valentine's party, with the exchange of many artistic valentines. Quite a few of the mothers came to this celebration. We were getting our academic work spread out before us now and applying ourselves full strength, as midterm had come and gone. We had all made it through midterm, and we were determined to do our best during the last half of the year.

When Easter came, our class was overage for the egg roll offered to us; instead we asked for a day at the Okefenokee Swamp. Our class would bear any expenses incurred for this trip. Our wish was granted, and we were provided with a school bus and bus driver. We provided our own lunch and gas. We had a lovely day. The students learned a lot, and I had everyone home before nightfall. By then, we had thirty more days of schooltime remaining, and we turned to our lessons to get everything in order to close out the term. I am glad to say the year was pleasant for all of us.

During this time my oldest brother, Francis Marion Mizell, aged eighty-nine, passed away, in the fall of 1958, at Savannah, Georgia. Mr. Puckett gave up his second eye after we had spent nine summers at McPherson's Hospital in Durham, North Carolina, trying to save it. He had lost the first one in a terrible accident in April 1931.

In the fall of 1959, I was back at Jesup Junior High with grade six. The Reverend James E. Bacon was its principal (Mr. Fordham had moved to Swainsboro to be the principal of a school there.) In this class I still had repeaters by the score. My enrollment was never under forty. My work was always heavy and demanding. With Jesup growing rapidly, many Catholic students were appearing here and there. I was usually asked to take them, as the word had gotten around that I knew how to handle them. I was able to keep order in the classroom and was able to prevent a "pecking order" from being established. I told my principal that I treated all my pupils with due respect, and I had learned long ago to tolerate all religions. I have never had any trouble in that field.

Television had come to stay. The state of Georgia had made special educational programs available to us, and I was sent to Waycross to see if they were any good. I brought back glowing accounts of these programs. Our PTA bought them for us. I hope everyone found the programs as helpful as I did.

As usual my students helped with the Halloween carnival. We were on PTA programs, and at one I was asked to speak and set forth what I believed in as a teacher. The thoughts I expressed during that address have been used many times as the basis of chapel talks by other teachers and school trustees.[1]

I was sixty-five in March 1962. I had planned to work until I was seventy, but Mr. Puckett told me that he could not stand to stay by himself any longer. So I retired in December 1962 after fifty years of teaching. I had loved every minute of it.

I began teaching in a log cabin in the Okefenokee Swamp in January 1913. I was paid one dollar a day for a two-and-a-half-month term. I taught in many schools in Wayne County, Georgia, and for five years in Pierce County. My salary had risen as I went from school to school down through the years. I worked at Empire School during Dick Russell's administration for no salary at all, and again for no salary during Eugene Talmadge's first term as governor (1933–35). It was Governor Talmadge who made it possible for us to receive our back pay during his second term (1935–37). I attended summer quarters of school at the University of Georgia and at Georgia Southern College and raised my license from a county license, granted by the county school superintendent, to a four-year-college life professional license, granted by the department of education of the state of Georgia. I still have all my licenses—I might have them framed someday— and I have pictures of most of the schoolhouses where I have taught.

On December 30, 1962, I held a party at my home, The Pines, to celebrate my golden jubilee of teaching. I sent invitations to every school and to the patrons who had been there when I had taught. I cordially invited them, one and all, to come. They came from every direction by the hundreds. Some of them were old and gray, as many were older than I when I began teaching at fifteen years of age. Every school was represented. The school that had the highest percentage in attendance was Sandy Hill, a small school in the Uncle Enoch Bennett settlement, where I had taught in 1916. Of course, many were from my most recent schools. In some cases, I had taught three generations, my early students, their children, and their children's children. It was always quite amusing when some child came in about the second day of school and said, "You taught my grandpa and grandma and my mother and daddy also." It was a gay, lovely party, with much reminiscing, talking, and laughter.

I enjoyed the last day I ever taught the same as all the others, but I could hardly keep back the tears. My principal, Mr. Bacon, knew it, but my pupils, my teacher friends, and the patrons did not. I pray I gave fifty years of my life directing children to the right pathway and teaching that all things hold fast to that which is good.

> Study to shew thyself approved unto God,
> a workman that needeth not to be ashamed,
> rightly dividing the word of truth.
> —*2 Timothy 2:15*

This I Believe

1. That our schools are operated for the purpose of teaching all students who come our way what they need to know to live happy, useful lives.

2. That schools are operated for the purpose of learning and should be conducted in such a way that there is a learning situation: a time for thinking, studying, and expressing our views.

3. That character-building is one of the great lessons of life, and honesty, integrity, thrift, joy, happiness, usefulness, and reverence are lessons that should be brought forward day by day in message, deed, and word.

4. That the language arts (reading, spelling, writing, talking, and speaking) are vitally important to any child. They should be brought in a joyous way so every child learns to embrace and love the great English language, with its thousands and hundreds of thousands of beautiful, expressive words. Then they might express themselves in any situation with ease, grace, and elegance in a charming, delightful manner, never forgetting that a well-read child is a knowing child. And our library should support this belief, affording the best of reading matter in all areas of study.

5. That mathematical knowledge is necessary so every boy and girl who comes our way will be able to carry on the everyday business of a well-rounded life; and that higher mathematics is vitally important in all fields of science, engineering, construction, industry, and research.

6. That health is vital to every human life and should be brought to bear on the lives of all children. They should know the great rules of health and that their body is the holy dwelling place of their soul; when the body is abused and is no more, the soul has to return to the Maker whence it came. Poor health is a personal problem, and it is also a community problem. Cooperation is necessary in this area of work.

7. That science is in the foreground today but not to the detriment of other fields of study. Therefore it should hold its place but not override all other fields of learning.

8. That the need to know social studies stands at the top of the ladder for all mankind. The more we can learn of the ways of our fellow man and the more we can respect those ways, the better off our world of brotherly understanding, love, and tolerance will be. I fear our social studies programs are too weak and should be enhanced by better maps, globes, films, literature, exchange students, travel, and study.

9. That the expressive arts are neglected because there is never time for painting, drawing, music, and modeling. Every child should have the opportunity to work with and through different media.

10. That all students need physical body build-up, not a selected few. Stature is very important in a child's life.

11. That public relations is our weakest point. School is a tax-supported institution. We are duty bound to give a good report of all monies consumed in the project. Parents have the right to know and to see the type of work their children are doing and to be able to compare one child's *F* with another child's *A* to discover why there is a wide variance in the grades. Parents must know the assignments their children are supposed to prepare day by day and know how well their children have covered their assignments and where and why they are falling short of the work expected of them. Does our method of reporting to the parents make this knowledge available to them? If not, why not? Is the work of every child available to the parents? Can our method of reporting to the parents be improved upon should they come asking where their child is failing? Do we hold that proof they could be shown? Or do we not know ourselves whether a child is failing or passing or superior? Can Jack spell? Can Betty handle zeros? Can John master foreign countries and peoples? Can Mary use the English language equal to Shakespeare? Can Albert do the science? Can Mollie promote healthy living? And on and on. Can we convince someone else we know what we are talking about when we grade?

12. That self-satisfaction is important. Are you satisfied with your profession? Do you feel that you have made lives better and opened rays of light to darkened, limited, benighted, narrow-thinking minds? Is what you are teaching needed in this world? Have you brought joy to ignorant families, wealth to poverty-ridden communities, health to disease-

racked districts? In other words, do you believe in education? Are you glad you are a part of that great continuous procession that must ever carry on so long as the race of man exists? In all this I do believe, and after forty-seven and a half years of labor I am still glad I am a teacher.

13. That our guide should ever be the record of the growth of the blessed Holy Child, "And Jesus increased in wisdom and in stature, and in favor with God and man" (Luke 2:52).

Martha M. Puckett, grade 6, section 1,
Jesup Junior High School, 1959–60

Schools at Which I Have Taught

Date	School	Location
1913	Burnt Bay	Hickox, Wayne Co.(now Brantley Co.)
1913	Long Ford	Broadhurst, Wayne Co.
1914	Dowling	Raybon, Wayne Co. (now Brantley Co.)
1914–16	Penholloway	Wayne Co.
1916	Sandy Hill	Wayne Co.
1916–17	Bamboo	Browntown, Wayne Co.
1917–18	O'Quinn	Screven, Wayne Co.
1918	Union	Grangerville, Wayne Co.
1918–19	Raybon	Raybon, Wayne Co. (now Brantley Co.)
1919	Goose Creek	Odum, Wayne Co.
1919–20	O'Quinn	Wayne Co.
1920	Red Hill	Redland, Wayne Co.
1920	Farm Life	Screven, Wayne Co.
1921–31	(Supply)	Jesup, Wayne Co.
1932–38	Empire	Jesup, Wayne Co.
1938–42	Gardi	Gardi, Wayne Co.
1942–46	Empire	Jesup, Wayne Co.
1946–50	Odum	Odum, Wayne Co.
1950–51	Veterans School	Screven
1951–52	Gardi	Wayne Co.
1952–53	Empire	Jesup, Wayne Co.
1953–58	Patterson	Pierce Co.
1958–62	Wayne County Junior High School	Jesup, Wayne Co.

CHAPTER 5. *Penholloway School*

1. While I was writing this, on April 5, 1971, I received a call telling me that Mr. Purcell had passed away at East Point, Georgia, at the age of eighty-nine. He had served there as superintendent of schools until he retired a few years earlier. Before going to East Point he had served for two years as superintendent of the Wayne County schools. We were requested to be at his funeral, but we were too feeble to go. Mr. Puckett was in his ninety-fourth year, and I was not far behind.

2. Dr. John Knight, the famous Baptist minister, is a son of the John Knight to whom I taught his ABCs when he was forty-two so that he could learn to read the Bible. The Dianne Waters who in 1971 starred in a Presbyterian play at Clinton, South Carolina, is a granddaughter of one of the Mannings I taught at Penholloway. George Westberry of Patterson, Pierce County, reaped many honors in FFA (Future Farmers of America); he is a grandson of Etta Manning, whom I taught letters. I could go on and on naming others who have reached notable places.

CHAPTER 6. *My Teaching at Sandy Hill*

1. In the late 1960s his wife came to a district garden club meeting in Jesup and said that the one thing she had to do before she returned home to Sylvania was to find Ernest's teacher, Mrs. Martha Mizell Puckett, and hug her neck and kiss her for him. He felt he owed her so much for helping him develop a foursquare life. I was one of the registrars at the door, so I spoke up and told her she would not have far to hunt, for she was now talking with the self-same lady she was supposed to find. So we had a joyous meeting, and I sent him my best regards for remembering me so beautifully. She brought me the message that all he was or ever hoped to be, he owed to me.

2. On June 5, 1971, I called Miss Beatrice and talked with her about the happy days of yore. She had turned eighty-eight on May 2 and still kept house and drove her own car. She lived in Jesup and kept a rooming house.

CHAPTER 13. *At Goose Creek*

1. Her brother, Elisha Sports (the father of Joe Sports, a top worker in the Democratic Party), was one of my finest students during this short school term. He has often told me he tried to put some of those good ideas of government I taught him into his son Joe's head.

CHAPTER 18. *I Marry, and My Life Is Changed*

1. Randal Tootle is now, in 1972, the principal at Odum Public School. He did a good job that night and is still doing a good job.
2. At our golden wedding anniversary, one of Mrs. Morgan's nieces reminded us that she remembered me doing all that sewing at her aunt's home in Screven.
3. Mr. and Mrs. Purcell were, indeed, among our dearest friends. They remembered us so beautifully at the celebration of our golden anniversary.

CHAPTER 22. *Empire Community School in World War II*

1. His last visit was when my garden club, Tacoma, gave a luncheon for Dorothy Biddie, who was in our town conducting a flower arranging school. Mr. Chaffin's wife, Lee Ollie Nichols Chaffin, was our Oleander District chairman at that time. This was in the 1960s. Our Wayne County Garden Club Council presented Mr. Chaffin with the annual county award for the wonderful work he did in home beautification while he was the county agent.
2. I have never been able to do any more 4-H work, as today, in 1972, I am in a wheelchair, and my husband, now ninety-four years old, is in failing health.

CHAPTER 26. *Back to Empire*

1. I just heard from two of my students from away back then, telling me that Christmas never came that they did not think of the beauty and joy of Christmas at Empire. It has been some twenty years, and as I write this in 1972, I get echoes of the glorious days at Empire.
2. My daughter, Lawrenna, came home last night (April 24, 1972) from the T. G. Ritch School PTA meeting. It is a school of some thirty teachers, with pupils and parents accordingly. She said there were only ten teachers and fewer than ten parents present at their final PTA meeting of the year. I cannot go along with calling that progress. The attitude of teachers and parents is "Let George do it," but it seems to me that George must have passed away many years ago. In fact, school busing has

long ago reached the point of no return. You can spend millions of dollars, haul them hundreds of miles, and they still do not know anything until they get to the teacher. Think of all the "pure blood" tax dollars spent and the hours of valuable time wasted by some ignorant, unknowing judges—and still more busing being demanded.

CHAPTER 28. *All Things Hold Fast*

1. See appendix "This I Believe." *Ed.*

Southern Voices from the Past:
Women's Letters, Diaries, and Writings

Time to Reconcile: The Odyssey of a Southern Baptist
Grace Bryan Holmes

Roots and Ever Green: The Selected Letters of Ina Dillard Russell
Ina Dillard Russell, edited by Sally Russell

Chained to the Rock of Adversity: To Be Free, Black, and Female in the Old South
edited by Virginia Meacham Gould

The Diary of Dolly Lunt Burge, 1848–1879
edited by Christine Jacobson Carter

A Heritage of Woe: The Civil War Diary of Grace Brown Elmore, 1861–1868
edited by Marli F. Weiner

Shadows on My Heart: The Civil War Diary of Lucy Rebecca Buck of Virginia
edited by Elizabeth R. Baer

Tokens of Affection: The Letters of a Planter's Daughter in the Old South
edited by Carol Bleser